REVELATIONS

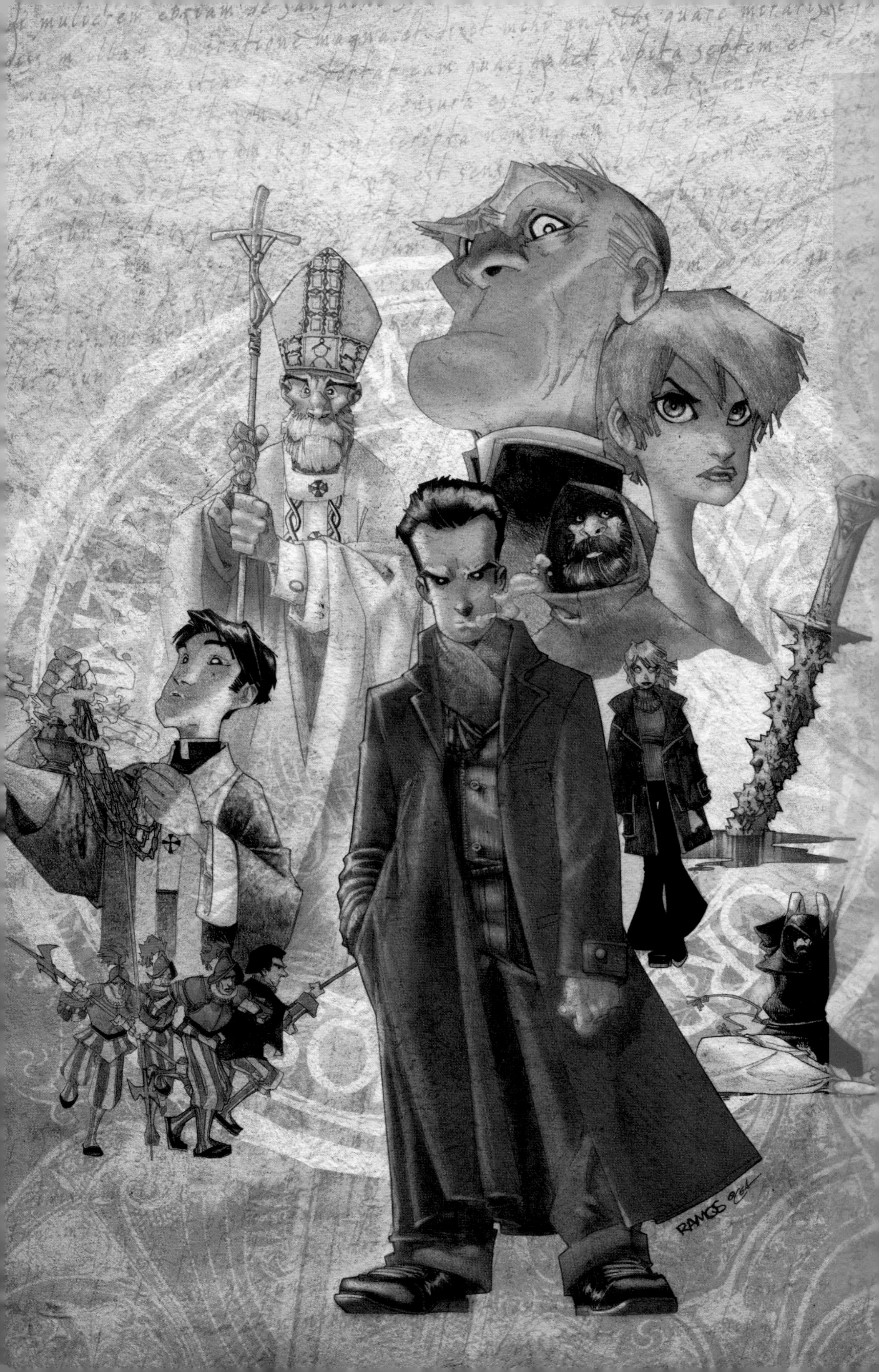
RAMOS

CREATED BY PAUL JENKINS
AND HUMBERTO RAMOS

Revelations™

STORY BY
PAUL JENKINS

ART BY
HUMBERTO RAMOS

COLORS BY
LEONARDO OLEA AND
EDGAR DELGADO

LETTERS BY
RICHARD STARKINGS
AND COMICRAFT

®

Dark Horse Books™

For Melinda, the woman I love.
—Paul Jenkins

*Our thanks to: Adriana Soria for her craft on calligraphy. Gavi Garpo, Alexa Garpo
and Silvia Ponce for their dedication. Edgar Delgado and Edgar Clement for their
support and jokes. Scott and Matt for guiding through the creation of this series.*
—Humberto Ramos & Leonardo Olea

PUBLISHER
Mike Richardson

LOGO DESIGNER
Leonardo Olea

COLLECTION DESIGNER
M. Joshua Elliott

ART DIRECTOR
Lia Ribacchi

ASSISTANT EDITORS
Matt Dryer AND
Dave Marshall

EDITOR
Scott Allie

PUBLISHED BY
Dark Horse Books
A DIVISION OF
Dark Horse Comics, Inc.
10956 SE Main Street
Milwaukie, OR 97222

First Edition: July 2006
ISBN 10: 1-59307-239-2
ISBN 13: 978-1-59307-239-1

I 3 5 7 9 10 8 6 4 2

PRINTED IN CHINA

THIS VOLUME COLLECTS ISSUES ONE THROUGH SIX OF THE DARK HORSE COMICS MINISERIES *REVELATIONS*.

INTRODUCTION

BY BOB HARRIS

"You can't run the Church on Hail Marys."
—Archbishop Paul "The Gorilla" Marcinkus, president of the Vatican Bank

We are being lied to.

This idea is no longer a "conspiracy" point of view. Listen closely: it's now a pervasive, unspoken premise in any modern political debate.

Who leaked what about which insider? Whose colossal screw-up caused the most recent giant pile of dead bodies? Did or did not the vice president use the lead pipe in the conservatory? Beyond the specifics of any frantic spaz du jour, it's usually a given for both sides that *we are being lied to*. The only real dispute: by whom?

Such a question should be easy to answer. Many of us now have resources beyond our wildest imaginings. Fifteen minutes with Google can give you anything from CIA assassination manuals to the U.S. president's insider-trading records to the Italian prime minister's membership in a secretive group linked to political violence, money laundering, and even bombings. All of these will be authentic and horrifying.

Hidden knowledge, weirdly enough, is often no longer hidden at all. It surrounds us. *Everything* connects, if you look. Indisputable facts about a dazzling array of horrors are available in such abundance that the most basic objective truths— roughly how many tens of thousands of civilians have died in a given country, say—should now be easy for everyone to agree on.

And yet we can't. All we do know is, yes, *we are being lied to.*

How can this be?

Maybe some of our own hidden connections can be pretty revealing, too.

As an exercise, I once tried to see how many steps it would take to connect myself, "Six Degrees of Separation"-style, to Hitler, Stalin, and Mao. Disturbingly, six steps were never necessary. Only in the case of Mao did I need more than four. To use Hitler as an example, one of my close friends is an investigative journalist (1) who has spent chunks of his free time with a notorious CIA agent (2) who worked for many years in Chile with a fugitive Nazi (3) who was close to, yes, (4) Hitler.

So am *I* connected to Hitler, Stalin, and Mao Tse-tung? This is a word I'm horrified to type, but must: yes. We can mince words about how many degrees matter, but the ultimate answer is plain enough.

As to Hitler: I *am* friends with my friend, and I *do* live willingly in a country which harbored war criminals, and I *have* benefited from the economic results of a brutal foreign policy. I *am* connected, in fact, two degrees further up the chain than I am comfortable realizing.

And now, still within six degrees of separation, *you're* connected, too.

Of course, you can choose never to see the paper trail detailing Nazi war criminals receiving CIA protection, or deny the historical record of U.S. support for brutal regimes at the behest of Wall Street. You can recoil, pretending that no degree of separation matters beyond the first. Obviously we are never responsible for what is done in our name. And then you're off the hook. (Congrats. I envy you.)

However, if you're more interested in the truth than your own comfort: you probably do live in the same country I do, and you've probably done just as little to change its ruthless exploitation of the developing world. So you're in for a couple of degrees yourself, at least a little.

So, now, the hard part: when any large institution acts in your name—whether or not you approve—how great is your responsibility? I think that's what a lot of the arguments around water coolers, on talk radio, and on the Sunday morning talk shows are really about.

Is global warming real? What kind of car do you drive, and how much gas do you use?

Are labor unions a good idea? What kind of work do you personally do?

Are tax breaks for the wealthy fair? How much money do you have, and how are your investments doing?

Any serious pursuit of political truths inevitably involves the examination of personal truths as well.

In religious terms, this is where the battle for our own soul begins. How much truth are we strong enough to seek? How much hardship will seeing the truth—all of it—force upon us, and are we willing to embrace it for the greater good? How much responsibility are we strong enough to take?

These are easy questions to run the hell away from. Such retreat is comforting, even pleasurable. But in these moments of withdrawal—of denying a connection to the world around us in our every act— I suggest, yes:

We are being lied to. By ourselves.

And it's in these moments that we, you and I, allow great wrongs to occur. Ironically, it's in the very instant of disavowing responsibility for tragedies in which we may become most responsible.

This may be the one hidden truth that you cannot find on the Internet.

In which case, things can only change when we do not flinch from our own flaws, when we stop trying to believe ourselves to be perfect and instead simply try to be good.

The actions we may take thereafter, whatever they might be, will be acts of faith—not in any deity, but in the potential virtue of humanity itself.

This is the story of Charlie Northern, one man who has more faith than even he himself believes. More than a detective story set amid various Vatican conspiracies, this is a journey into the darkness of the human soul. Beings with a lesser sense of responsibility and truth may confront Charlie Northern at every turn. But while his faith in an institution may be shaken, his faith in the necessity of good is not.

I hope all of us, together, may soon find the courage to take a similar journey as well.

CHAPTER ONE

A Fall from Grace

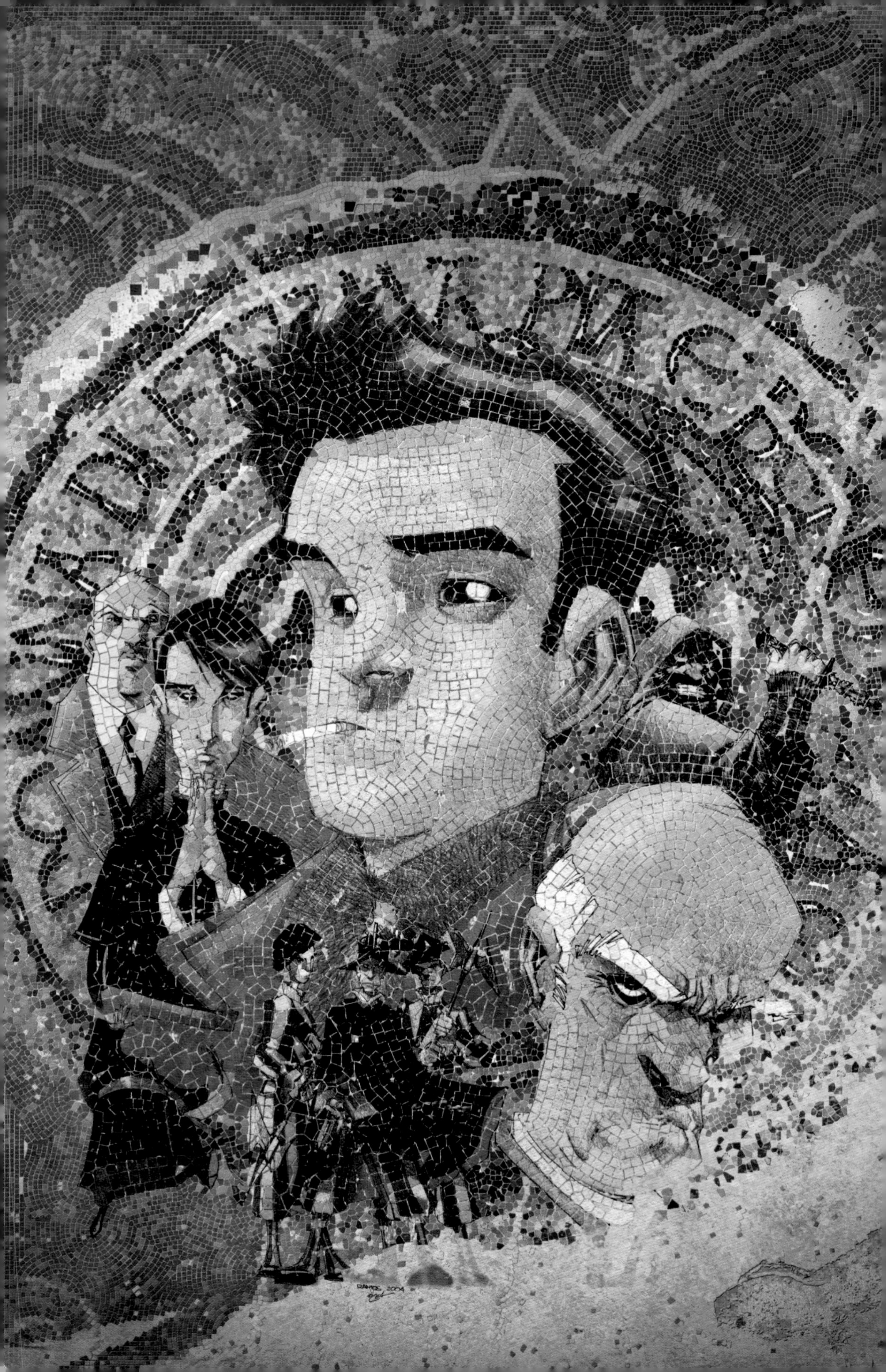
RAMOS 2004

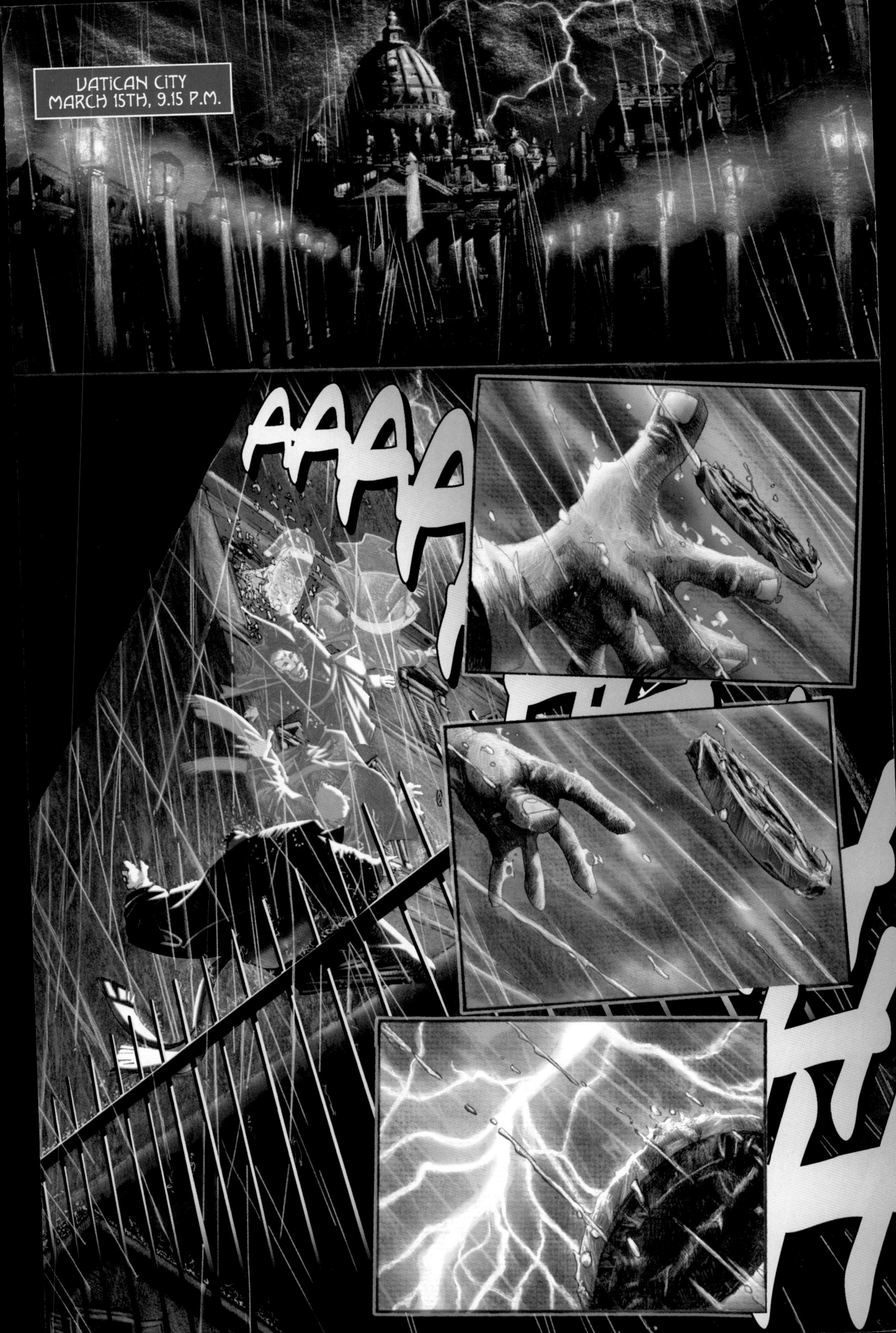
VATICAN CITY
MARCH 15TH, 9.15 P.M.
AAAA

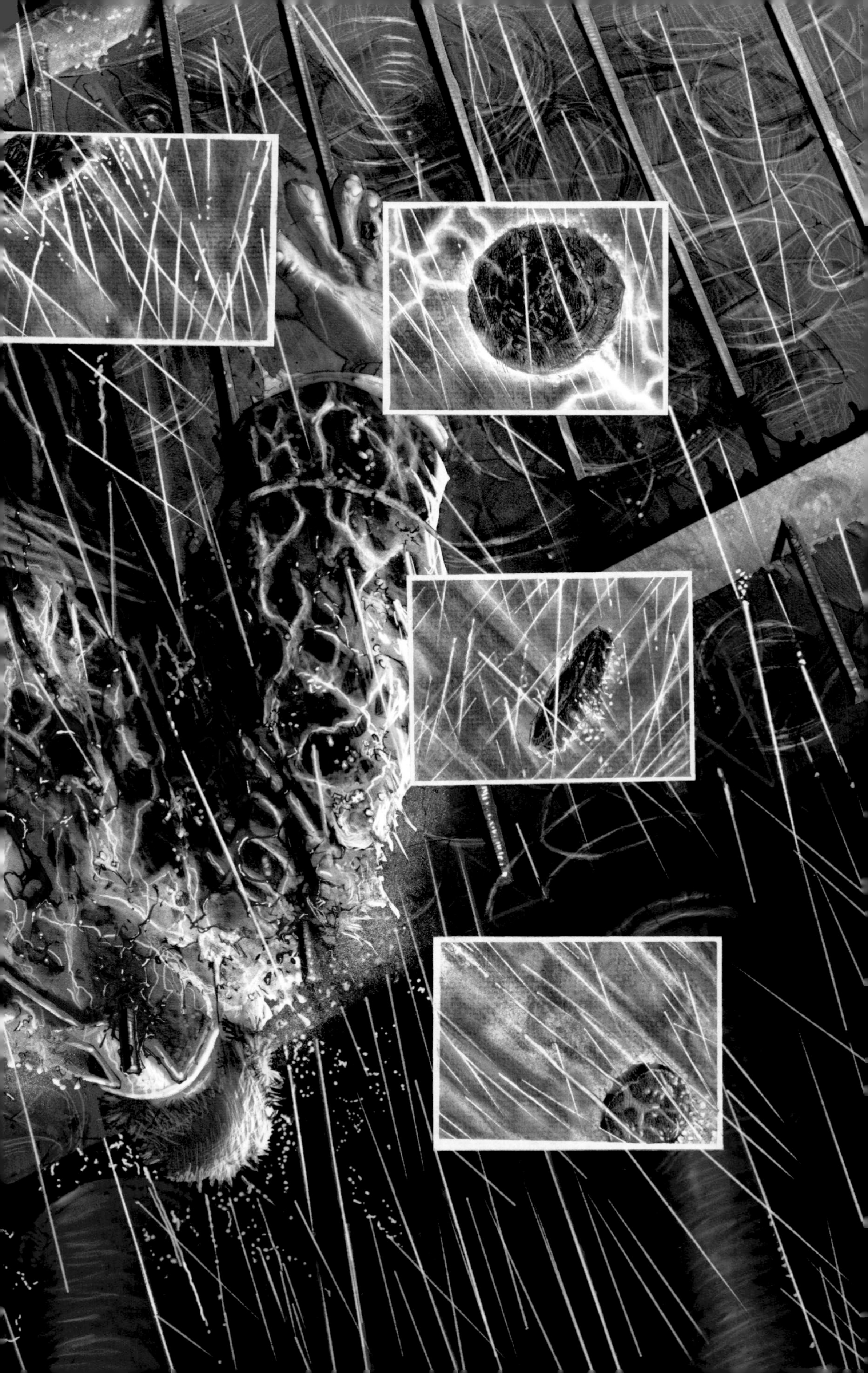

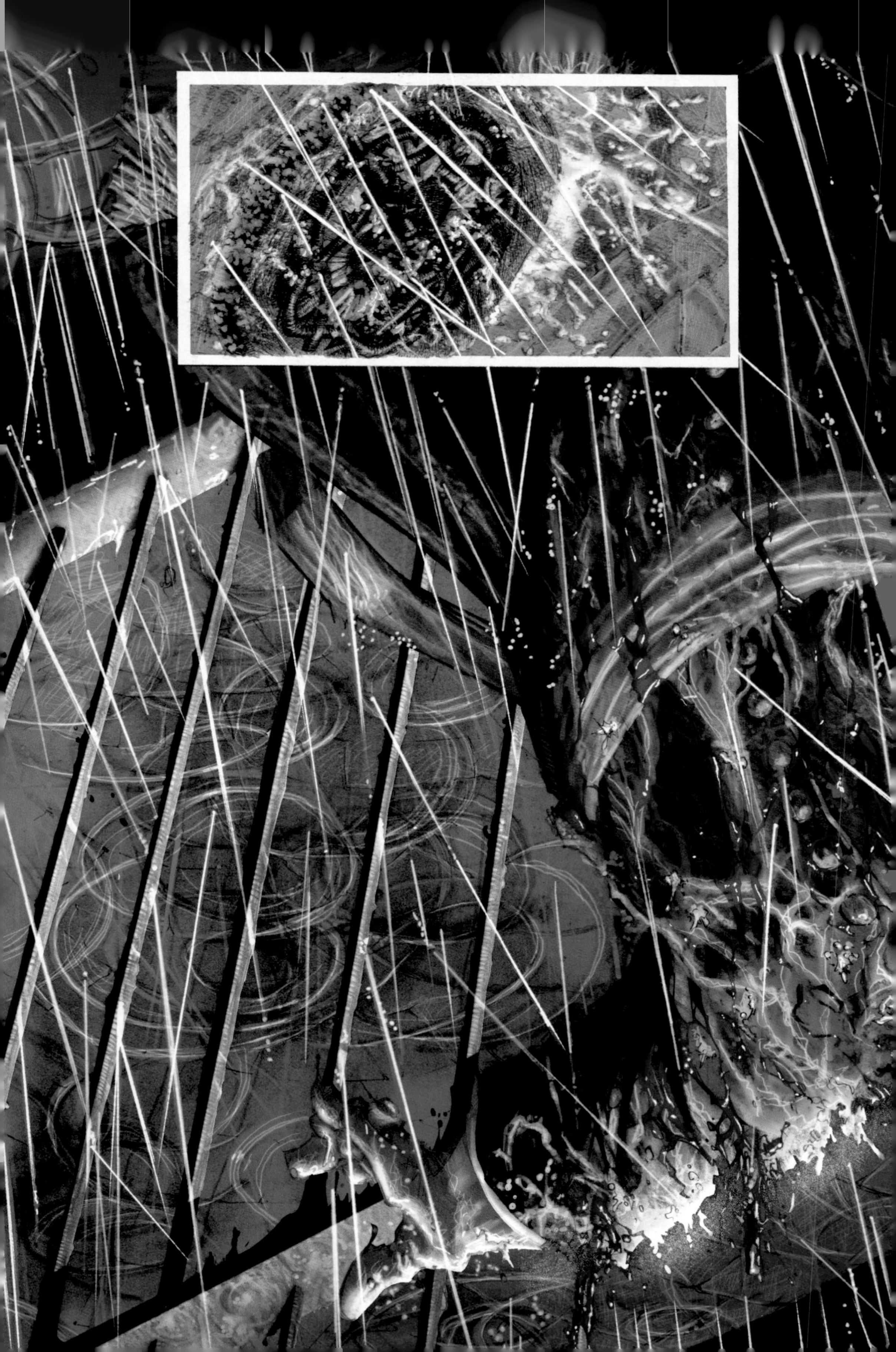

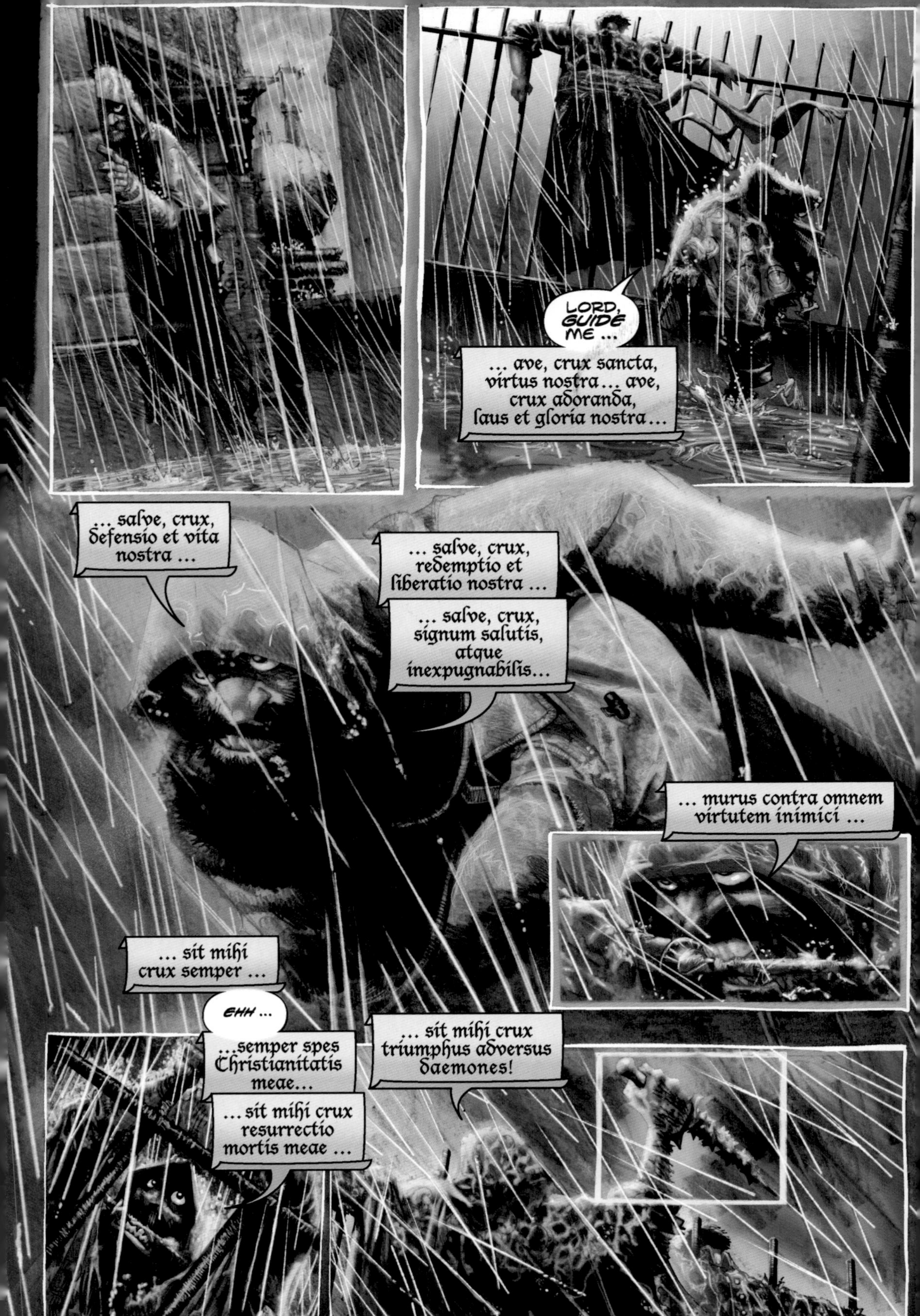
LORD, GUIDE ME ...
... ave, crux sancta, virtus nostra ... ave, crux adoranda, laus et gloria nostra ...
... salve, crux, defensio et vita nostra ...
... salve, crux, redemptio et liberatio nostra ...
... salve, crux, signum salutis, atque inexpugnabilis ...
... murus contra omnem virtutem inimici ...
... sit mihi crux semper ...
EHH ...
... semper spes Christianitatis meae ...
... sit mihi crux resurrectio mortis meae ...
... sit mihi crux triumphus adversus daemones!

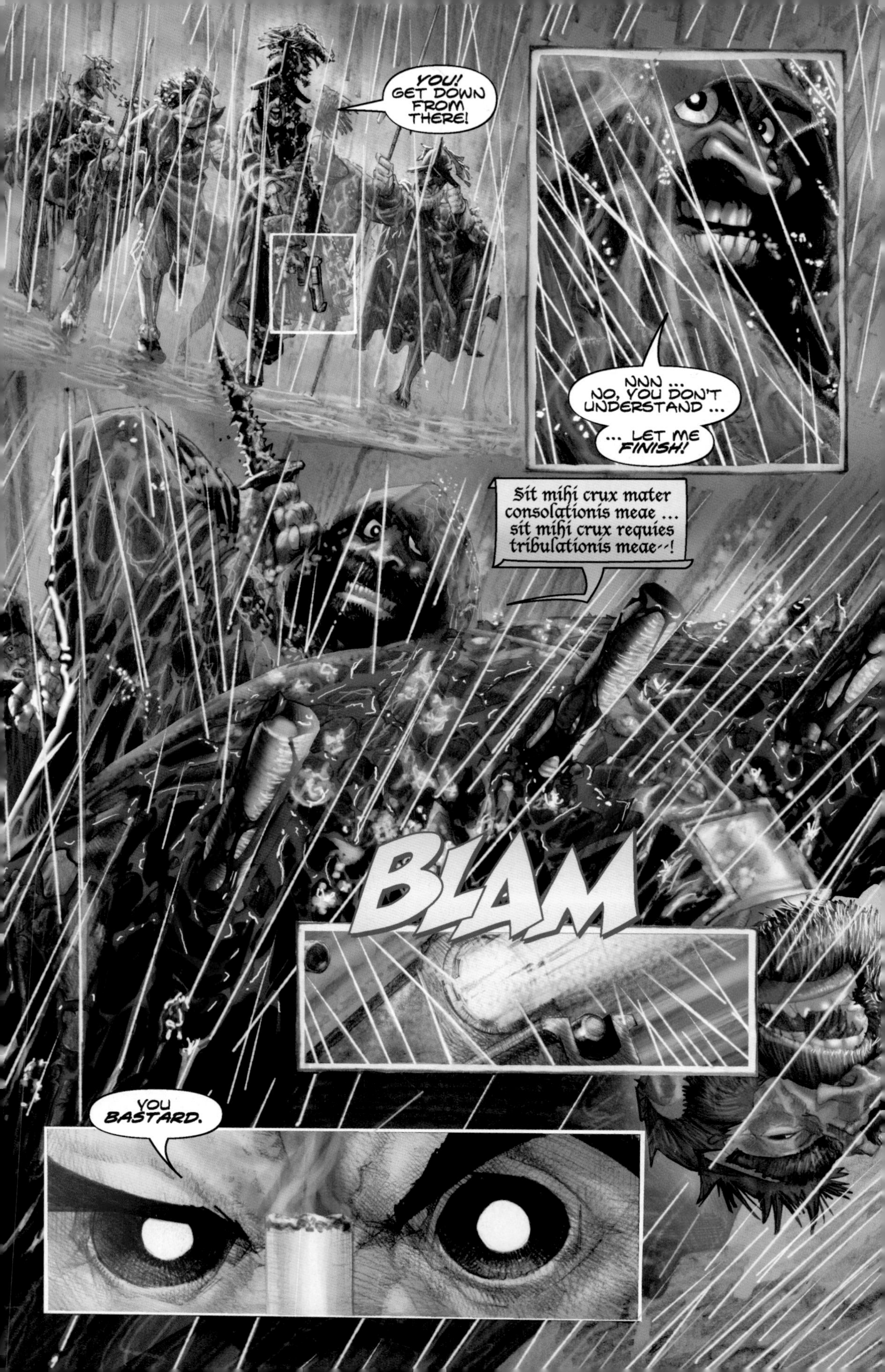
YOU! GET DOWN FROM THERE!
NNN ... NO, YOU DON'T UNDERSTAND ...
... LET ME FINISH!
Sit mihi crux mater consolationis meae ... sit mihi crux requies tribulationis meae--!
BLAM
YOU BASTARD.

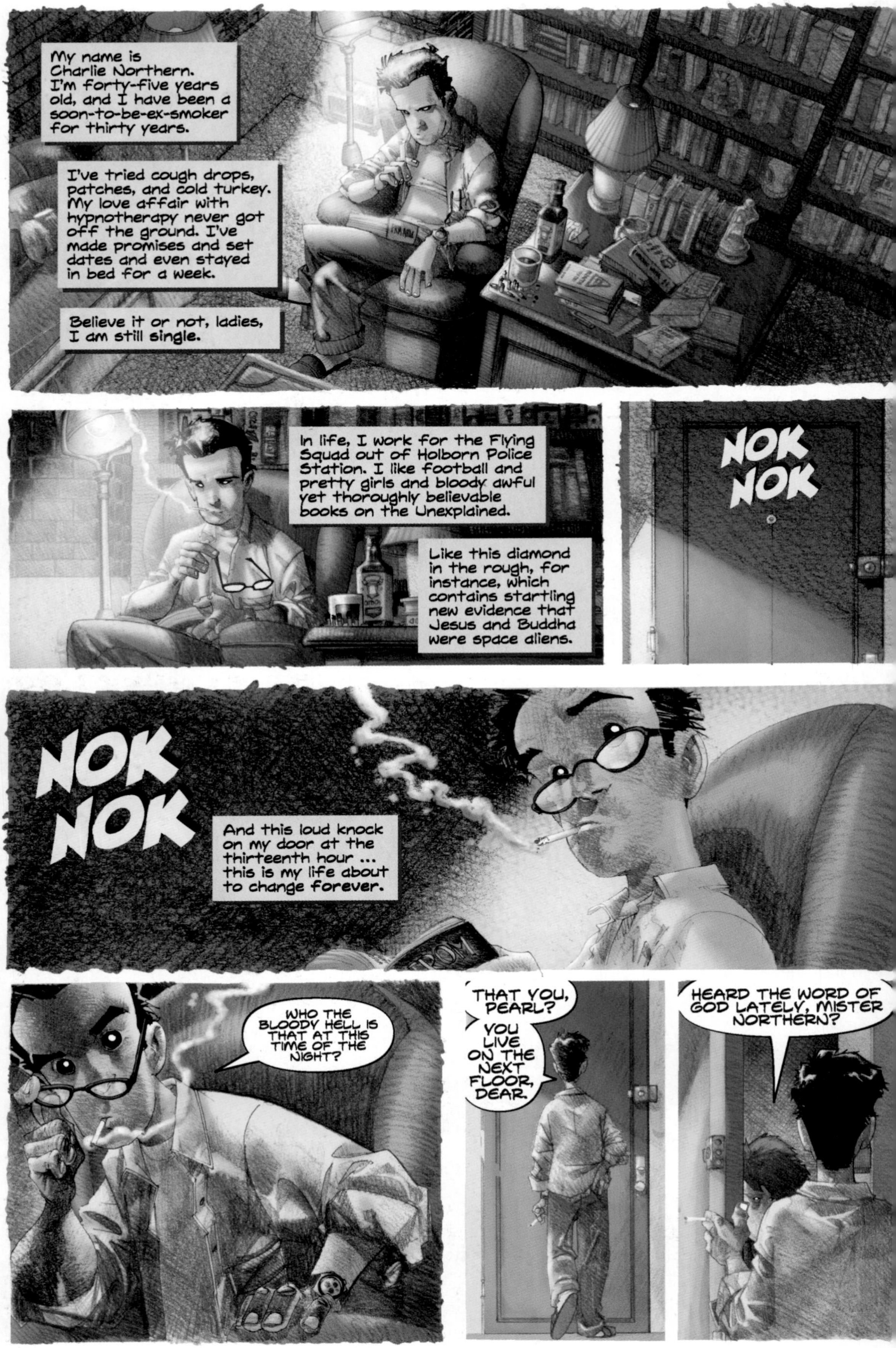
My name is Charlie Northern. I'm forty-five years old, and I have been a soon-to-be-ex-smoker for thirty years.
I've tried cough drops, patches, and cold turkey. My love affair with hypnotherapy never got off the ground. I've made promises and set dates and even stayed in bed for a week.
Believe it or not, ladies, I am still single.
In life, I work for the Flying Squad out of Holborn Police Station. I like football and pretty girls and bloody awful yet thoroughly believable books on the Unexplained.
Like this diamond in the rough, for instance, which contains startling new evidence that Jesus and Buddha were space aliens.
NOK NOK
NOK NOK
And this loud knock on my door at the thirteenth hour ... this is my life about to change forever.
WHO THE BLOODY HELL IS THAT AT THIS TIME OF THE NIGHT?
THAT YOU, PEARL?
YOU LIVE ON THE NEXT FLOOR, DEAR.
HEARD THE WORD OF GOD LATELY, MISTER NORTHERN?

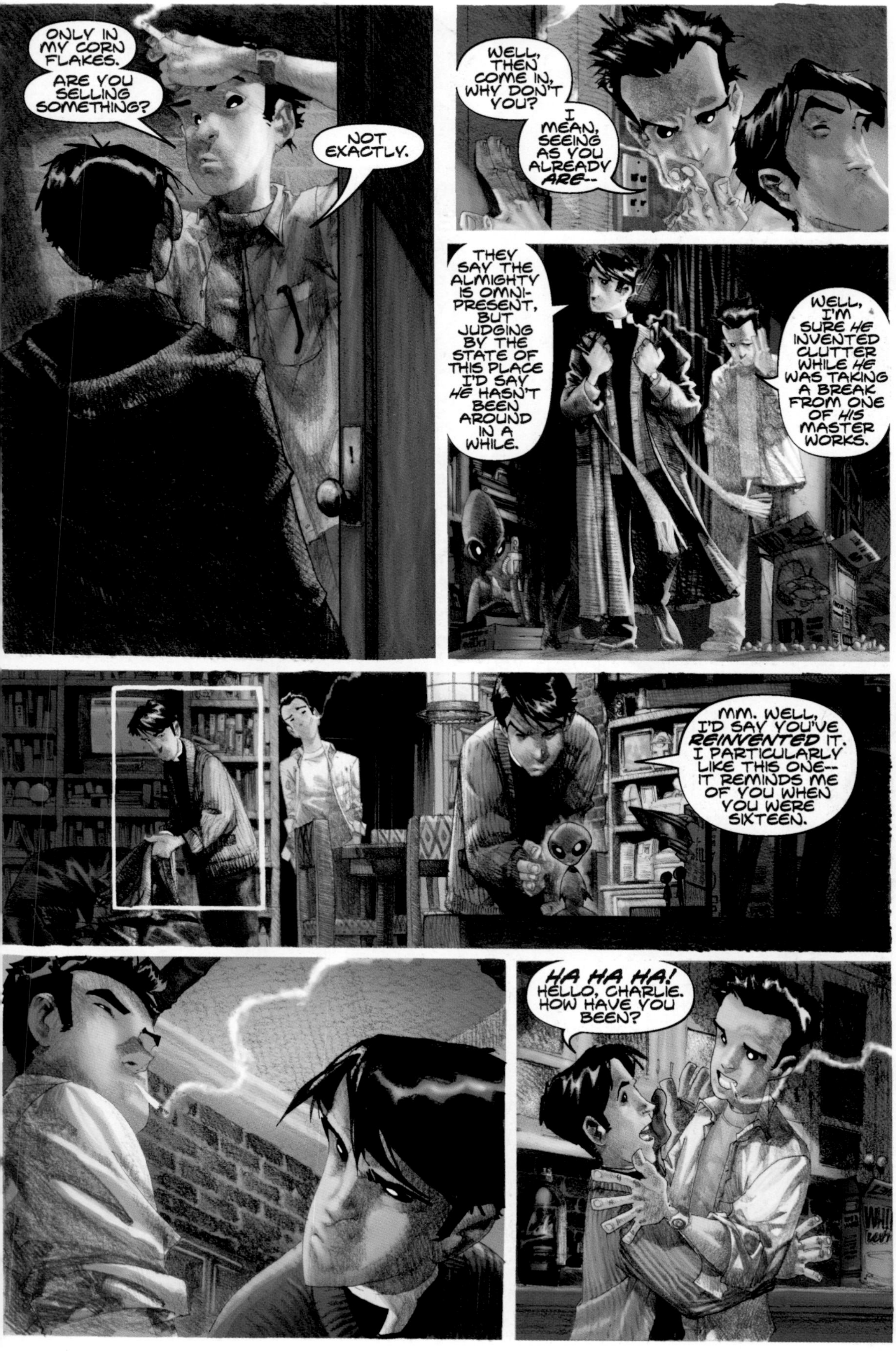
ONLY IN MY CORN FLAKES.
ARE YOU SELLING SOMETHING?
NOT EXACTLY.
WELL, THEN COME IN, WHY DON'T YOU?
I MEAN, SEEING AS YOU ALREADY *ARE*--
THEY SAY THE ALMIGHTY IS OMNI-PRESENT, BUT JUDGING BY THE STATE OF THIS PLACE I'D SAY *HE* HASN'T BEEN AROUND IN A WHILE.
WELL, I'M SURE *HE* INVENTED CLUTTER WHILE *HE* WAS TAKING A BREAK FROM ONE OF *HIS* MASTER WORKS.
MM. WELL, I'D SAY YOU'VE ***REINVENTED*** IT. I PARTICULARLY LIKE THIS ONE-- IT REMINDS ME OF YOU WHEN YOU WERE SIXTEEN.
HA HA HA! HELLO, CHARLIE. HOW HAVE YOU BEEN?

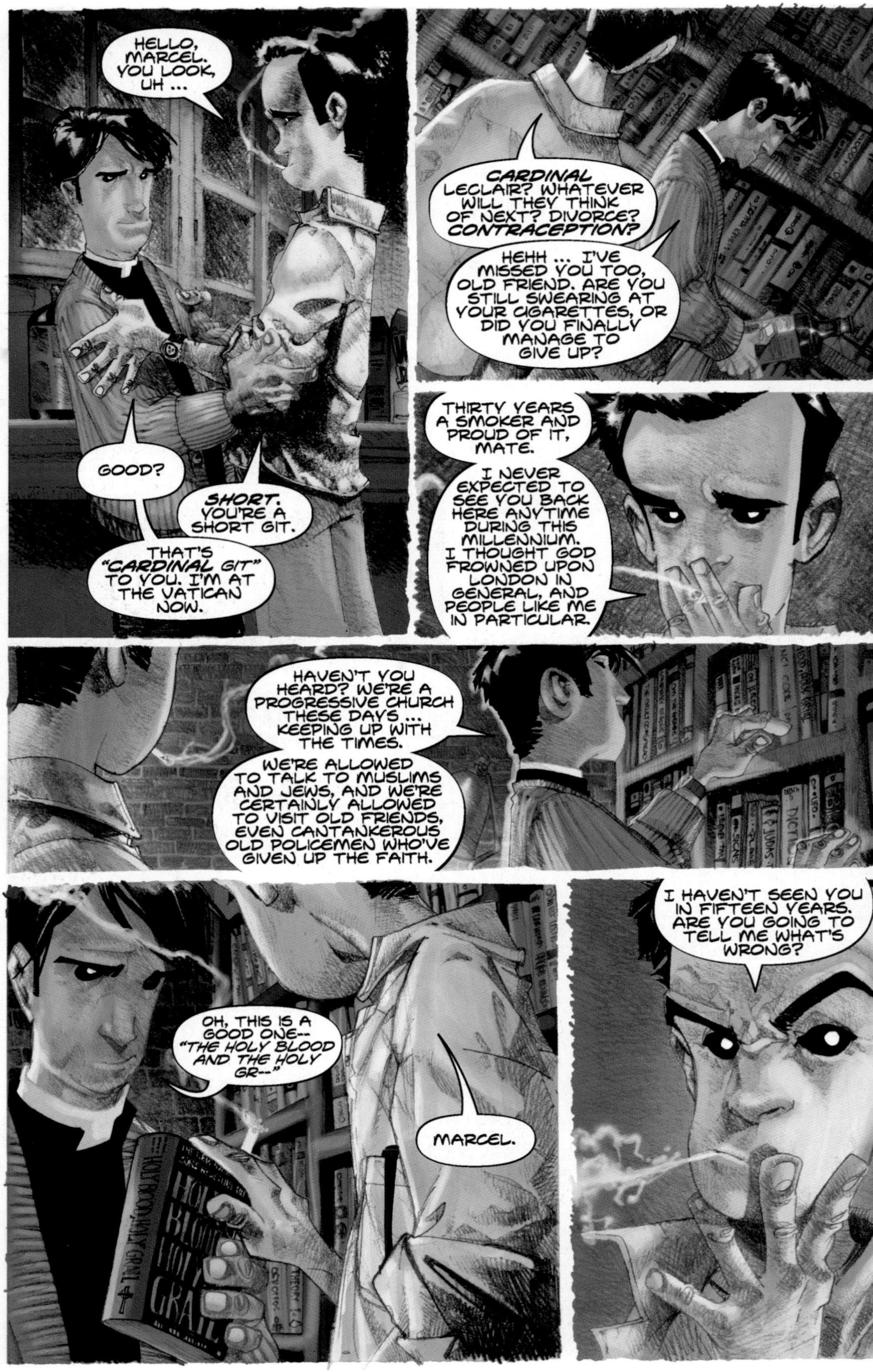

HELLO, MARCEL. YOU LOOK, UH ...
GOOD?
SHORT. YOU'RE A SHORT GIT.
THAT'S "CARDINAL GIT" TO YOU. I'M AT THE VATICAN NOW.
CARDINAL LECLAIR? WHATEVER WILL THEY THINK OF NEXT? DIVORCE? CONTRACEPTION?
HEHH ... I'VE MISSED YOU TOO, OLD FRIEND. ARE YOU STILL SWEARING AT YOUR CIGARETTES, OR DID YOU FINALLY MANAGE TO GIVE UP?
THIRTY YEARS A SMOKER AND PROUD OF IT, MATE.
I NEVER EXPECTED TO SEE YOU BACK HERE ANYTIME DURING THIS MILLENNIUM. I THOUGHT GOD FROWNED UPON LONDON IN GENERAL, AND PEOPLE LIKE ME IN PARTICULAR.
HAVEN'T YOU HEARD? WE'RE A PROGRESSIVE CHURCH THESE DAYS ... KEEPING UP WITH THE TIMES.
WE'RE ALLOWED TO TALK TO MUSLIMS AND JEWS, AND WE'RE CERTAINLY ALLOWED TO VISIT OLD FRIENDS, EVEN CANTANKEROUS OLD POLICEMEN WHO'VE GIVEN UP THE FAITH.
OH, THIS IS A GOOD ONE-- "THE HOLY BLOOD AND THE HOLY GR--"
MARCEL.
I HAVEN'T SEEN YOU IN FIFTEEN YEARS. ARE YOU GOING TO TELL ME WHAT'S WRONG?

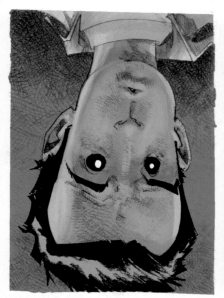

WILLIAM RICHLEAU IS DEAD.

WAIT A SECOND ... WHAT KIND OF "MAJOR EVENT"?

I MANAGED TO FINAGLE GETTING YOU AWAY FROM THE STATION FOR A WHILE. TECHNICALLY, THE VATICAN IS A COUNTRY, SO THIS IS SEEN AS AN EXERCISE IN INTERNATIONAL COOPERATION.

TRUST ME WITH WHAT?

I NEED YOUR HELP ON THIS ONE, CHARLIE. BELIEVE IT OR NOT, I THINK YOU MIGHT BE THE ONLY PERSON I CAN TRUST.

WHEN PEOPLE TURN ON THEIR TELEVISION SETS TOMORROW THEY'RE GOING TO LEARN OF A MAJOR EVENT THAT'S TAKEN PLACE AT THE VATICAN. WE'VE KEPT IT AS QUIET AS WE CAN BUT OUR TIME'S RUN OUT.

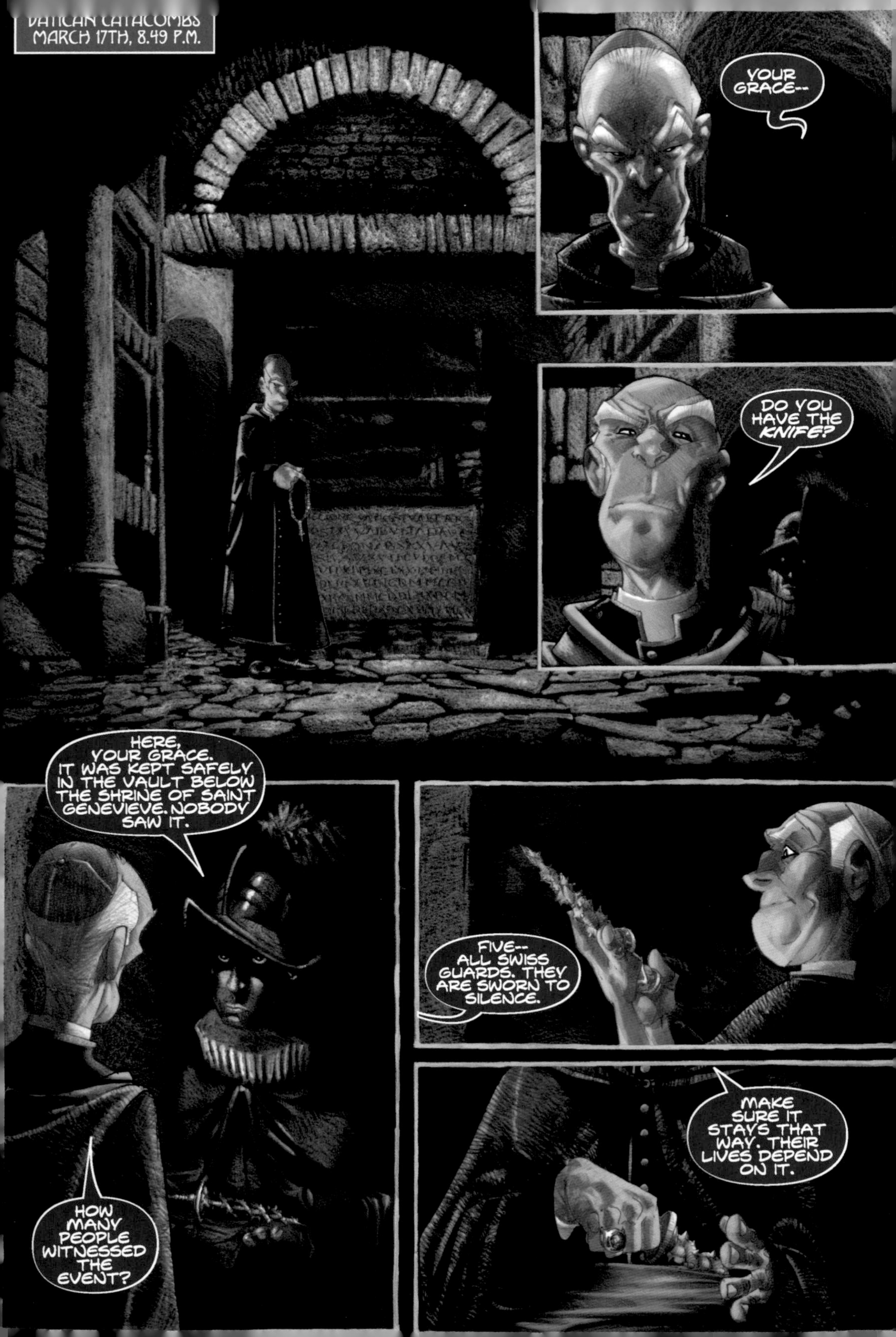
VATICAN CATACOMBS
MARCH 17TH, 8.49 P.M.
YOUR GRACE--
DO YOU HAVE THE KNIFE?
HERE, YOUR GRACE. IT WAS KEPT SAFELY IN THE VAULT BELOW THE SHRINE OF SAINT GENEVIEVE. NOBODY SAW IT.
HOW MANY PEOPLE WITNESSED THE EVENT?
FIVE-- ALL SWISS GUARDS. THEY ARE SWORN TO SILENCE.
MAKE SURE IT STAYS THAT WAY. THEIR LIVES DEPEND ON IT.

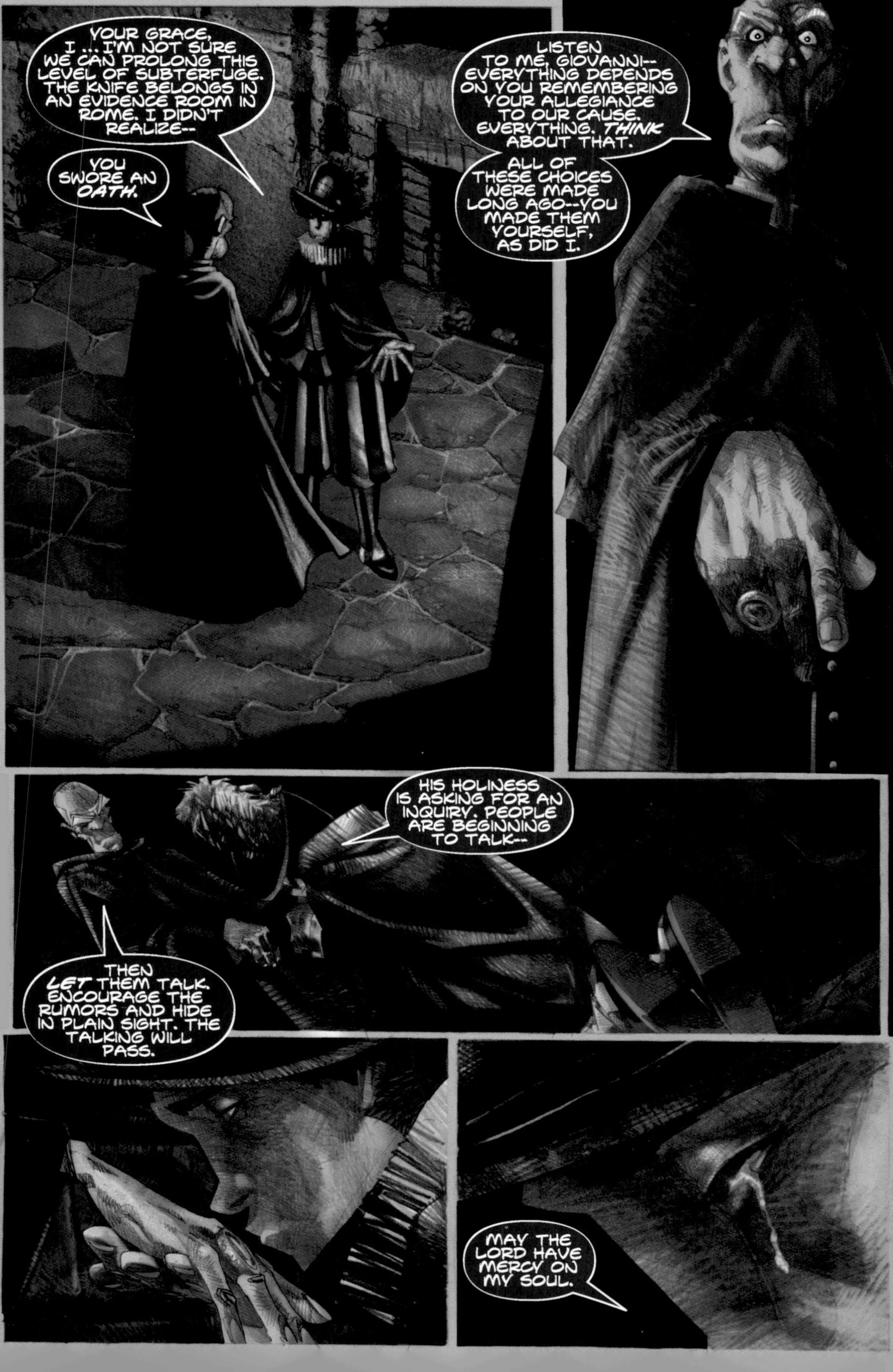
YOUR GRACE, I ... I'M NOT SURE WE CAN PROLONG THIS LEVEL OF SUBTERFUGE. THE KNIFE BELONGS IN AN EVIDENCE ROOM IN ROME. I DIDN'T REALIZE--
YOU SWORE AN *OATH.*
LISTEN TO ME, GIOVANNI-- EVERYTHING DEPENDS ON YOU REMEMBERING YOUR ALLEGIANCE TO OUR CAUSE. EVERYTHING. *THINK* ABOUT THAT.
ALL OF THESE CHOICES WERE MADE LONG AGO--YOU MADE THEM YOURSELF, AS DID I.
HIS HOLINESS IS ASKING FOR AN INQUIRY. PEOPLE ARE BEGINNING TO TALK--
THEN *LET* THEM TALK. ENCOURAGE THE RUMORS AND HIDE IN PLAIN SIGHT. THE TALKING WILL PASS.
MAY THE LORD HAVE MERCY ON MY SOUL.

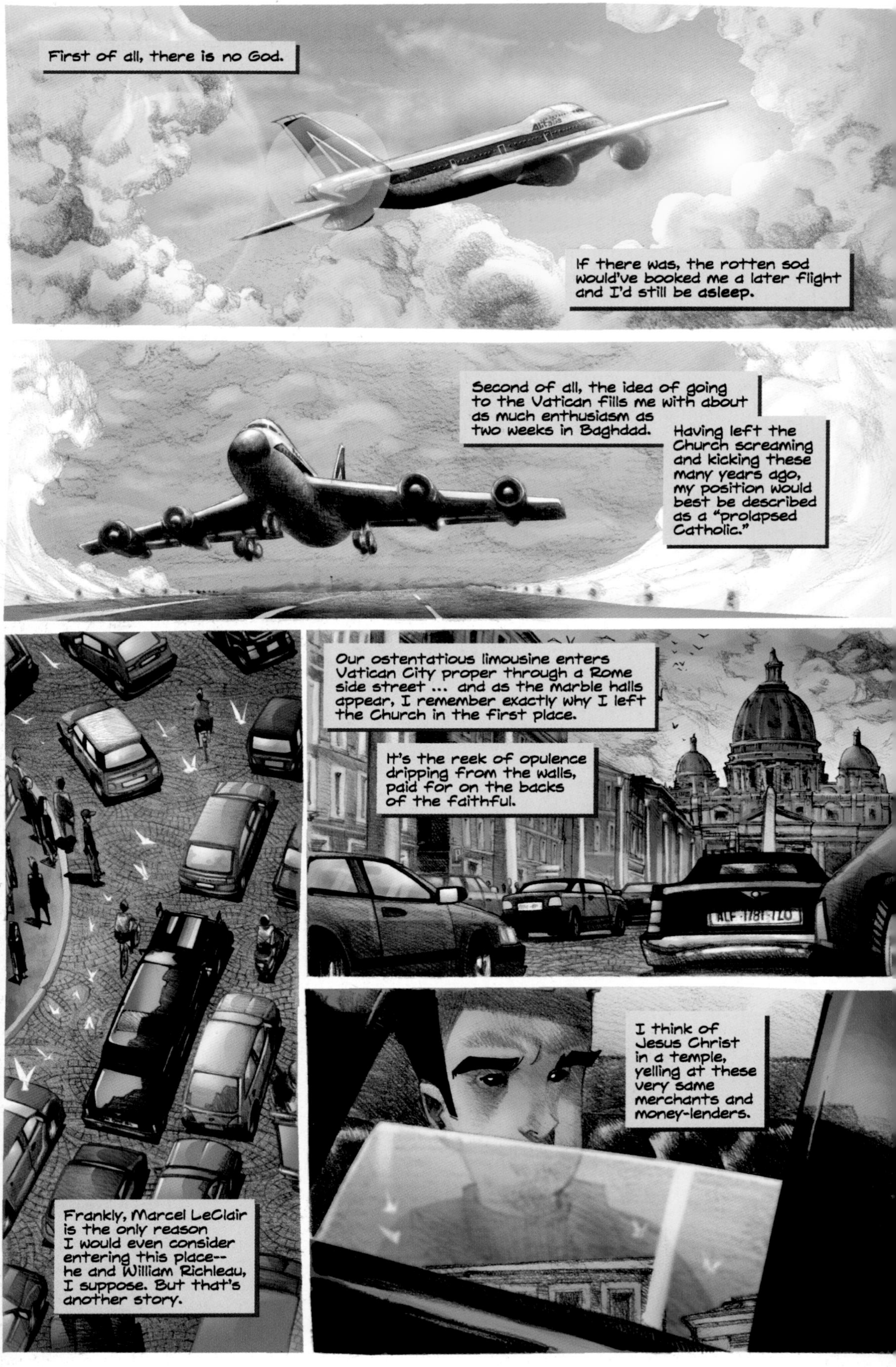
First of all, there is no God.
If there was, the rotten sod would've booked me a later flight and I'd still be asleep.
Second of all, the idea of going to the Vatican fills me with about as much enthusiasm as two weeks in Baghdad.
Having left the Church screaming and kicking these many years ago, my position would best be described as a "prolapsed Catholic."
Frankly, Marcel LeClair is the only reason I would even consider entering this place-- he and William Richleau, I suppose. But that's another story.
Our ostentatious limousine enters Vatican City proper through a Rome side street ... and as the marble halls appear, I remember exactly why I left the Church in the first place.
It's the reek of opulence dripping from the walls, paid for on the backs of the faithful.
I think of Jesus Christ in a temple, yelling at these very same merchants and money-lenders.

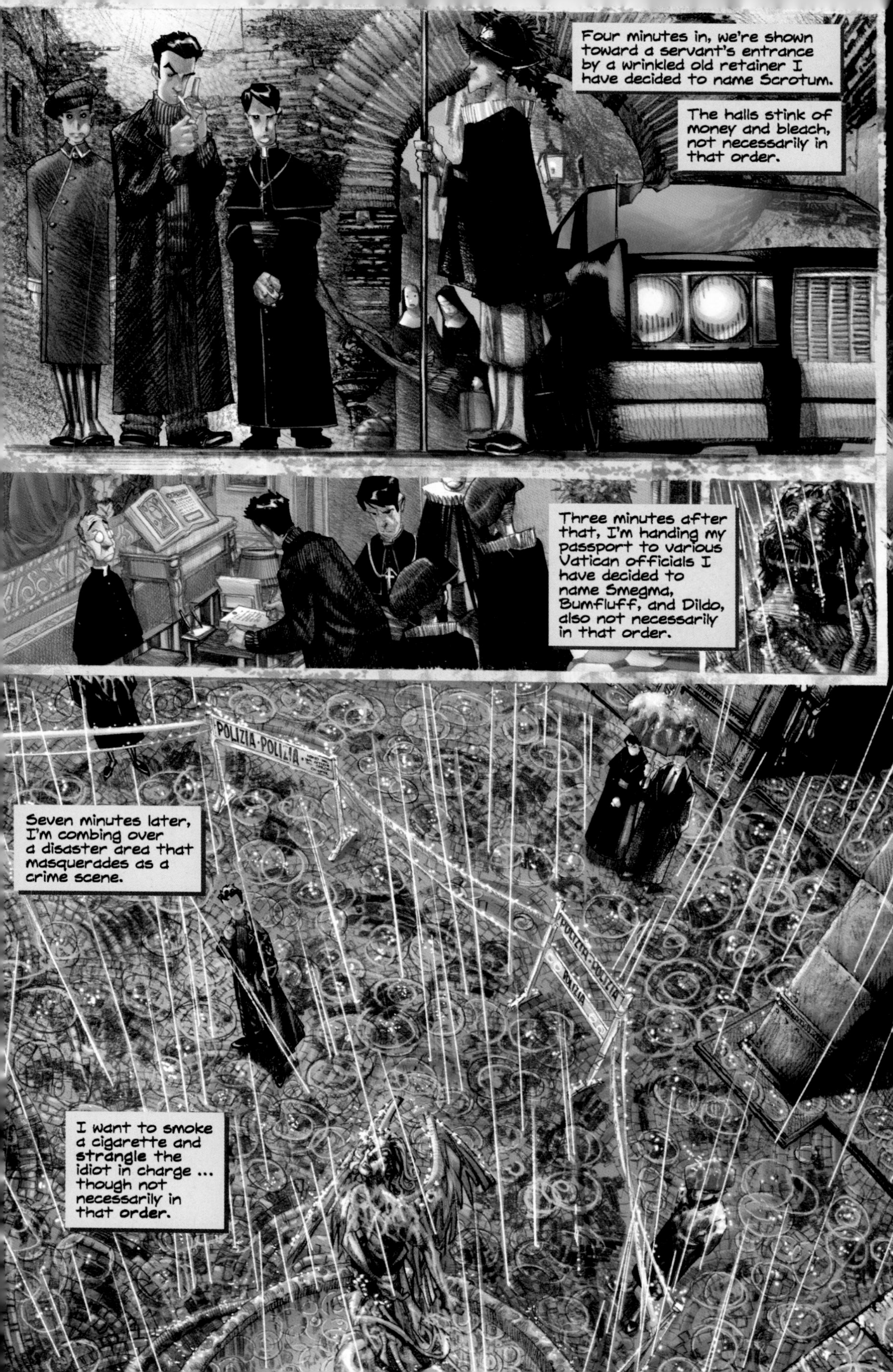
Four minutes in, we're shown toward a servant's entrance by a wrinkled old retainer I have decided to name Scrotum.
The halls stink of money and bleach, not necessarily in that order.
Three minutes after that, I'm handing my passport to various Vatican officials I have decided to name Smegma, Bumfluff, and Dildo, also not necessarily in that order.
POLIZIA·POLIZIA
Seven minutes later, I'm combing over a disaster area that masquerades as a crime scene.
I want to smoke a cigarette and strangle the idiot in charge ... though not necessarily in that order.

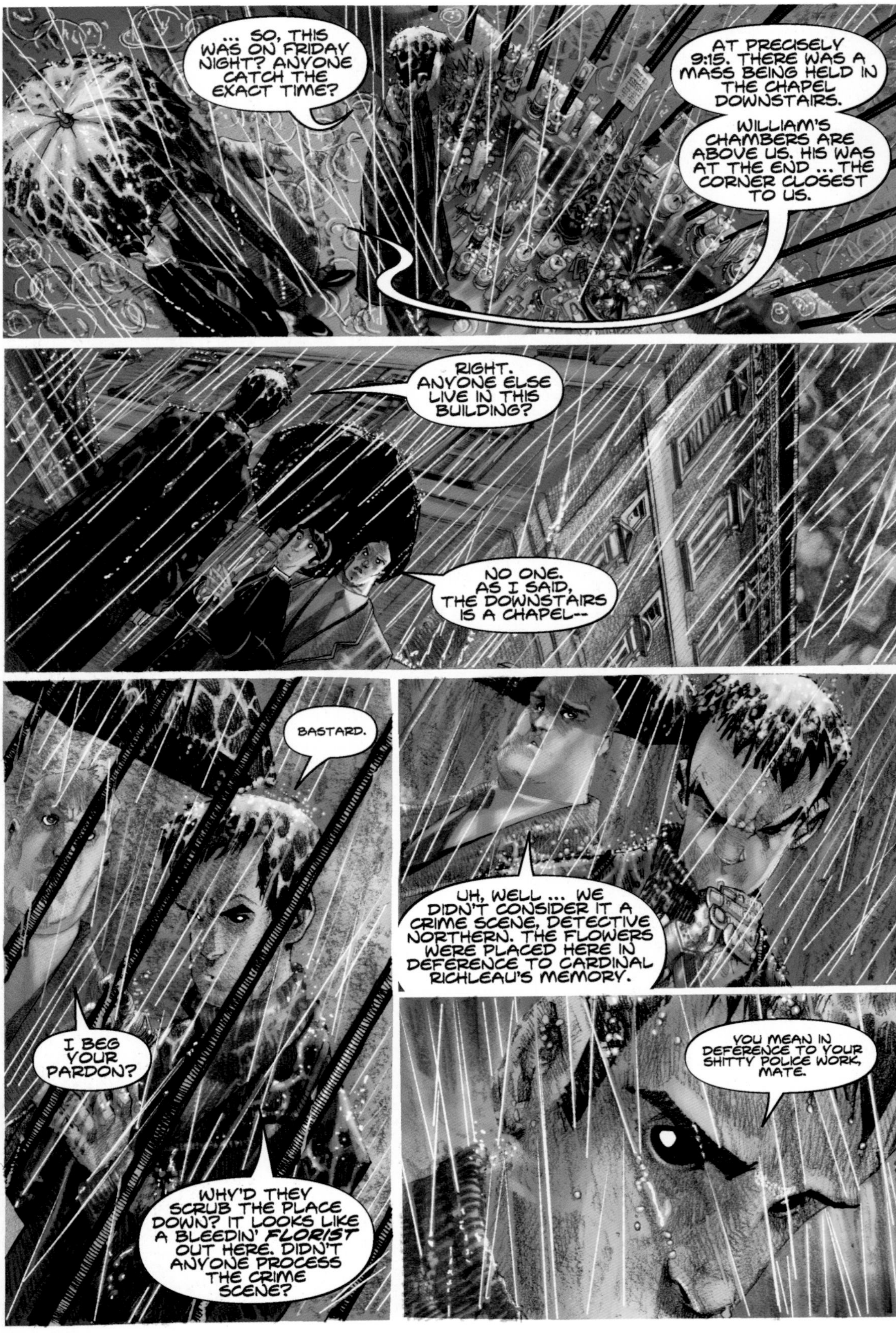
... SO, THIS WAS ON FRIDAY NIGHT? ANYONE CATCH THE EXACT TIME?
AT PRECISELY 9:15. THERE WAS A MASS BEING HELD IN THE CHAPEL DOWNSTAIRS.
WILLIAM'S CHAMBERS ARE ABOVE US. HIS WAS AT THE END ... THE CORNER CLOSEST TO US.
RIGHT. ANYONE ELSE LIVE IN THIS BUILDING?
NO ONE. AS I SAID, THE DOWNSTAIRS IS A CHAPEL--
BASTARD.
WHY'D THEY SCRUB THE PLACE DOWN? IT LOOKS LIKE A BLEEDIN' *FLORIST* OUT HERE. DIDN'T ANYONE PROCESS THE CRIME SCENE?
I BEG YOUR PARDON?
UH, WELL ... WE DIDN'T CONSIDER IT A CRIME SCENE, DETECTIVE NORTHERN. THE FLOWERS WERE PLACED HERE IN DEFERENCE TO CARDINAL RICHLEAU'S MEMORY.
YOU MEAN IN DEFERENCE TO YOUR SHITTY POLICE WORK, MATE.

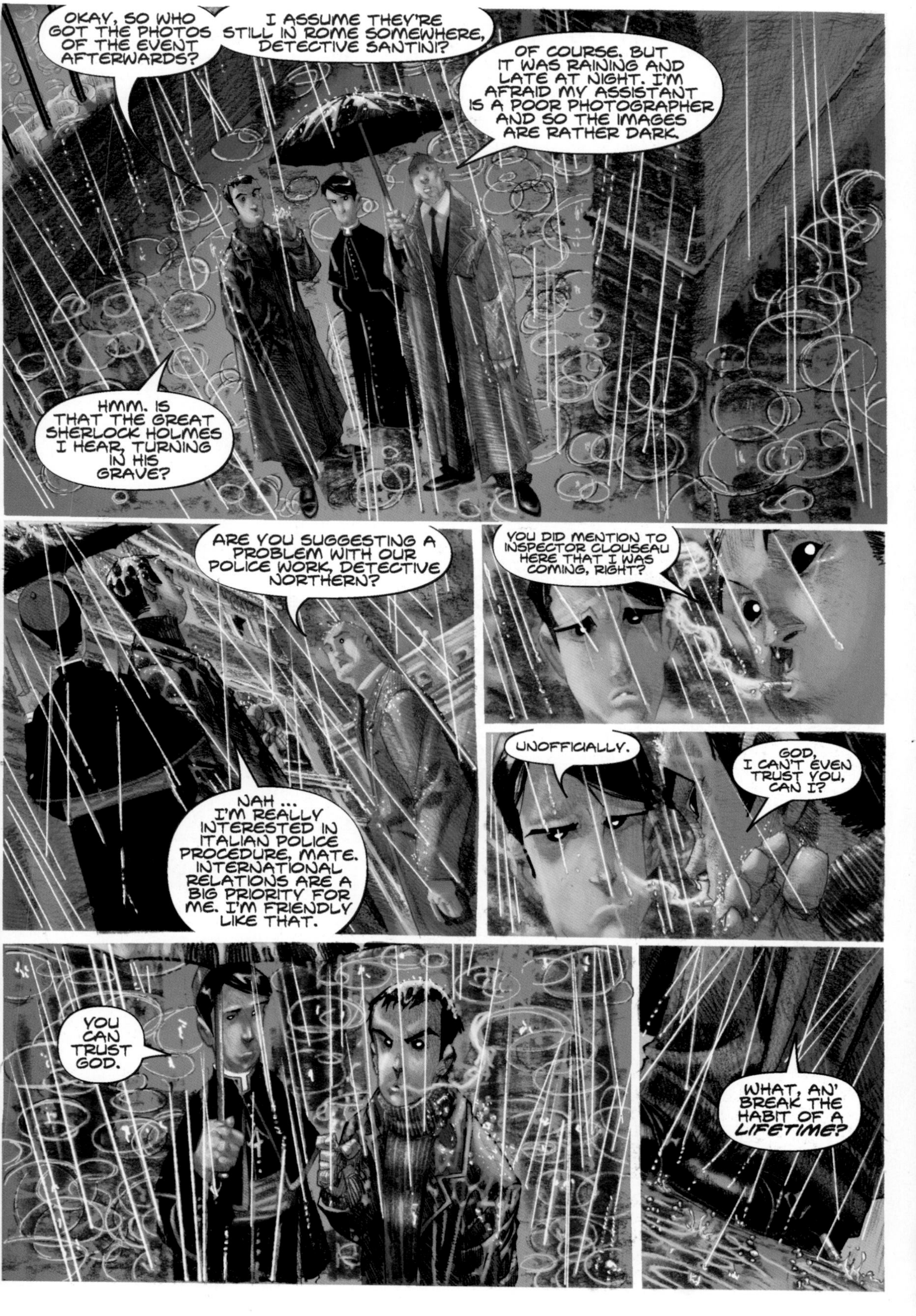

OKAY, SO WHO GOT THE PHOTOS OF THE EVENT AFTERWARDS?
I ASSUME THEY'RE STILL IN ROME SOMEWHERE, DETECTIVE SANTINI?
OF COURSE. BUT IT WAS RAINING AND LATE AT NIGHT. I'M AFRAID MY ASSISTANT IS A POOR PHOTOGRAPHER AND SO THE IMAGES ARE RATHER DARK.
HMM. IS THAT THE GREAT SHERLOCK HOLMES I HEAR, TURNING IN HIS GRAVE?
ARE YOU SUGGESTING A PROBLEM WITH OUR POLICE WORK, DETECTIVE NORTHERN?
NAH ... I'M REALLY INTERESTED IN ITALIAN POLICE PROCEDURE, MATE. INTERNATIONAL RELATIONS ARE A BIG PRIORITY FOR ME. I'M FRIENDLY LIKE THAT.
YOU DID MENTION TO INSPECTOR CLOUSEAU HERE THAT I WAS COMING, RIGHT?
UNOFFICIALLY.
GOD, I CAN'T EVEN TRUST YOU, CAN I?
YOU CAN TRUST GOD.
WHAT, AN' BREAK THE HABIT OF A *LIFETIME?*

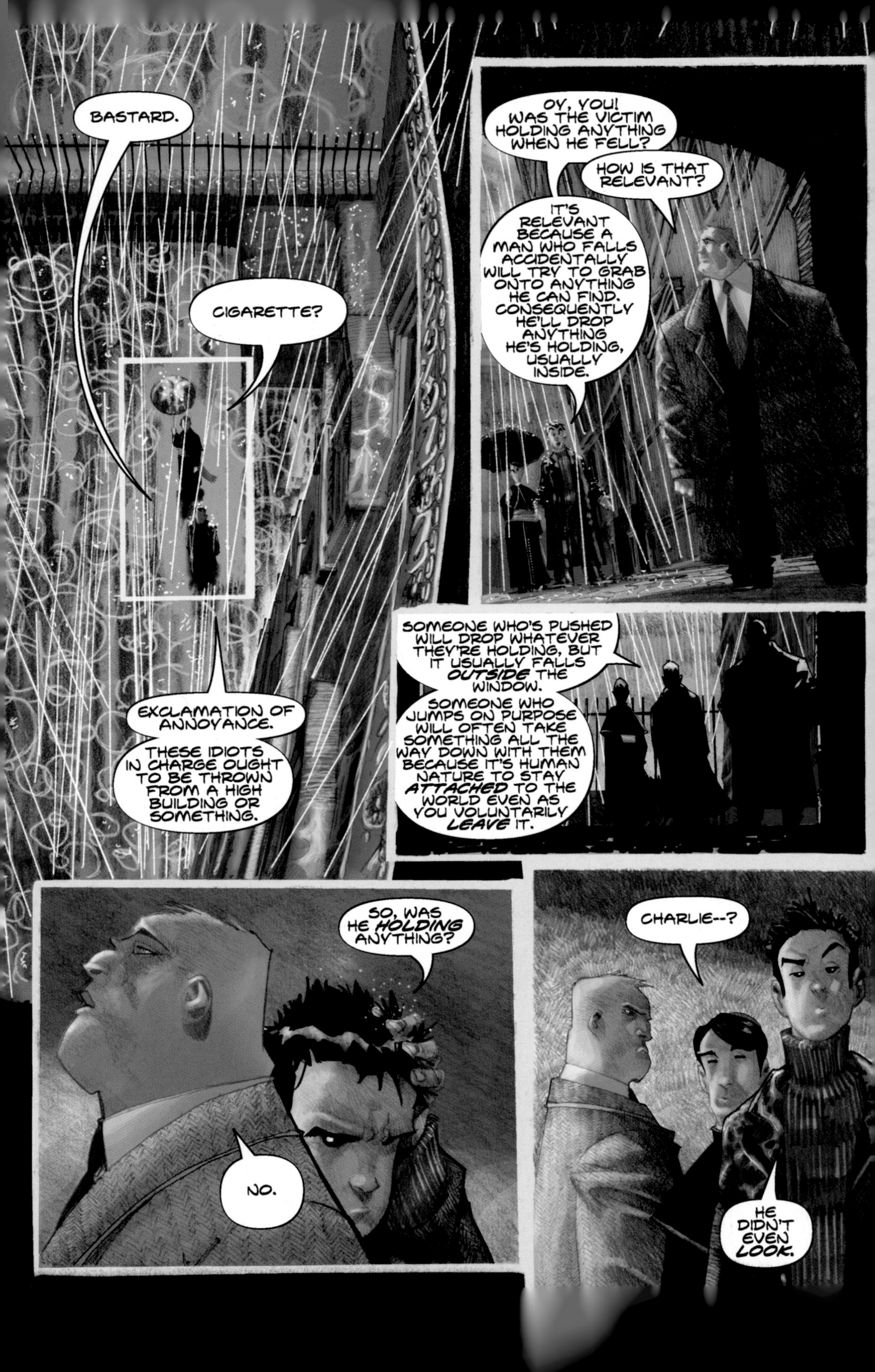
BASTARD.
CIGARETTE?
EXCLAMATION OF ANNOYANCE.
THESE IDIOTS IN CHARGE OUGHT TO BE THROWN FROM A HIGH BUILDING OR SOMETHING.
OY, YOU! WAS THE VICTIM HOLDING ANYTHING WHEN HE FELL?
HOW IS THAT RELEVANT?
IT'S RELEVANT BECAUSE A MAN WHO FALLS ACCIDENTALLY WILL TRY TO GRAB ONTO ANYTHING HE CAN FIND. CONSEQUENTLY HE'LL DROP ANYTHING HE'S HOLDING, USUALLY INSIDE.
SOMEONE WHO'S PUSHED WILL DROP WHATEVER THEY'RE HOLDING, BUT IT USUALLY FALLS *OUTSIDE* THE WINDOW.
SOMEONE WHO JUMPS ON PURPOSE WILL OFTEN TAKE SOMETHING ALL THE WAY DOWN WITH THEM BECAUSE IT'S HUMAN NATURE TO STAY *ATTACHED* TO THE WORLD EVEN AS YOU VOLUNTARILY *LEAVE* IT.
SO, WAS HE *HOLDING* ANYTHING?
NO.
CHARLIE--?
HE DIDN'T EVEN *LOOK*.

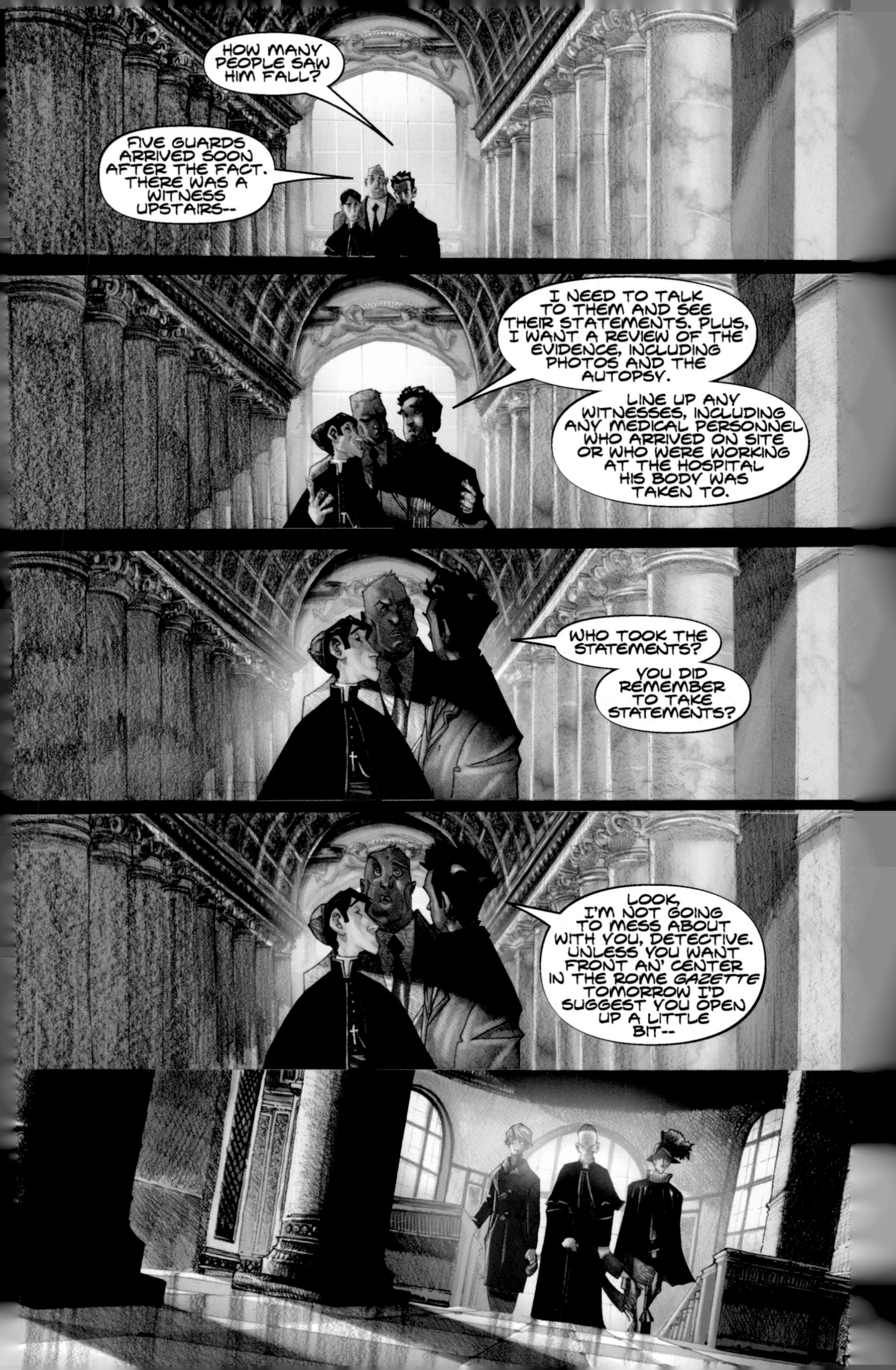
HOW MANY PEOPLE SAW HIM FALL?
FIVE GUARDS ARRIVED SOON AFTER THE FACT. THERE WAS A WITNESS UPSTAIRS--
I NEED TO TALK TO THEM AND SEE THEIR STATEMENTS. PLUS, I WANT A REVIEW OF THE EVIDENCE, INCLUDING PHOTOS AND THE AUTOPSY.
LINE UP ANY WITNESSES, INCLUDING ANY MEDICAL PERSONNEL WHO ARRIVED ON SITE OR WHO WERE WORKING AT THE HOSPITAL HIS BODY WAS TAKEN TO.
WHO TOOK THE STATEMENTS?
YOU DID REMEMBER TO TAKE STATEMENTS?
LOOK, I'M NOT GOING TO MESS ABOUT WITH YOU, DETECTIVE. UNLESS YOU WANT FRONT AN' CENTER IN THE ROME *GAZETTE* TOMORROW I'D SUGGEST YOU OPEN UP A LITTLE BIT--

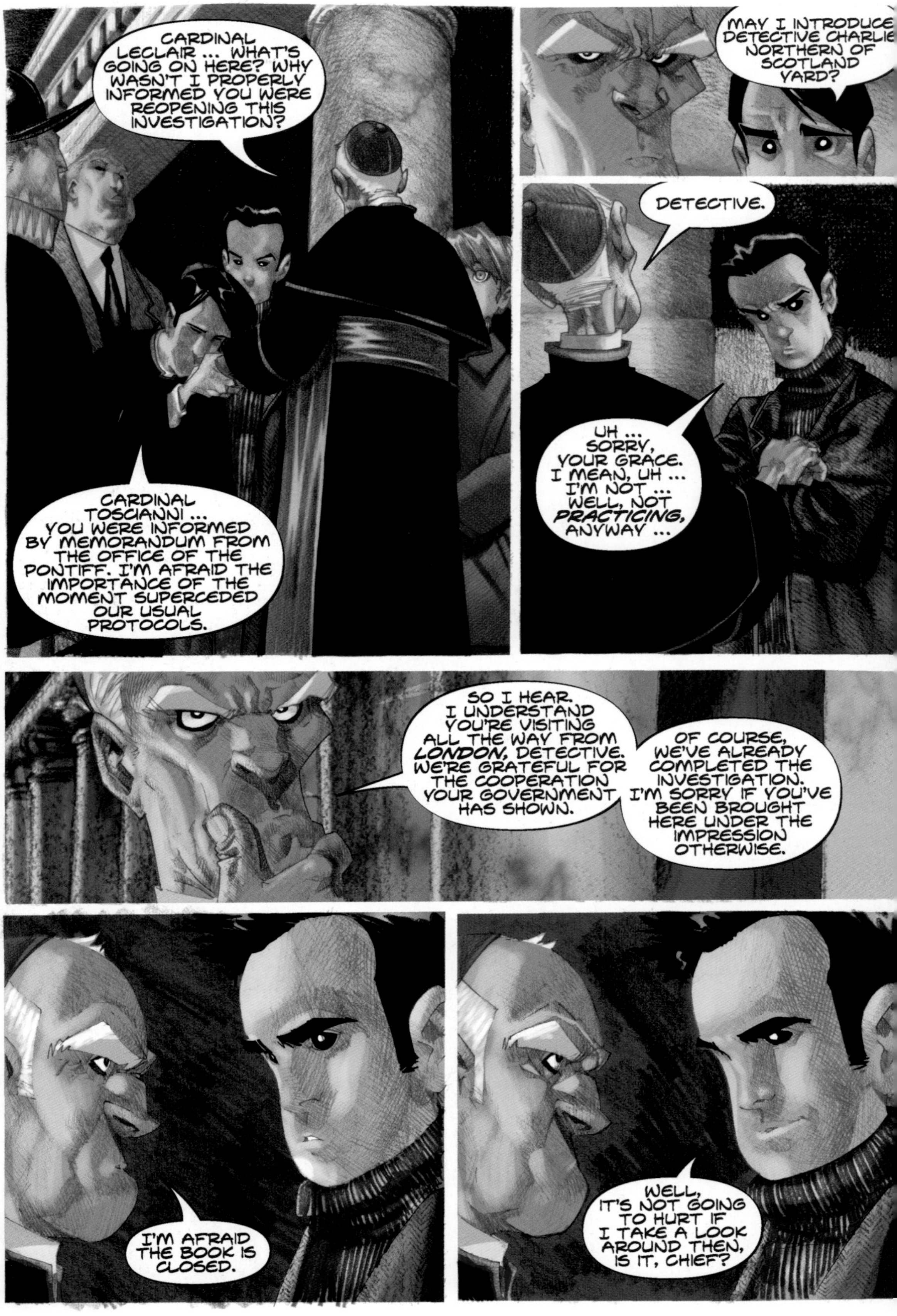
CARDINAL LECLAIR ... WHAT'S GOING ON HERE? WHY WASN'T I PROPERLY INFORMED YOU WERE REOPENING THIS INVESTIGATION?
CARDINAL TOSCIANNI ... YOU WERE INFORMED BY MEMORANDUM FROM THE OFFICE OF THE PONTIFF. I'M AFRAID THE IMPORTANCE OF THE MOMENT SUPERCEDED OUR USUAL PROTOCOLS.
MAY I INTRODUCE DETECTIVE CHARLIE NORTHERN OF SCOTLAND YARD?
DETECTIVE.
UH ... SORRY, YOUR GRACE. I MEAN, UH ... I'M NOT ... WELL, NOT *PRACTICING,* ANYWAY ...
SO I HEAR. I UNDERSTAND YOU'RE VISITING ALL THE WAY FROM *LONDON,* DETECTIVE. WE'RE GRATEFUL FOR THE COOPERATION YOUR GOVERNMENT HAS SHOWN.
OF COURSE, WE'VE ALREADY COMPLETED THE INVESTIGATION. I'M SORRY IF YOU'VE BEEN BROUGHT HERE UNDER THE IMPRESSION OTHERWISE.
I'M AFRAID THE BOOK IS CLOSED.
WELL, IT'S NOT GOING TO HURT IF I TAKE A LOOK AROUND THEN, IS IT, CHIEF?

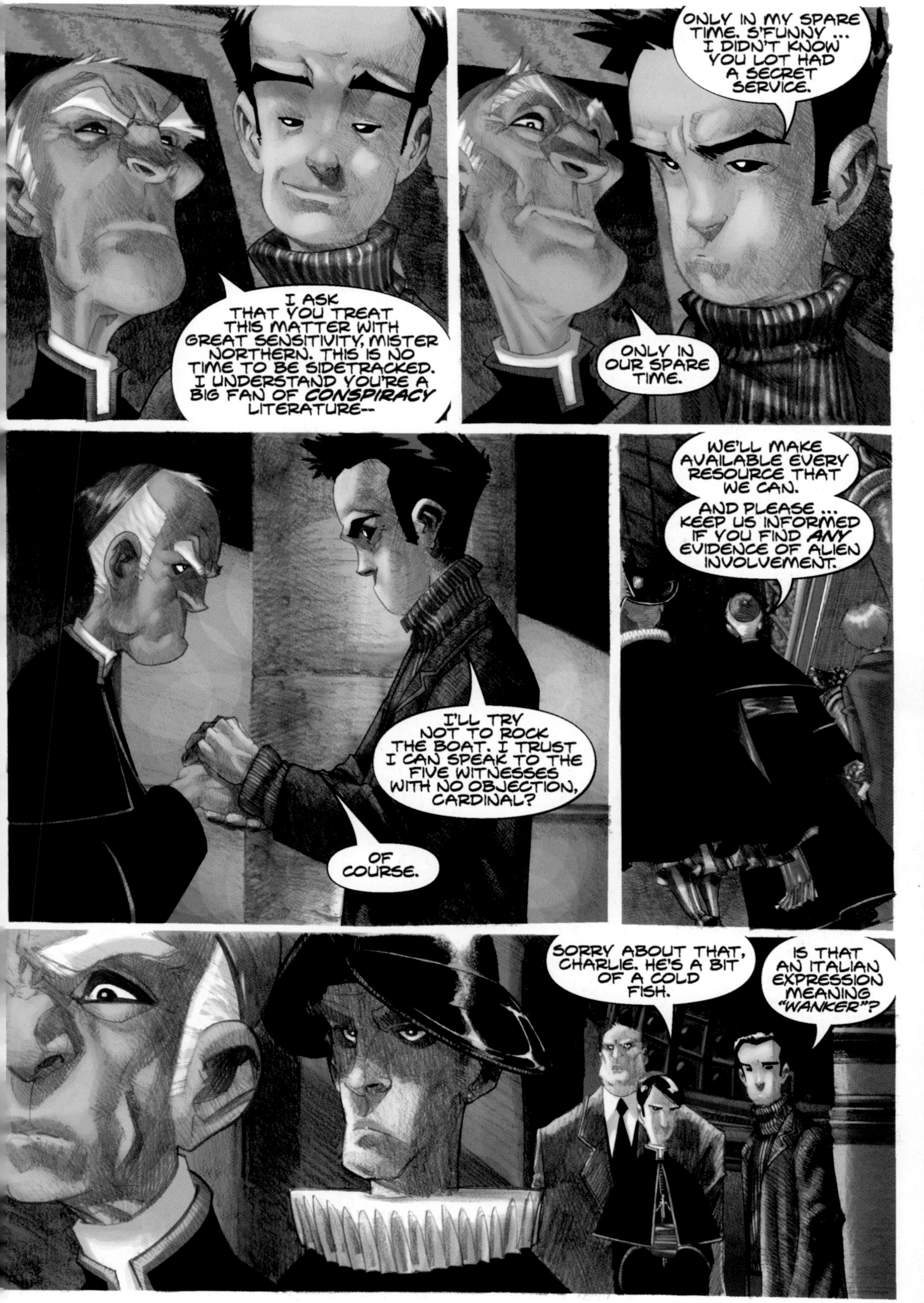
I ASK THAT YOU TREAT THIS MATTER WITH GREAT SENSITIVITY, MISTER NORTHERN. THIS IS NO TIME TO BE SIDETRACKED. I UNDERSTAND YOU'RE A BIG FAN OF CONSPIRACY LITERATURE--
ONLY IN MY SPARE TIME. S'FUNNY ... I DIDN'T KNOW YOU LOT HAD A SECRET SERVICE.
ONLY IN OUR SPARE TIME.
I'LL TRY NOT TO ROCK THE BOAT. I TRUST I CAN SPEAK TO THE FIVE WITNESSES WITH NO OBJECTION, CARDINAL?
OF COURSE.
WE'LL MAKE AVAILABLE EVERY RESOURCE THAT WE CAN.
AND PLEASE ... KEEP US INFORMED IF YOU FIND ANY EVIDENCE OF ALIEN INVOLVEMENT.
SORRY ABOUT THAT, CHARLIE. HE'S A BIT OF A COLD FISH.
IS THAT AN ITALIAN EXPRESSION MEANING "WANKER"?

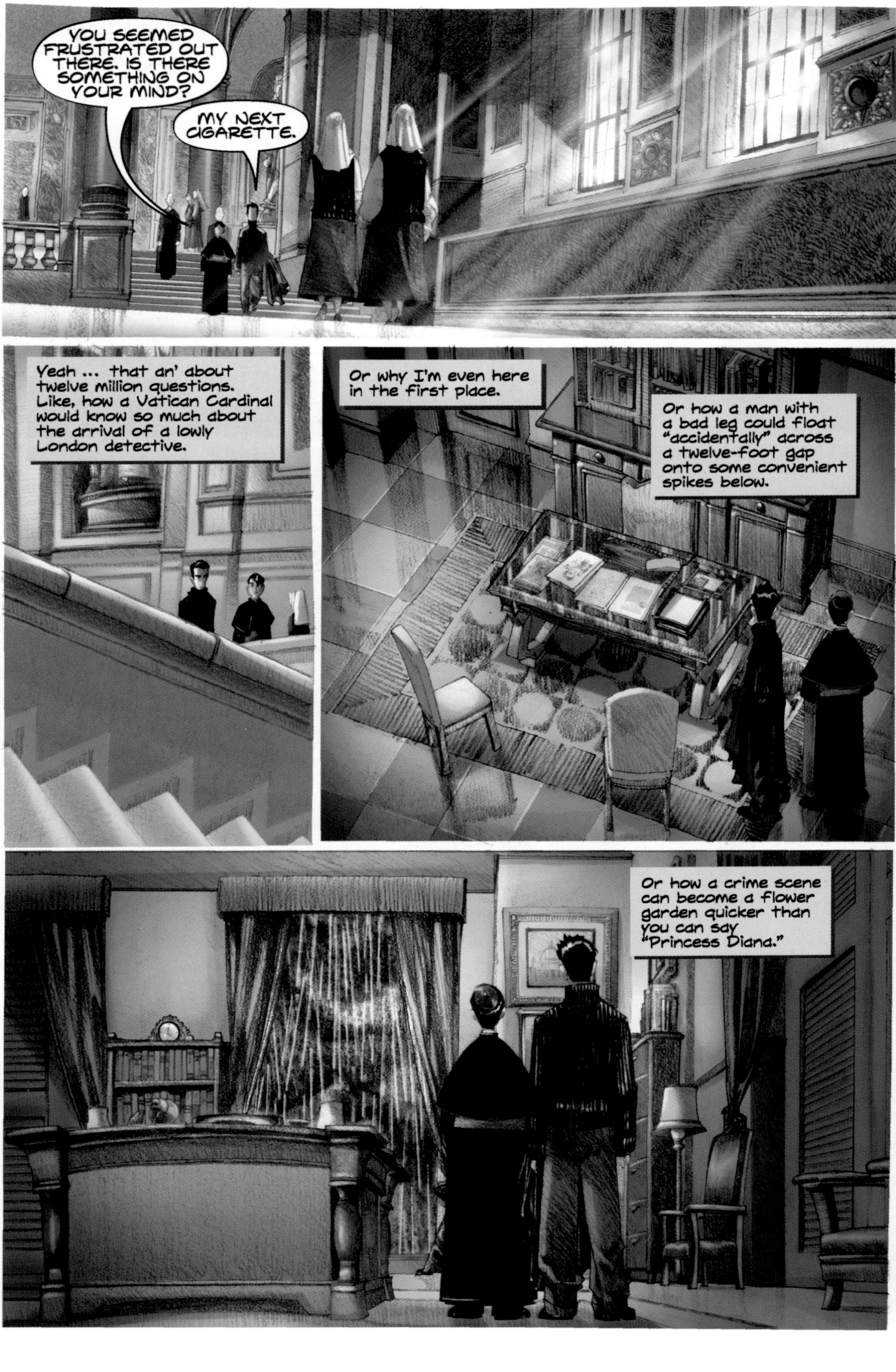
YOU SEEMED FRUSTRATED OUT THERE. IS THERE SOMETHING ON YOUR MIND?
MY NEXT CIGARETTE.
Yeah ... that an' about twelve million questions. Like, how a Vatican Cardinal would know so much about the arrival of a lowly London detective.
Or why I'm even here in the first place.
Or how a man with a bad leg could float "accidentally" across a twelve-foot gap onto some convenient spikes below.
Or how a crime scene can become a flower garden quicker than you can say "Princess Diana."

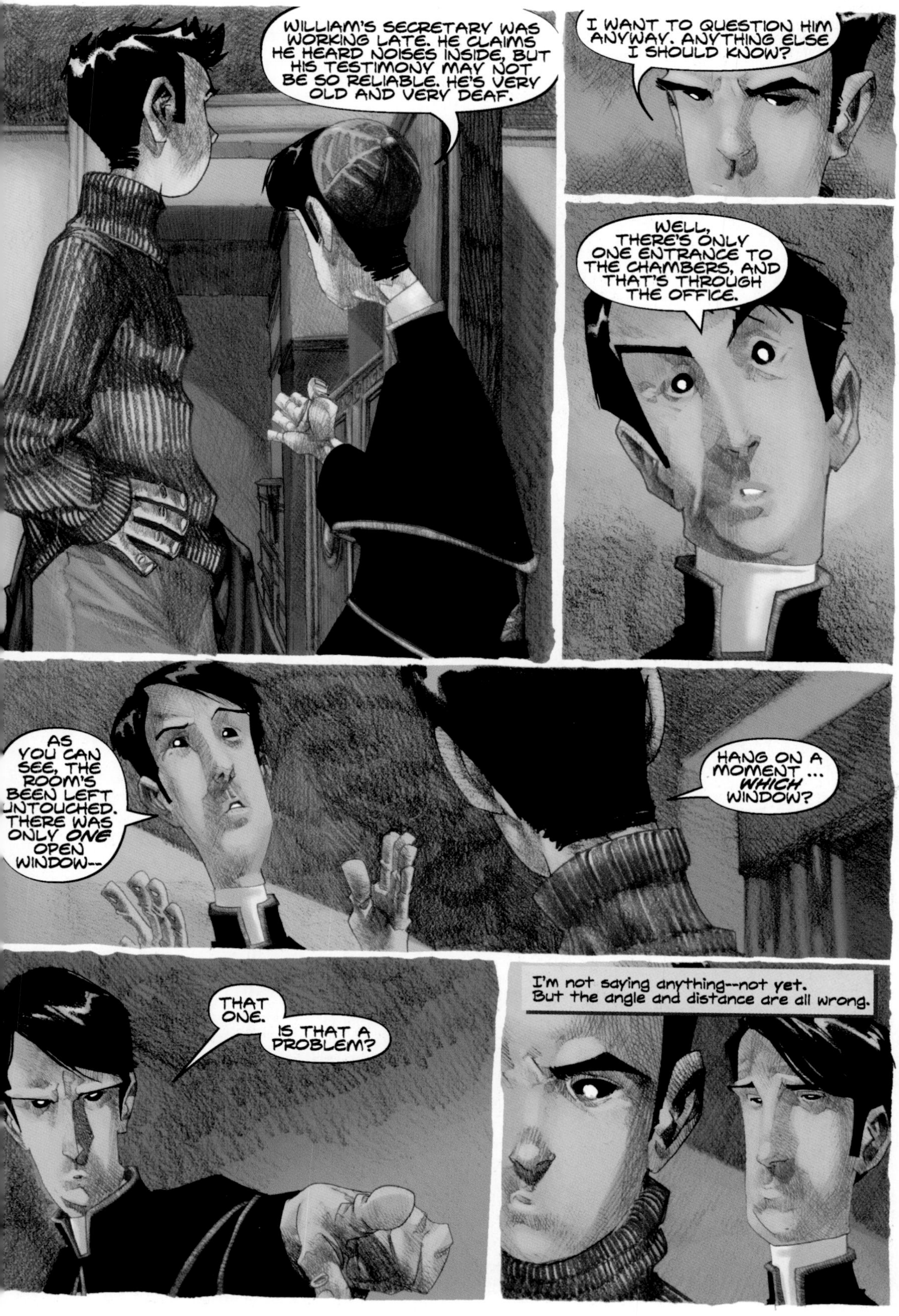
WILLIAM'S SECRETARY WAS WORKING LATE. HE CLAIMS HE HEARD NOISES INSIDE, BUT HIS TESTIMONY MAY NOT BE SO RELIABLE. HE'S VERY OLD AND VERY DEAF.
I WANT TO QUESTION HIM ANYWAY. ANYTHING ELSE I SHOULD KNOW?
WELL, THERE'S ONLY ONE ENTRANCE TO THE CHAMBERS, AND THAT'S THROUGH THE OFFICE.
AS YOU CAN SEE, THE ROOM'S BEEN LEFT UNTOUCHED. THERE WAS ONLY *ONE* OPEN WINDOW--
HANG ON A MOMENT ... *WHICH* WINDOW?
THAT ONE.
IS THAT A PROBLEM?
I'm not saying anything--not yet.
But the angle and distance are all wrong.

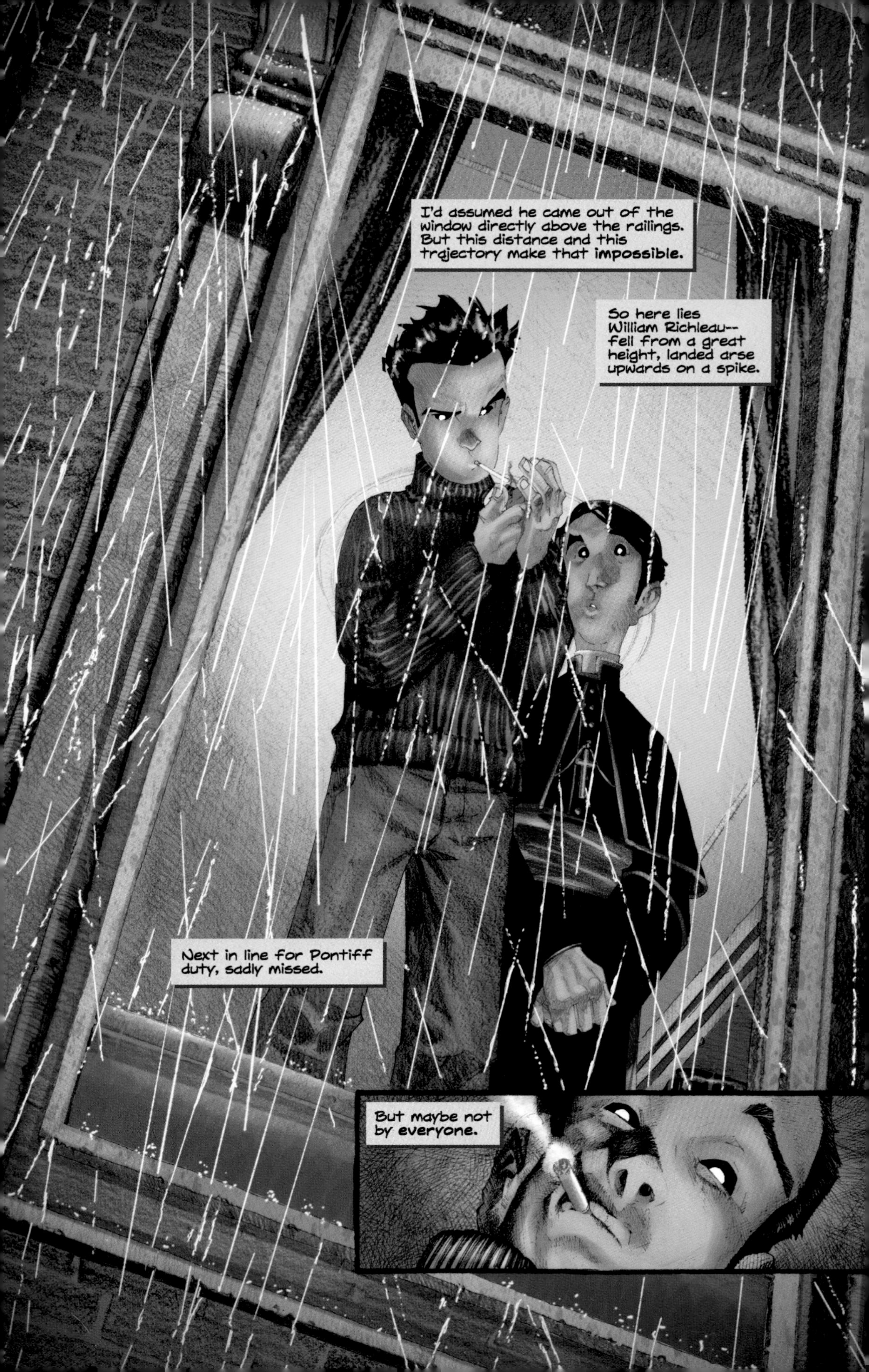
I'd assumed he came out of the window directly above the railings. But this distance and this trajectory make that impossible.
So here lies William Richleau--fell from a great height, landed arse upwards on a spike.
Next in line for Pontiff duty, sadly missed.
But maybe not by everyone.

CHAPTER TWO

Assisted Suicide

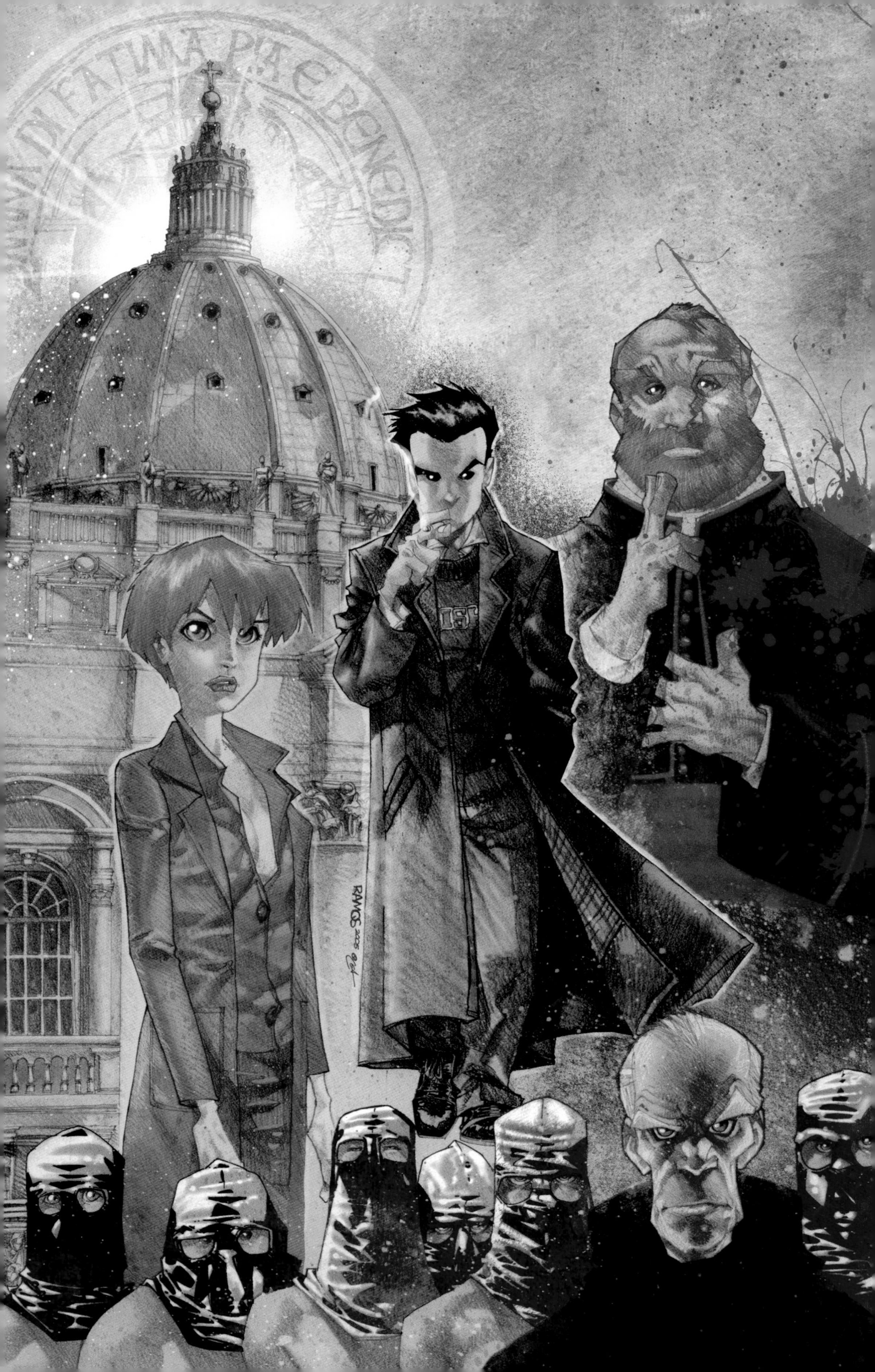
RAMOS 2005

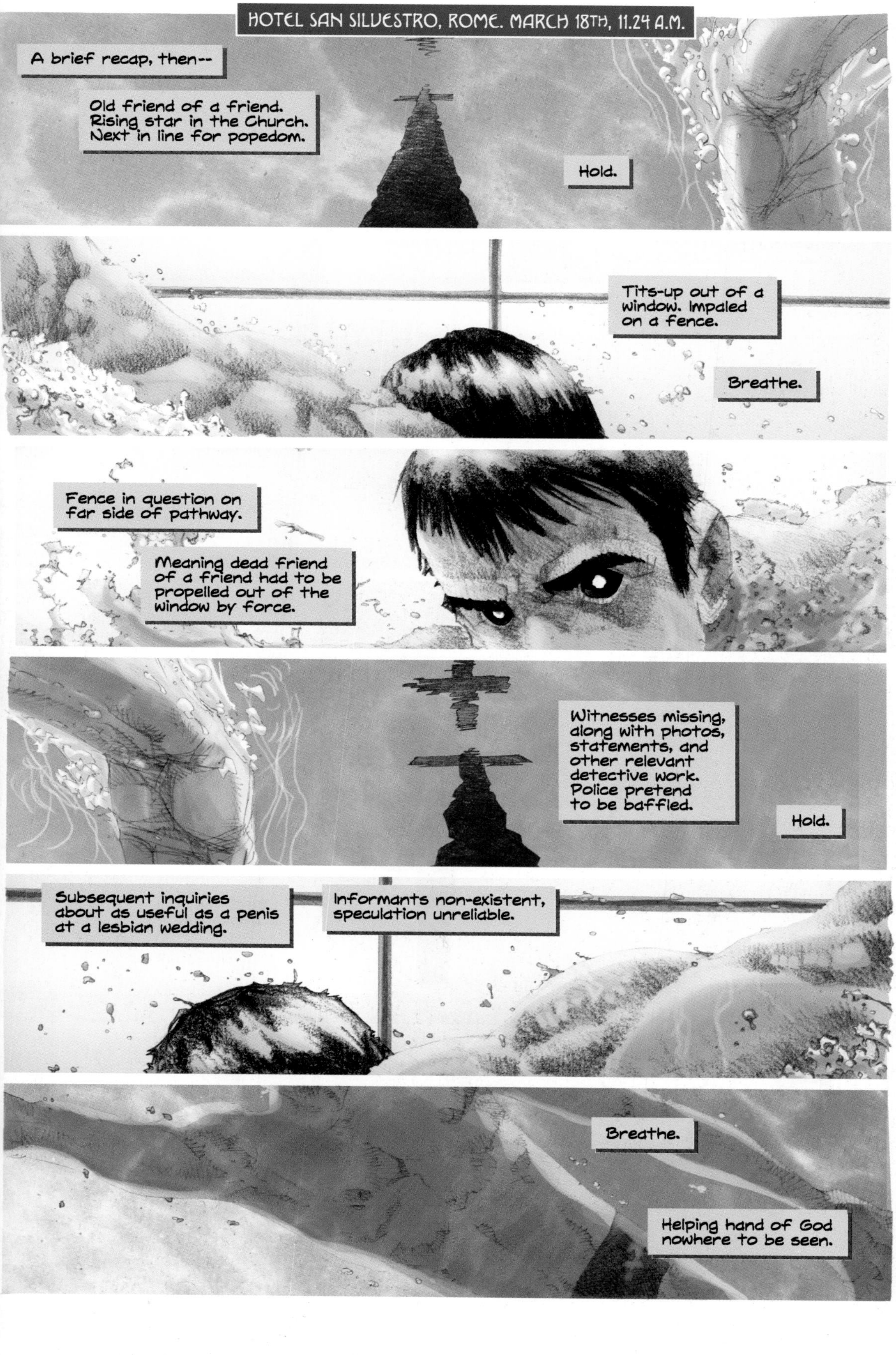
HOTEL SAN SILVESTRO, ROME. MARCH 18TH, 11.24 A.M.
A brief recap, then--
Old friend of a friend. Rising star in the Church. Next in line for popedom.
Hold.
Tits-up out of a window. Impaled on a fence.
Breathe.
Fence in question on far side of pathway.
Meaning dead friend of a friend had to be propelled out of the window by force.
Witnesses missing, along with photos, statements, and other relevant detective work. Police pretend to be baffled.
Hold.
Subsequent inquiries about as useful as a penis at a lesbian wedding.
Informants non-existent, speculation unreliable.
Breathe.
Helping hand of God nowhere to be seen.

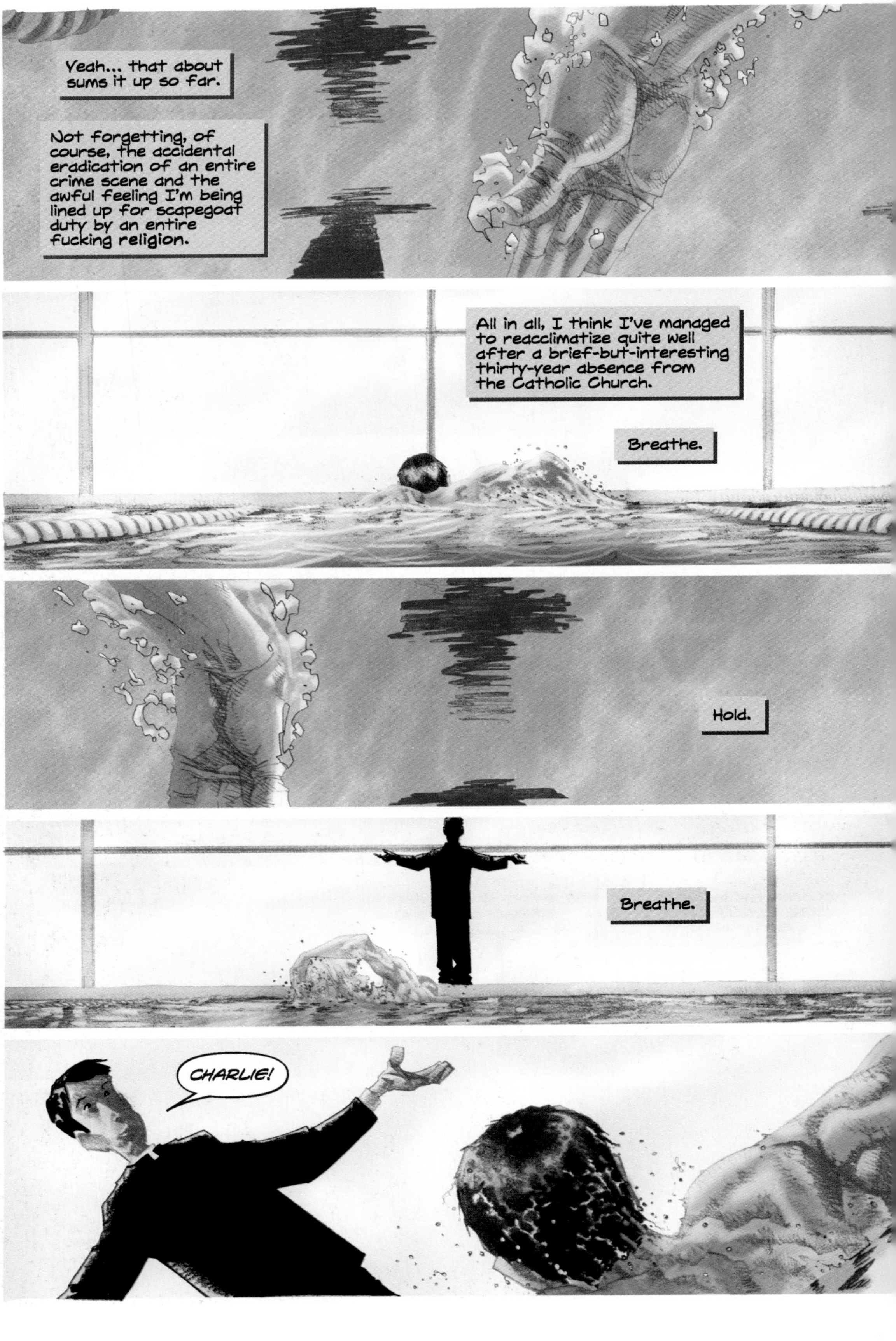
Yeah... that about sums it up so far.
Not forgetting, of course, the accidental eradication of an entire crime scene and the awful feeling I'm being lined up for scapegoat duty by an entire fucking religion.
All in all, I think I've managed to reacclimatize quite well after a brief-but-interesting thirty-year absence from the Catholic Church.
Breathe.
Hold.
Breathe.
CHARLIE!

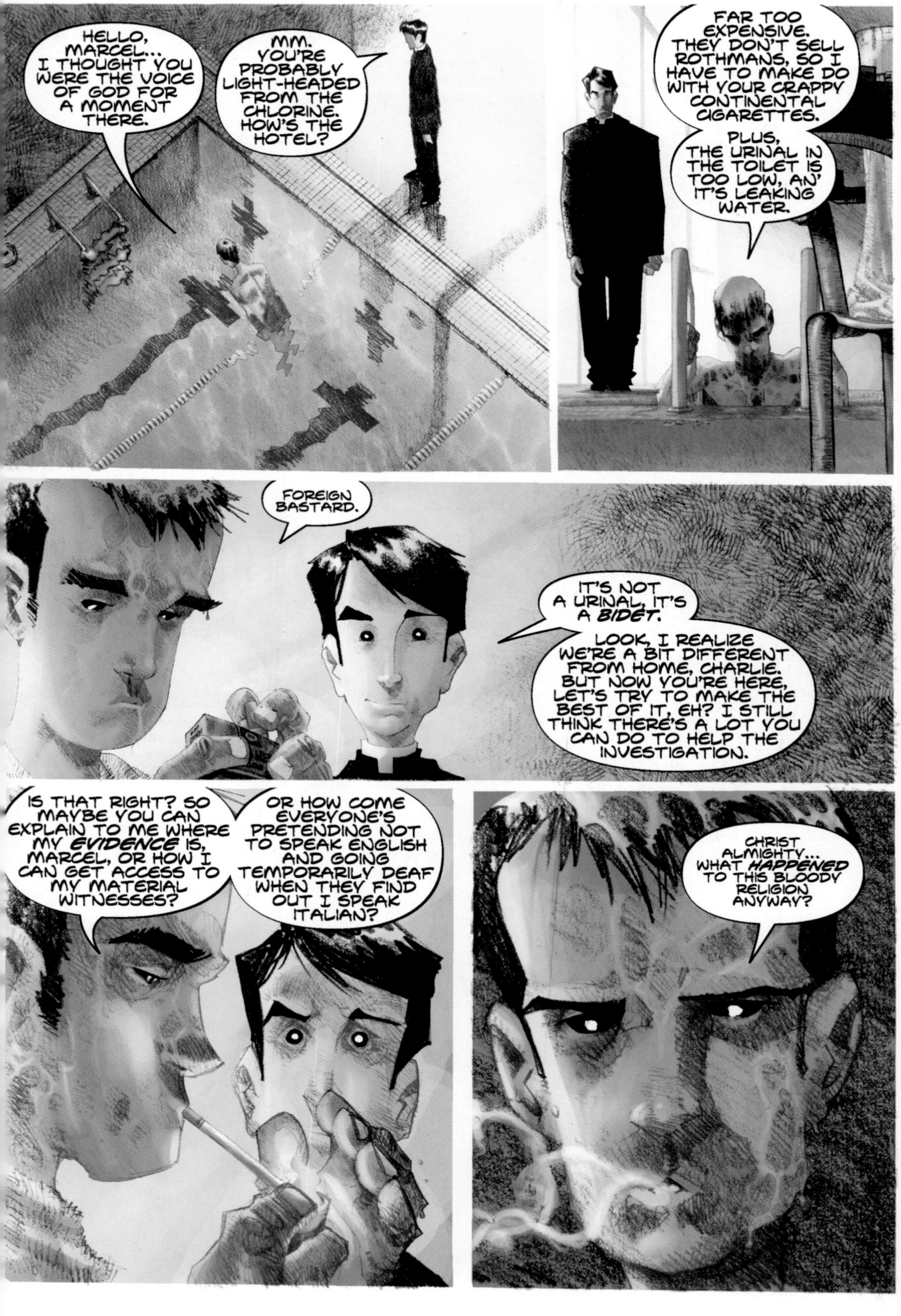
HELLO, MARCEL... I THOUGHT YOU WERE THE VOICE OF GOD FOR A MOMENT THERE.
MM. YOU'RE PROBABLY LIGHT-HEADED FROM THE CHLORINE. HOW'S THE HOTEL?
FAR TOO EXPENSIVE. THEY DON'T SELL ROTHMANS, SO I HAVE TO MAKE DO WITH YOUR CRAPPY CONTINENTAL CIGARETTES.
PLUS, THE URINAL IN THE TOILET IS TOO LOW, AN' IT'S LEAKING WATER.
FOREIGN BASTARD.
IT'S NOT A URINAL, IT'S A *BIDET*.
LOOK, I REALIZE WE'RE A BIT DIFFERENT FROM HOME, CHARLIE. BUT NOW YOU'RE HERE, LET'S TRY TO MAKE THE BEST OF IT, EH? I STILL THINK THERE'S A LOT YOU CAN DO TO HELP THE INVESTIGATION.
IS THAT RIGHT? SO MAYBE YOU CAN EXPLAIN TO ME WHERE MY *EVIDENCE* IS, MARCEL, OR HOW I CAN GET ACCESS TO MY MATERIAL WITNESSES?
OR HOW COME EVERYONE'S PRETENDING NOT TO SPEAK ENGLISH AND GOING TEMPORARILY DEAF WHEN THEY FIND OUT I SPEAK ITALIAN?
CHRIST ALMIGHTY... WHAT *HAPPENED* TO THIS BLOODY RELIGION ANYWAY?

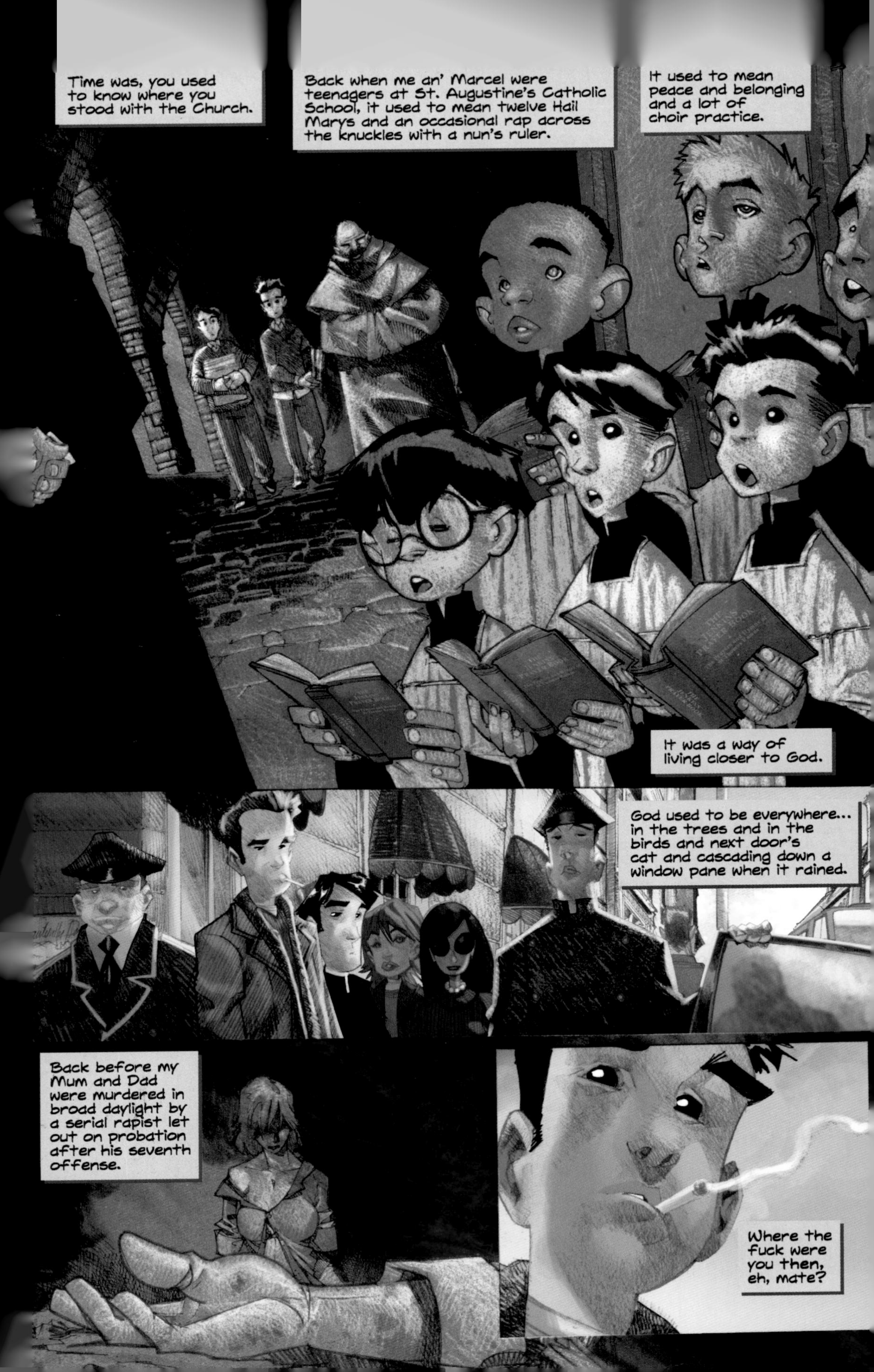
Time was, you used to know where you stood with the Church.
Back when me an' Marcel were teenagers at St. Augustine's Catholic School, it used to mean twelve Hail Marys and an occasional rap across the knuckles with a nun's ruler.
It used to mean peace and belonging and a lot of choir practice.
It was a way of living closer to God.
God used to be everywhere... in the trees and in the birds and next door's cat and cascading down a window pane when it rained.
Back before my Mum and Dad were murdered in broad daylight by a serial rapist let out on probation after his seventh offense.
Where the fuck were you then, eh, mate?

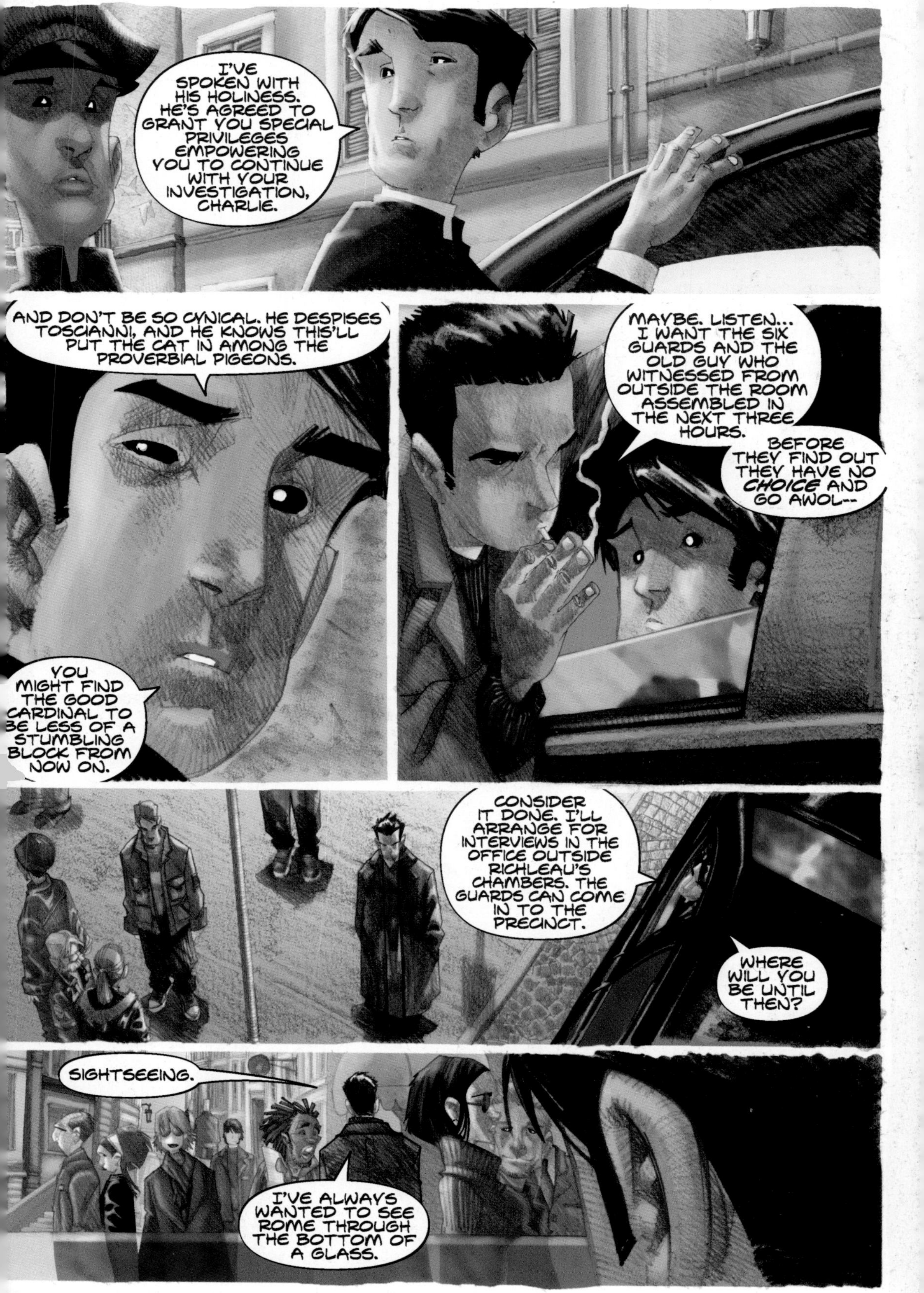
I'VE SPOKEN WITH HIS HOLINESS. HE'S AGREED TO GRANT YOU SPECIAL PRIVILEGES EMPOWERING YOU TO CONTINUE WITH YOUR INVESTIGATION, CHARLIE.
AND DON'T BE SO CYNICAL. HE DESPISES TOSCIANNI, AND HE KNOWS THIS'LL PUT THE CAT IN AMONG THE PROVERBIAL PIGEONS.
YOU MIGHT FIND THE GOOD CARDINAL TO BE LESS OF A STUMBLING BLOCK FROM NOW ON.
MAYBE. LISTEN... I WANT THE SIX GUARDS AND THE OLD GUY WHO WITNESSED FROM OUTSIDE THE ROOM ASSEMBLED IN THE NEXT THREE HOURS.
BEFORE THEY FIND OUT THEY HAVE NO *CHOICE* AND GO AWOL--
CONSIDER IT DONE. I'LL ARRANGE FOR INTERVIEWS IN THE OFFICE OUTSIDE RICHLEAU'S CHAMBERS. THE GUARDS CAN COME IN TO THE PRECINCT.
WHERE WILL YOU BE UNTIL THEN?
SIGHTSEEING.
I'VE ALWAYS WANTED TO SEE ROME THROUGH THE BOTTOM OF A GLASS.

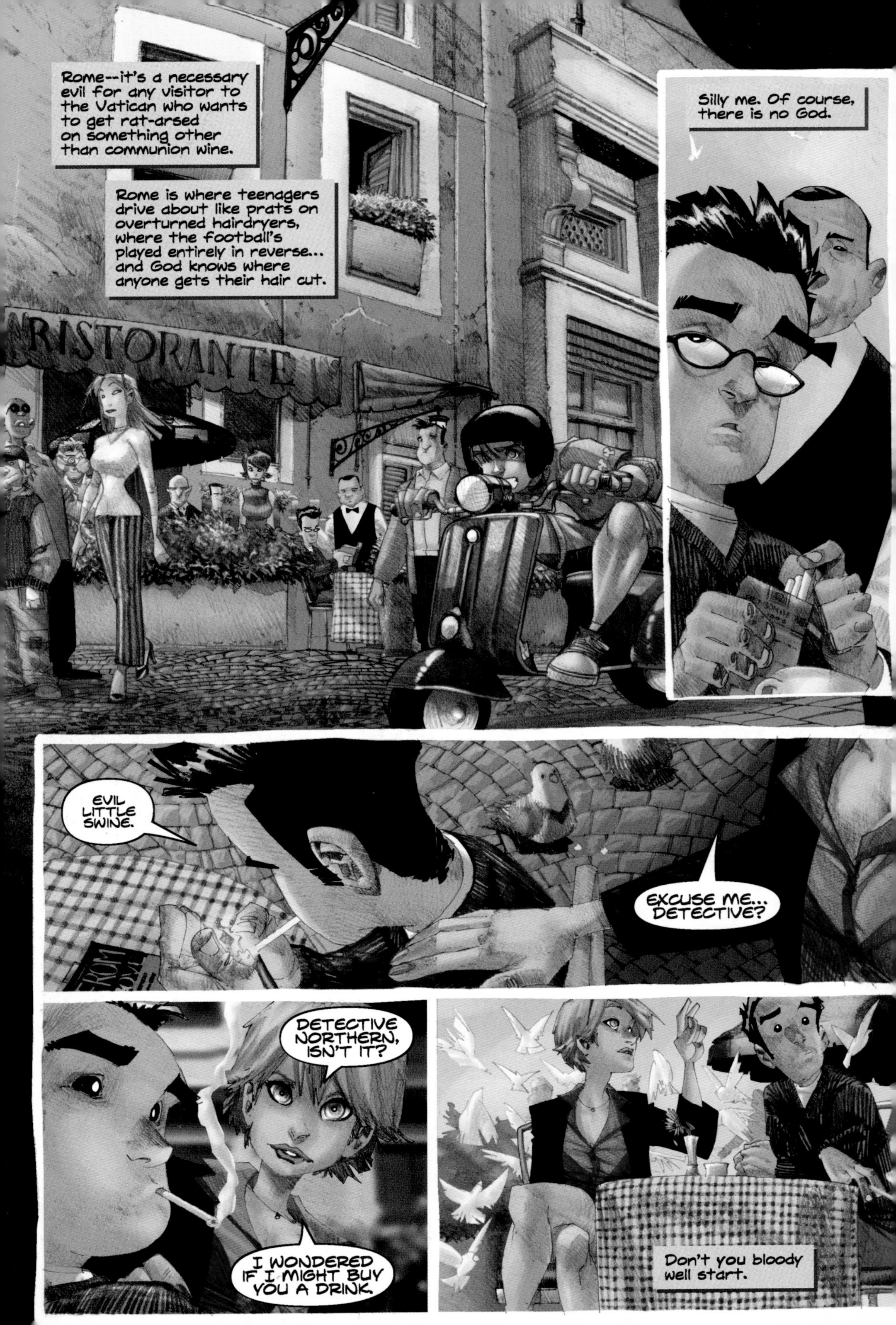

Rome--it's a necessary evil for any visitor to the Vatican who wants to get rat-arsed on something other than communion wine.
Rome is where teenagers drive about like prats on overturned hairdryers, where the football's played entirely in reverse... and God knows where anyone gets their hair cut.
RISTORANTE
Silly me. Of course, there is no God.
EVIL LITTLE SWINE.
EXCUSE ME... DETECTIVE?
DETECTIVE NORTHERN, ISN'T IT?
I WONDERED IF I MIGHT BUY YOU A DRINK.
Don't you bloody well start.

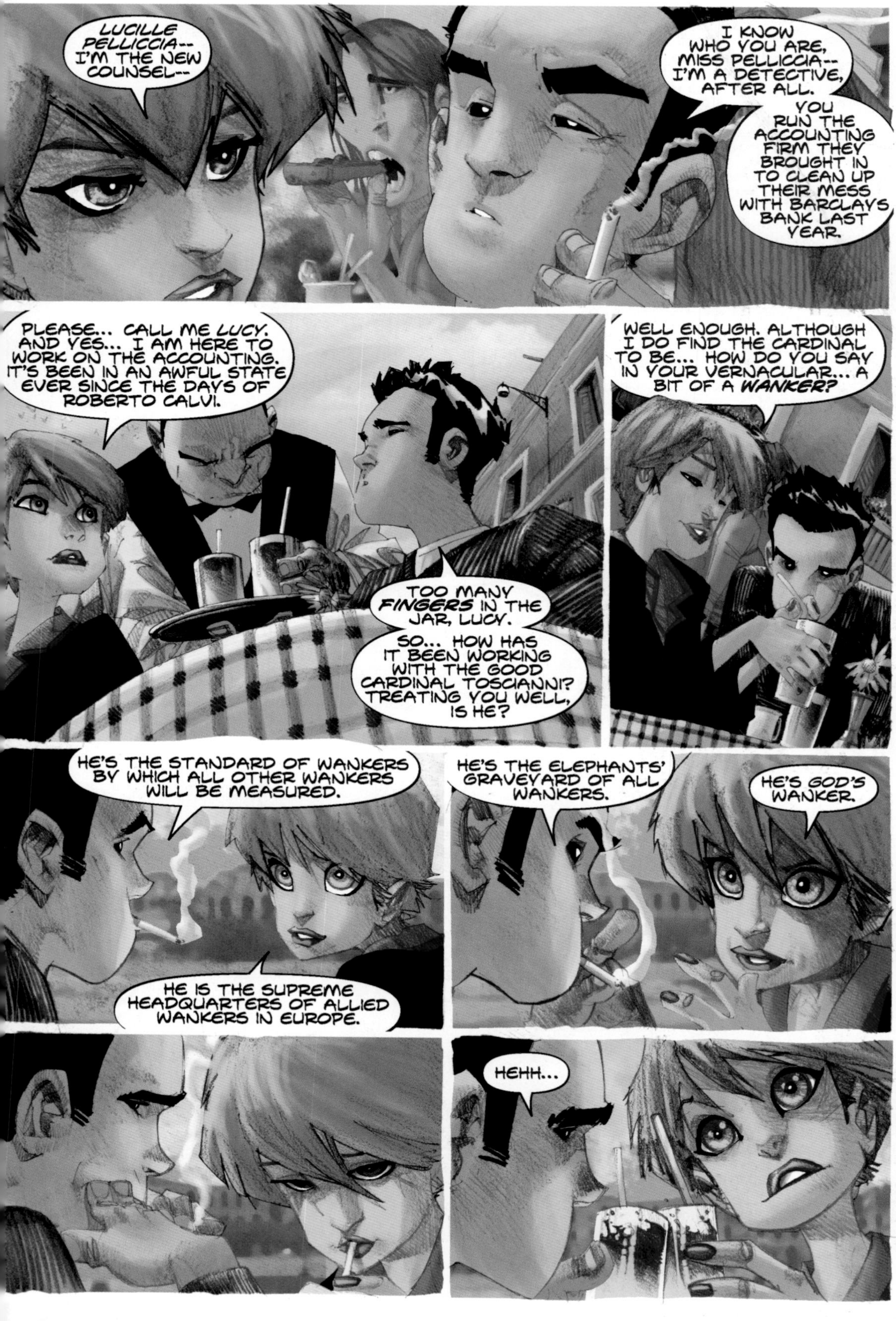
LUCILLE PELLICCIA-- I'M THE NEW COUNSEL--
I KNOW WHO YOU ARE, MISS PELLICCIA-- I'M A DETECTIVE, AFTER ALL.
YOU RUN THE ACCOUNTING FIRM THEY BROUGHT IN TO CLEAN UP THEIR MESS WITH BARCLAYS BANK LAST YEAR.
PLEASE... CALL ME LUCY. AND YES... I AM HERE TO WORK ON THE ACCOUNTING. IT'S BEEN IN AN AWFUL STATE EVER SINCE THE DAYS OF ROBERTO CALVI.
TOO MANY FINGERS IN THE JAR, LUCY.
SO... HOW HAS IT BEEN WORKING WITH THE GOOD CARDINAL TOSCIANNI? TREATING YOU WELL, IS HE?
WELL ENOUGH. ALTHOUGH I DO FIND THE CARDINAL TO BE... HOW DO YOU SAY IN YOUR VERNACULAR... A BIT OF A WANKER?
HE'S THE STANDARD OF WANKERS BY WHICH ALL OTHER WANKERS WILL BE MEASURED.
HE IS THE SUPREME HEADQUARTERS OF ALLIED WANKERS IN EUROPE.
HE'S THE ELEPHANTS' GRAVEYARD OF ALL WANKERS.
HE'S GOD'S WANKER.
HEHH...

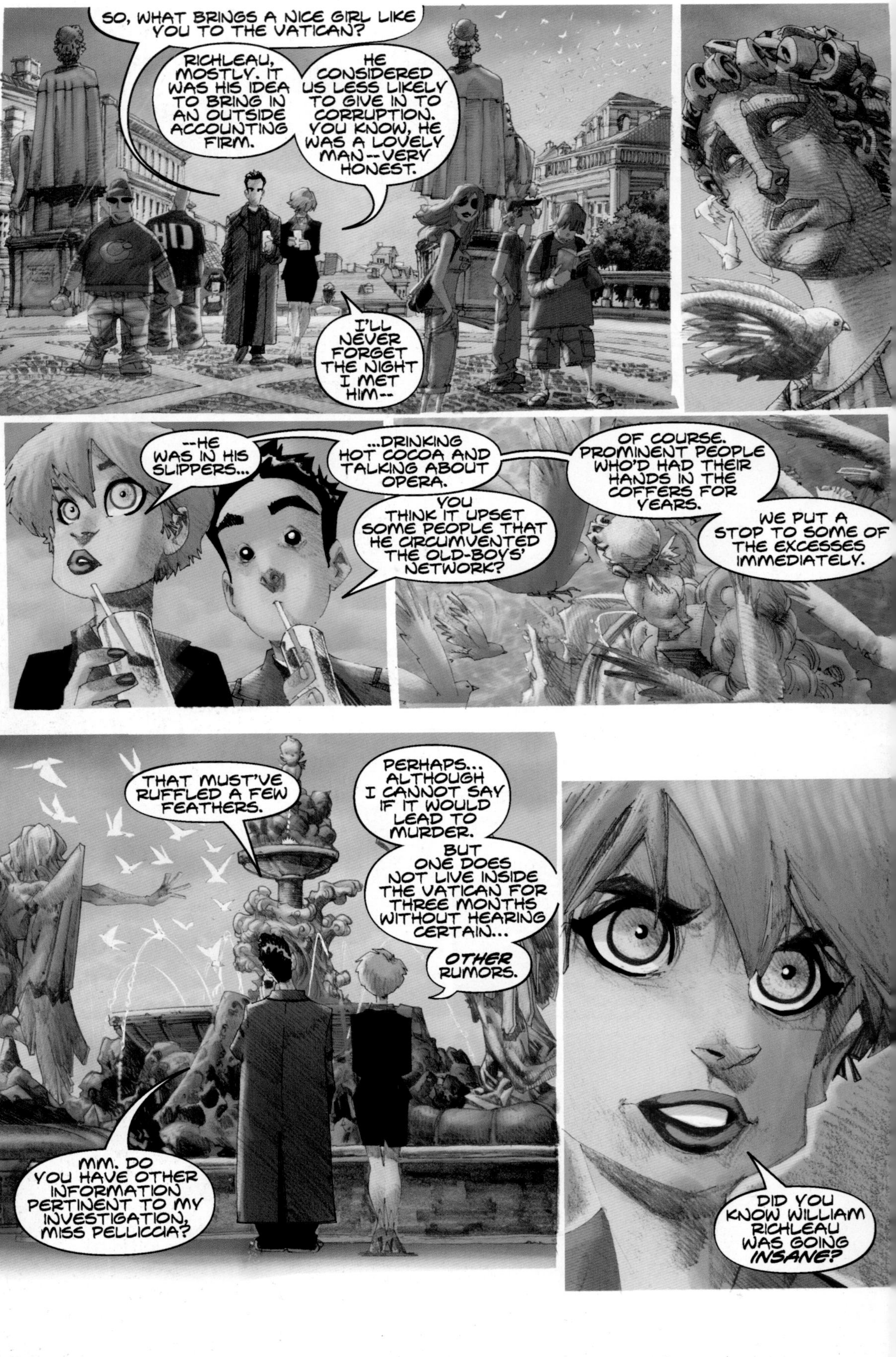
SO, WHAT BRINGS A NICE GIRL LIKE YOU TO THE VATICAN?
RICHLEAU, MOSTLY. IT WAS HIS IDEA TO BRING IN AN OUTSIDE ACCOUNTING FIRM.
HE CONSIDERED US LESS LIKELY TO GIVE IN TO CORRUPTION. YOU KNOW, HE WAS A LOVELY MAN--VERY HONEST.
I'LL NEVER FORGET THE NIGHT I MET HIM--
--HE WAS IN HIS SLIPPERS...
...DRINKING HOT COCOA AND TALKING ABOUT OPERA.
YOU THINK IT UPSET SOME PEOPLE THAT HE CIRCUMVENTED THE OLD-BOYS' NETWORK?
OF COURSE. PROMINENT PEOPLE WHO'D HAD THEIR HANDS IN THE COFFERS FOR YEARS.
WE PUT A STOP TO SOME OF THE EXCESSES IMMEDIATELY.
THAT MUST'VE RUFFLED A FEW FEATHERS.
PERHAPS... ALTHOUGH I CANNOT SAY IF IT WOULD LEAD TO MURDER.
BUT ONE DOES NOT LIVE INSIDE THE VATICAN FOR THREE MONTHS WITHOUT HEARING CERTAIN...
OTHER RUMORS.
MM. DO YOU HAVE OTHER INFORMATION PERTINENT TO MY INVESTIGATION, MISS PELLICCIA?
DID YOU KNOW WILLIAM RICHLEAU WAS GOING INSANE?

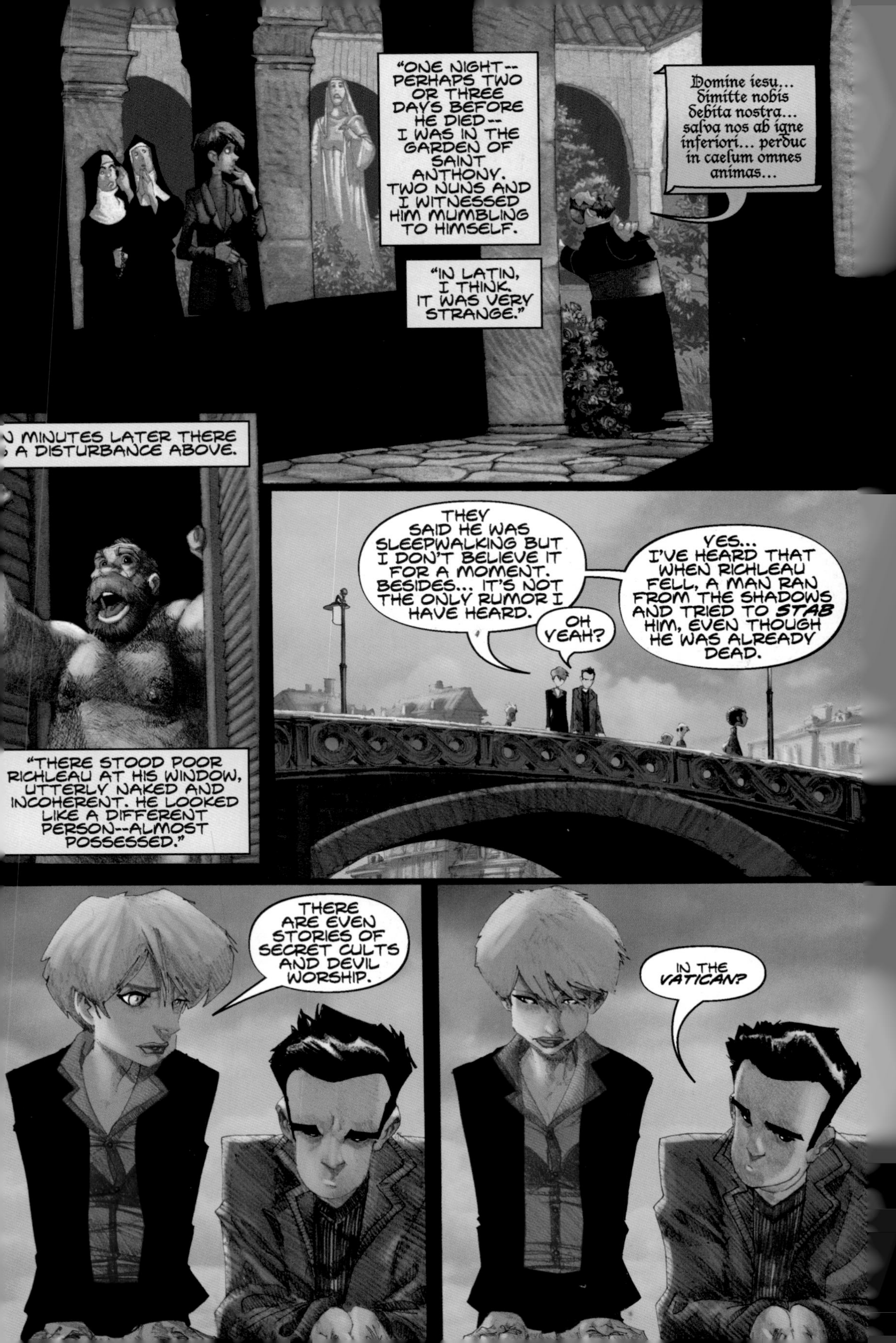
"ONE NIGHT-- PERHAPS TWO OR THREE DAYS BEFORE HE DIED-- I WAS IN THE GARDEN OF SAINT ANTHONY. TWO NUNS AND I WITNESSED HIM MUMBLING TO HIMSELF.
Domine iesu... dimitte nobis debita nostra... salva nos ab igne inferiori... perduc in caelum omnes animas...
"IN LATIN, I THINK. IT WAS VERY STRANGE."
N MINUTES LATER THERE A DISTURBANCE ABOVE.
"THERE STOOD POOR RICHLEAU AT HIS WINDOW, UTTERLY NAKED AND INCOHERENT. HE LOOKED LIKE A DIFFERENT PERSON--ALMOST POSSESSED."
THEY SAID HE WAS SLEEPWALKING BUT I DON'T BELIEVE IT FOR A MOMENT. BESIDES... IT'S NOT THE ONLY RUMOR I HAVE HEARD.
OH YEAH?
YES... I'VE HEARD THAT WHEN RICHLEAU FELL, A MAN RAN FROM THE SHADOWS AND TRIED TO STAB HIM, EVEN THOUGH HE WAS ALREADY DEAD.
THERE ARE EVEN STORIES OF SECRET CULTS AND DEVIL WORSHIP.
IN THE VATICAN?

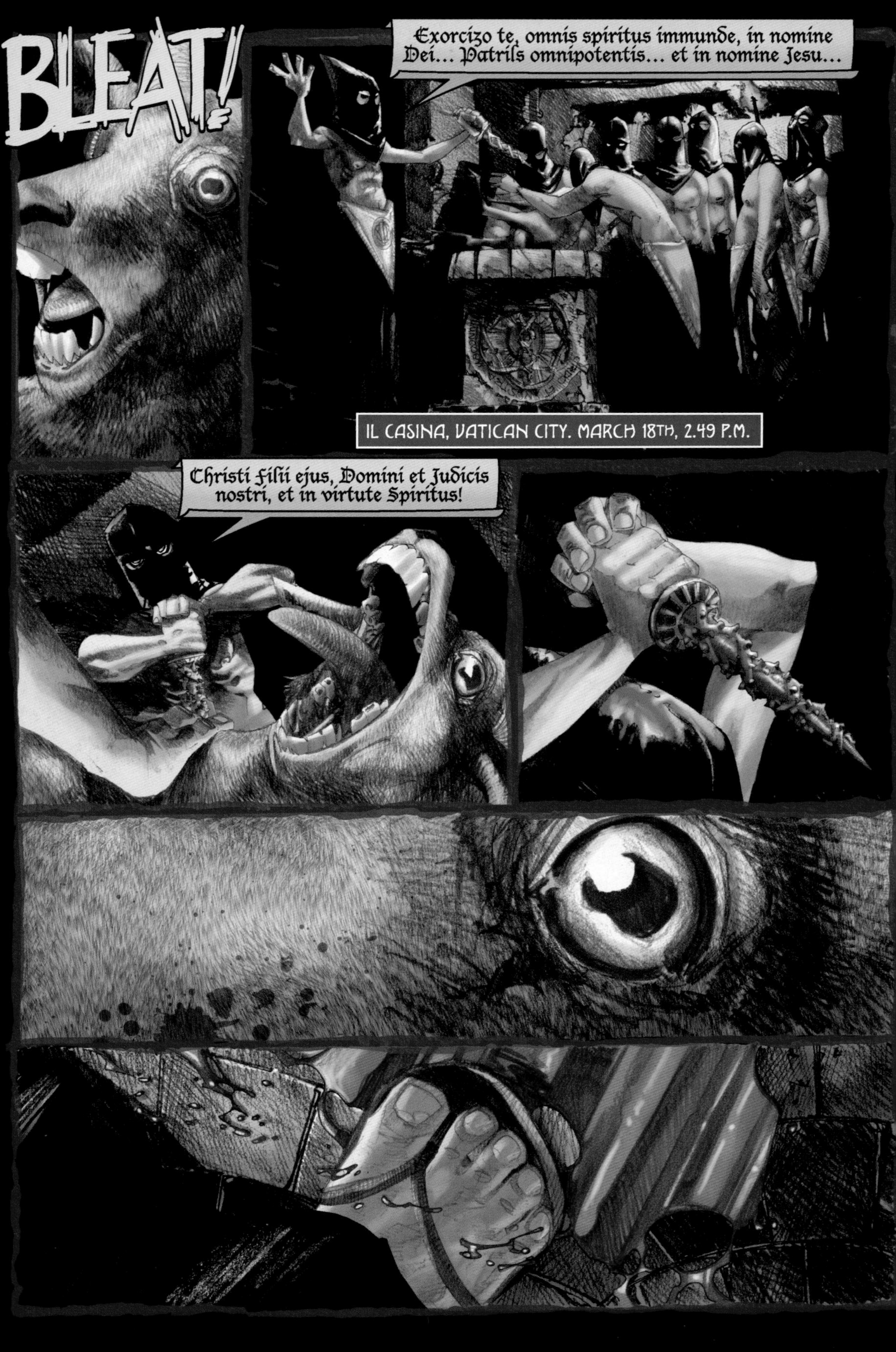
BLEAT!
Exorcizo te, omnis spiritus immunde, in nomine Dei... Patris omnipotentis... et in nomine Jesu...
IL CASINA, VATICAN CITY. MARCH 18TH, 2.49 P.M.
Christi Filii ejus, Domini et Judicis nostri, et in virtute Spiritus!

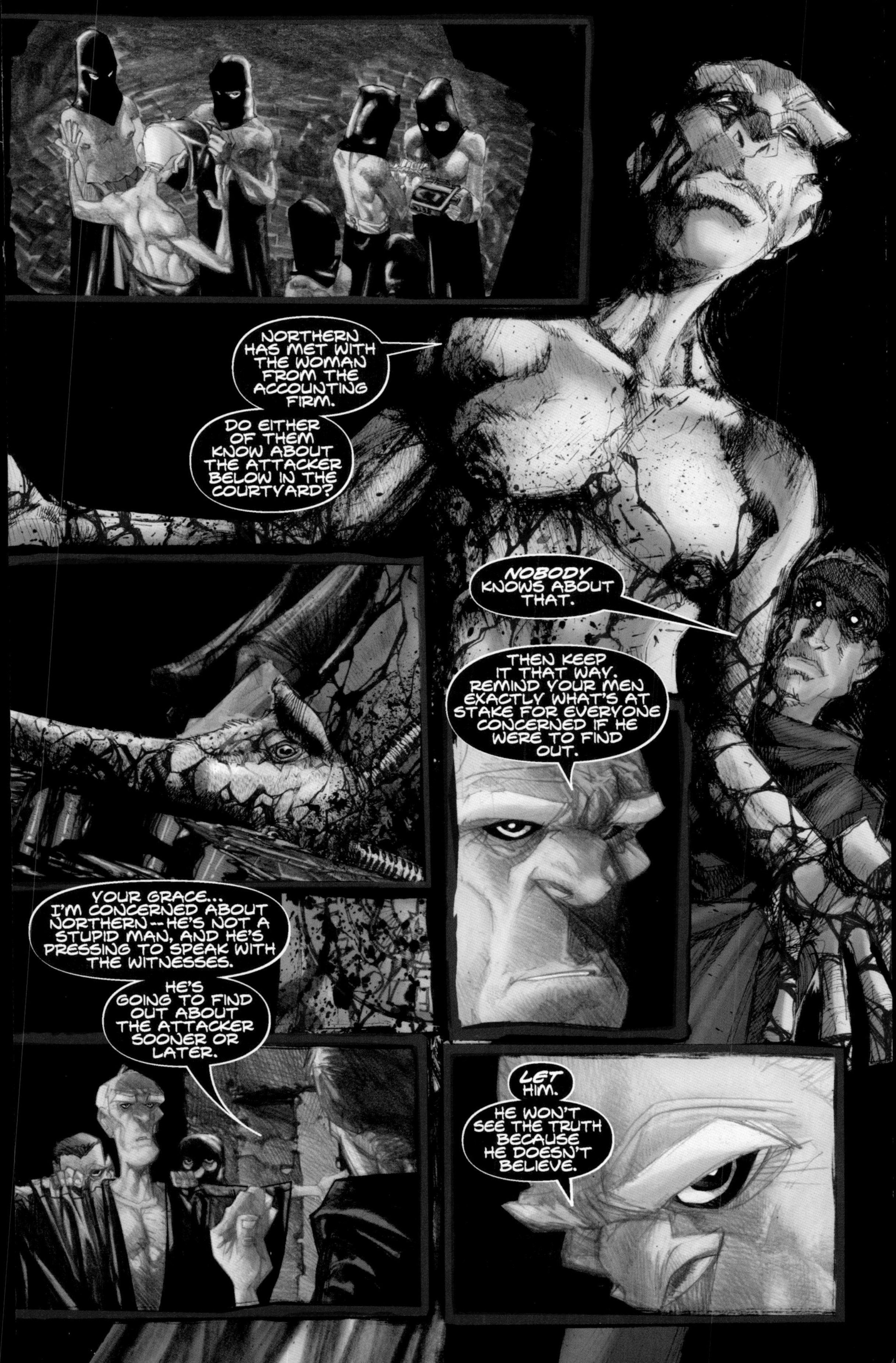
NORTHERN HAS MET WITH THE WOMAN FROM THE ACCOUNTING FIRM.
DO EITHER OF THEM KNOW ABOUT THE ATTACKER BELOW IN THE COURTYARD?
NOBODY KNOWS ABOUT THAT.
THEN KEEP IT THAT WAY. REMIND YOUR MEN EXACTLY WHAT'S AT STAKE FOR EVERYONE CONCERNED IF HE WERE TO FIND OUT.
YOUR GRACE... I'M CONCERNED ABOUT NORTHERN--HE'S NOT A STUPID MAN, AND HE'S PRESSING TO SPEAK WITH THE WITNESSES.
HE'S GOING TO FIND OUT ABOUT THE ATTACKER SOONER OR LATER.
LET HIM.
HE WON'T SEE THE TRUTH BECAUSE HE DOESN'T BELIEVE.

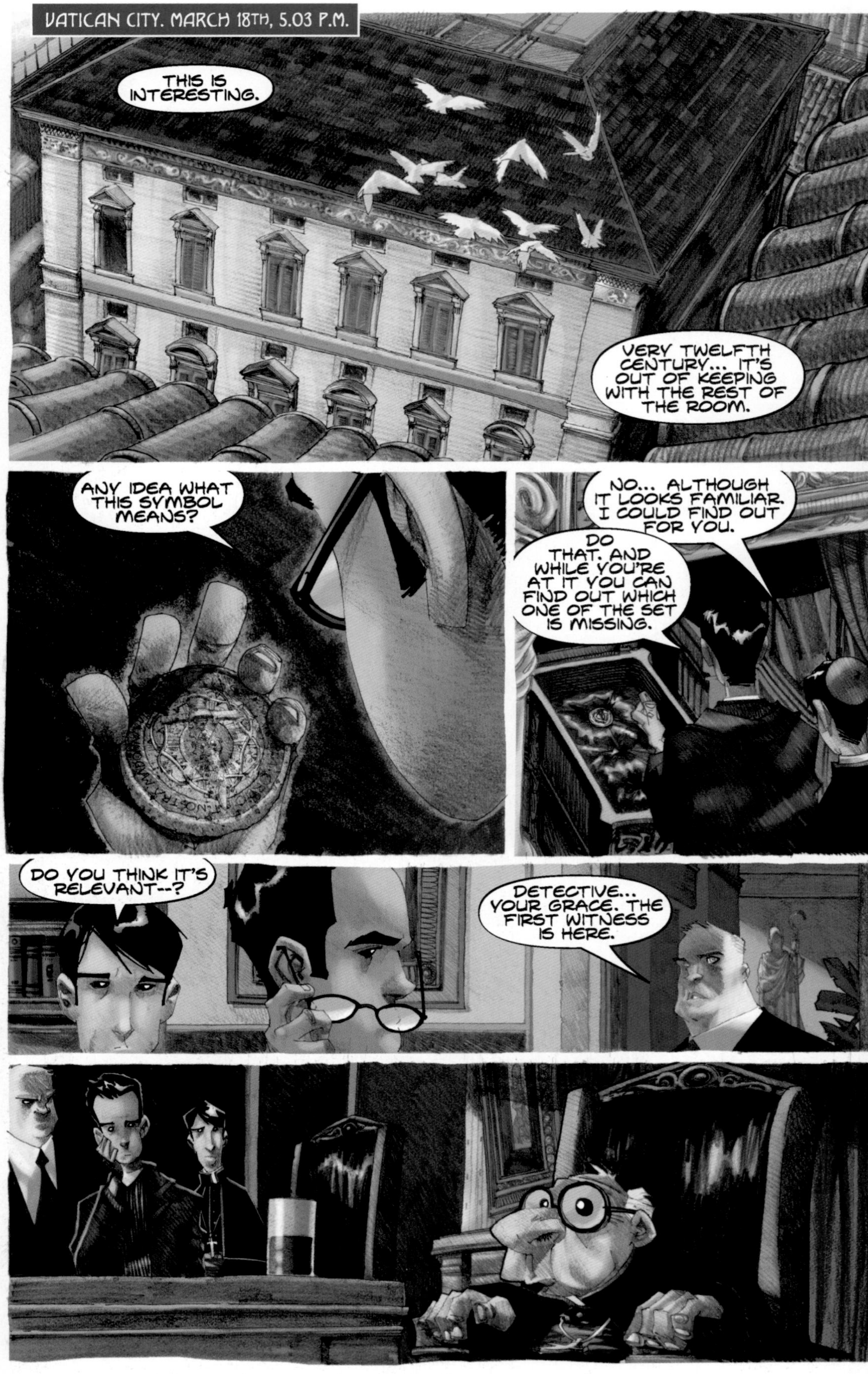
VATICAN CITY. MARCH 18TH, 5.03 P.M.
THIS IS INTERESTING.
VERY TWELFTH CENTURY... IT'S OUT OF KEEPING WITH THE REST OF THE ROOM.
ANY IDEA WHAT THIS SYMBOL MEANS?
NO... ALTHOUGH IT LOOKS FAMILIAR. I COULD FIND OUT FOR YOU.
DO THAT. AND WHILE YOU'RE AT IT YOU CAN FIND OUT WHICH ONE OF THE SET IS MISSING.
DO YOU THINK IT'S RELEVANT--?
DETECTIVE... YOUR GRACE. THE FIRST WITNESS IS HERE.

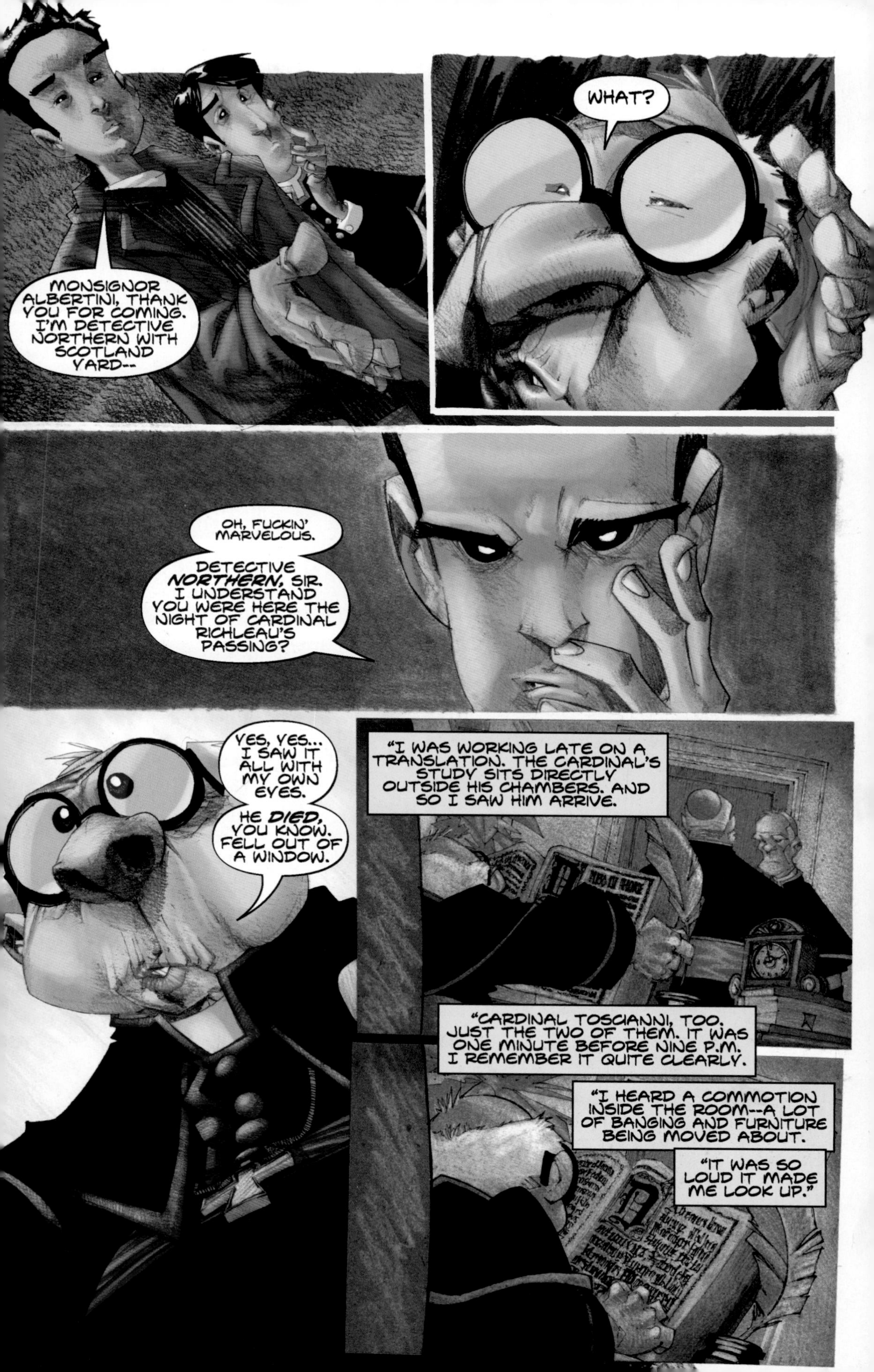
MONSIGNOR ALBERTINI, THANK YOU FOR COMING. I'M DETECTIVE NORTHERN WITH SCOTLAND YARD--
WHAT?
OH, FUCKIN' MARVELOUS.
DETECTIVE ***NORTHERN,*** SIR. I UNDERSTAND YOU WERE HERE THE NIGHT OF CARDINAL RICHLEAU'S PASSING?
YES, YES... I SAW IT ALL WITH MY OWN EYES.
HE ***DIED,*** YOU KNOW. FELL OUT OF A WINDOW.
"I WAS WORKING LATE ON A TRANSLATION. THE CARDINAL'S STUDY SITS DIRECTLY OUTSIDE HIS CHAMBERS. AND SO I SAW HIM ARRIVE.
"CARDINAL TOSCIANNI, TOO. JUST THE TWO OF THEM. IT WAS ONE MINUTE BEFORE NINE P.M. I REMEMBER IT QUITE CLEARLY.
"I HEARD A COMMOTION INSIDE THE ROOM--A LOT OF BANGING AND FURNITURE BEING MOVED ABOUT.
"IT WAS SO LOUD IT MADE ME LOOK UP."

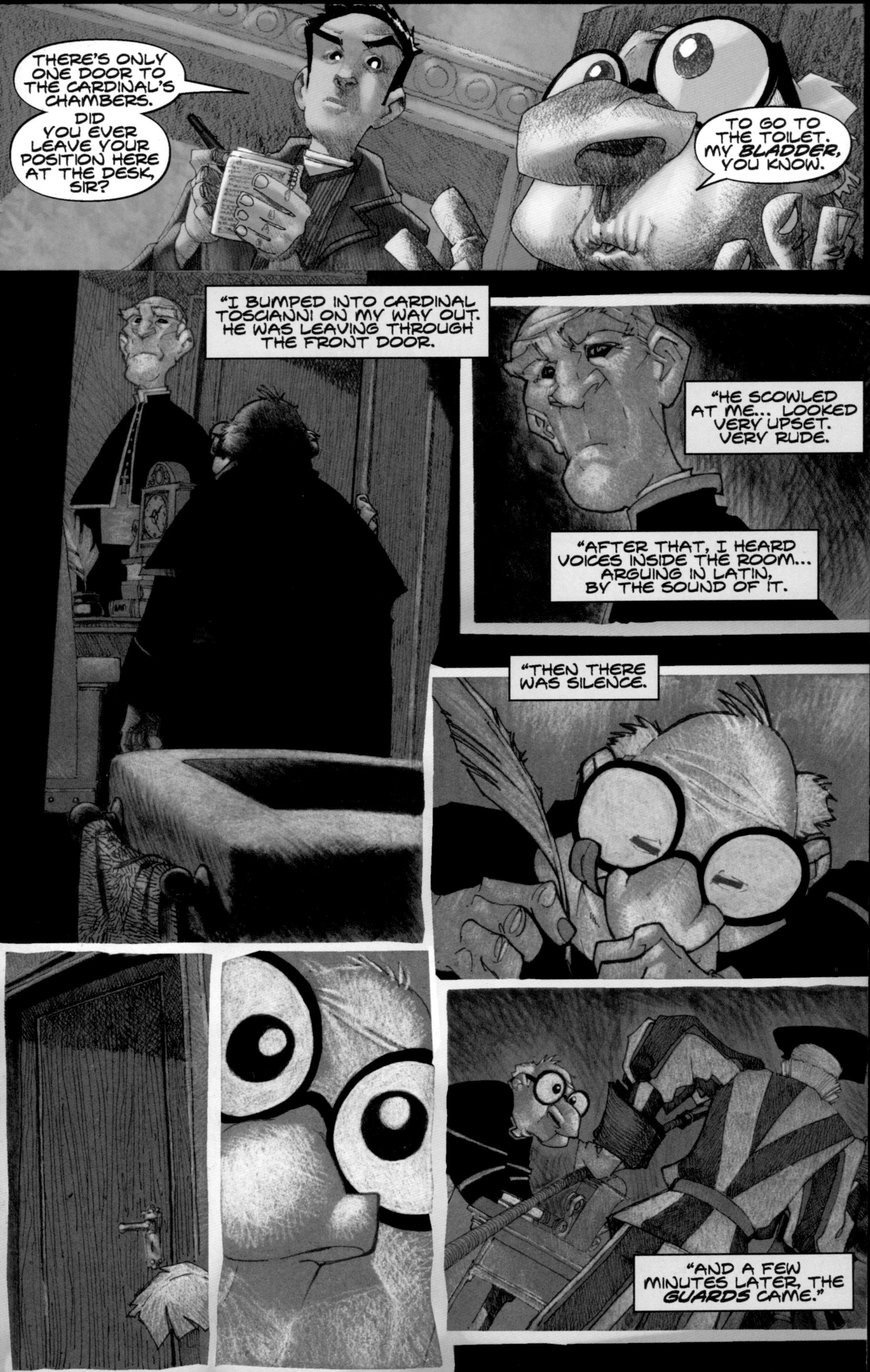
THERE'S ONLY ONE DOOR TO THE CARDINAL'S CHAMBERS.
DID YOU EVER LEAVE YOUR POSITION HERE AT THE DESK, SIR?
TO GO TO THE TOILET. MY *BLADDER*, YOU KNOW.
"I BUMPED INTO CARDINAL TOSCIANNI ON MY WAY OUT. HE WAS LEAVING THROUGH THE FRONT DOOR.
"HE SCOWLED AT ME... LOOKED VERY UPSET. VERY RUDE.
"AFTER THAT, I HEARD VOICES INSIDE THE ROOM... ARGUING IN LATIN, BY THE SOUND OF IT.
"THEN THERE WAS SILENCE.
"AND A FEW MINUTES LATER, THE *GUARDS* CAME."

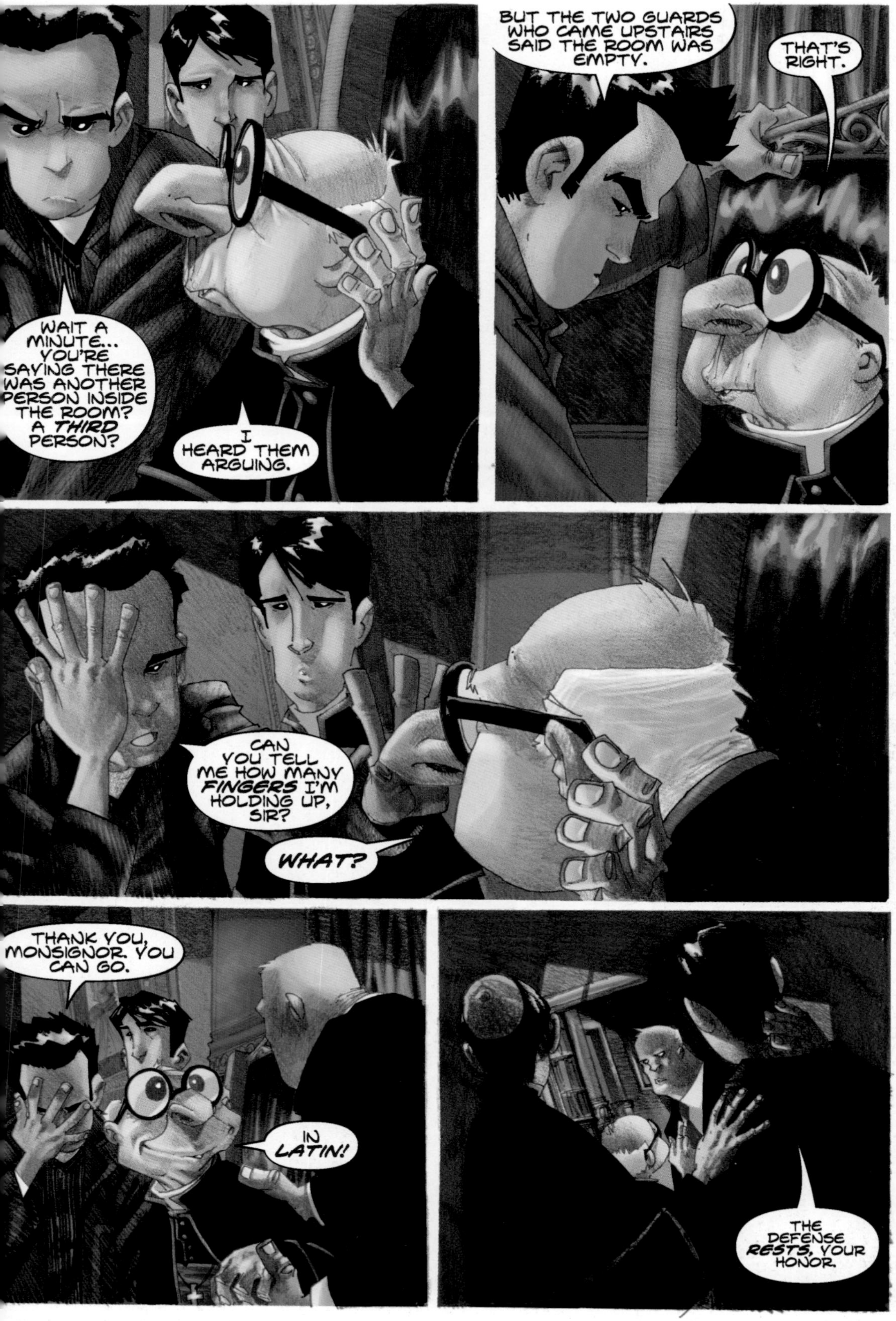
WAIT A MINUTE... YOU'RE SAYING THERE WAS ANOTHER PERSON INSIDE THE ROOM? A *THIRD* PERSON?
I HEARD THEM ARGUING.
BUT THE TWO GUARDS WHO CAME UPSTAIRS SAID THE ROOM WAS EMPTY.
THAT'S RIGHT.
CAN YOU TELL ME HOW MANY *FINGERS* I'M HOLDING UP, SIR?
WHAT?
THANK YOU, MONSIGNOR. YOU CAN GO.
IN *LATIN!*
THE DEFENSE *RESTS,* YOUR HONOR.

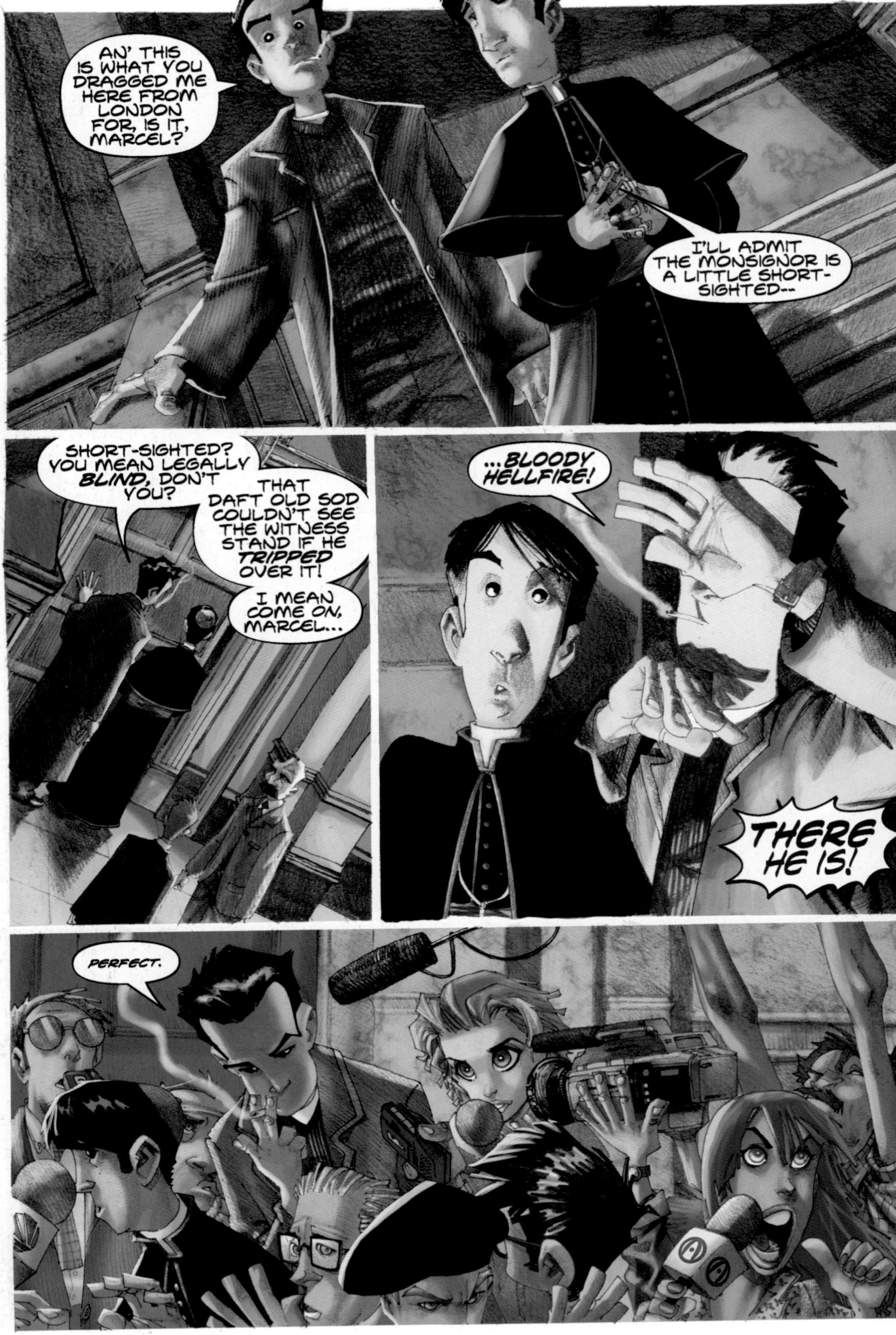
AN' THIS IS WHAT YOU DRAGGED ME HERE FROM LONDON FOR, IS IT, MARCEL?
I'LL ADMIT THE MONSIGNOR IS A LITTLE SHORT-SIGHTED--
SHORT-SIGHTED? YOU MEAN LEGALLY BLIND, DON'T YOU?
THAT DAFT OLD SOD COULDN'T SEE THE WITNESS STAND IF HE TRIPPED OVER IT!
I MEAN COME ON, MARCEL...
...BLOODY HELLFIRE!
THERE HE IS!
PERFECT.

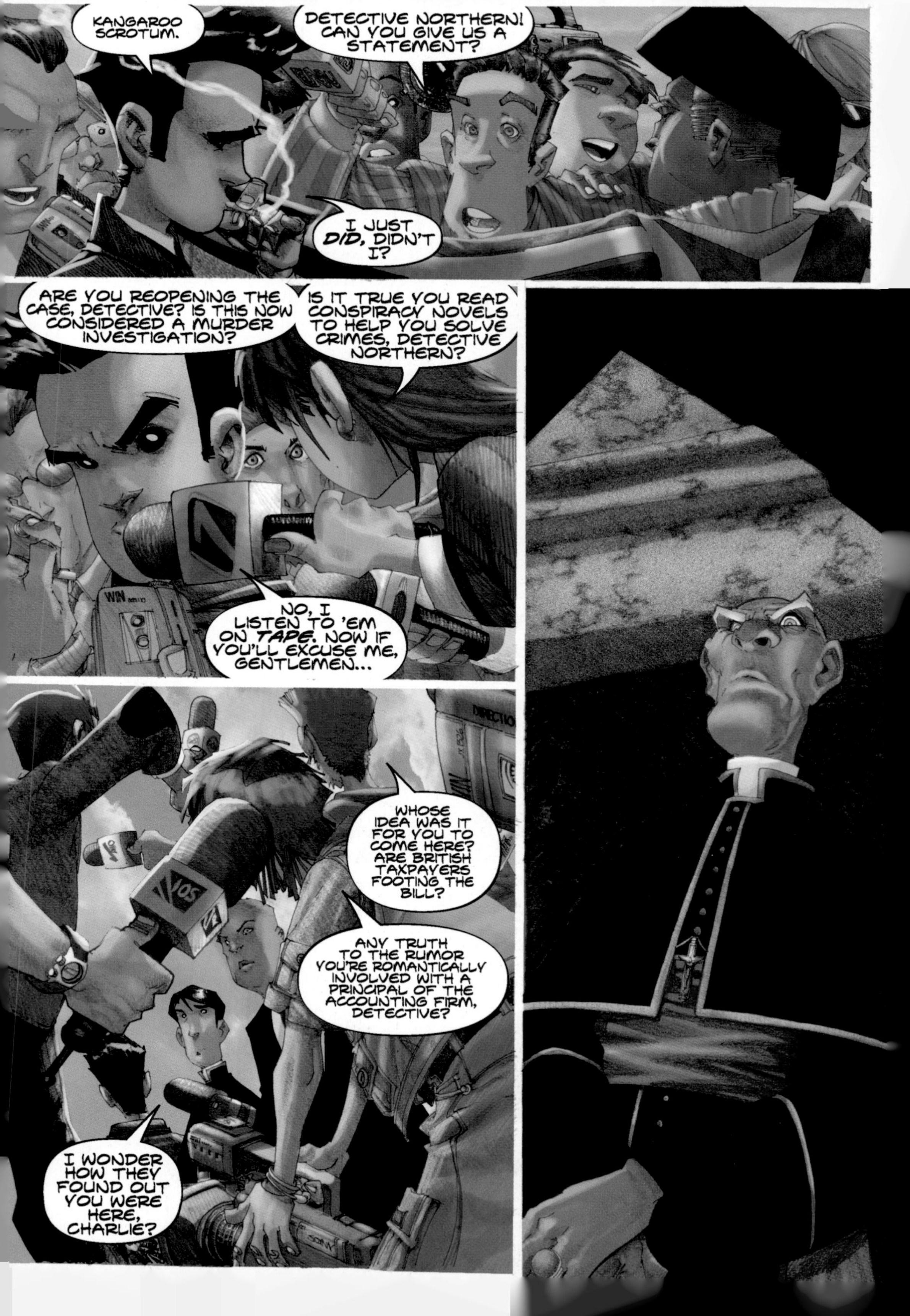
KANGAROO SCROTUM.
DETECTIVE NORTHERN! CAN YOU GIVE US A STATEMENT?
I JUST **DID**, DIDN'T I?
ARE YOU REOPENING THE CASE, DETECTIVE? IS THIS NOW CONSIDERED A MURDER INVESTIGATION?
IS IT TRUE YOU READ CONSPIRACY NOVELS TO HELP YOU SOLVE CRIMES, DETECTIVE NORTHERN?
NO, I LISTEN TO 'EM ON **TAPE**. NOW IF YOU'LL EXCUSE ME, GENTLEMEN...
WHOSE IDEA WAS IT FOR YOU TO COME HERE? ARE BRITISH TAXPAYERS FOOTING THE BILL?
ANY TRUTH TO THE RUMOR YOU'RE ROMANTICALLY INVOLVED WITH A PRINCIPAL OF THE ACCOUNTING FIRM, DETECTIVE?
I WONDER HOW THEY FOUND OUT YOU WERE HERE, CHARLIE?

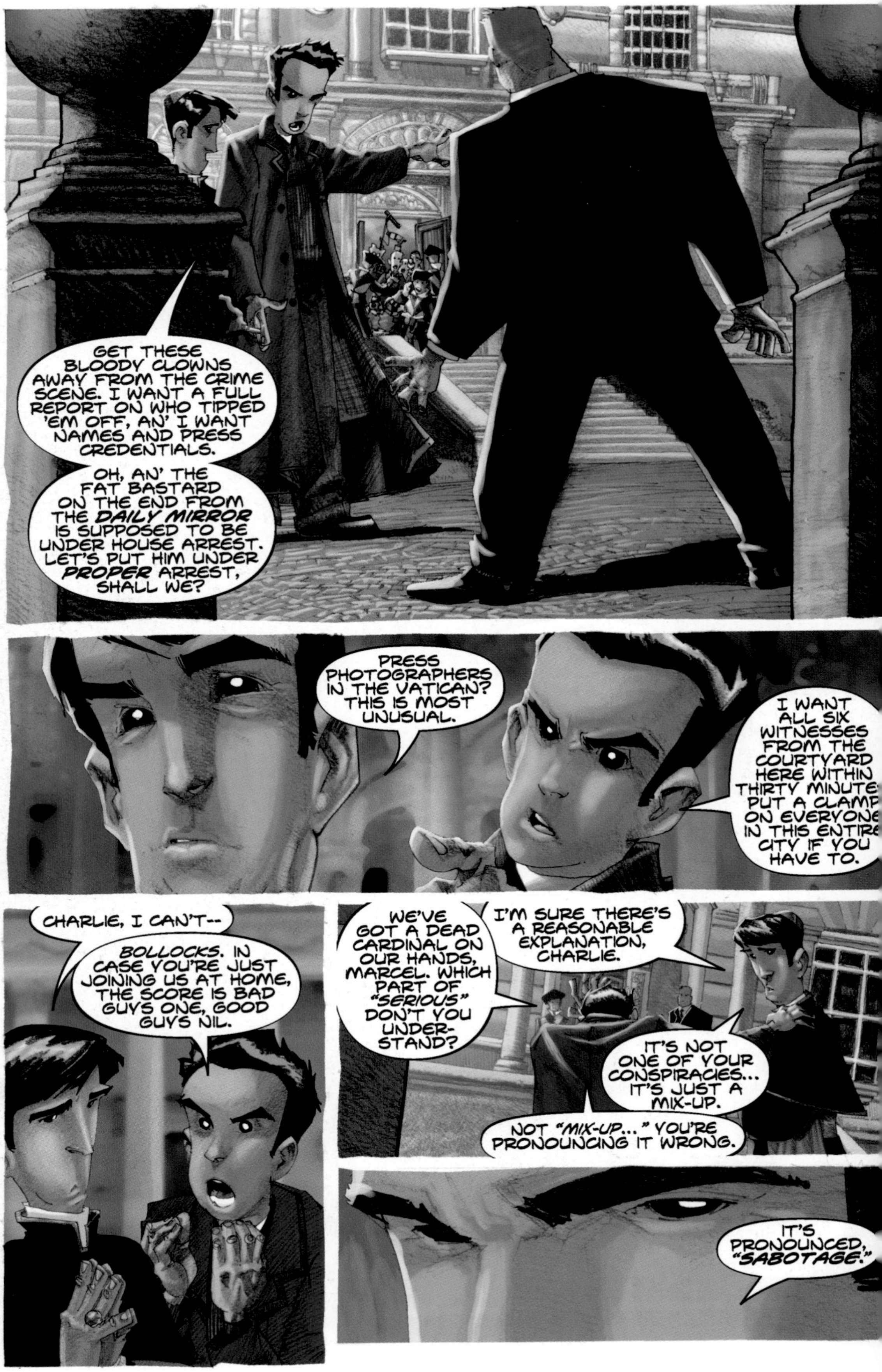
GET THESE BLOODY CLOWNS AWAY FROM THE CRIME SCENE. I WANT A FULL REPORT ON WHO TIPPED 'EM OFF, AN' I WANT NAMES AND PRESS CREDENTIALS.
OH, AN' THE FAT BASTARD ON THE END FROM THE *DAILY MIRROR* IS SUPPOSED TO BE UNDER HOUSE ARREST. LET'S PUT HIM UNDER *PROPER* ARREST, SHALL WE?
PRESS PHOTOGRAPHERS IN THE VATICAN? THIS IS MOST UNUSUAL.
I WANT ALL SIX WITNESSES FROM THE COURTYARD HERE WITHIN THIRTY MINUTES. PUT A CLAMP ON EVERYONE IN THIS ENTIRE CITY IF YOU HAVE TO.
CHARLIE, I CAN'T--
BOLLOCKS. IN CASE YOU'RE JUST JOINING US AT HOME, THE SCORE IS BAD GUYS ONE, GOOD GUYS NIL.
I'M SURE THERE'S A REASONABLE EXPLANATION, CHARLIE.
WE'VE GOT A DEAD CARDINAL ON OUR HANDS, MARCEL. WHICH PART OF "*SERIOUS*" DON'T YOU UNDER-STAND?
IT'S NOT ONE OF YOUR CONSPIRACIES... IT'S JUST A MIX-UP.
NOT "*MIX-UP...*" YOU'RE PRONOUNCING IT WRONG.
IT'S PRONOUNCED, "*SABOTAGE.*"

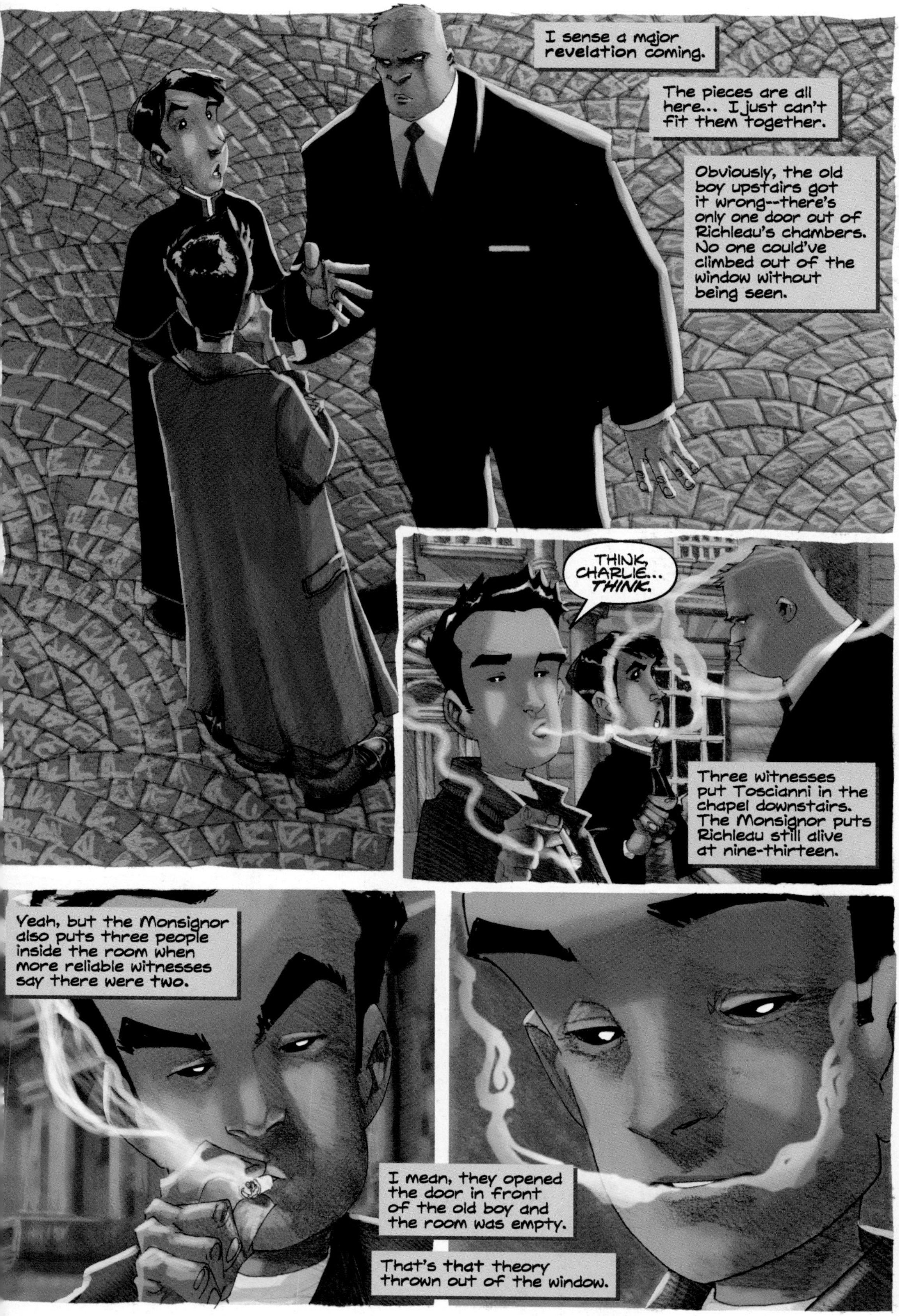
I sense a major revelation coming.
The pieces are all here... I just can't fit them together.
Obviously, the old boy upstairs got it wrong--there's only one door out of Richleau's chambers. No one could've climbed out of the window without being seen.
THINK, CHARLIE... THINK.
Three witnesses put Toscianni in the chapel downstairs. The Monsignor puts Richleau still alive at nine-thirteen.
Yeah, but the Monsignor also puts three people inside the room when more reliable witnesses say there were two.
I mean, they opened the door in front of the old boy and the room was empty.
That's that theory thrown out of the window.

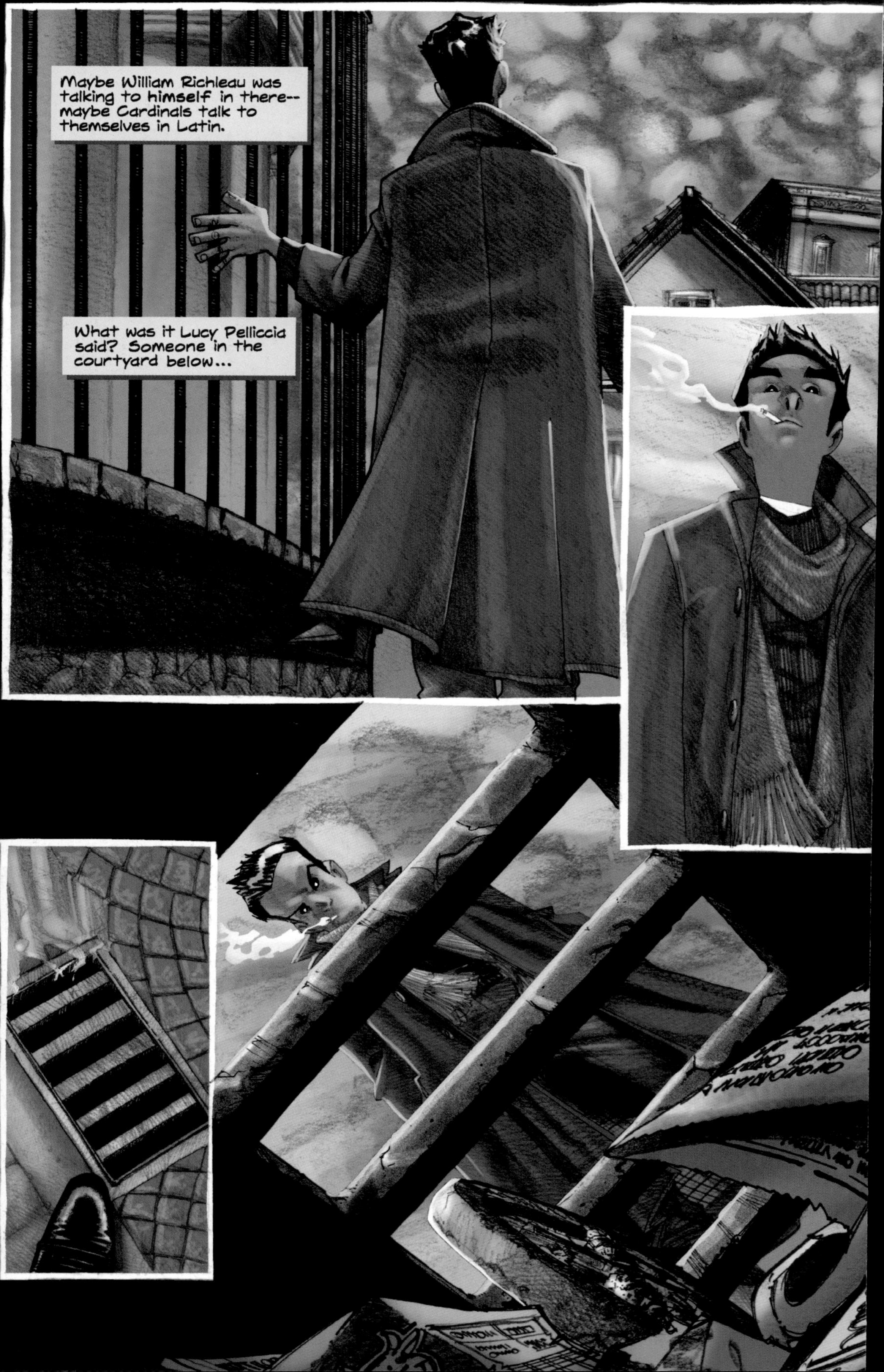

Maybe William Richleau was talking to himself in there-- maybe Cardinals talk to themselves in Latin.
What was it Lucy Pelliccia said? Someone in the courtyard below...

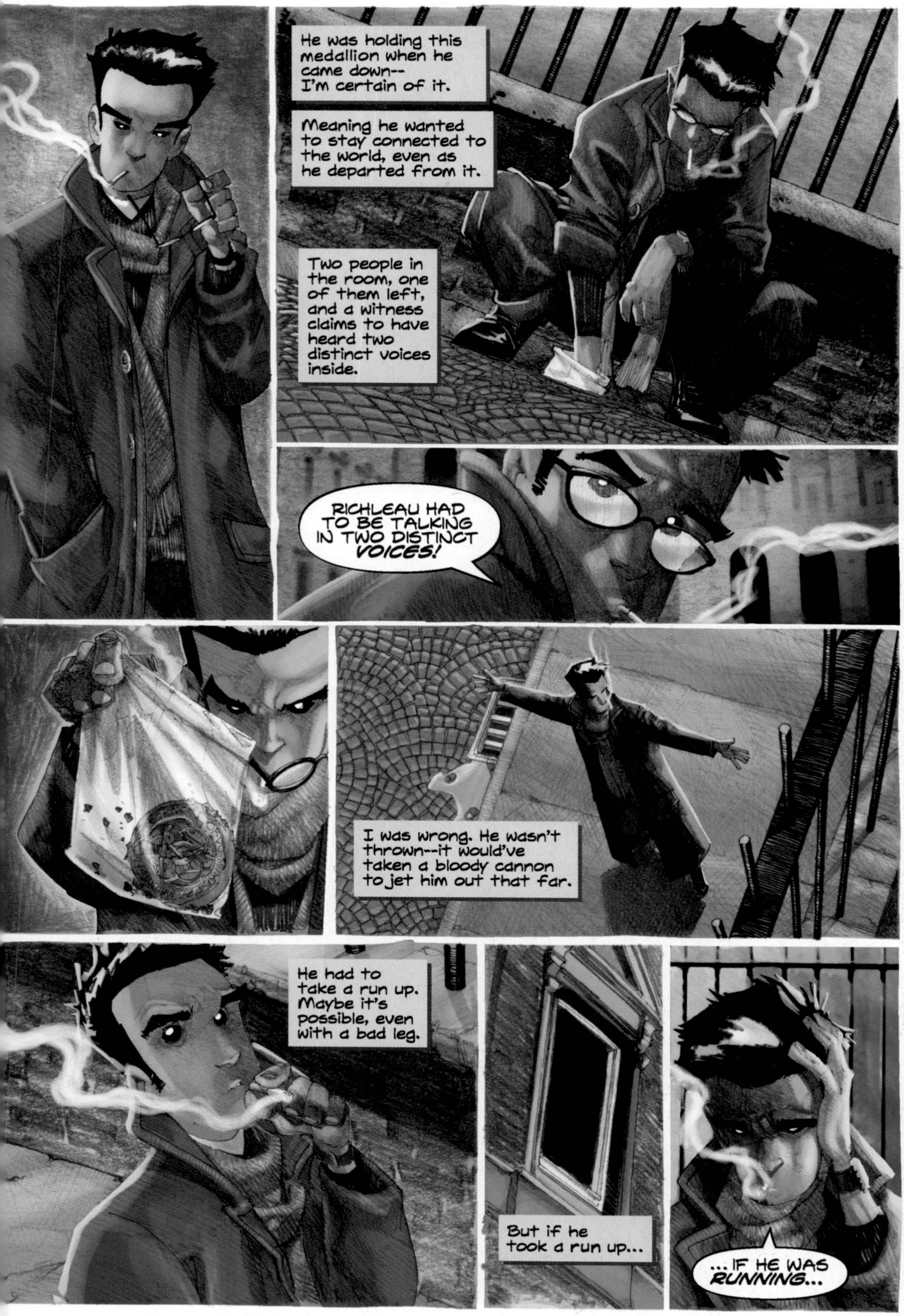
He was holding this medallion when he came down-- I'm certain of it.
Meaning he wanted to stay connected to the world, even as he departed from it.
Two people in the room, one of them left, and a witness claims to have heard two distinct voices inside.
RICHLEAU HAD TO BE TALKING IN TWO DISTINCT ***VOICES!***
I was wrong. He wasn't thrown--it would've taken a bloody cannon to jet him out that far.
He had to take a run up. Maybe it's possible, even with a bad leg.
But if he took a run up...
...IF HE WAS ***RUNNING...***

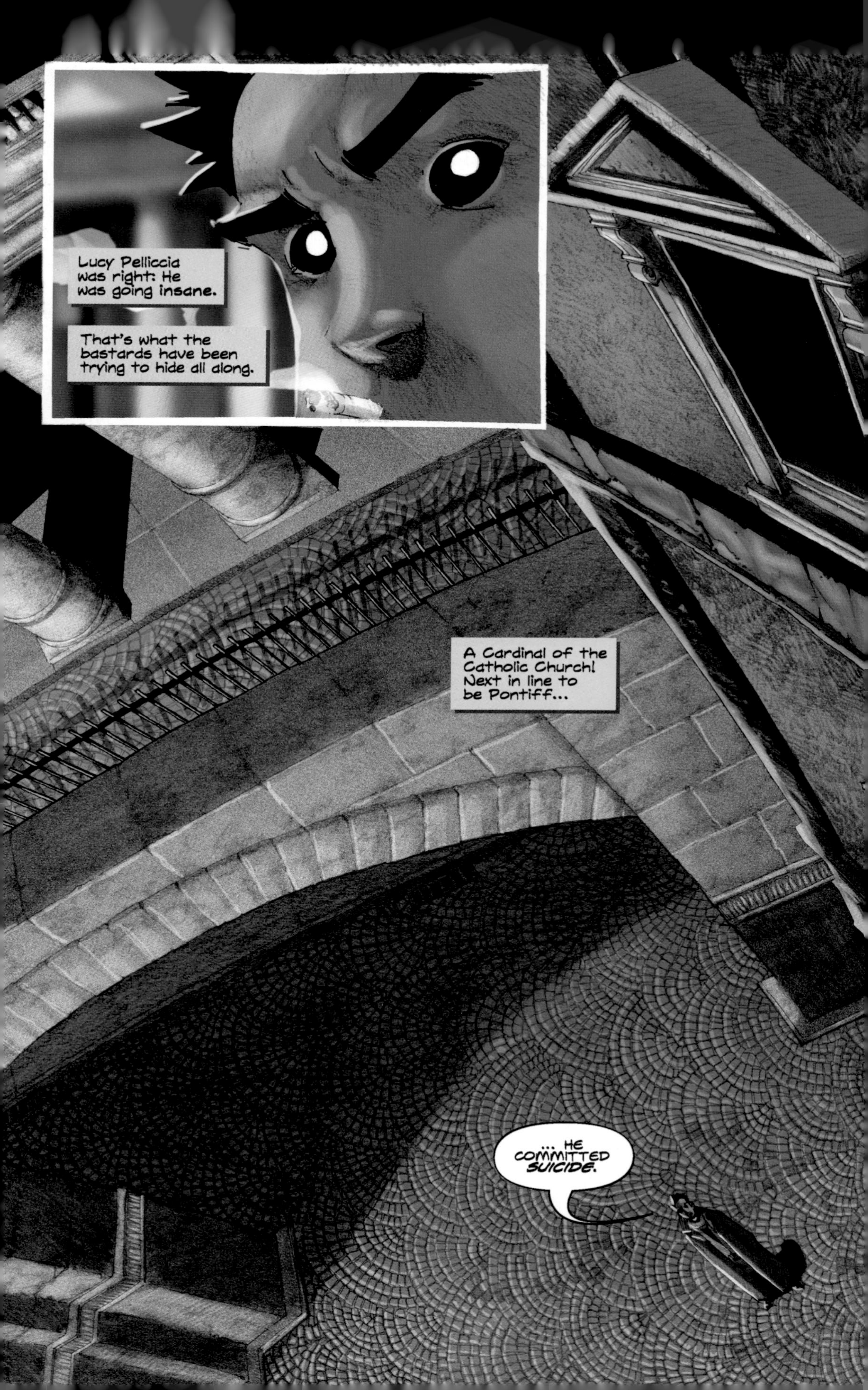
Lucy Pelliccia was right: He was going insane.
That's what the bastards have been trying to hide all along.
A Cardinal of the Catholic Church! Next in line to be Pontiff...
... HE COMMITTED SUICIDE.

CHAPTER THREE

Trace Evidence

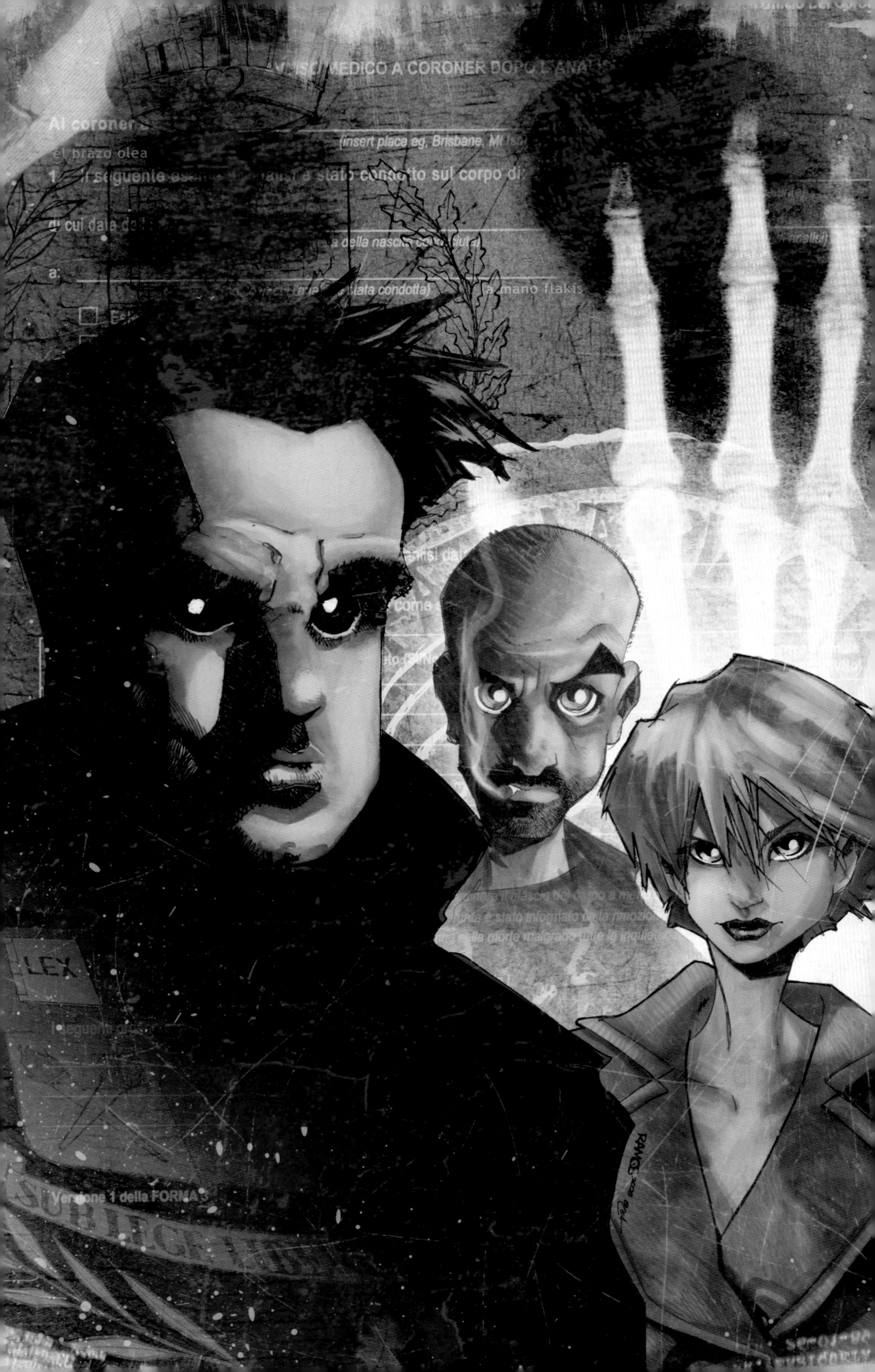
MEDICO A CORONER DOPO
Al coroner
(insert place eg, Brisbane, Mt Isa
el brazo olea
stato condotto sul corpo di
di cui data
della nascita
a:
condotta)
mano flakis
coma
LEX
Versione 1 della FORMA 3
RAMOS 2008

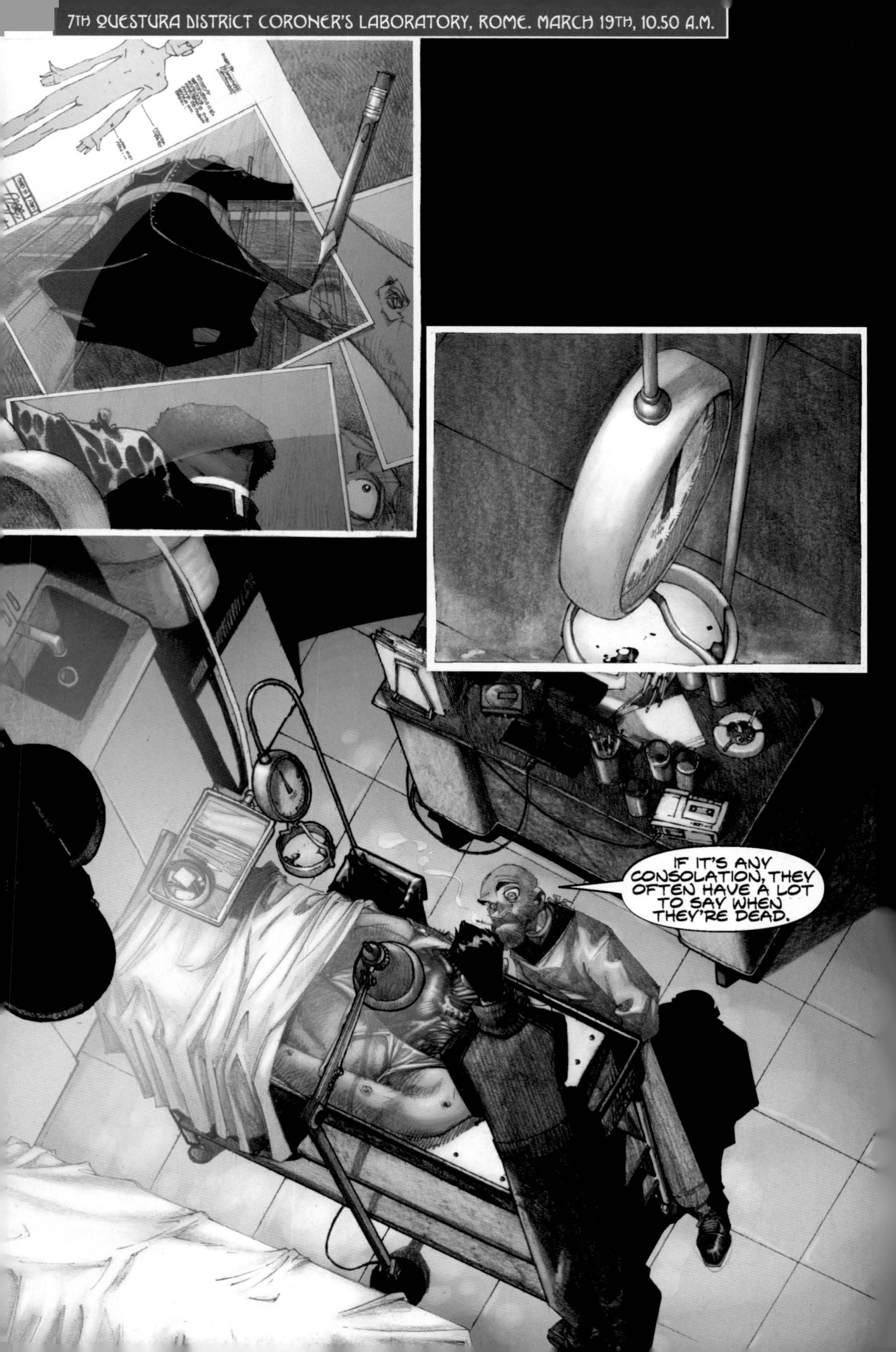
7TH QUESTURA DISTRICT CORONER'S LABORATORY, ROME. MARCH 19TH, 10.50 A.M.
IF IT'S ANY CONSOLATION, THEY OFTEN HAVE A LOT TO SAY WHEN THEY'RE DEAD.

MMF. ONE QUICK LOOK AT THE BODY EXPLAINS WHY THEY NEVER FAXED ME THAT AUTOPSY REPORT I REQUESTED BEFORE I GOT ON THE PLANE.
OH YEAH? WHY'S THAT?
'CAUSE THEY NEVER FUCKIN' PERFORMED ONE, CHARLIE, THAT'S WHY. WENT STRAIGHT TO EMBALMING.
TAKES A PROFESSIONAL LIKE ME TO SPOT THE TOTAL LACK OF HEART, LUNGS, AND KIDNEYS. AND THE FORMALDEHYDE SMELL'S A DEAD GIVEAWAY.
WELL, SCREW THAT FOR A GAME OF SOLDIERS. AREN'T THEY LEGALLY REQUIRED TO DO AN AUTOPSY?
I SEE IT ALL THE TIME--RANK BLOODY AMATEURS SOME OF THESE PROVINCIALS.
'ERE Y'ARE, LOOK-- THAT'S QUITE INTERESTING.
WHAT IS?

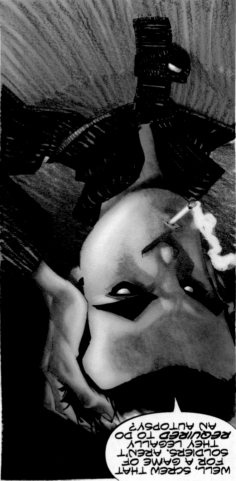

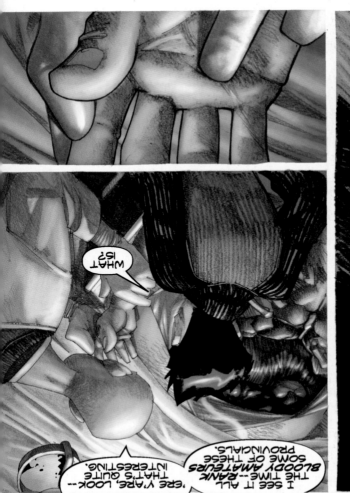

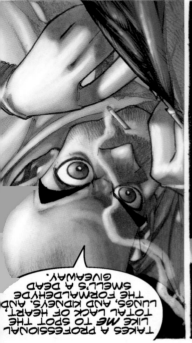

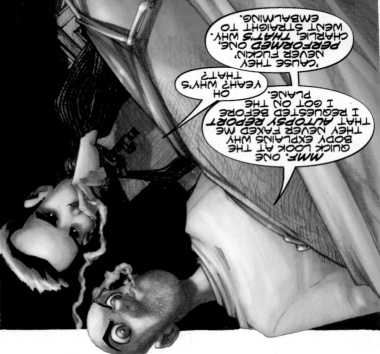

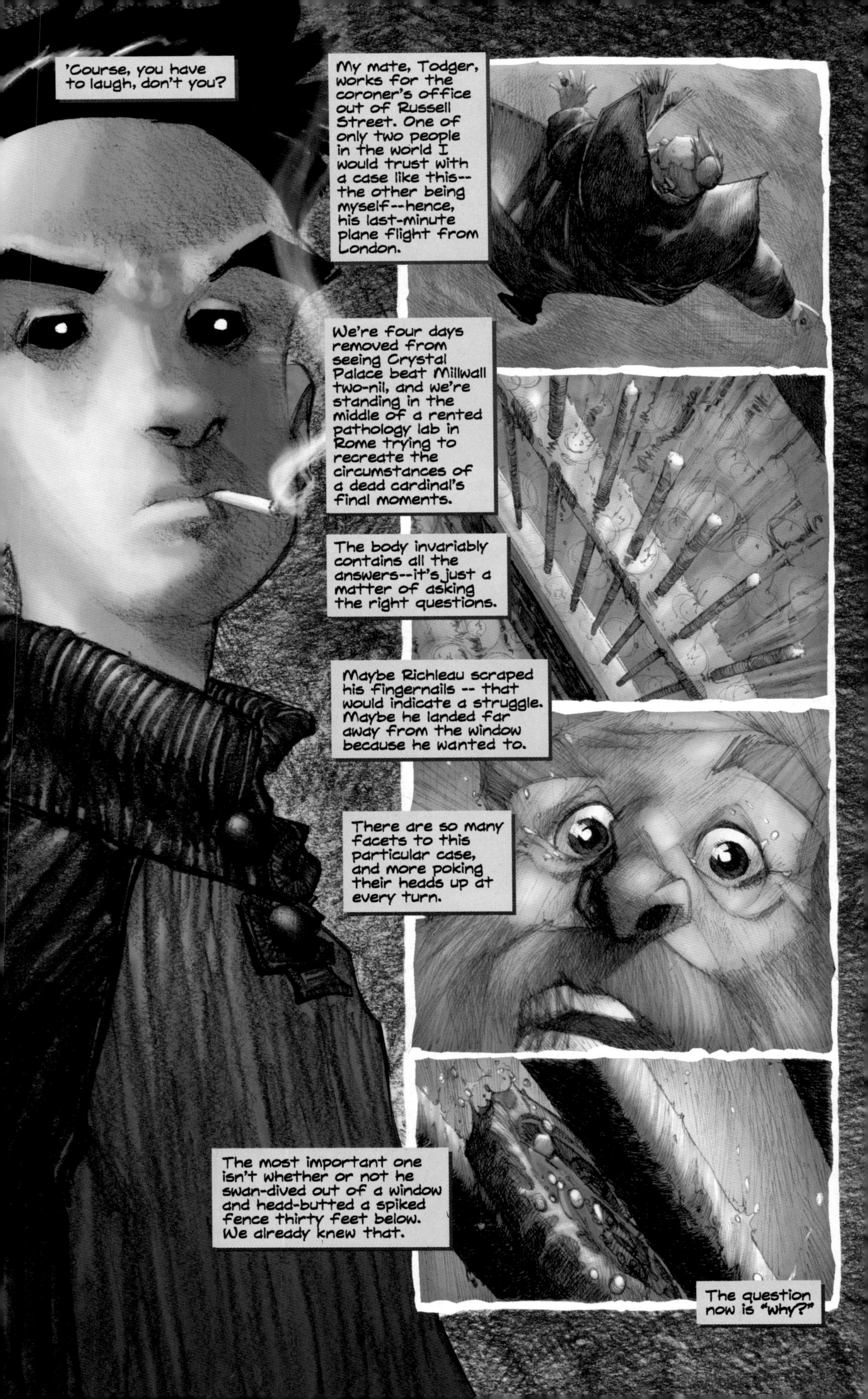
'Course, you have to laugh, don't you?
My mate, Todger, works for the coroner's office out of Russell Street. One of only two people in the world I would trust with a case like this--the other being myself--hence, his last-minute plane flight from London.
We're four days removed from seeing Crystal Palace beat Millwall two-nil, and we're standing in the middle of a rented pathology lab in Rome trying to recreate the circumstances of a dead cardinal's final moments.
The body invariably contains all the answers--it's just a matter of asking the right questions.
Maybe Richleau scraped his fingernails -- that would indicate a struggle. Maybe he landed far away from the window because he wanted to.
There are so many facets to this particular case, and more poking their heads up at every turn.
The most important one isn't whether or not he swan-dived out of a window and head-butted a spiked fence thirty feet below. We already knew that.
The question now is "why?"

ANY CHANCE *THIS* COULD'VE MADE THOSE MARKS, TODGE?
I'M NOT A DERMAPATHOLOGIST, CHARLIE, BUT I'D SAY THE CHANCES ARE PRETTY DECENT. THE SERRATED EDGE MATCHES THE DERMAL ABRASIONS.
WHERE'D YOU GET IT?
FELL OFF THE BACK OF A CARDINAL. LANDED ABOUT TWELVE YARDS FROM THE BODY. MY GUESS IS HE WAS HOLDING IT FOR SOME REASON WHEN HE TOOK THE QUICK WAY DOWN.
ANYTHING ELSE STRIKE YOU AS ODD?
NOT REALLY. NOTHING UNDER THE NAILS ... NO OTHER EVIDENCE OF TRAUMA TO THE SKIN. HE HIT THE SPIKES PRETTY CLEANLY, SO THEY STOPPED HIS FALL.
IF THERE'D BEEN A FIGHT WE'D HAVE SEEN POST-MORTEM LIVIDITY ON HIS SKIN IN THE AREAS WHERE HE WAS INJURED.
I SUPPOSE HE *MIGHT'VE* BEEN PRACTICING HIS LONG JUMP, BUT HE DOESN'T LOOK LIKE HE WAS MUCH OF AN ATHLETE.
NEITHER WOULD YOU WITH YOUR INSIDES RIPPED OUT, TODGE.

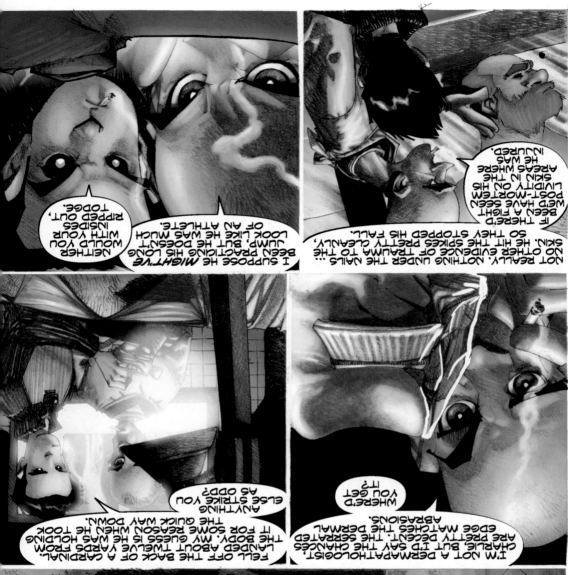

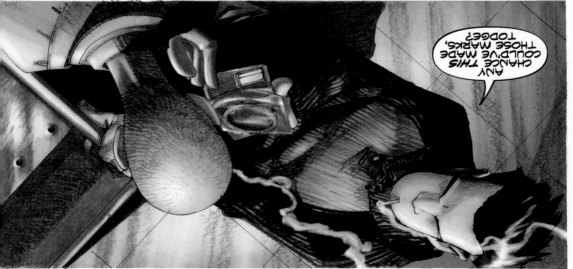

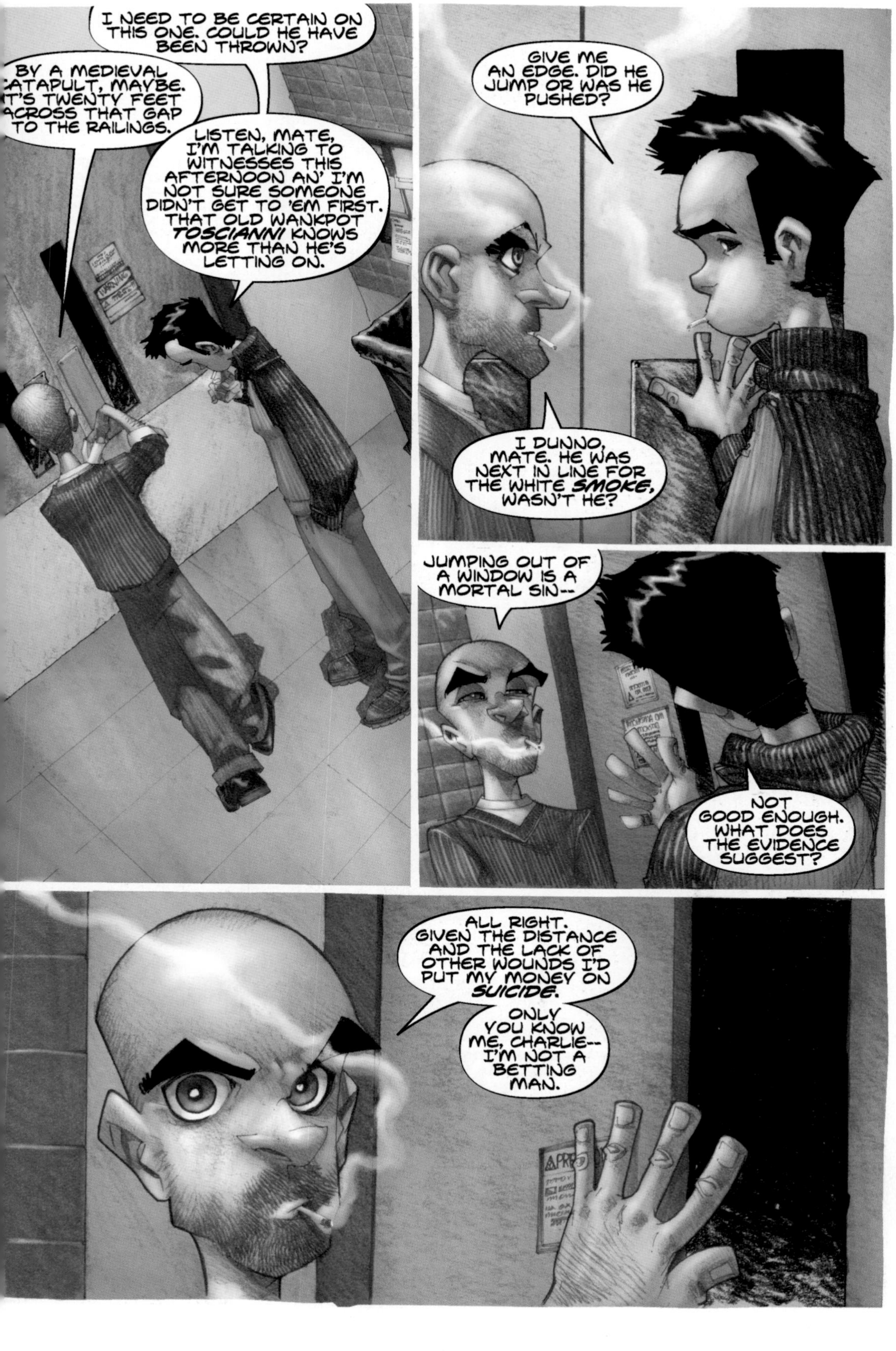
I NEED TO BE CERTAIN ON THIS ONE. COULD HE HAVE BEEN THROWN?
BY A MEDIEVAL CATAPULT, MAYBE. IT'S TWENTY FEET ACROSS THAT GAP TO THE RAILINGS.
LISTEN, MATE, I'M TALKING TO WITNESSES THIS AFTERNOON AN' I'M NOT SURE SOMEONE DIDN'T GET TO 'EM FIRST. THAT OLD WANKPOT ***TOSCIANNI*** KNOWS MORE THAN HE'S LETTING ON.
GIVE ME AN EDGE. DID HE JUMP OR WAS HE PUSHED?
I DUNNO, MATE. HE WAS NEXT IN LINE FOR THE WHITE ***SMOKE,*** WASN'T HE?
JUMPING OUT OF A WINDOW IS A MORTAL SIN--
NOT GOOD ENOUGH. WHAT DOES THE EVIDENCE SUGGEST?
ALL RIGHT. GIVEN THE DISTANCE AND THE LACK OF OTHER WOUNDS I'D PUT MY MONEY ON ***SUICIDE***.
ONLY YOU KNOW ME, CHARLIE-- I'M NOT A BETTING MAN.

"I WILL, MATE. SEE, THE PROBLEM WITH THAT SCENARIO IS THAT IT BEGS THE QUESTION OF WHO CALLED FOR HELP."

"CERTAINLY NOT THE CARDINAL, SINCE HE WAS ALREADY DEAD."

"NO ONE. I SWEAR IT. ASK ESTERMANN."

"WAIT A MINUTE, SERGEANT SCHULTZ... YOU HEARD A CRY FOR HELP AND WHEN YOU GOT THERE NO ONE WAS THERE?"

"THERE WAS NO ONE IN SIGHT. THREE OR FOUR OTHER GUARDS HEARD THE NOISE AND CAME WITHIN MINUTES."

"WE FOUND CARDINAL RICHLEAU IMPALED AT THE BASE OF THE APARTMENTS."

OVER THERE.

HELP! SOMEBODY HELP! THE FENCE!

"...I WAS WITH CORPORAL ESTERMANN AT THE MARESCIALLO COURTYARD. WE WERE PATROLLING TOWARDS THE ROYAL STAIRWAY WHEN THE NOISE CAME. WE ALL HEARD IT..."

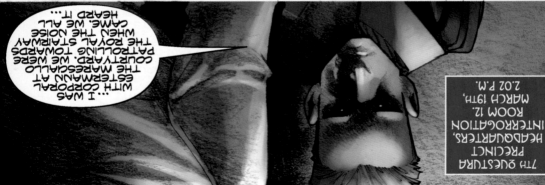

7TH QUESTURA PRECINCT HEADQUARTERS, INTERROGATION ROOM 12, MARCH 19TH, 2.02 P.M.

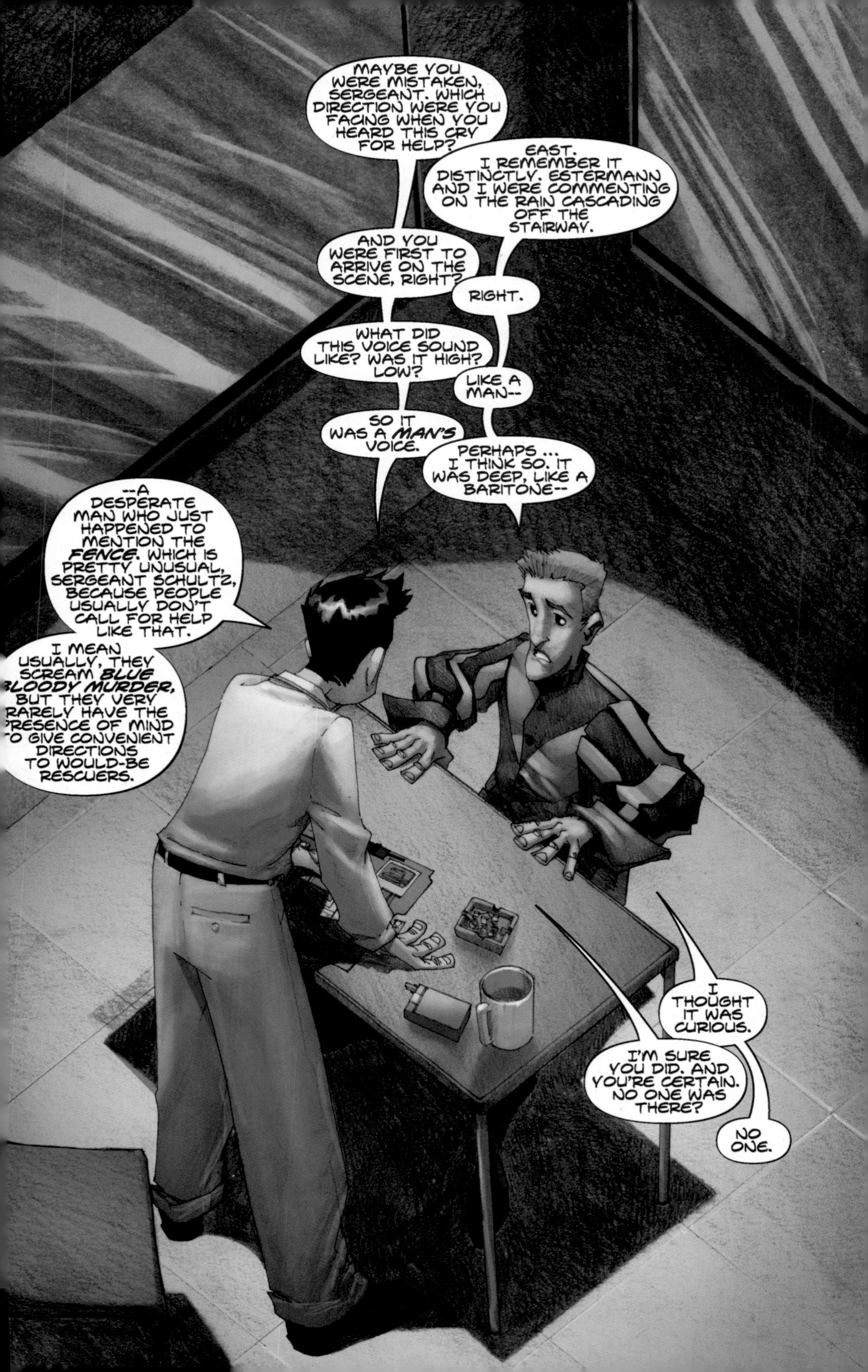
MAYBE YOU WERE MISTAKEN, SERGEANT. WHICH DIRECTION WERE YOU FACING WHEN YOU HEARD THIS CRY FOR HELP?
EAST. I REMEMBER IT DISTINCTLY. ESTERMANN AND I WERE COMMENTING ON THE RAIN CASCADING OFF THE STAIRWAY.
AND YOU WERE FIRST TO ARRIVE ON THE SCENE, RIGHT?
RIGHT.
WHAT DID THIS VOICE SOUND LIKE? WAS IT HIGH? LOW?
LIKE A MAN--
SO IT WAS A *MAN'S* VOICE.
PERHAPS ... I THINK SO. IT WAS DEEP, LIKE A BARITONE--
--A DESPERATE MAN WHO JUST HAPPENED TO MENTION THE *FENCE*. WHICH IS PRETTY UNUSUAL, SERGEANT SCHULTZ, BECAUSE PEOPLE USUALLY DON'T CALL FOR HELP LIKE THAT.
I MEAN USUALLY, THEY SCREAM *BLUE BLOODY MURDER,* BUT THEY VERY RARELY HAVE THE PRESENCE OF MIND TO GIVE CONVENIENT DIRECTIONS TO WOULD-BE RESCUERS.
I THOUGHT IT WAS CURIOUS.
I'M SURE YOU DID. AND YOU'RE CERTAIN. NO ONE WAS THERE?
NO ONE.

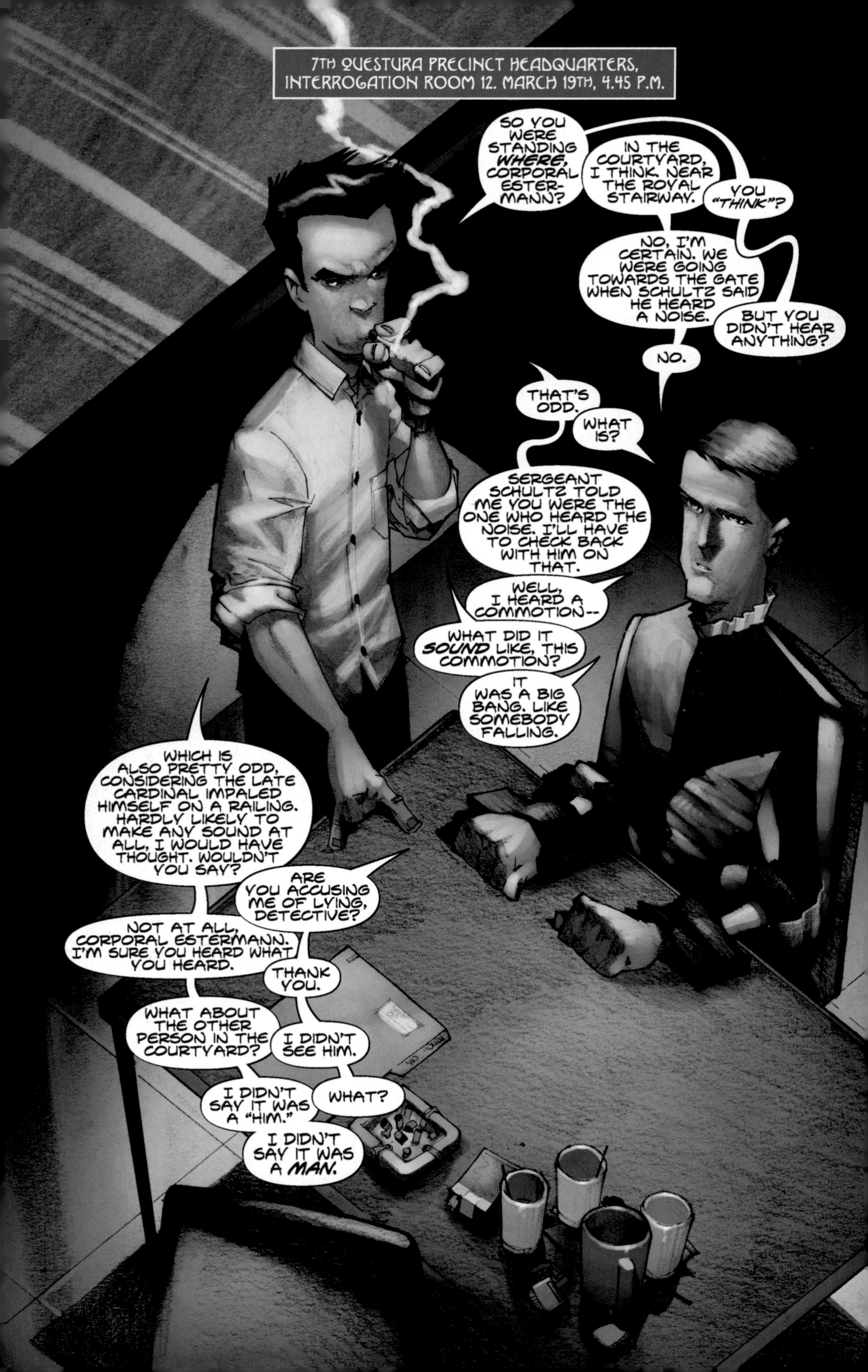
7TH QUESTURA PRECINCT HEADQUARTERS, INTERROGATION ROOM 12. MARCH 19TH, 4.45 P.M.
SO YOU WERE STANDING *WHERE*, CORPORAL ESTER-MANN?
IN THE COURTYARD, I THINK. NEAR THE ROYAL STAIRWAY.
YOU *"THINK"*?
NO, I'M CERTAIN. WE WERE GOING TOWARDS THE GATE WHEN SCHULTZ SAID HE HEARD A NOISE.
BUT YOU DIDN'T HEAR ANYTHING?
NO.
THAT'S ODD.
WHAT IS?
SERGEANT SCHULTZ TOLD ME YOU WERE THE ONE WHO HEARD THE NOISE. I'LL HAVE TO CHECK BACK WITH HIM ON THAT.
WELL, I HEARD A COMMOTION--
WHAT DID IT *SOUND* LIKE, THIS COMMOTION?
IT WAS A BIG BANG. LIKE SOMEBODY FALLING.
WHICH IS ALSO PRETTY ODD, CONSIDERING THE LATE CARDINAL IMPALED HIMSELF ON A RAILING. HARDLY LIKELY TO MAKE ANY SOUND AT ALL, I WOULD HAVE THOUGHT. WOULDN'T YOU SAY?
ARE YOU ACCUSING ME OF LYING, DETECTIVE?
NOT AT ALL, CORPORAL ESTERMANN. I'M SURE YOU HEARD WHAT YOU HEARD.
THANK YOU.
WHAT ABOUT THE OTHER PERSON IN THE COURTYARD?
I DIDN'T SEE HIM.
I DIDN'T SAY IT WAS A "HIM."
WHAT?
I DIDN'T SAY IT WAS A *MAN*.

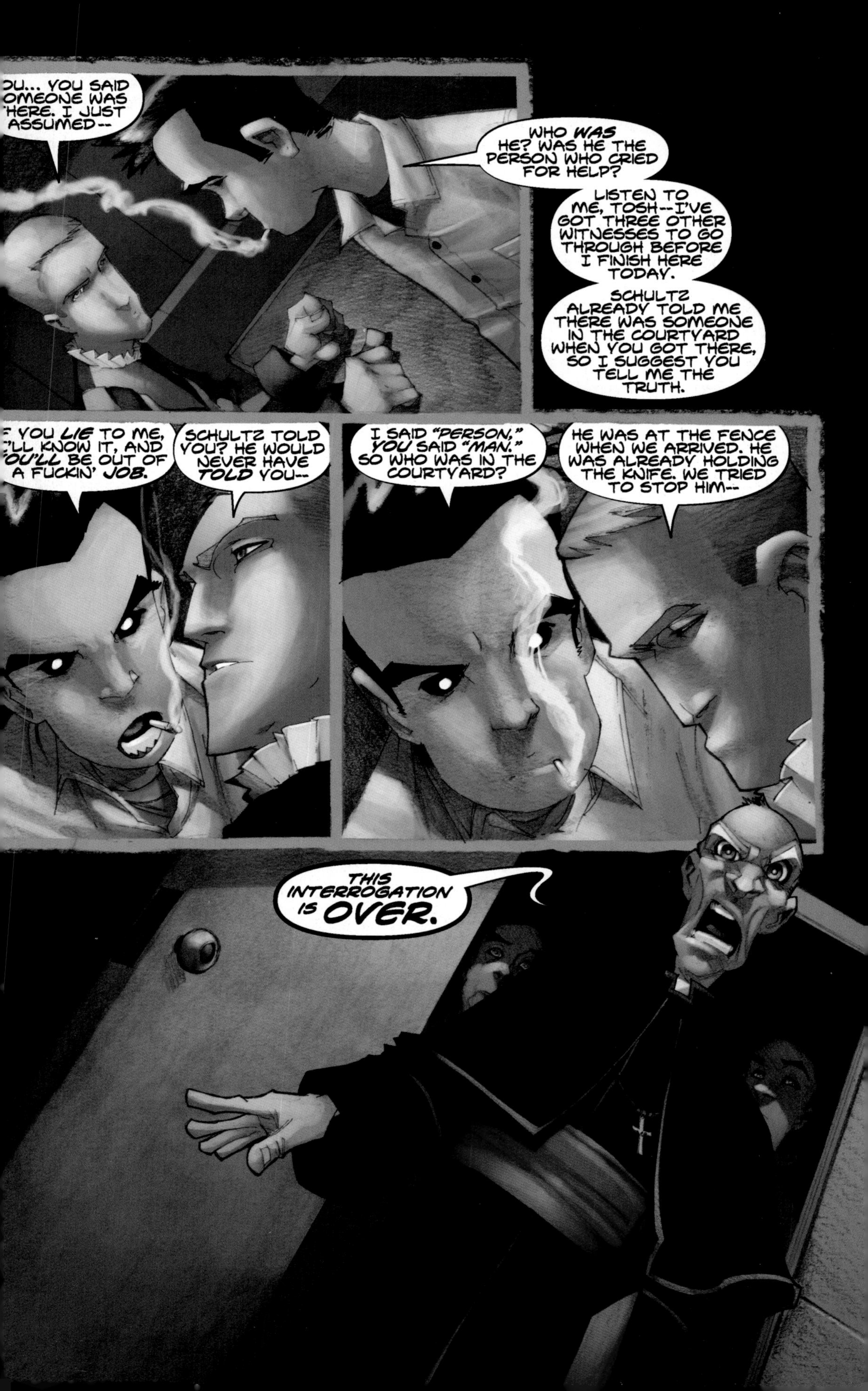
OU... YOU SAID OMEONE WAS HERE. I JUST ASSUMED--
WHO *WAS* HE? WAS HE THE PERSON WHO CRIED FOR HELP?
LISTEN TO ME, TOSH--I'VE GOT THREE OTHER WITNESSES TO GO THROUGH BEFORE I FINISH HERE TODAY.
SCHULTZ ALREADY TOLD ME THERE WAS SOMEONE IN THE COURTYARD WHEN YOU GOT THERE, SO I SUGGEST YOU TELL ME THE TRUTH.
F YOU *LIE* TO ME, 'LL KNOW IT, AND *OU'LL* BE OUT OF A FUCKIN' *JOB.*
SCHULTZ TOLD YOU? HE WOULD NEVER HAVE *TOLD* YOU--
I SAID *"PERSON," YOU* SAID *"MAN."* SO WHO WAS IN THE COURTYARD?
HE WAS AT THE FENCE WHEN WE ARRIVED. HE WAS ALREADY HOLDING THE KNIFE. WE TRIED TO STOP HIM--
THIS INTERROGATION IS OVER.

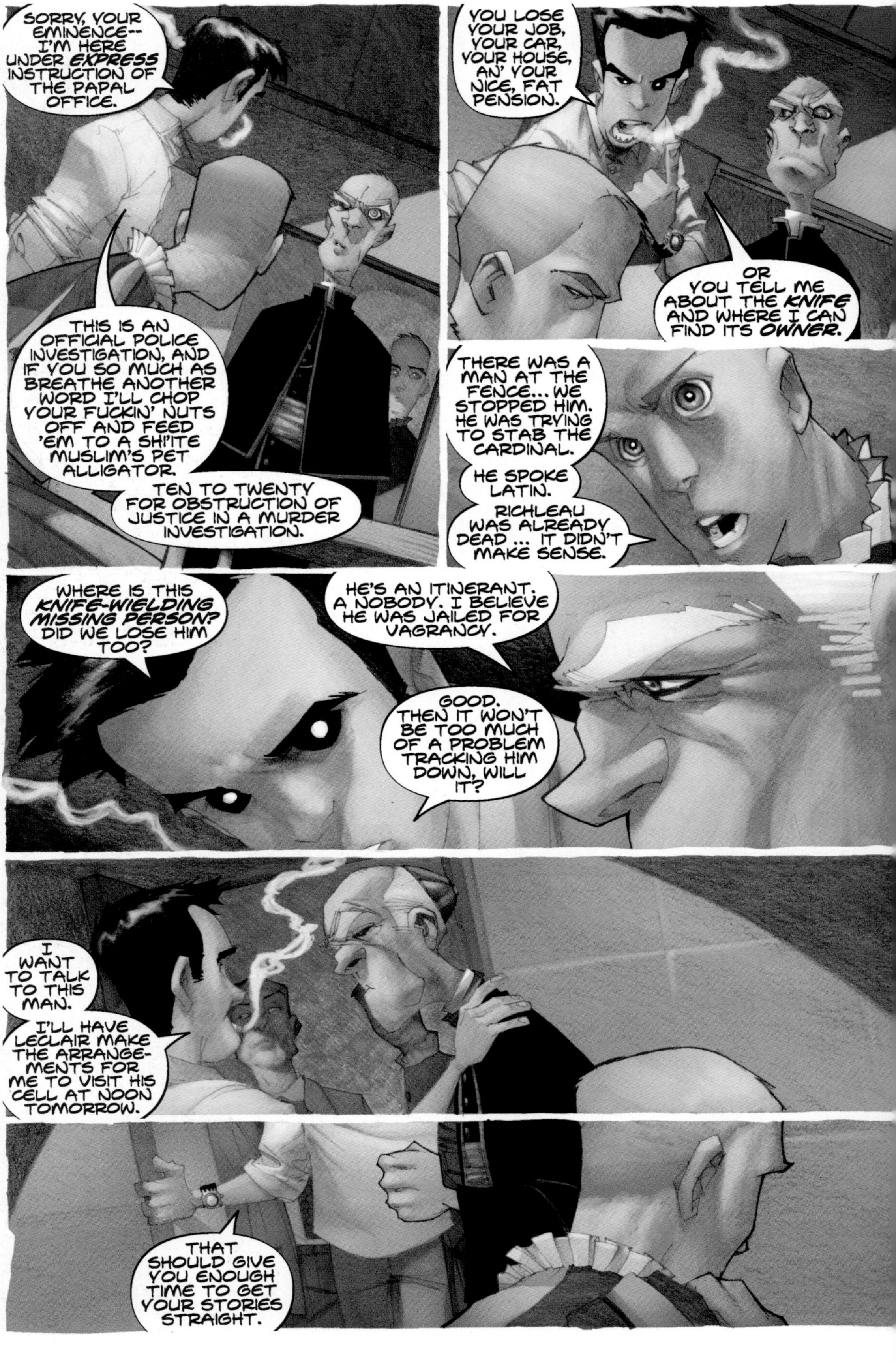
SORRY, YOUR EMINENCE-- I'M HERE UNDER ***EXPRESS*** INSTRUCTION OF THE PAPAL OFFICE.
THIS IS AN OFFICIAL POLICE INVESTIGATION, AND IF YOU SO MUCH AS BREATHE ANOTHER WORD I'LL CHOP YOUR FUCKIN' NUTS OFF AND FEED 'EM TO A SHI'ITE MUSLIM'S PET ALLIGATOR.
TEN TO TWENTY FOR OBSTRUCTION OF JUSTICE IN A MURDER INVESTIGATION.
YOU LOSE YOUR JOB, YOUR CAR, YOUR HOUSE, AN' YOUR NICE, FAT PENSION.
OR YOU TELL ME ABOUT THE ***KNIFE*** AND WHERE I CAN FIND ITS ***OWNER***.
THERE WAS A MAN AT THE FENCE... WE STOPPED HIM. HE WAS TRYING TO STAB THE CARDINAL.
HE SPOKE LATIN.
RICHLEAU WAS ALREADY DEAD ... IT DIDN'T MAKE SENSE.
WHERE IS THIS ***KNIFE-WIELDING MISSING PERSON?*** DID WE LOSE HIM TOO?
HE'S AN ITINERANT. A NOBODY. I BELIEVE HE WAS JAILED FOR VAGRANCY.
GOOD. THEN IT WON'T BE TOO MUCH OF A PROBLEM TRACKING HIM DOWN, WILL IT?
I WANT TO TALK TO THIS MAN.
I'LL HAVE LECLAIR MAKE THE ARRANGEMENTS FOR ME TO VISIT HIS CELL AT NOON TOMORROW.
THAT SHOULD GIVE YOU ENOUGH TIME TO GET YOUR STORIES STRAIGHT.

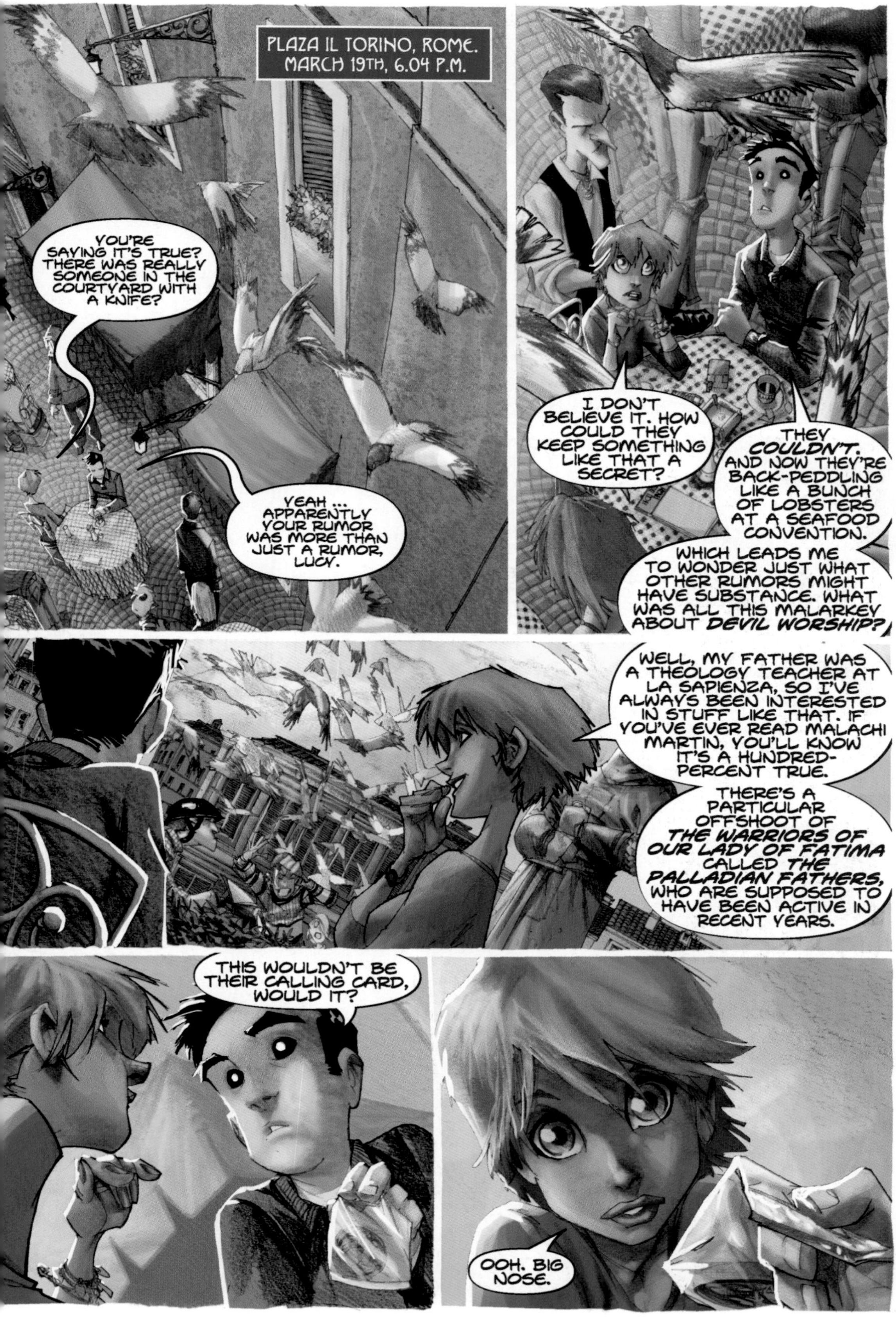
PLAZA IL TORINO, ROME. MARCH 19TH, 6.04 P.M.
YOU'RE SAYING IT'S TRUE? THERE WAS REALLY SOMEONE IN THE COURTYARD WITH A KNIFE?
YEAH ... APPARENTLY YOUR RUMOR WAS MORE THAN JUST A RUMOR, LUCY.
I DON'T BELIEVE IT. HOW COULD THEY KEEP SOMETHING LIKE THAT A SECRET?
THEY *COULDN'T.* AND NOW THEY'RE BACK-PEDDLING LIKE A BUNCH OF LOBSTERS AT A SEAFOOD CONVENTION.
WHICH LEADS ME TO WONDER JUST WHAT OTHER RUMORS MIGHT HAVE SUBSTANCE. WHAT WAS ALL THIS MALARKEY ABOUT *DEVIL WORSHIP?*
WELL, MY FATHER WAS A THEOLOGY TEACHER AT LA SAPIENZA, SO I'VE ALWAYS BEEN INTERESTED IN STUFF LIKE THAT. IF YOU'VE EVER READ MALACHI MARTIN, YOU'LL KNOW IT'S A HUNDRED-PERCENT TRUE.
THERE'S A PARTICULAR OFFSHOOT OF *THE WARRIORS OF OUR LADY OF FATIMA* CALLED *THE PALLADIAN FATHERS,* WHO ARE SUPPOSED TO HAVE BEEN ACTIVE IN RECENT YEARS.
THIS WOULDN'T BE THEIR CALLING CARD, WOULD IT?
OOH. BIG NOSE.

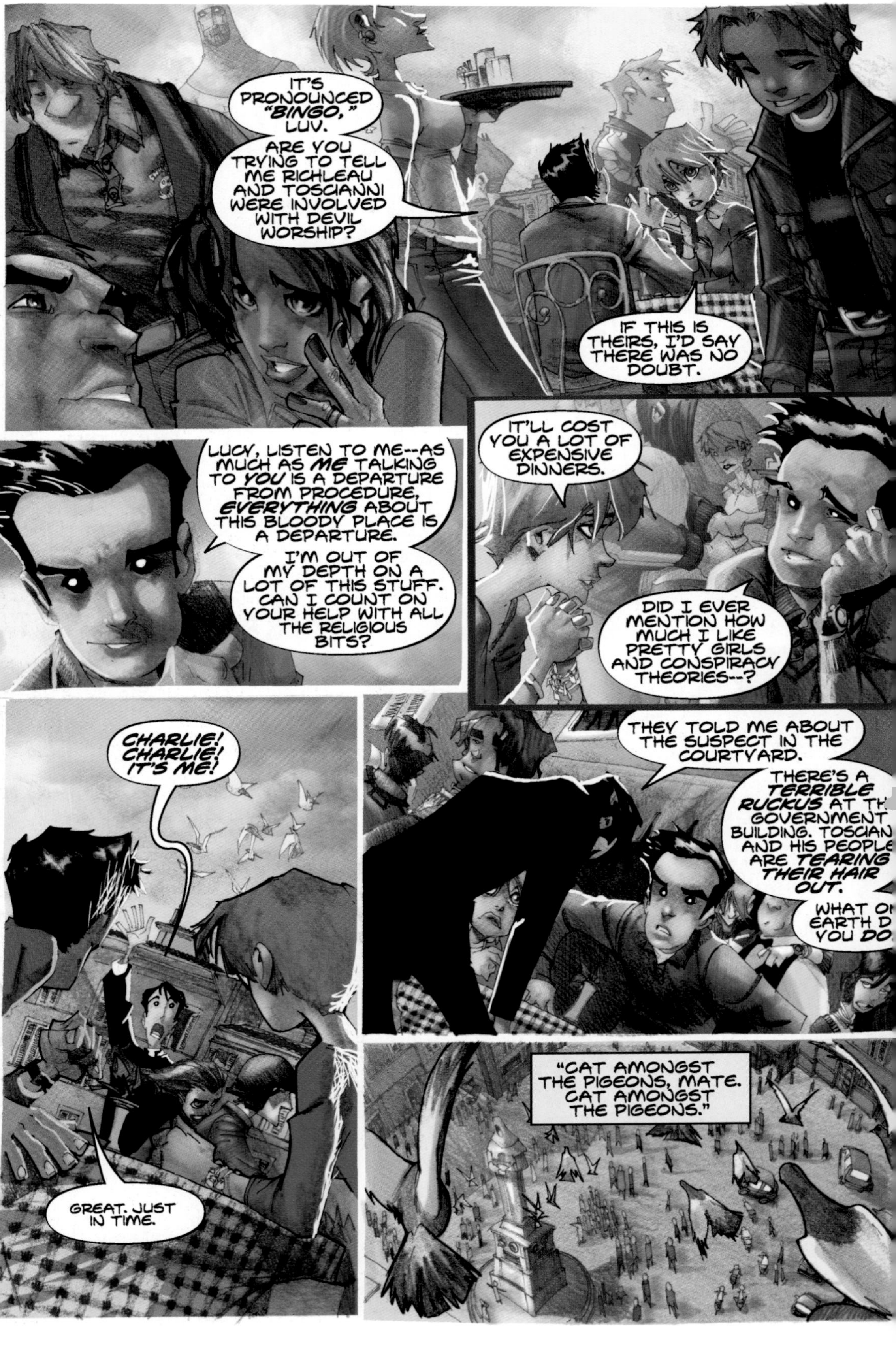
IT'S PRONOUNCED "BINGO," LUV.
ARE YOU TRYING TO TELL ME RICHLEAU AND TOSCIANNI WERE INVOLVED WITH DEVIL WORSHIP?
IF THIS IS THEIRS, I'D SAY THERE WAS NO DOUBT.
LUCY, LISTEN TO ME--AS MUCH AS ME TALKING TO YOU IS A DEPARTURE FROM PROCEDURE, EVERYTHING ABOUT THIS BLOODY PLACE IS A DEPARTURE.
I'M OUT OF MY DEPTH ON A LOT OF THIS STUFF. CAN I COUNT ON YOUR HELP WITH ALL THE RELIGIOUS BITS?
IT'LL COST YOU A LOT OF EXPENSIVE DINNERS.
DID I EVER MENTION HOW MUCH I LIKE PRETTY GIRLS AND CONSPIRACY THEORIES--?
CHARLIE! CHARLIE! IT'S ME!
GREAT. JUST IN TIME.
THEY TOLD ME ABOUT THE SUSPECT IN THE COURTYARD.
THERE'S A TERRIBLE RUCKUS AT TH GOVERNMENT BUILDING. TOSCIAN AND HIS PEOPLE ARE TEARING THEIR HAIR OUT.
WHAT O EARTH D YOU DO
"CAT AMONGST THE PIGEONS, MATE. CAT AMONGST THE PIGEONS."

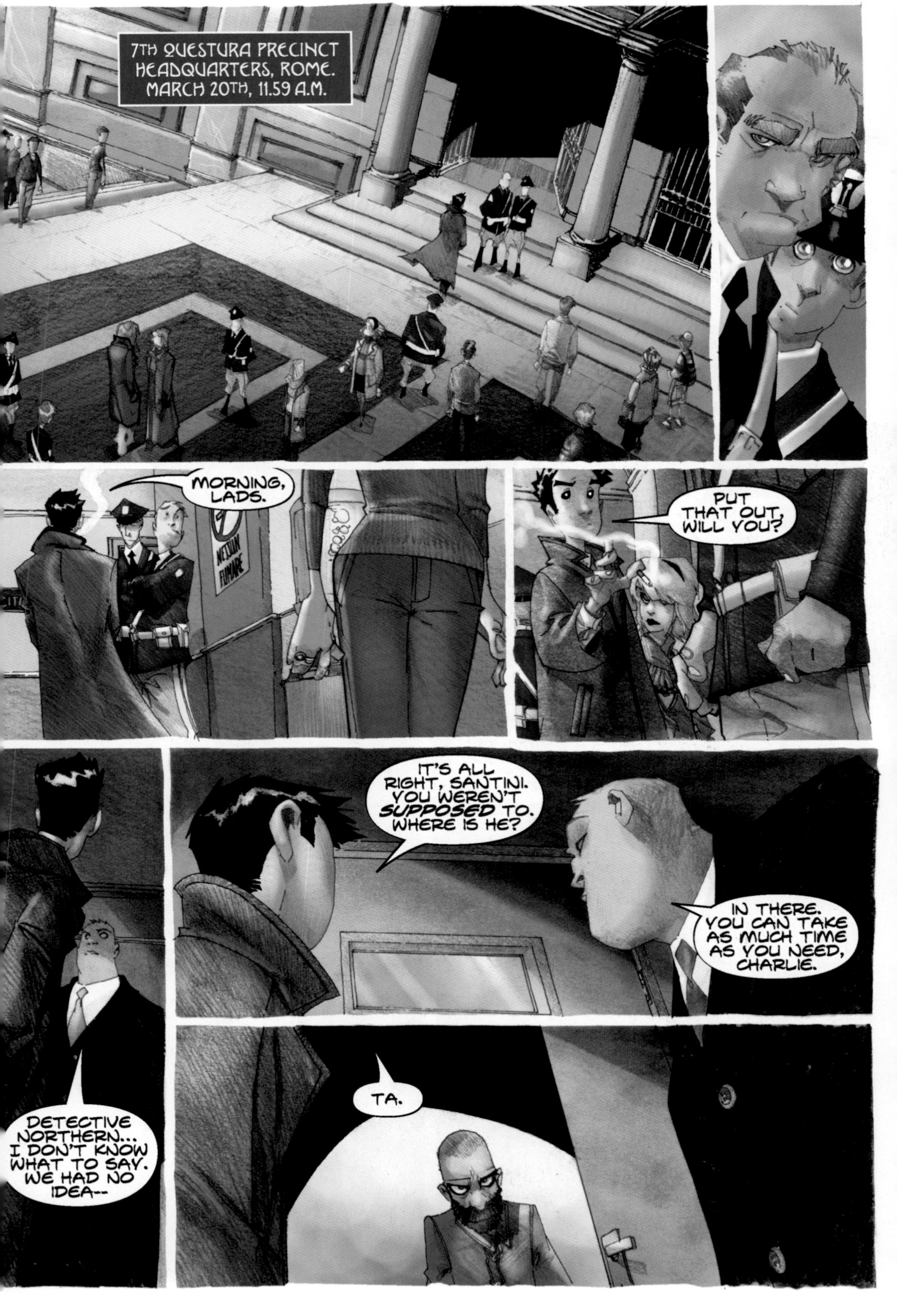
7TH QUESTURA PRECINCT HEADQUARTERS, ROME. MARCH 20TH, 11.59 A.M.
MORNING, LADS.
NESSUN FUMARE
PUT THAT OUT, WILL YOU?
DETECTIVE NORTHERN... I DON'T KNOW WHAT TO SAY. WE HAD NO IDEA--
IT'S ALL RIGHT, SANTINI. YOU WEREN'T *SUPPOSED* TO. WHERE IS HE?
IN THERE. YOU CAN TAKE AS MUCH TIME AS YOU NEED, CHARLIE.
TA.

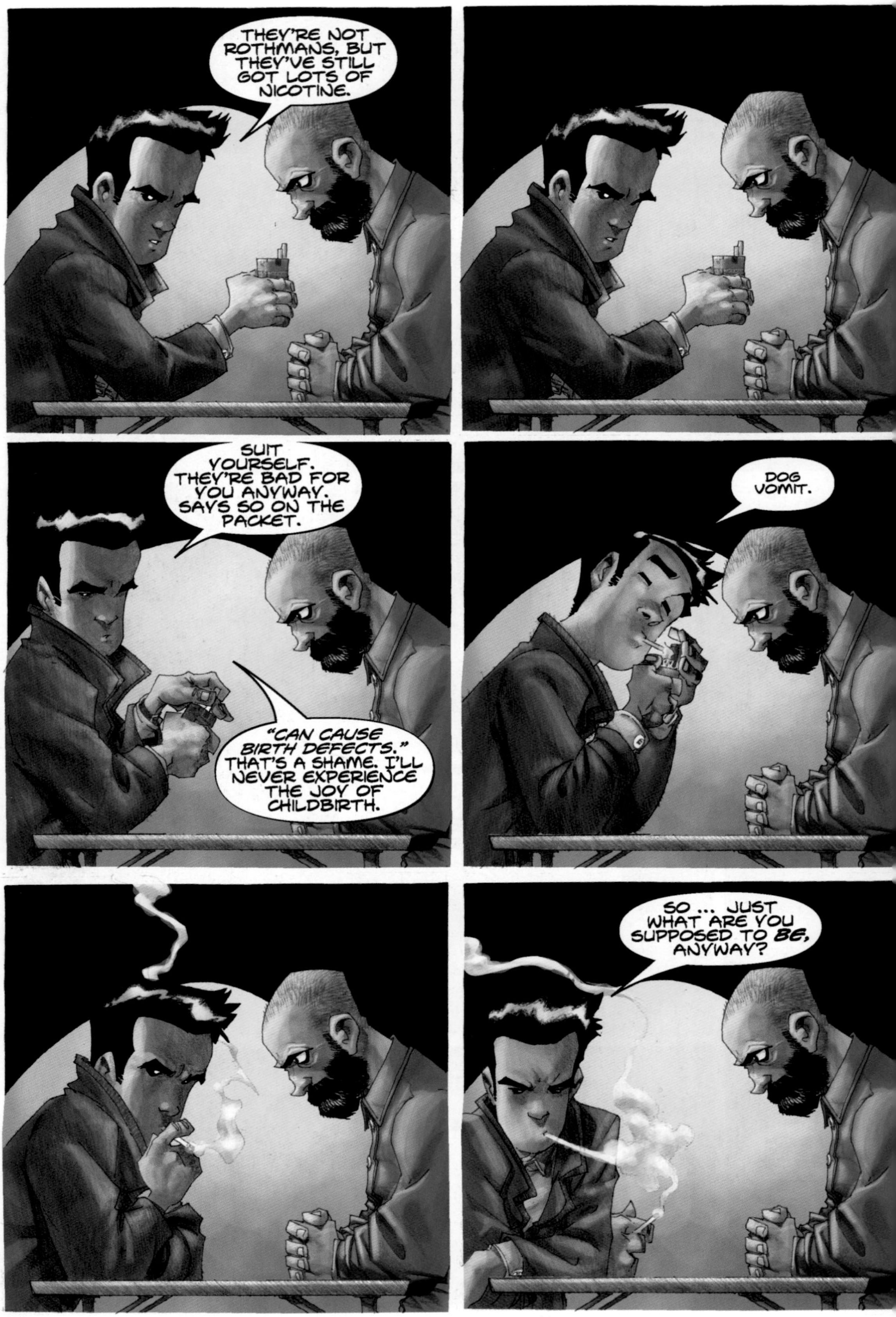
THEY'RE NOT ROTHMANS, BUT THEY'VE STILL GOT LOTS OF NICOTINE.
SUIT YOURSELF. THEY'RE BAD FOR YOU ANYWAY. SAYS SO ON THE PACKET.
"CAN CAUSE BIRTH DEFECTS." THAT'S A SHAME. I'LL NEVER EXPERIENCE THE JOY OF CHILDBIRTH.
DOG VOMIT.
SO ... JUST WHAT ARE YOU SUPPOSED TO BE, ANYWAY?

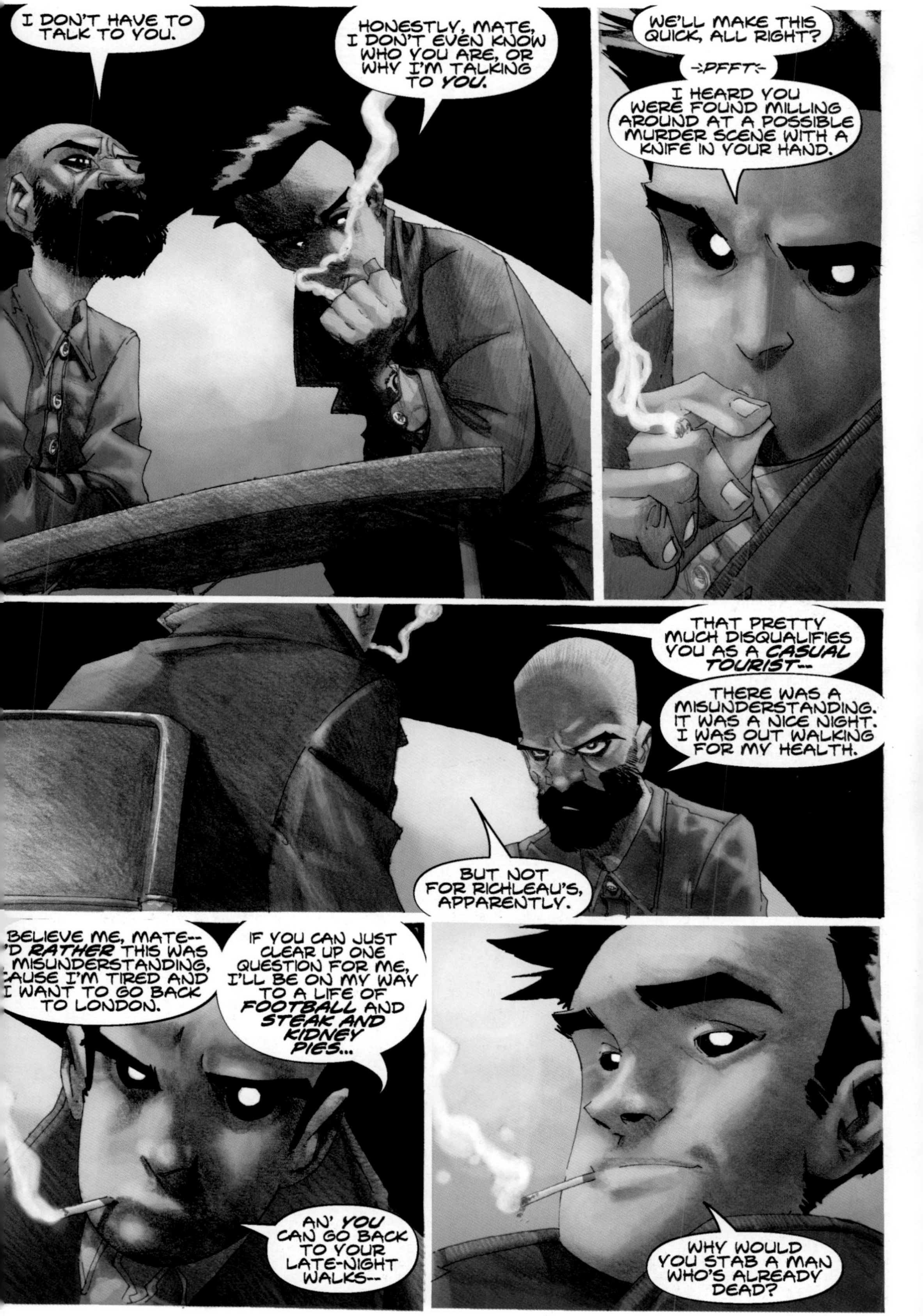
I DON'T HAVE TO TALK TO YOU.
HONESTLY, MATE, I DON'T EVEN KNOW WHO YOU ARE, OR WHY I'M TALKING TO *YOU.*
WE'LL MAKE THIS QUICK, ALL RIGHT?
-PFFT-
I HEARD YOU WERE FOUND MILLING AROUND AT A POSSIBLE MURDER SCENE WITH A KNIFE IN YOUR HAND.
THAT PRETTY MUCH DISQUALIFIES YOU AS A *CASUAL TOURIST*--
THERE WAS A MISUNDERSTANDING. IT WAS A NICE NIGHT. I WAS OUT WALKING FOR MY HEALTH.
BUT NOT FOR RICHLEAU'S, APPARENTLY.
BELIEVE ME, MATE-- 'D *RATHER* THIS WAS MISUNDERSTANDING, CAUSE I'M TIRED AND I WANT TO GO BACK TO LONDON.
IF YOU CAN JUST CLEAR UP ONE QUESTION FOR ME, I'LL BE ON MY WAY TO A LIFE OF *FOOTBALL* AND *STEAK AND KIDNEY PIES...*
AN' *YOU* CAN GO BACK TO YOUR LATE-NIGHT WALKS--
WHY WOULD YOU STAB A MAN WHO'S ALREADY DEAD?

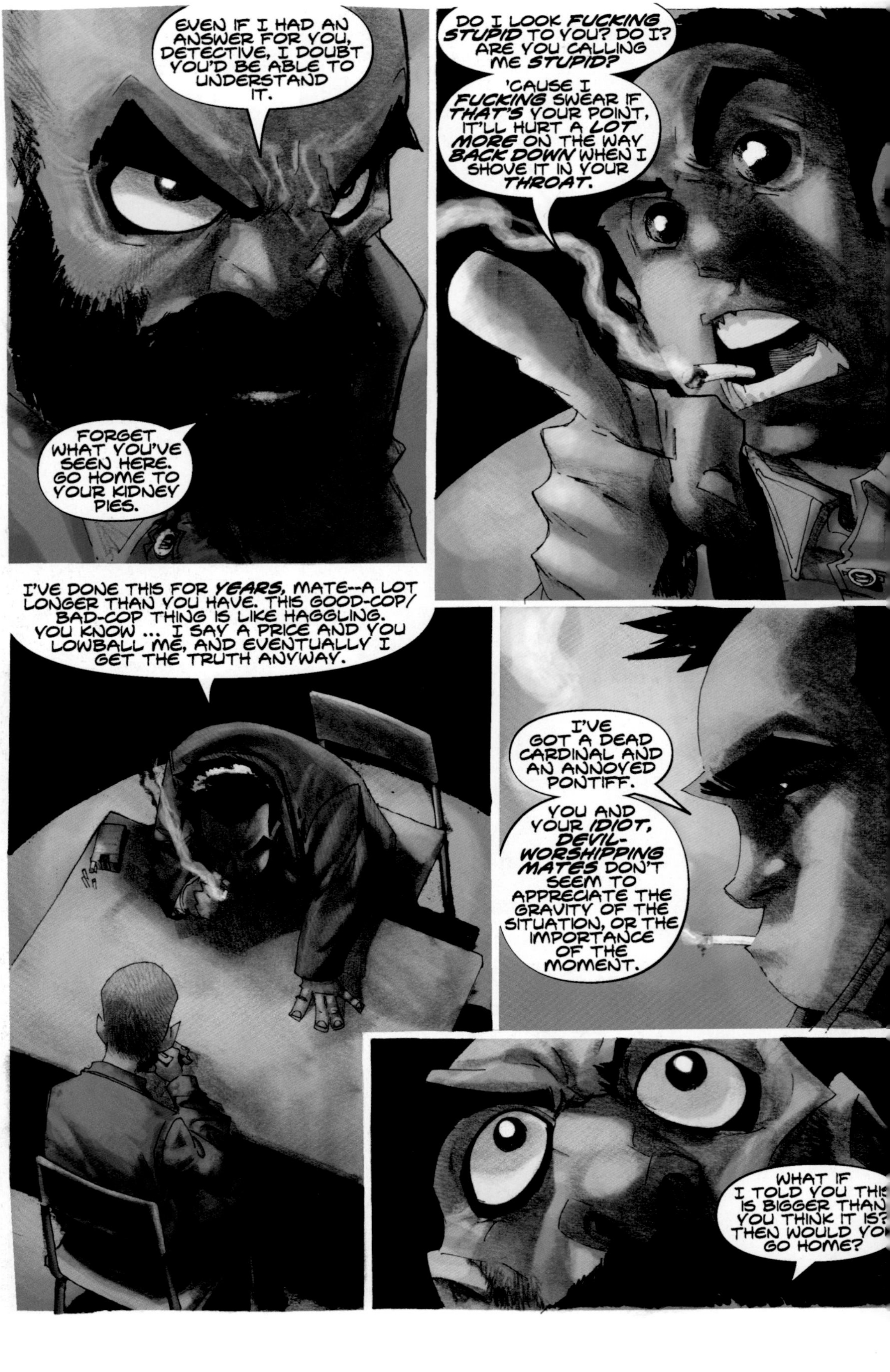
EVEN IF I HAD AN ANSWER FOR YOU, DETECTIVE, I DOUBT YOU'D BE ABLE TO UNDERSTAND IT.
FORGET WHAT YOU'VE SEEN HERE. GO HOME TO YOUR KIDNEY PIES.
DO I LOOK *FUCKING STUPID* TO YOU? DO I? ARE YOU CALLING ME *STUPID?*
'CAUSE I *FUCKING* SWEAR IF *THAT'S* YOUR POINT, IT'LL HURT A *LOT MORE* ON THE WAY *BACK DOWN* WHEN I SHOVE IT IN YOUR *THROAT*.
I'VE DONE THIS FOR *YEARS*, MATE--A LOT LONGER THAN YOU HAVE. THIS GOOD-COP/BAD-COP THING IS LIKE HAGGLING. YOU KNOW ... I SAY A PRICE AND YOU LOWBALL ME, AND EVENTUALLY I GET THE TRUTH ANYWAY.
I'VE GOT A DEAD CARDINAL AND AN ANNOYED PONTIFF.
YOU AND YOUR *IDIOT, DEVIL-WORSHIPPING MATES* DON'T SEEM TO APPRECIATE THE GRAVITY OF THE SITUATION, OR THE IMPORTANCE OF THE MOMENT.
WHAT IF I TOLD YOU THI IS BIGGER THAN YOU THINK IT IS? THEN WOULD YO GO HOME?

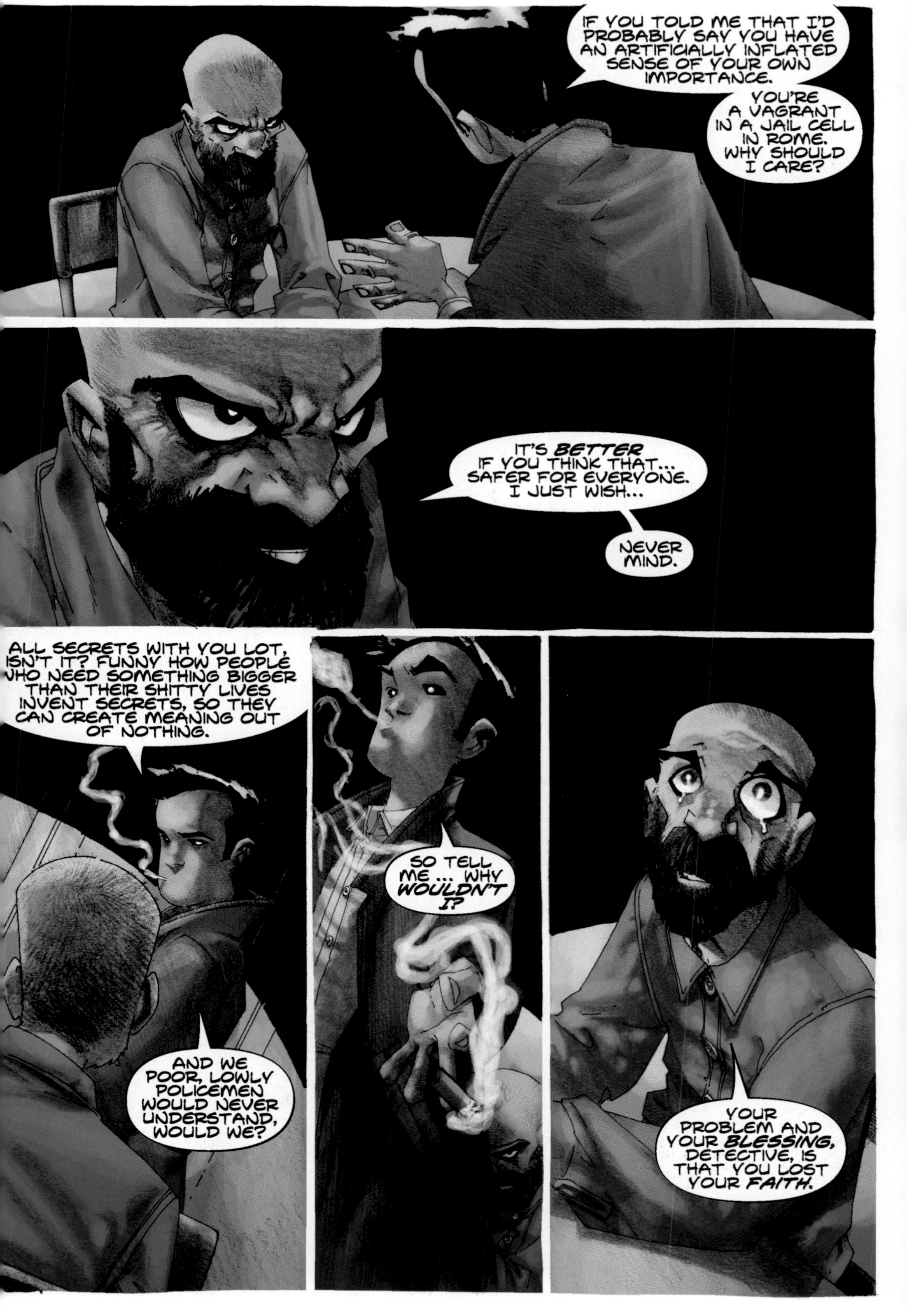
IF YOU TOLD ME THAT I'D PROBABLY SAY YOU HAVE AN ARTIFICIALLY INFLATED SENSE OF YOUR OWN IMPORTANCE.
YOU'RE A VAGRANT IN A JAIL CELL IN ROME. WHY SHOULD I CARE?
IT'S *BETTER* IF YOU THINK THAT... SAFER FOR EVERYONE. I JUST WISH...
NEVER MIND.
ALL SECRETS WITH YOU LOT, ISN'T IT? FUNNY HOW PEOPLE WHO NEED SOMETHING BIGGER THAN THEIR SHITTY LIVES INVENT SECRETS, SO THEY CAN CREATE MEANING OUT OF NOTHING.
AND WE POOR, LOWLY POLICEMEN WOULD NEVER UNDERSTAND, WOULD WE?
SO TELL ME ... WHY *WOULDN'T I?*
YOUR PROBLEM AND YOUR *BLESSING*, DETECTIVE, IS THAT YOU LOST YOUR *FAITH*.

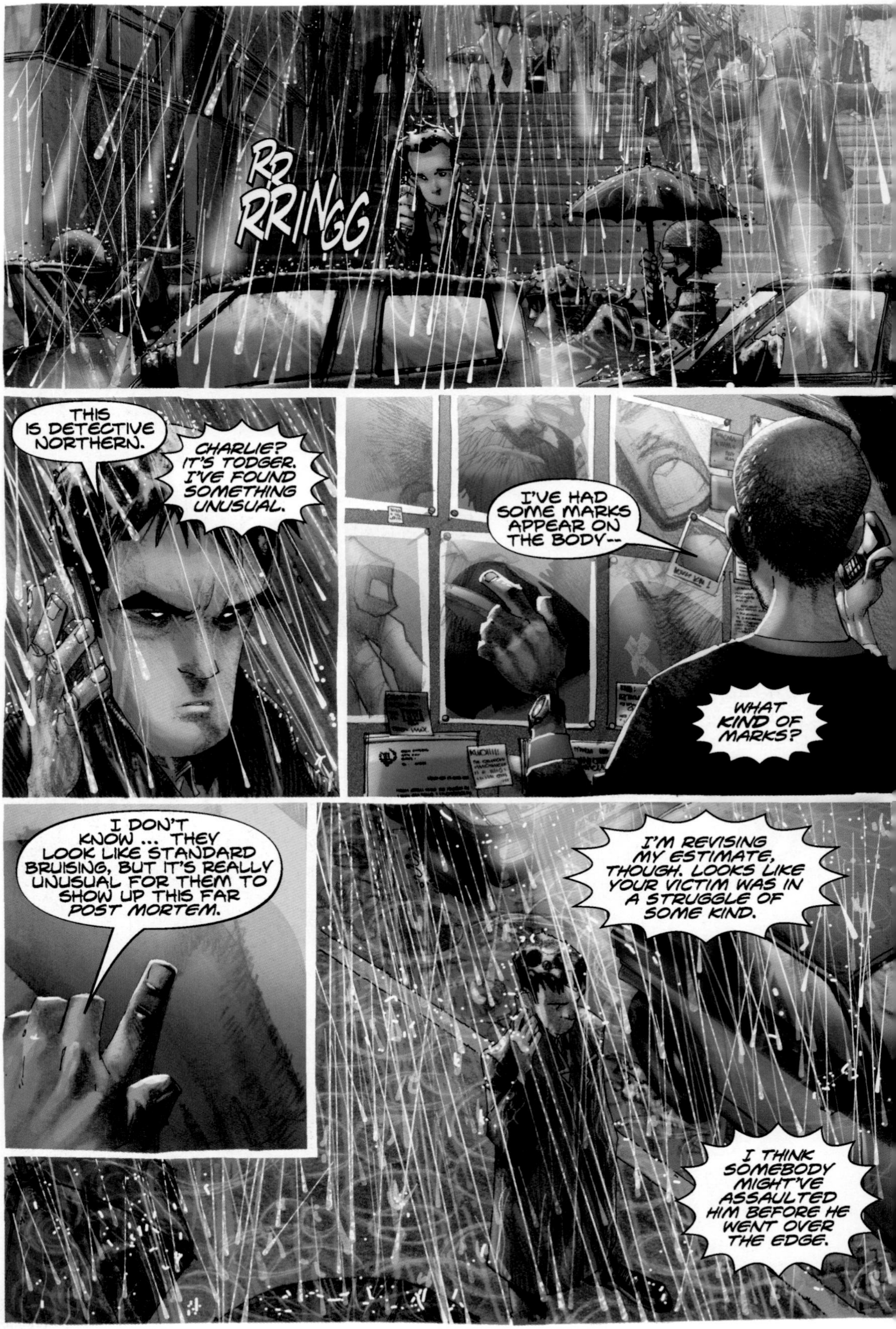
RRRINGG
THIS IS DETECTIVE NORTHERN.
CHARLIE? IT'S TODGER. I'VE FOUND SOMETHING UNUSUAL.
I'VE HAD SOME MARKS APPEAR ON THE BODY--
WHAT KIND OF MARKS?
I DON'T KNOW ... THEY LOOK LIKE STANDARD BRUISING, BUT IT'S REALLY UNUSUAL FOR THEM TO SHOW UP THIS FAR POST MORTEM.
I'M REVISING MY ESTIMATE, THOUGH. LOOKS LIKE YOUR VICTIM WAS IN A STRUGGLE OF SOME KIND.
I THINK SOMEBODY MIGHT'VE ASSAULTED HIM BEFORE HE WENT OVER THE EDGE.

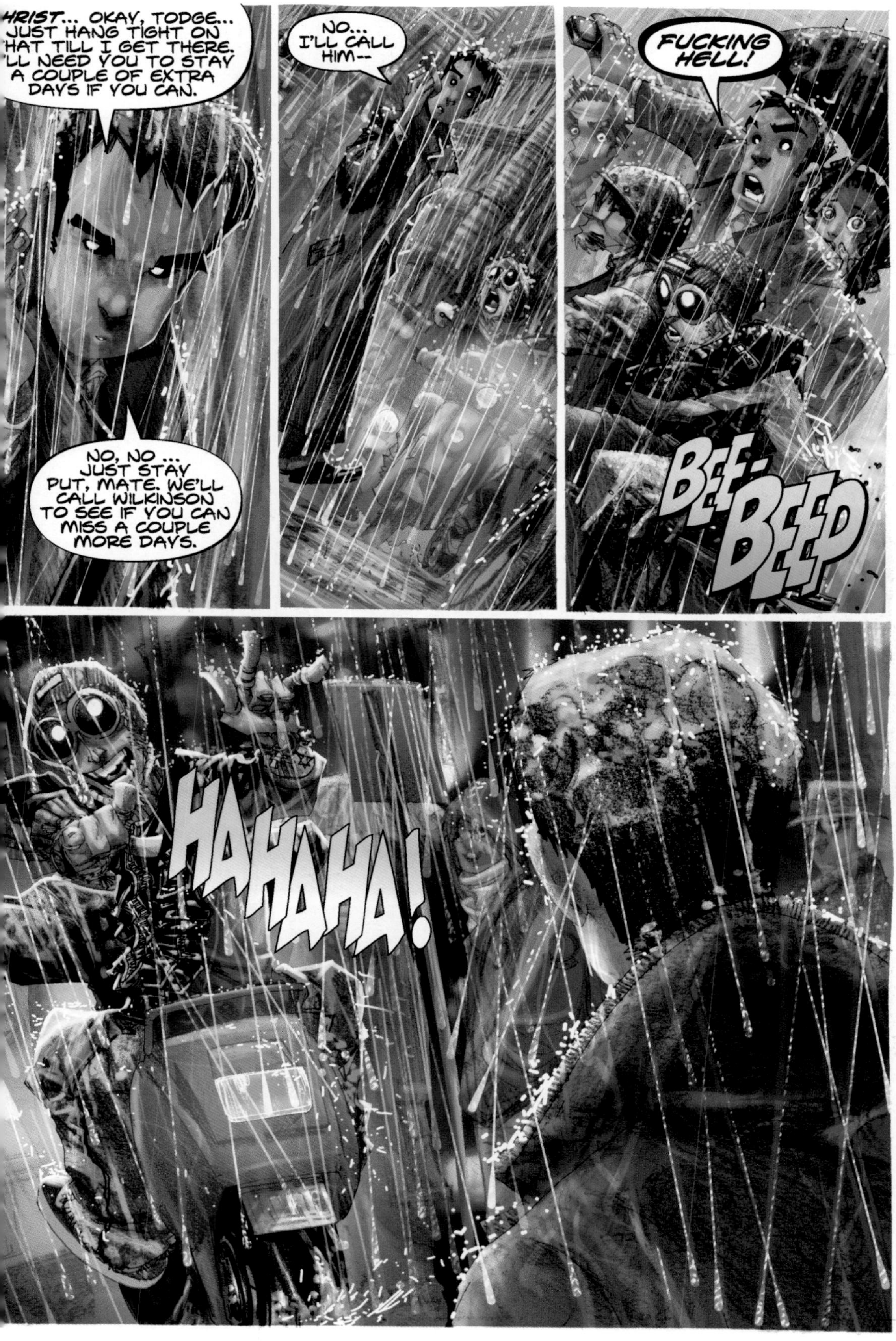
HRIST... OKAY, TODGE... JUST HANG TIGHT ON HAT TILL I GET THERE. 'LL NEED YOU TO STAY A COUPLE OF EXTRA DAYS IF YOU CAN.
NO, NO ... JUST STAY PUT, MATE. WE'LL CALL WILKINSON TO SEE IF YOU CAN MISS A COUPLE MORE DAYS.
NO... I'LL CALL HIM--
FUCKING HELL!
BEE-BEEP
HAHAHA!

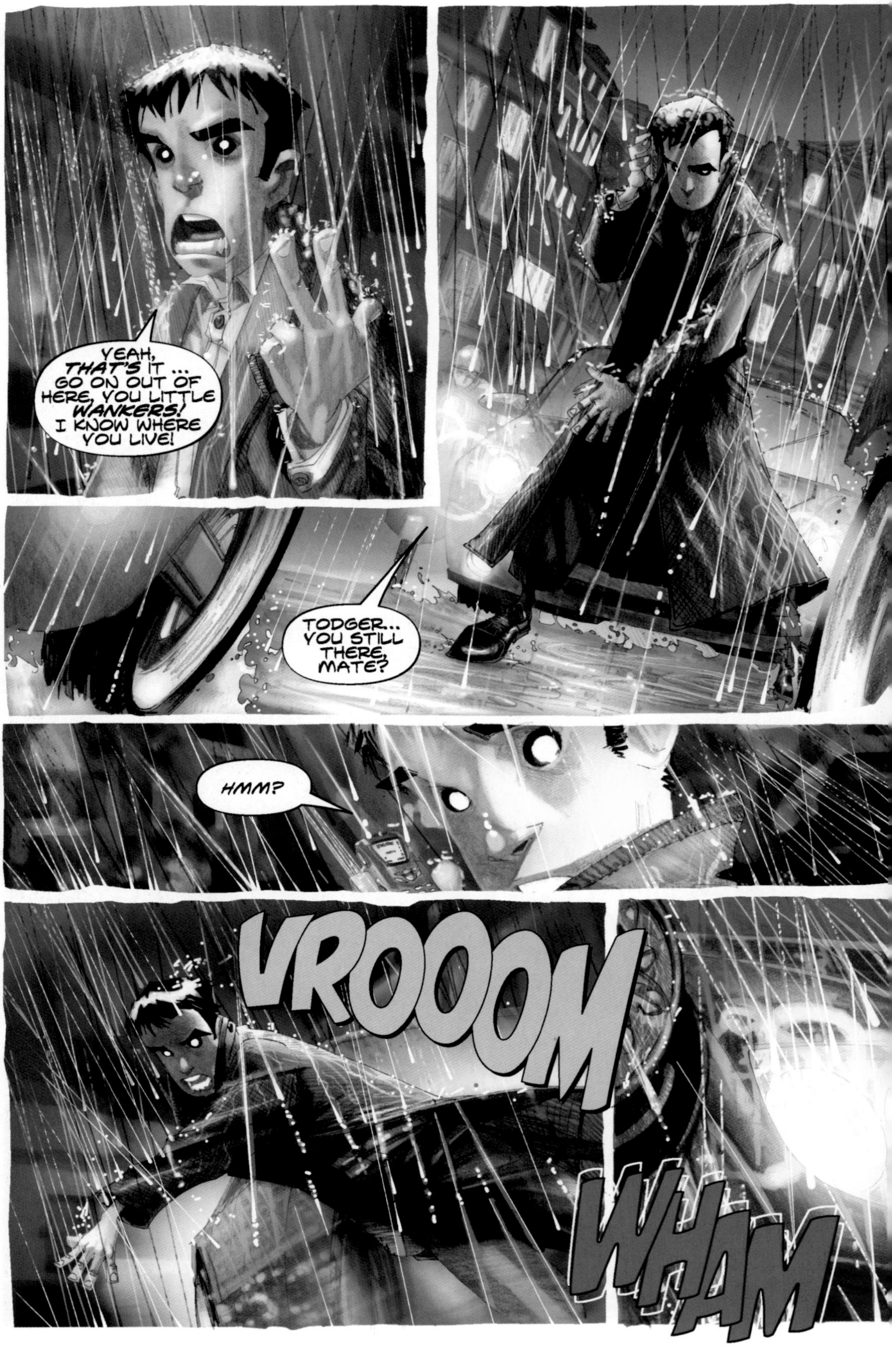
YEAH, *THAT'S* IT ... GO ON OUT OF HERE, YOU LITTLE *WANKERS!* I KNOW WHERE YOU LIVE!
TODGER... YOU STILL THERE, MATE?
HMM?
VROOOM
WHAM

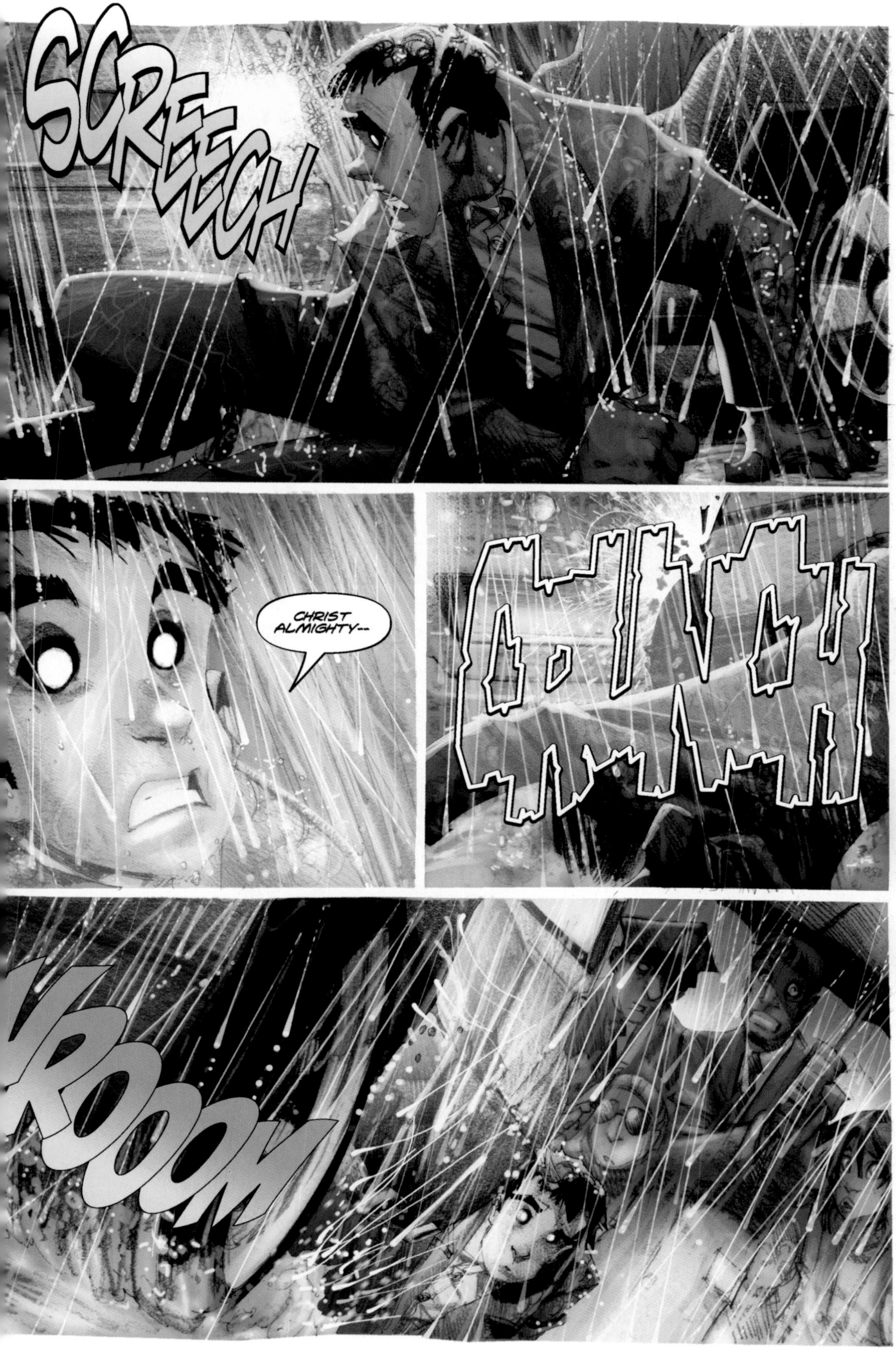
SCREECH
CHRIST ALMIGHTY--
KROOOM

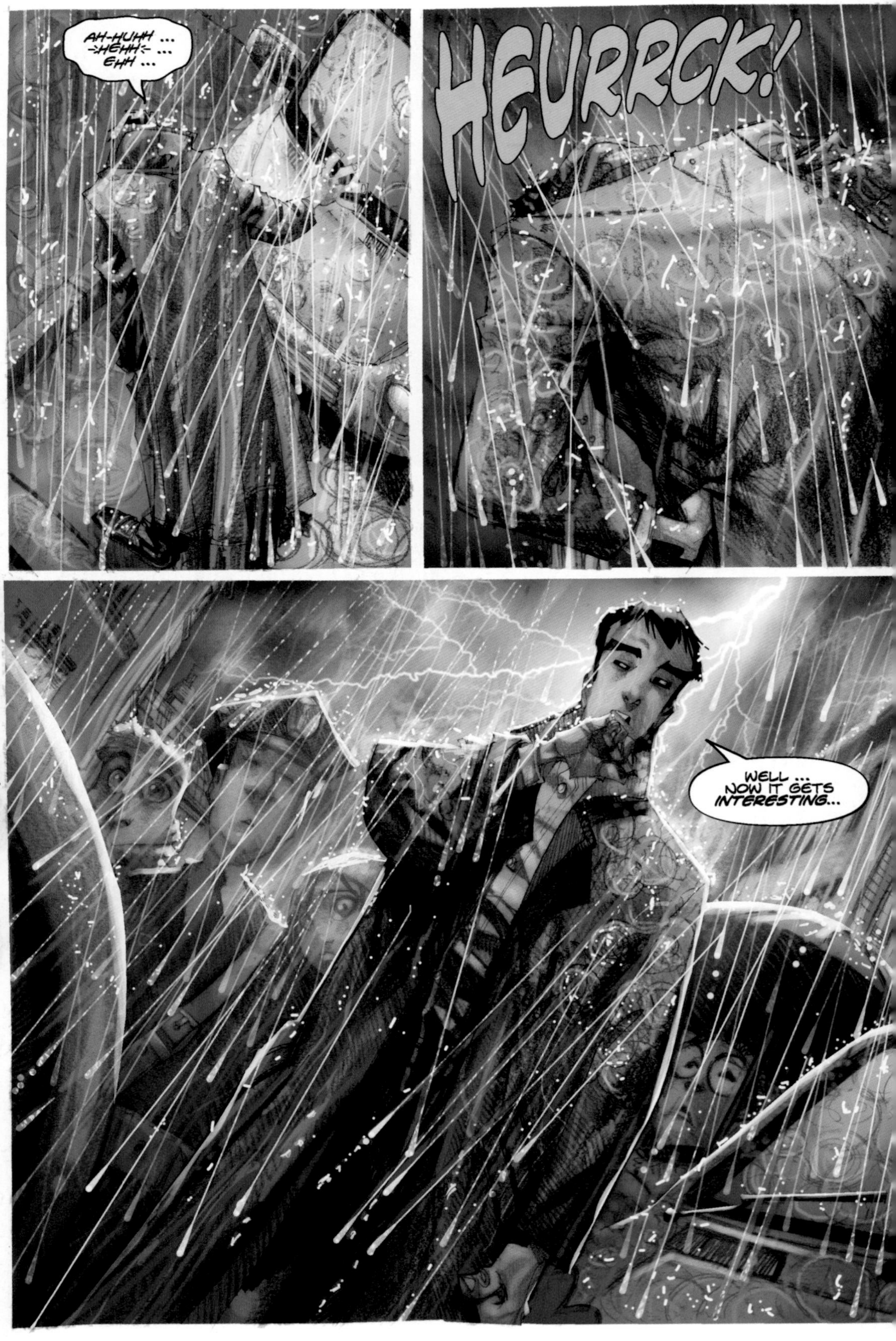
AH-HUHH ... -HEHH- ... EHH ...
HEURRCK!
WELL ... NOW IT GETS INTERESTING...

CHAPTER FOUR

Dead to Rights

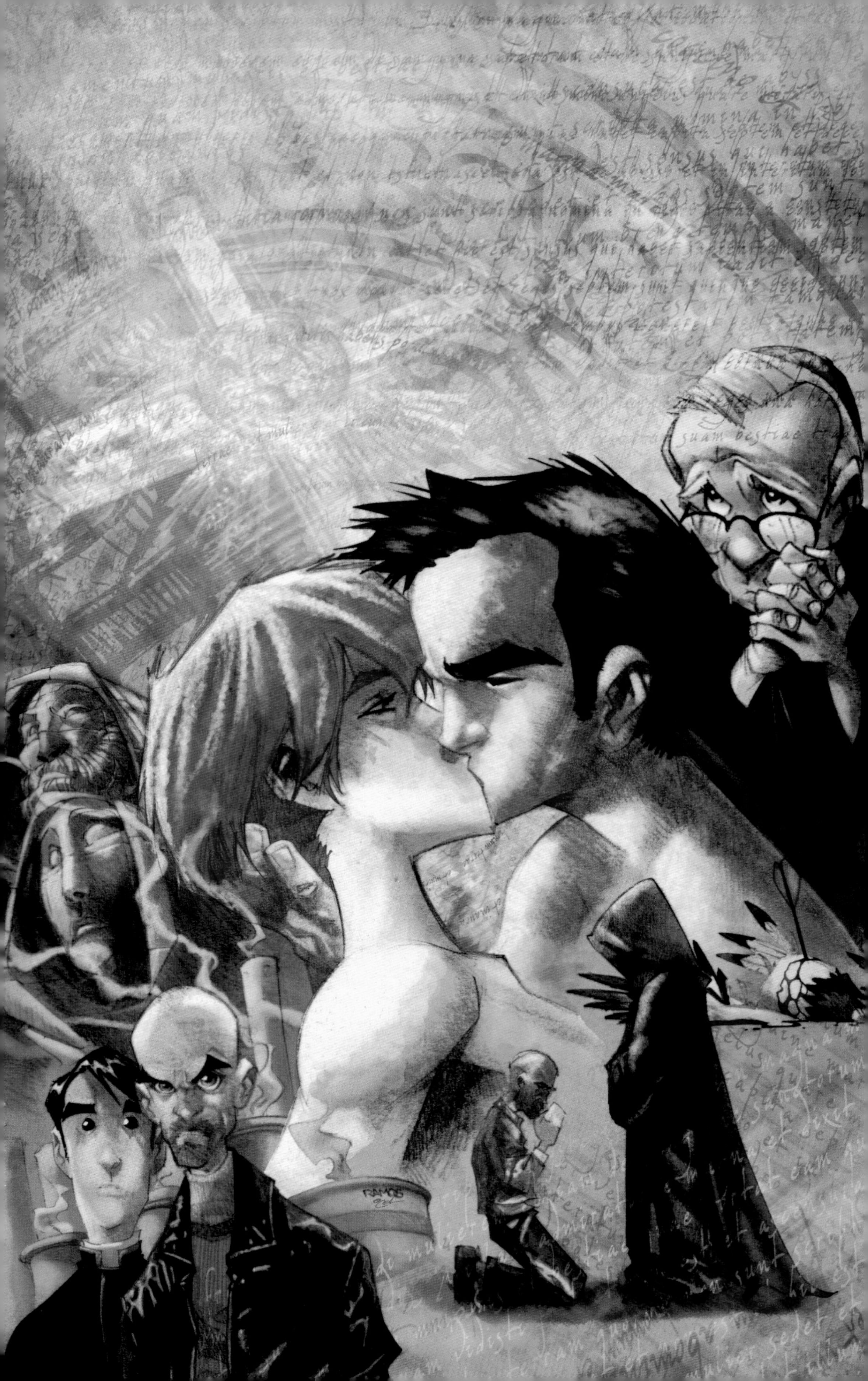

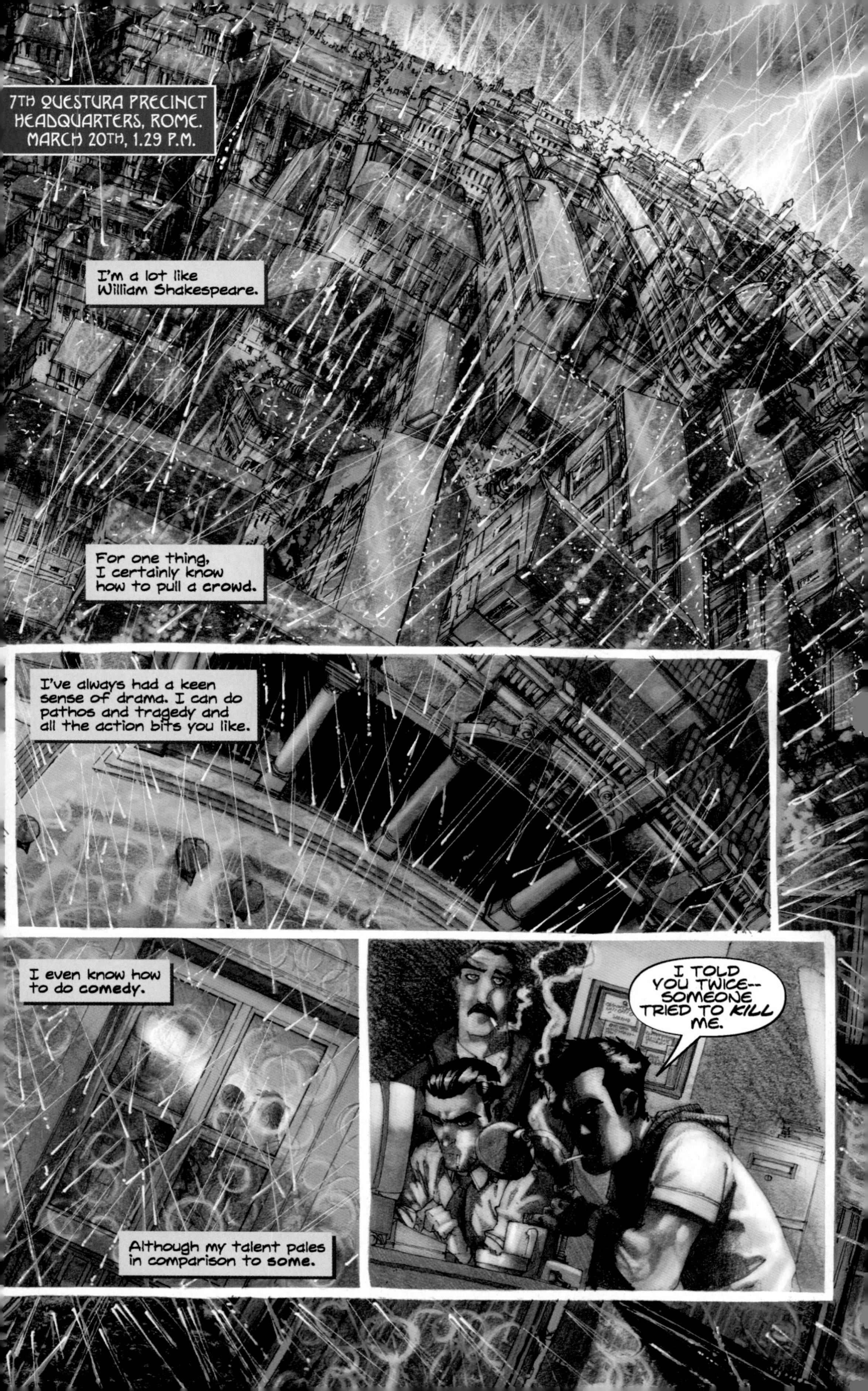
7TH QUESTURA PRECINCT HEADQUARTERS, ROME. MARCH 20TH, 1.29 P.M.
I'm a lot like William Shakespeare.
For one thing, I certainly know how to pull a crowd.
I've always had a keen sense of drama. I can do pathos and tragedy and all the action bits you like.
I even know how to do comedy.
Although my talent pales in comparison to some.
I TOLD YOU TWICE-- SOMEONE TRIED TO KILL ME.

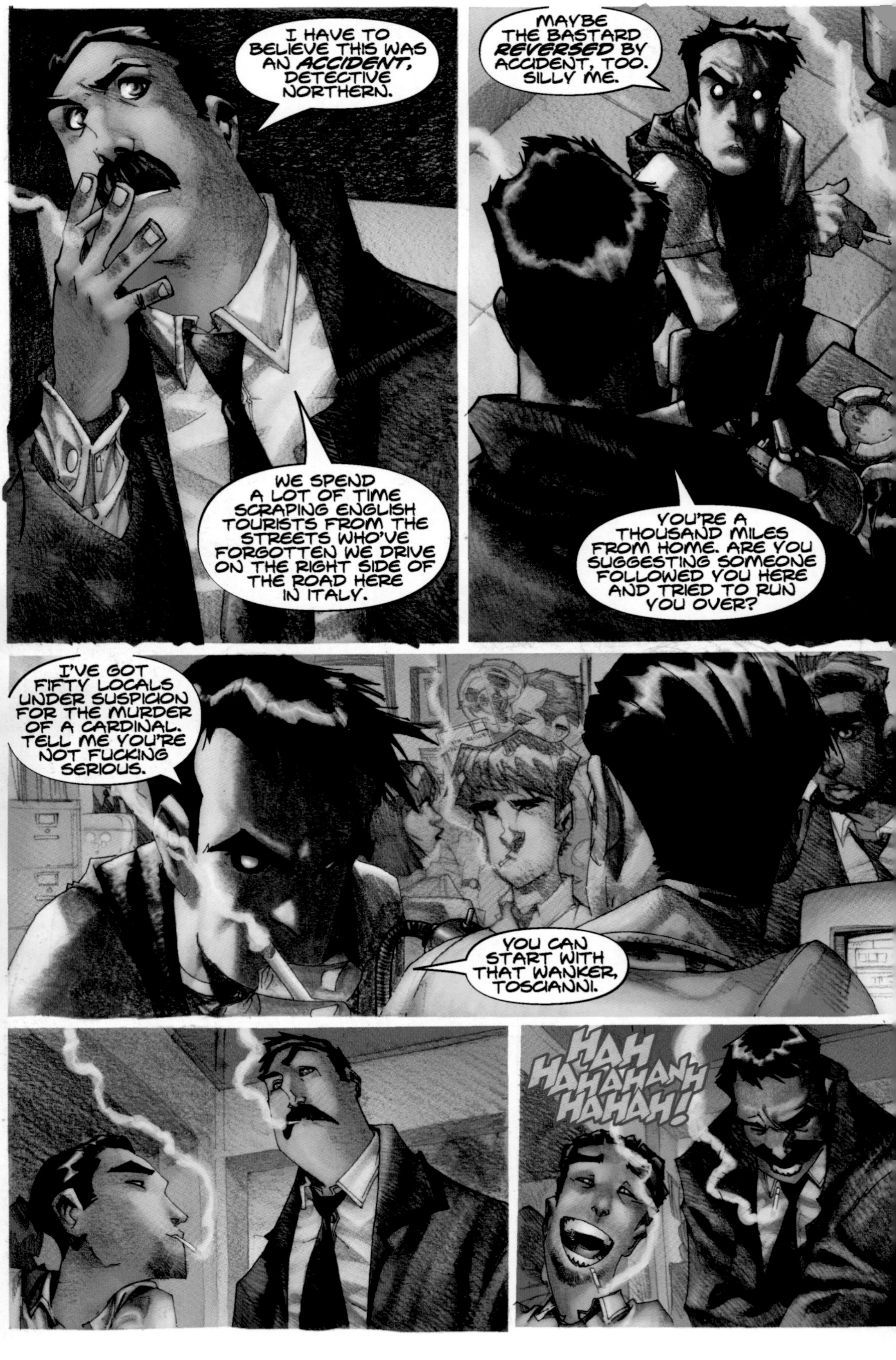
I HAVE TO BELIEVE THIS WAS AN *ACCIDENT*, DETECTIVE NORTHERN.
WE SPEND A LOT OF TIME SCRAPING ENGLISH TOURISTS FROM THE STREETS WHO'VE FORGOTTEN WE DRIVE ON THE RIGHT SIDE OF THE ROAD HERE IN ITALY.
MAYBE THE BASTARD *REVERSED* BY ACCIDENT, TOO. SILLY ME.
YOU'RE A THOUSAND MILES FROM HOME. ARE YOU SUGGESTING SOMEONE FOLLOWED YOU HERE AND TRIED TO RUN YOU OVER?
I'VE GOT FIFTY LOCALS UNDER SUSPICION FOR THE MURDER OF A CARDINAL. TELL ME YOU'RE NOT FUCKING SERIOUS.
YOU CAN START WITH THAT WANKER, TOSCIANNI.
HAH HAHAHANH HAHAH!

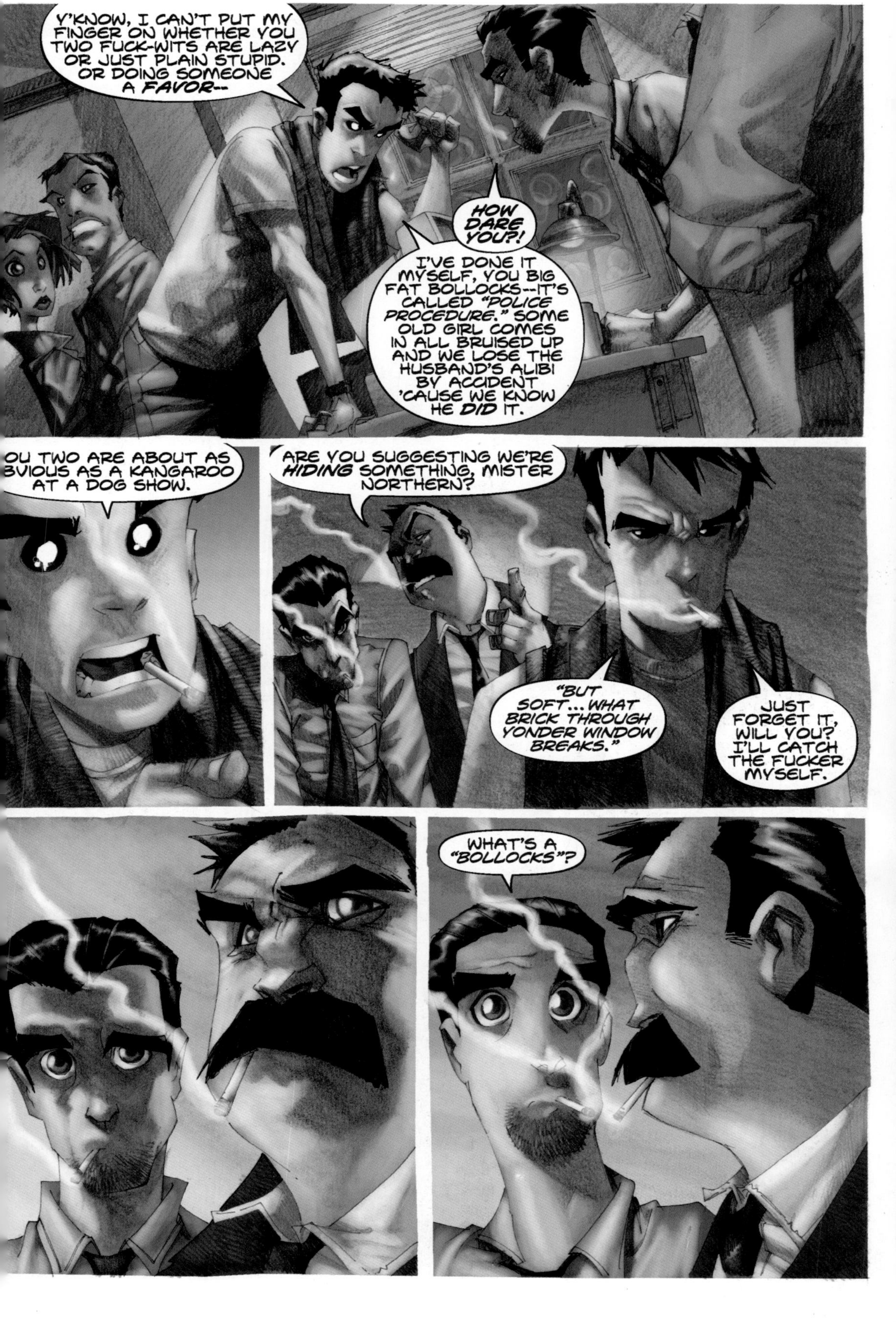
Y'KNOW, I CAN'T PUT MY FINGER ON WHETHER YOU TWO FUCK-WITS ARE LAZY OR JUST PLAIN STUPID. OR DOING SOMEONE A *FAVOR*--
HOW DARE YOU?!
I'VE DONE IT MYSELF, YOU BIG FAT BOLLOCKS--IT'S CALLED *"POLICE PROCEDURE."* SOME OLD GIRL COMES IN ALL BRUISED UP AND WE LOSE THE HUSBAND'S ALIBI BY ACCIDENT 'CAUSE WE KNOW HE *DID* IT.
OU TWO ARE ABOUT AS BVIOUS AS A KANGAROO AT A DOG SHOW.
ARE YOU SUGGESTING WE'RE *HIDING* SOMETHING, MISTER NORTHERN?
"BUT SOFT... WHAT BRICK THROUGH YONDER WINDOW BREAKS."
JUST FORGET IT, WILL YOU? I'LL CATCH THE FUCKER MYSELF.
WHAT'S A "BOLLOCKS"?

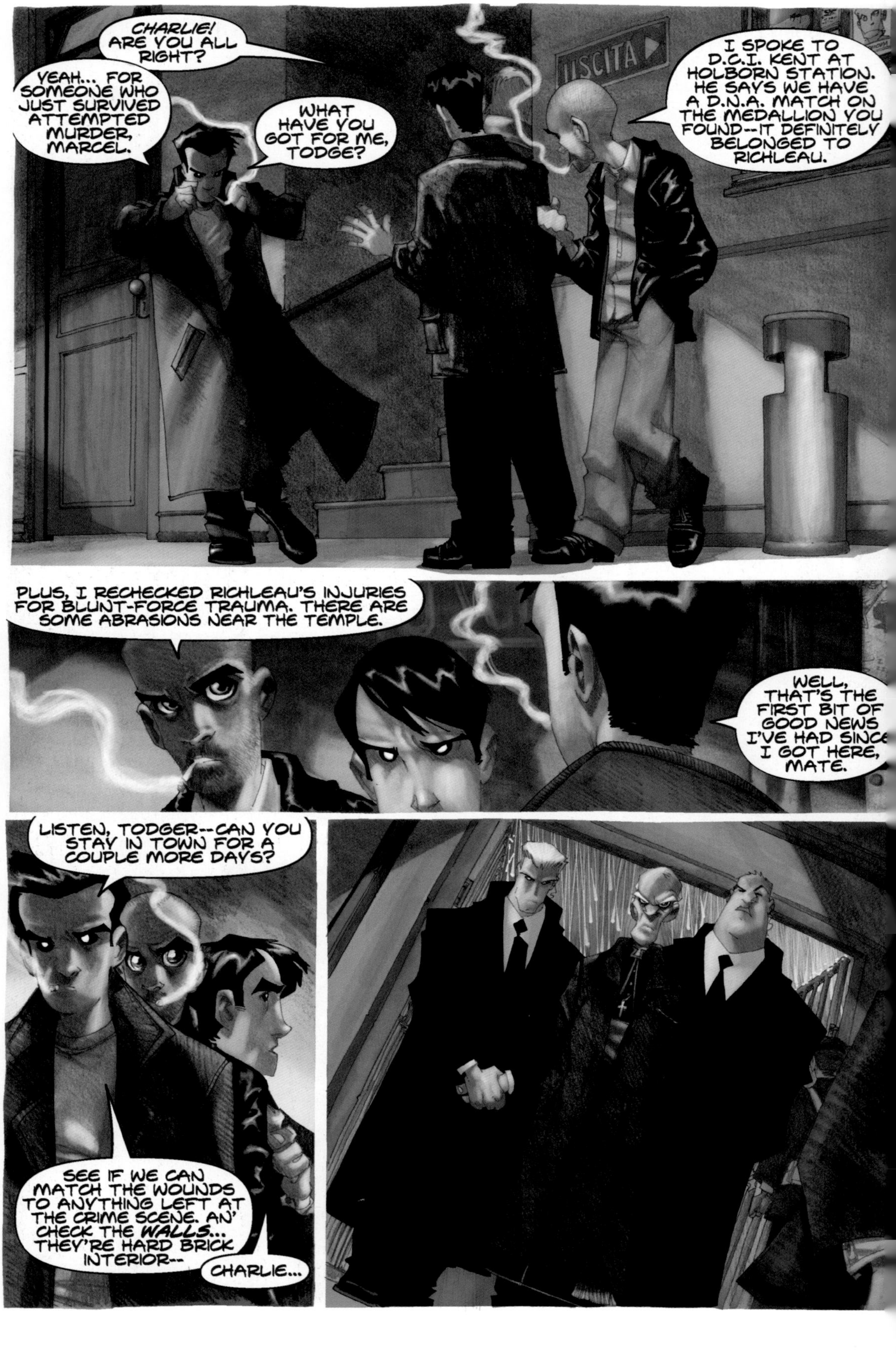
CHARLIE! ARE YOU ALL RIGHT?
YEAH... FOR SOMEONE WHO JUST SURVIVED ATTEMPTED MURDER, MARCEL.
WHAT HAVE YOU GOT FOR ME, TODGE?
USCITA
I SPOKE TO D.C.I. KENT AT HOLBORN STATION. HE SAYS WE HAVE A D.N.A. MATCH ON THE MEDALLION YOU FOUND--IT DEFINITELY BELONGED TO RICHLEAU.
PLUS, I RECHECKED RICHLEAU'S INJURIES FOR BLUNT-FORCE TRAUMA. THERE ARE SOME ABRASIONS NEAR THE TEMPLE.
WELL, THAT'S THE FIRST BIT OF GOOD NEWS I'VE HAD SINCE I GOT HERE, MATE.
LISTEN, TODGER--CAN YOU STAY IN TOWN FOR A COUPLE MORE DAYS?
SEE IF WE CAN MATCH THE WOUNDS TO ANYTHING LEFT AT THE CRIME SCENE. AN' CHECK THE *WALLS*... THEY'RE HARD BRICK INTERIOR--
CHARLIE...

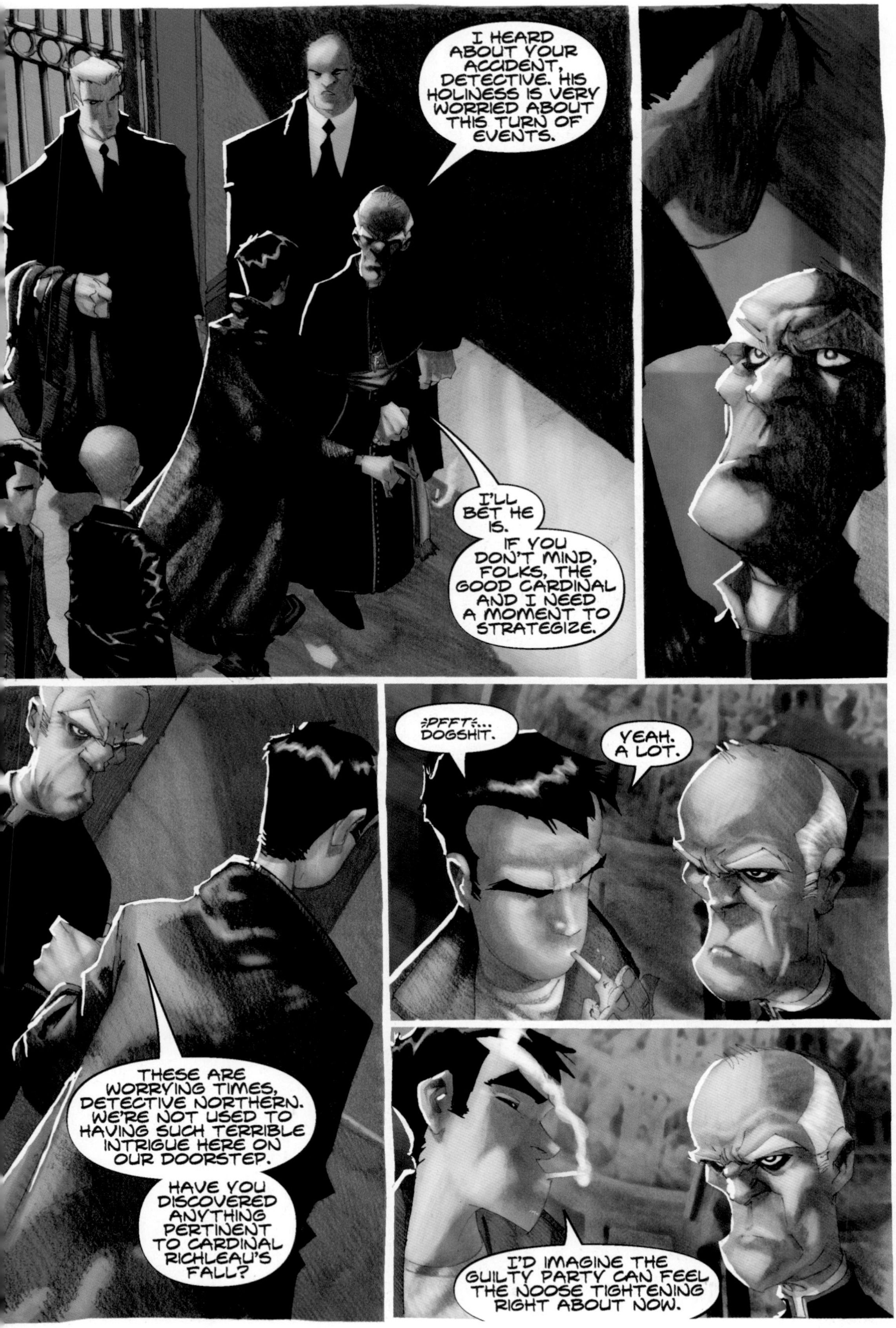
I HEARD ABOUT YOUR ACCIDENT, DETECTIVE. HIS HOLINESS IS VERY WORRIED ABOUT THIS TURN OF EVENTS.
I'LL BET HE IS.
IF YOU DON'T MIND, FOLKS, THE GOOD CARDINAL AND I NEED A MOMENT TO STRATEGIZE.
THESE ARE WORRYING TIMES, DETECTIVE NORTHERN. WE'RE NOT USED TO HAVING SUCH TERRIBLE INTRIGUE HERE ON OUR DOORSTEP.
HAVE YOU DISCOVERED ANYTHING PERTINENT TO CARDINAL RICHLEAU'S FALL?
PFFT... DOGSHIT.
YEAH. A LOT.
I'D IMAGINE THE GUILTY PARTY CAN FEEL THE NOOSE TIGHTENING RIGHT ABOUT NOW.

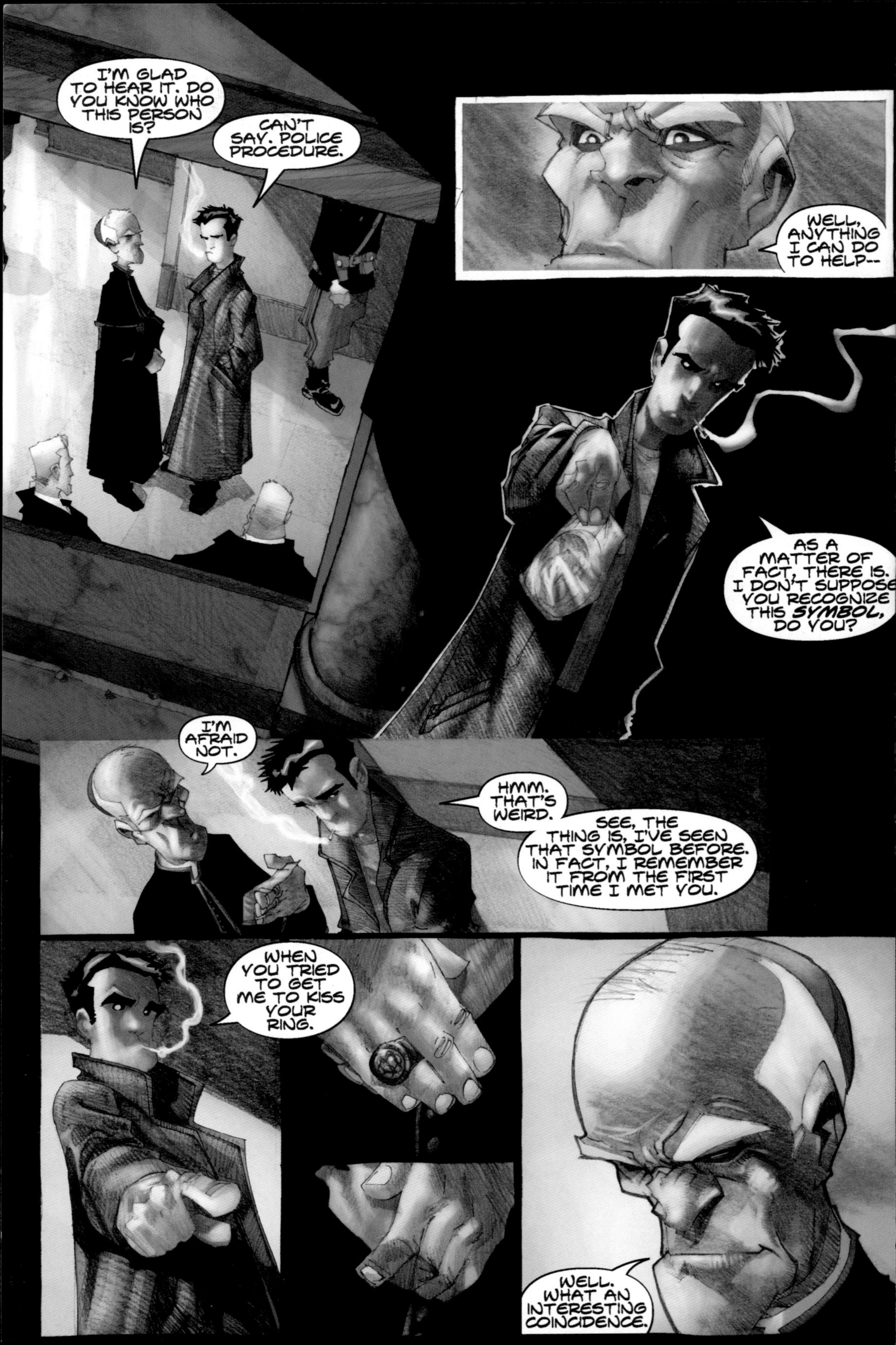
I'M GLAD TO HEAR IT. DO YOU KNOW WHO THIS PERSON IS?
CAN'T SAY. POLICE PROCEDURE.
WELL, ANYTHING I CAN DO TO HELP--
AS A MATTER OF FACT, THERE IS. I DON'T SUPPOSE YOU RECOGNIZE THIS *SYMBOL*, DO YOU?
I'M AFRAID NOT.
HMM. THAT'S WEIRD.
SEE, THE THING IS, I'VE SEEN THAT SYMBOL BEFORE. IN FACT, I REMEMBER IT FROM THE FIRST TIME I MET YOU.
WHEN YOU TRIED TO GET ME TO KISS YOUR RING.
WELL. WHAT AN INTERESTING COINCIDENCE.

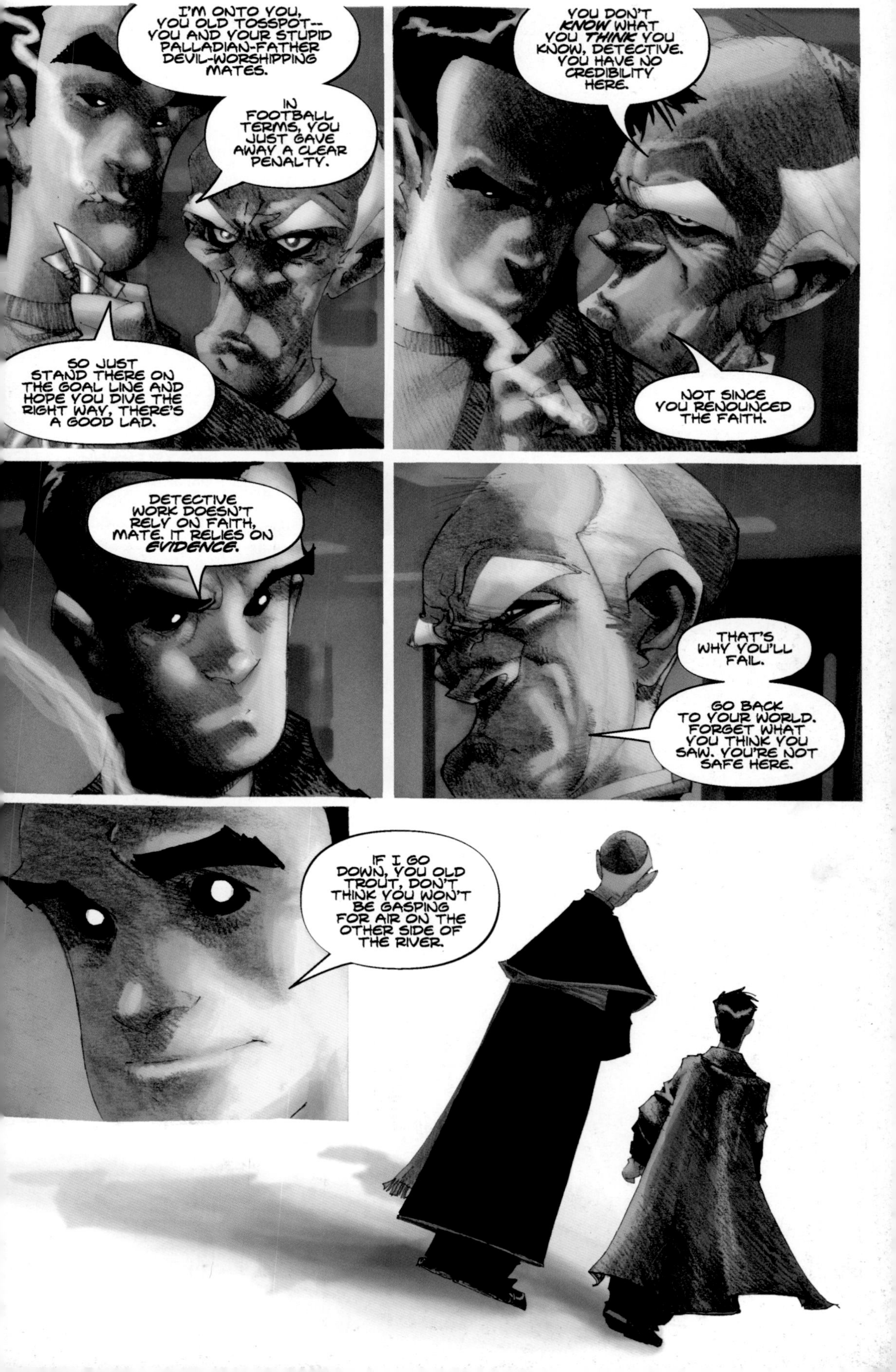

I'M ONTO YOU, YOU OLD TOSSPOT-- YOU AND YOUR STUPID PALLADIAN-FATHER DEVIL-WORSHIPPING MATES.
IN FOOTBALL TERMS, YOU JUST GAVE AWAY A CLEAR PENALTY.
SO JUST STAND THERE ON THE GOAL LINE AND HOPE YOU DIVE THE RIGHT WAY, THERE'S A GOOD LAD.
YOU DON'T *KNOW* WHAT YOU *THINK* YOU KNOW, DETECTIVE. YOU HAVE NO CREDIBILITY HERE.
NOT SINCE YOU RENOUNCED THE FAITH.
DETECTIVE WORK DOESN'T RELY ON FAITH, MATE. IT RELIES ON *EVIDENCE.*
THAT'S WHY YOU'LL FAIL.
GO BACK TO YOUR WORLD. FORGET WHAT YOU THINK YOU SAW. YOU'RE NOT SAFE HERE.
IF I GO DOWN, YOU OLD TROUT, DON'T THINK YOU WON'T BE GASPING FOR AIR ON THE OTHER SIDE OF THE RIVER.

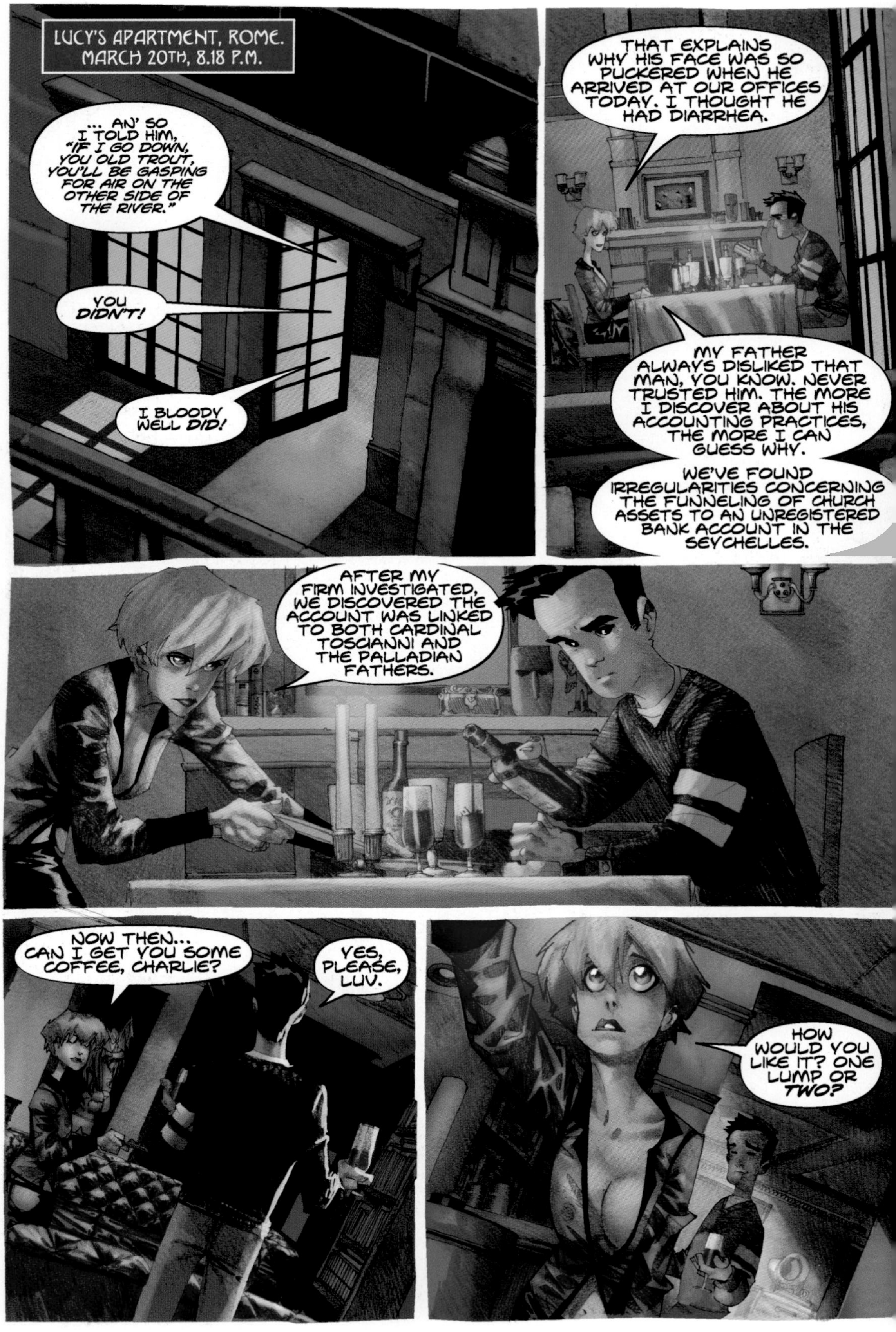
LUCY'S APARTMENT, ROME. MARCH 20TH, 8.18 P.M.
... AN' SO I TOLD HIM, "IF I GO DOWN, YOU OLD TROUT, YOU'LL BE GASPING FOR AIR ON THE OTHER SIDE OF THE RIVER."
YOU DIDN'T!
I BLOODY WELL DID!
THAT EXPLAINS WHY HIS FACE WAS SO PUCKERED WHEN HE ARRIVED AT OUR OFFICES TODAY. I THOUGHT HE HAD DIARRHEA.
MY FATHER ALWAYS DISLIKED THAT MAN, YOU KNOW. NEVER TRUSTED HIM. THE MORE I DISCOVER ABOUT HIS ACCOUNTING PRACTICES, THE MORE I CAN GUESS WHY.
WE'VE FOUND IRREGULARITIES CONCERNING THE FUNNELING OF CHURCH ASSETS TO AN UNREGISTERED BANK ACCOUNT IN THE SEYCHELLES.
AFTER MY FIRM INVESTIGATED, WE DISCOVERED THE ACCOUNT WAS LINKED TO BOTH CARDINAL TOSCIANNI AND THE PALLADIAN FATHERS.
NOW THEN... CAN I GET YOU SOME COFFEE, CHARLIE?
YES, PLEASE, LUV.
HOW WOULD YOU LIKE IT? ONE LUMP OR TWO?

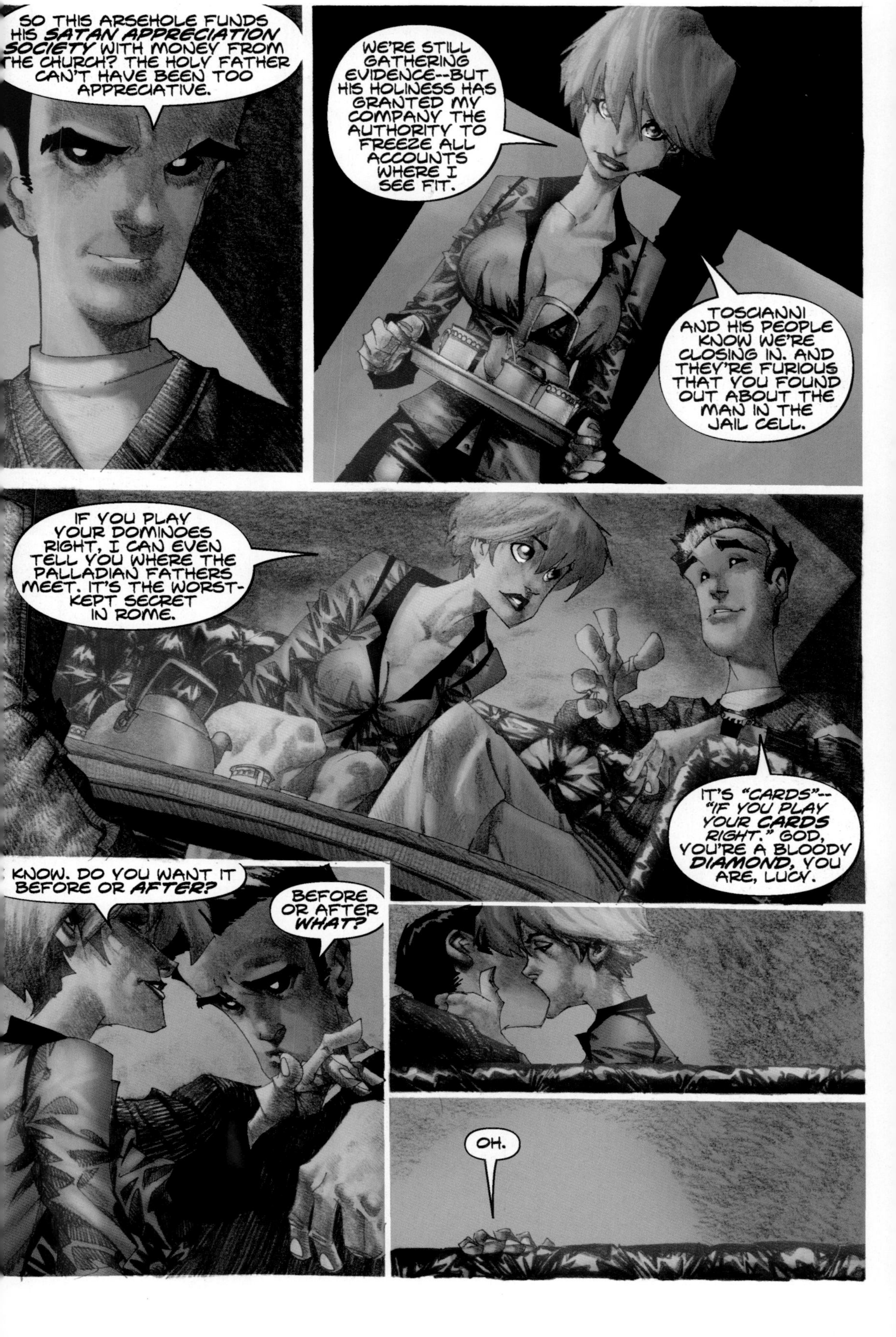
SO THIS ARSEHOLE FUNDS HIS *SATAN APPRECIATION SOCIETY* WITH MONEY FROM THE CHURCH? THE HOLY FATHER CAN'T HAVE BEEN TOO APPRECIATIVE.
WE'RE STILL GATHERING EVIDENCE--BUT HIS HOLINESS HAS GRANTED MY COMPANY THE AUTHORITY TO FREEZE ALL ACCOUNTS WHERE I SEE FIT.
TOSCIANNI AND HIS PEOPLE KNOW WE'RE CLOSING IN. AND THEY'RE FURIOUS THAT YOU FOUND OUT ABOUT THE MAN IN THE JAIL CELL.
IF YOU PLAY YOUR DOMINOES RIGHT, I CAN EVEN TELL YOU WHERE THE PALLADIAN FATHERS MEET. IT'S THE WORST-KEPT SECRET IN ROME.
IT'S "CARDS"--"IF YOU PLAY YOUR **CARDS** RIGHT." GOD, YOU'RE A BLOODY ***DIAMOND***, YOU ARE, LUCY.
KNOW. DO YOU WANT IT BEFORE OR *AFTER?*
BEFORE OR AFTER ***WHAT?***
OH.

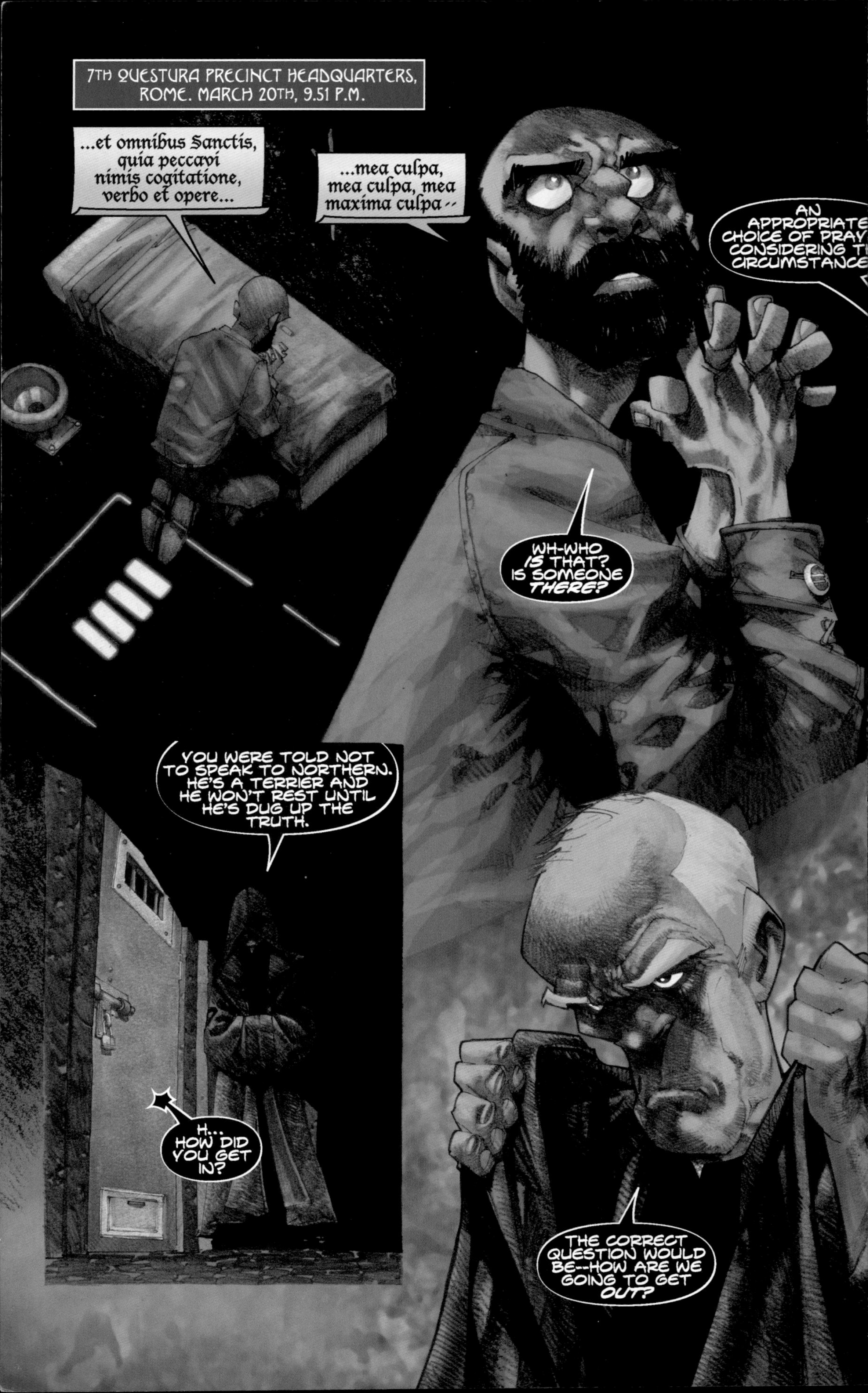
7TH QUESTURA PRECINCT HEADQUARTERS, ROME. MARCH 20TH, 9.51 P.M.
...et omnibus Sanctis, quia peccavi nimis cogitatione, verbo et opere...
...mea culpa, mea culpa, mea maxima culpa--
WH-WHO *IS* THAT? IS SOMEONE *THERE?*
YOU WERE TOLD NOT TO SPEAK TO NORTHERN. HE'S A TERRIER AND HE WON'T REST UNTIL HE'S DUG UP THE TRUTH.
H... HOW DID YOU GET IN?
THE CORRECT QUESTION WOULD BE--HOW ARE WE GOING TO GET *OUT?*

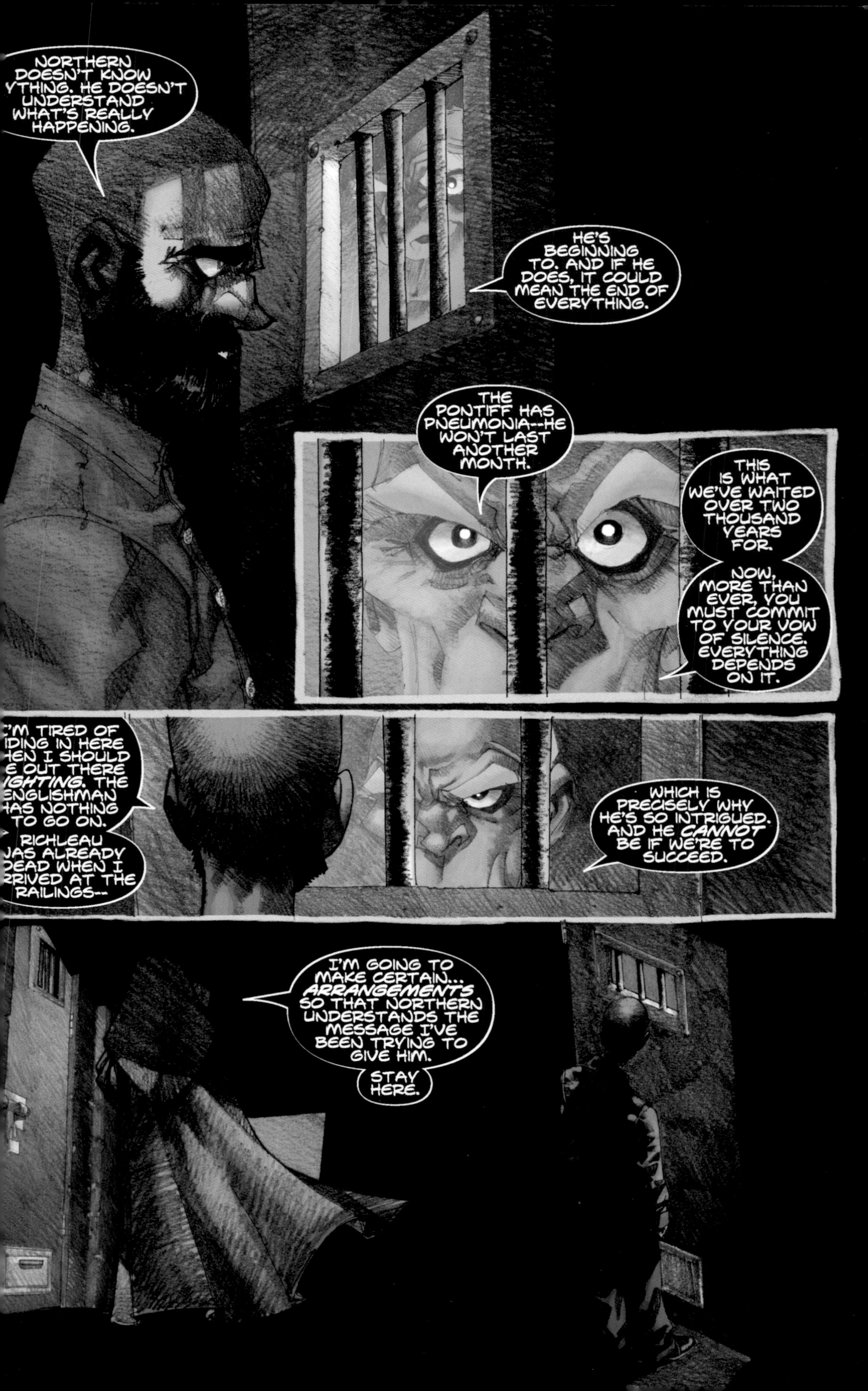
NORTHERN DOESN'T KNOW YTHING. HE DOESN'T UNDERSTAND WHAT'S REALLY HAPPENING.
HE'S BEGINNING TO. AND IF HE DOES, IT COULD MEAN THE END OF EVERYTHING.
THE PONTIFF HAS PNEUMONIA--HE WON'T LAST ANOTHER MONTH.
THIS IS WHAT WE'VE WAITED OVER TWO THOUSAND YEARS FOR.
NOW, MORE THAN EVER, YOU MUST COMMIT TO YOUR VOW OF SILENCE. EVERYTHING DEPENDS ON IT.
'M TIRED OF IDING IN HERE HEN I SHOULD E OUT THERE IGHTING. THE ENGLISHMAN HAS NOTHING TO GO ON.
RICHLEAU JAS ALREADY DEAD WHEN I RRIVED AT THE RAILINGS--
WHICH IS PRECISELY WHY HE'S SO INTRIGUED. AND HE CANNOT BE IF WE'RE TO SUCCEED.
I'M GOING TO MAKE CERTAIN... ARRANGEMENTS SO THAT NORTHERN UNDERSTANDS THE MESSAGE I'VE BEEN TRYING TO GIVE HIM.
STAY HERE.

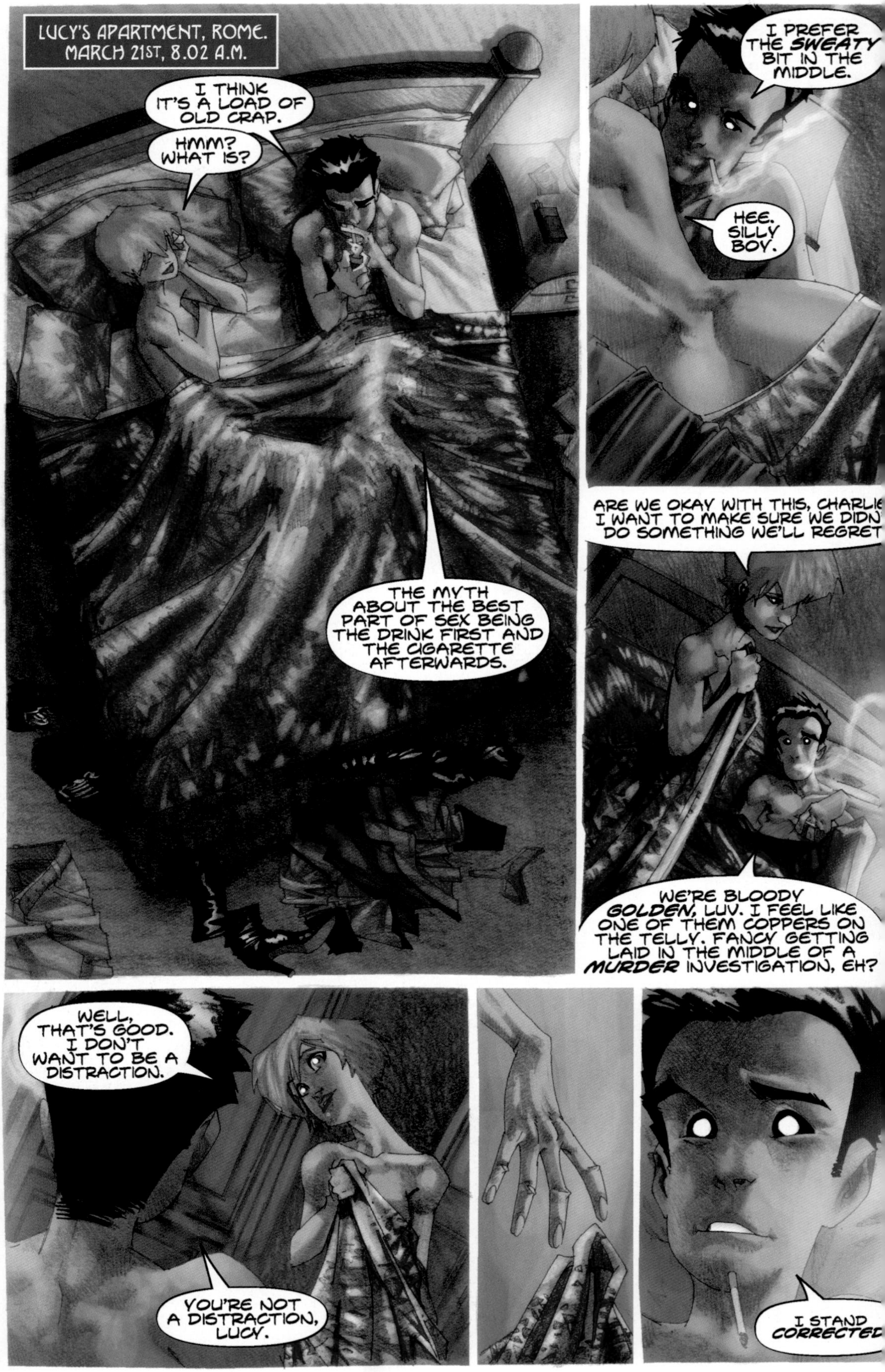
LUCY'S APARTMENT, ROME.
MARCH 21ST, 8.02 A.M.
I THINK IT'S A LOAD OF OLD CRAP.
HMM? WHAT IS?
THE MYTH ABOUT THE BEST PART OF SEX BEING THE DRINK FIRST AND THE CIGARETTE AFTERWARDS.
I PREFER THE SWEATY BIT IN THE MIDDLE.
HEE. SILLY BOY.
ARE WE OKAY WITH THIS, CHARLIE I WANT TO MAKE SURE WE DIDN DO SOMETHING WE'LL REGRET
WE'RE BLOODY GOLDEN, LUV. I FEEL LIKE ONE OF THEM COPPERS ON THE TELLY. FANCY GETTING LAID IN THE MIDDLE OF A MURDER INVESTIGATION, EH?
WELL, THAT'S GOOD. I DON'T WANT TO BE A DISTRACTION.
YOU'RE NOT A DISTRACTION, LUCY.
I STAND CORRECTED

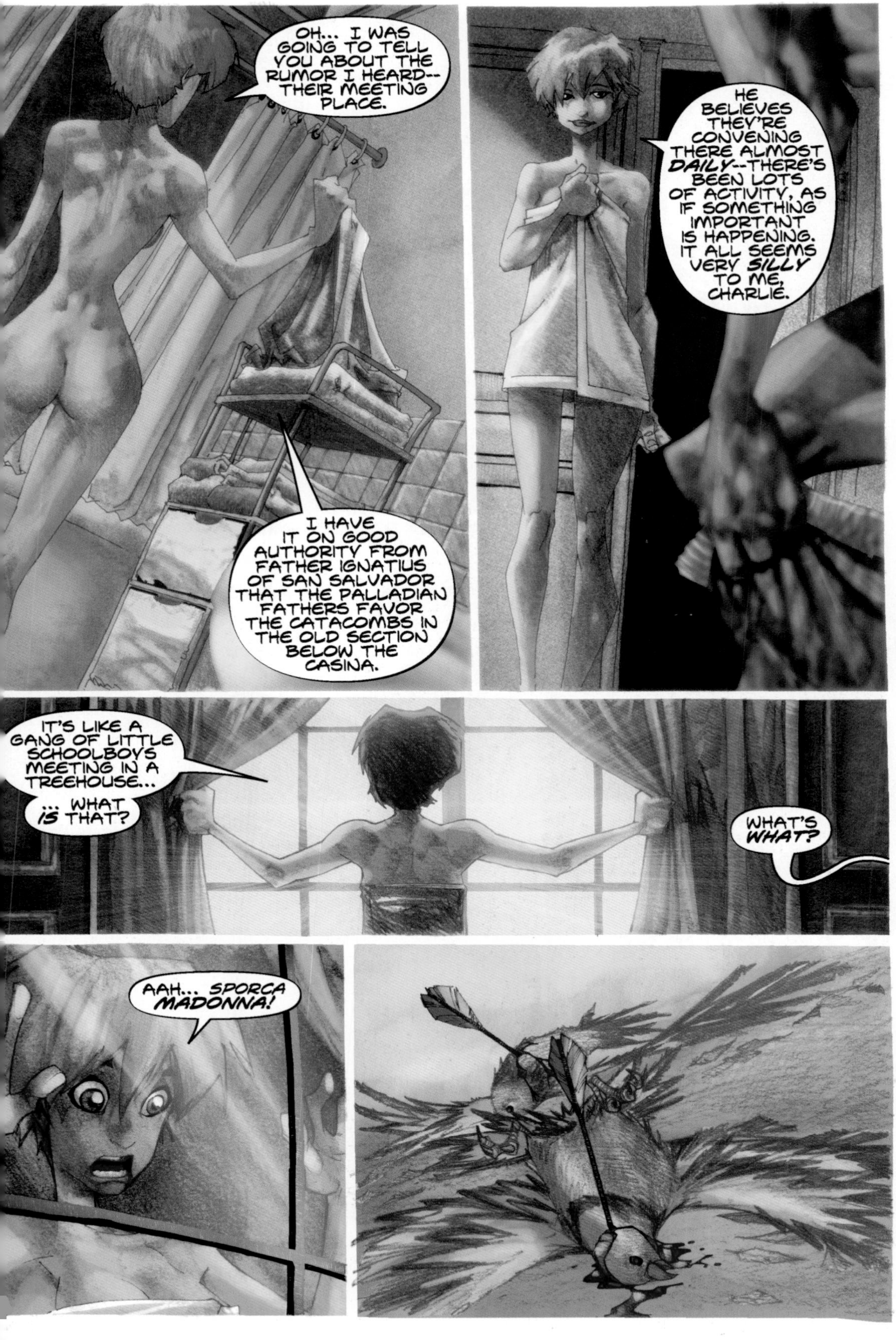
OH... I WAS GOING TO TELL YOU ABOUT THE RUMOR I HEARD-- THEIR MEETING PLACE.
I HAVE IT ON GOOD AUTHORITY FROM FATHER IGNATIUS OF SAN SALVADOR THAT THE PALLADIAN FATHERS FAVOR THE CATACOMBS IN THE OLD SECTION BELOW THE CASINA.
HE BELIEVES THEY'RE CONVENING THERE ALMOST *DAILY*--THERE'S BEEN LOTS OF ACTIVITY, AS IF SOMETHING IMPORTANT IS HAPPENING. IT ALL SEEMS VERY *SILLY* TO ME, CHARLIE.
IT'S LIKE A GANG OF LITTLE SCHOOLBOYS MEETING IN A TREEHOUSE...
... WHAT *IS* THAT?
WHAT'S *WHAT?*
AAH... SPORCA *MADONNA!*

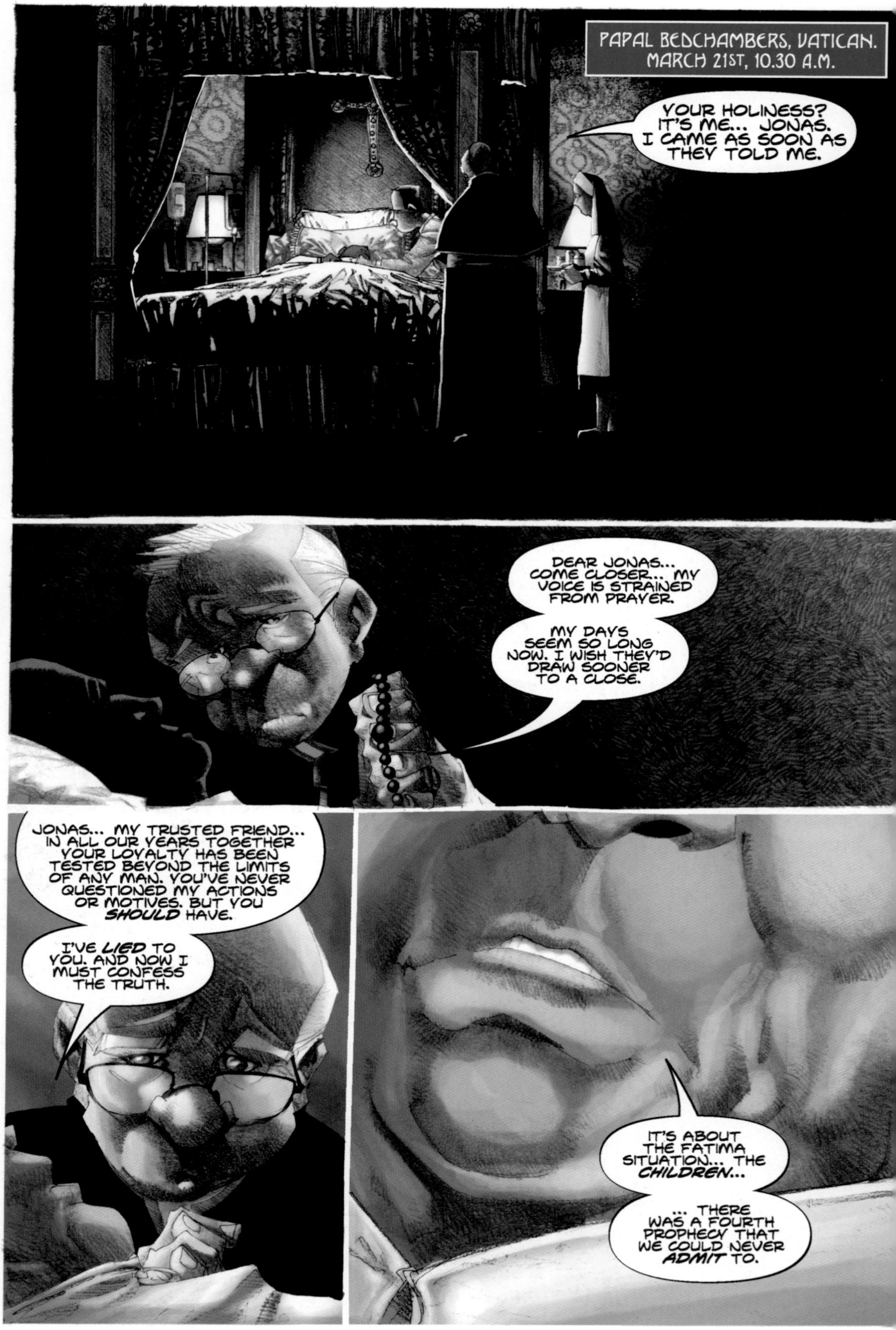
PAPAL BEDCHAMBERS, VATICAN. MARCH 21ST, 10.30 A.M.
YOUR HOLINESS? IT'S ME... JONAS. I CAME AS SOON AS THEY TOLD ME.
DEAR JONAS... COME CLOSER... MY VOICE IS STRAINED FROM PRAYER.
MY DAYS SEEM SO LONG NOW. I WISH THEY'D DRAW SOONER TO A CLOSE.
JONAS... MY TRUSTED FRIEND... IN ALL OUR YEARS TOGETHER YOUR LOYALTY HAS BEEN TESTED BEYOND THE LIMITS OF ANY MAN. YOU'VE NEVER QUESTIONED MY ACTIONS OR MOTIVES. BUT YOU *SHOULD* HAVE.
I'VE *LIED* TO YOU. AND NOW I MUST CONFESS THE TRUTH.
IT'S ABOUT THE FATIMA SITUATION... THE *CHILDREN*...
... THERE WAS A FOURTH PROPHECY THAT WE COULD NEVER *ADMIT* TO.

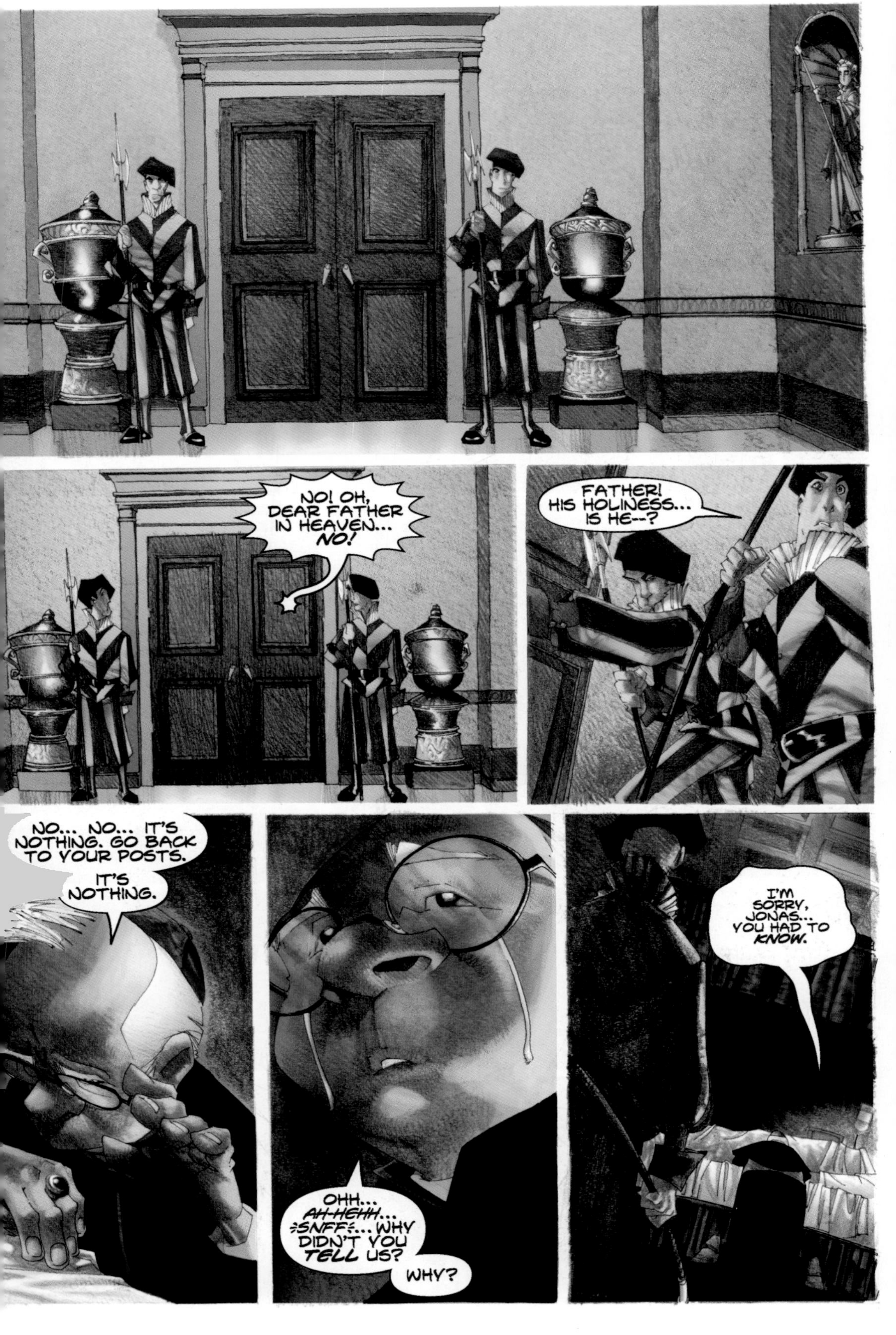
NO! OH, DEAR FATHER IN HEAVEN... NO!
FATHER! HIS HOLINESS... IS HE--?
NO... NO... IT'S NOTHING. GO BACK TO YOUR POSTS.
IT'S NOTHING.
OHH... AH-HEHH... SNFF... WHY DIDN'T YOU TELL US?
WHY?
I'M SORRY, JONAS... YOU HAD TO KNOW.

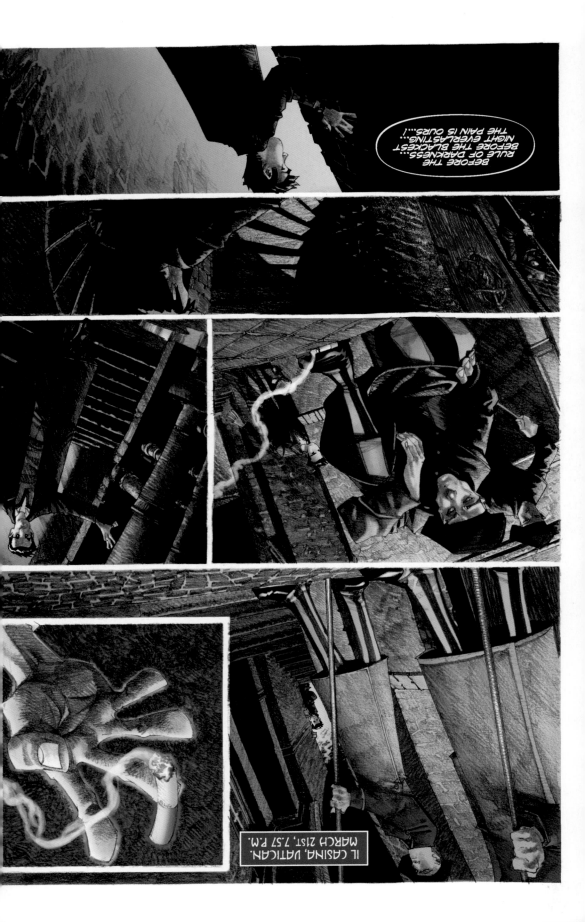

BEFORE THE
RULE OF DARKNESS...
BEFORE THE BLACKEST
NIGHT EVERLASTING...
THE PAIN IS OURS...!

IL CASINA, VATICAN.
MARCH 21ST, 7:57 P.M.

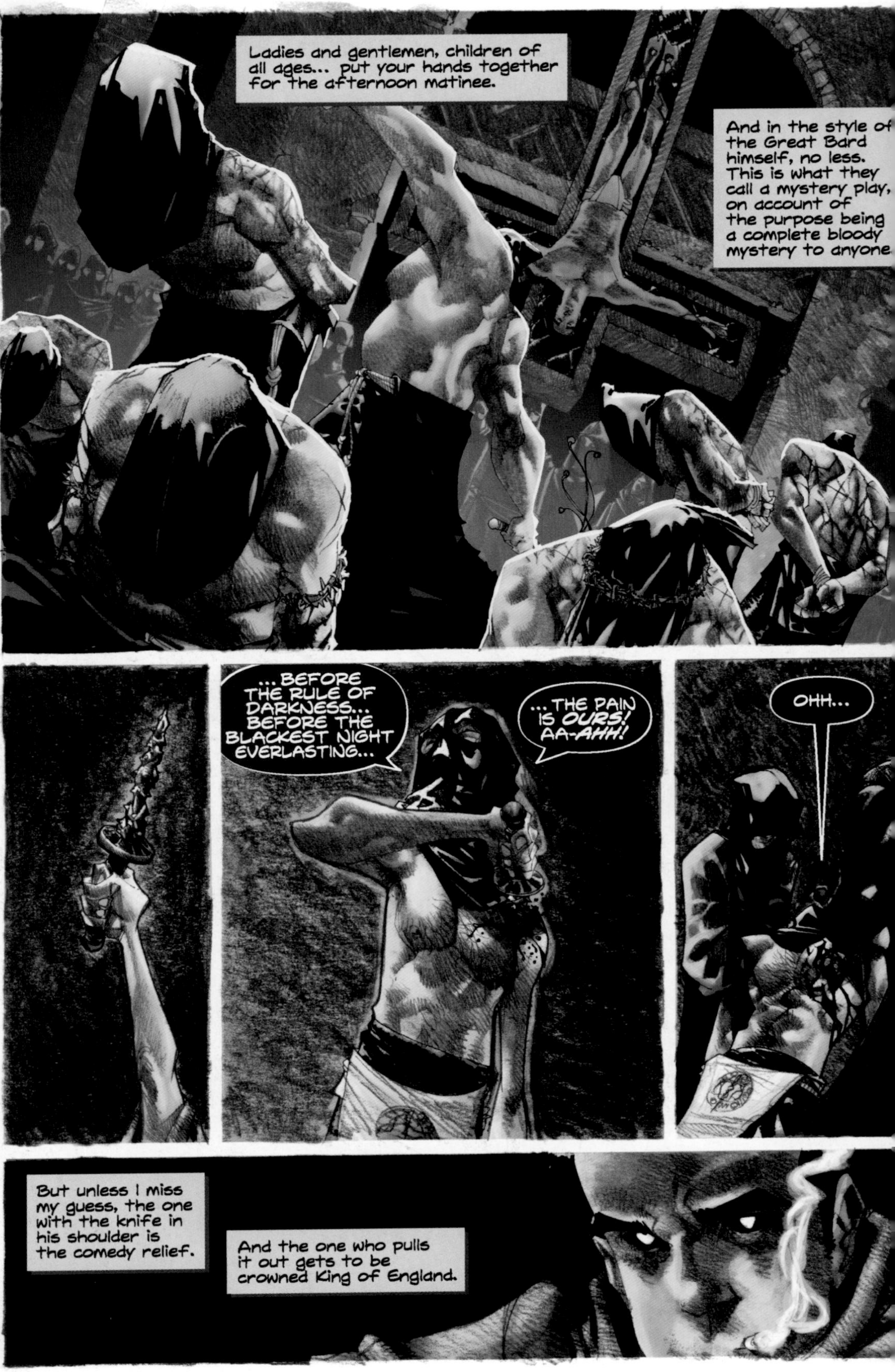
Ladies and gentlemen, children of all ages... put your hands together for the afternoon matinee.
And in the style of the Great Bard himself, no less. This is what they call a mystery play, on account of the purpose being a complete bloody mystery to anyone
...BEFORE THE RULE OF DARKNESS... BEFORE THE BLACKEST NIGHT EVERLASTING...
...THE PAIN IS OURS! AA-AHH!
OHH...
But unless I miss my guess, the one with the knife in his shoulder is the comedy relief.
And the one who pulls it out gets to be crowned King of England.

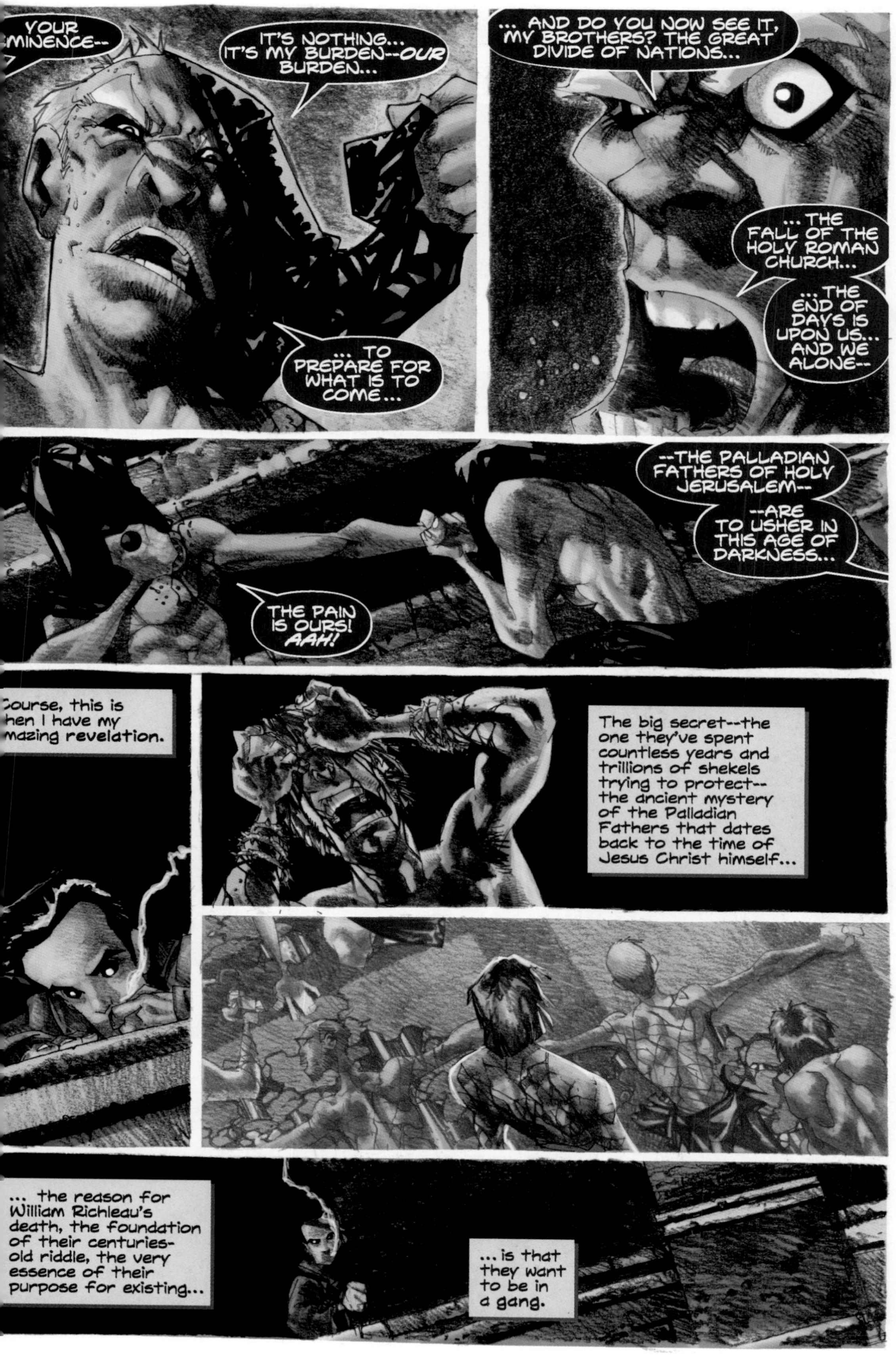
YOUR
MINENCE--
IT'S NOTHING... IT'S MY BURDEN--OUR BURDEN...
... TO PREPARE FOR WHAT IS TO COME...
... AND DO YOU NOW SEE IT, MY BROTHERS? THE GREAT DIVIDE OF NATIONS...
... THE FALL OF THE HOLY ROMAN CHURCH...
... THE END OF DAYS IS UPON US... AND WE ALONE--
--THE PALLADIAN FATHERS OF HOLY JERUSALEM--
--ARE TO USHER IN THIS AGE OF DARKNESS...
THE PAIN IS OURS! AAH!
ourse, this is
hen I have my
mazing revelation.
The big secret--the one they've spent countless years and trillions of shekels trying to protect--the ancient mystery of the Palladian Fathers that dates back to the time of Jesus Christ himself...
... the reason for William Richleau's death, the foundation of their centuries-old riddle, the very essence of their purpose for existing...
... is that they want to be in a gang.

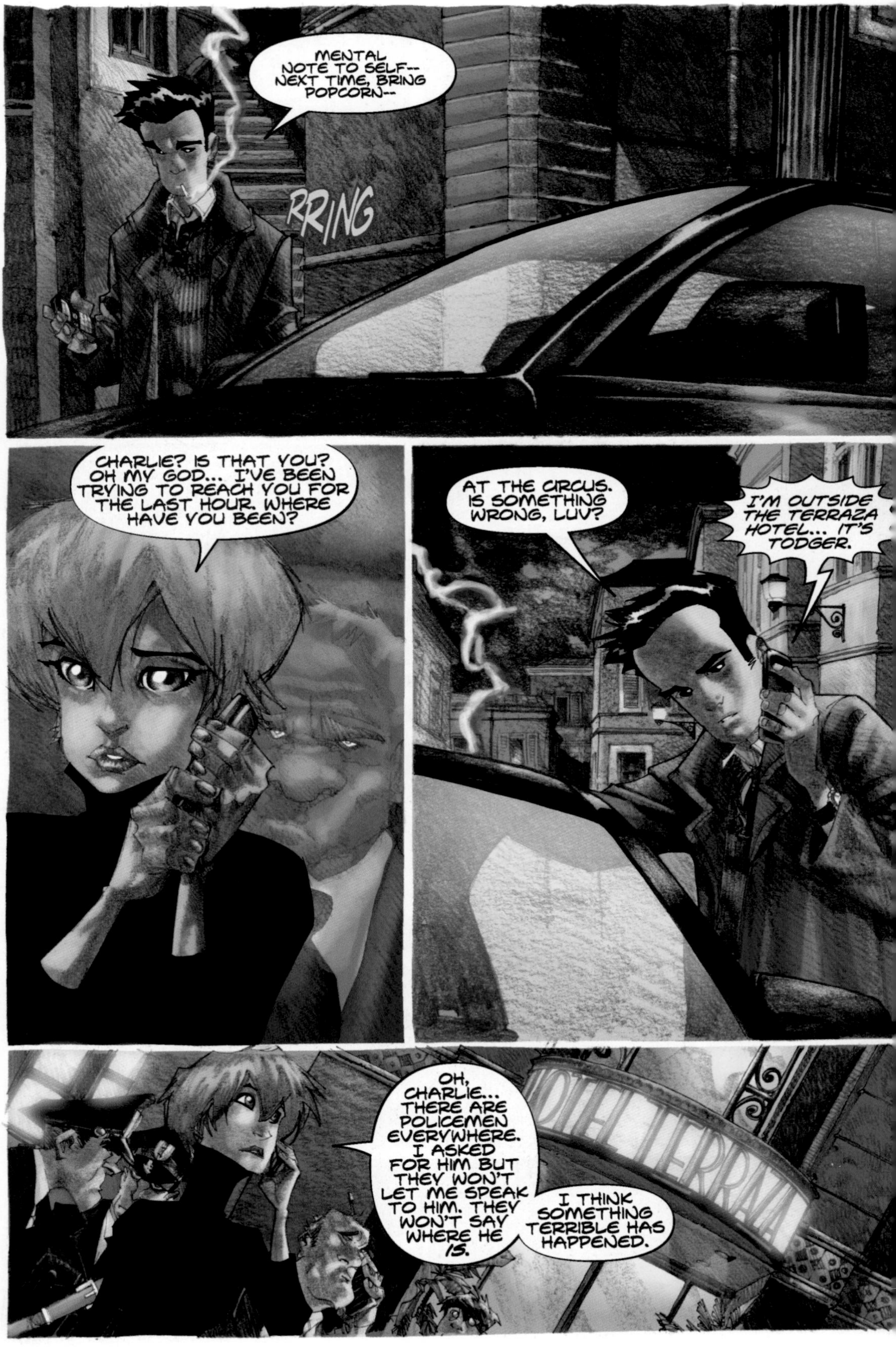
MENTAL NOTE TO SELF-- NEXT TIME, BRING POPCORN--
RRING
CHARLIE? IS THAT YOU? OH MY GOD... I'VE BEEN TRYING TO REACH YOU FOR THE LAST HOUR. WHERE HAVE YOU BEEN?
AT THE CIRCUS. IS SOMETHING WRONG, LUV?
I'M OUTSIDE THE TERRAZA HOTEL... IT'S TODGER.
OH, CHARLIE... THERE ARE POLICEMEN EVERYWHERE. I ASKED FOR HIM BUT THEY WON'T LET ME SPEAK TO HIM. THEY WON'T SAY WHERE HE IS.
I THINK SOMETHING TERRIBLE HAS HAPPENED.

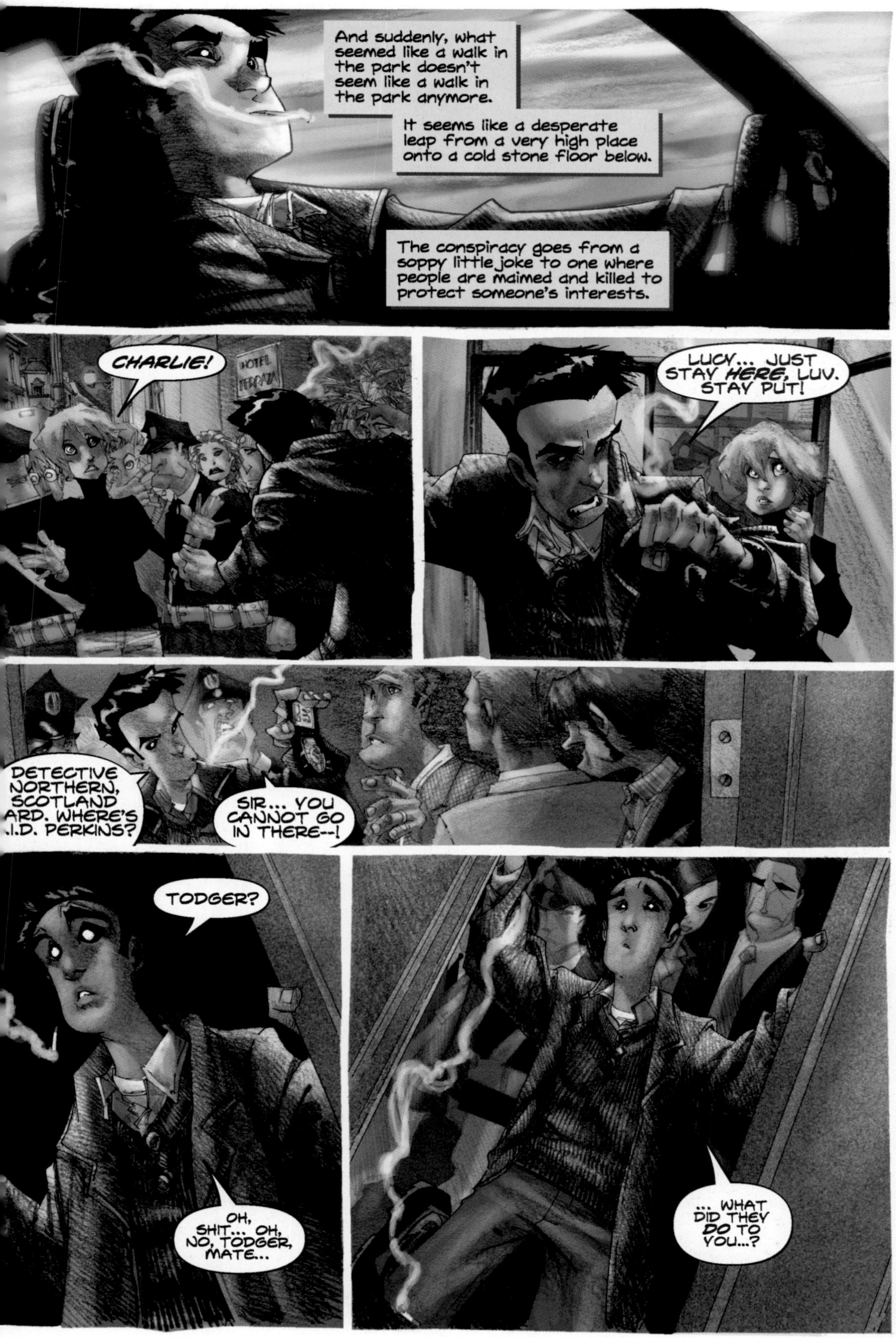
And suddenly, what seemed like a walk in the park doesn't seem like a walk in the park anymore.
It seems like a desperate leap from a very high place onto a cold stone floor below.
The conspiracy goes from a soppy little joke to one where people are maimed and killed to protect someone's interests.
CHARLIE!
HOTEL TERRAZA
LUCY... JUST STAY *HERE*, LUV. STAY PUT!
DETECTIVE NORTHERN, SCOTLAND ARD. WHERE'S .I.D. PERKINS?
SIR... YOU CANNOT GO IN THERE--!
TODGER?
OH, SHIT... OH, NO, TODGER, MATE...
... WHAT DID THEY *DO* TO YOU...?

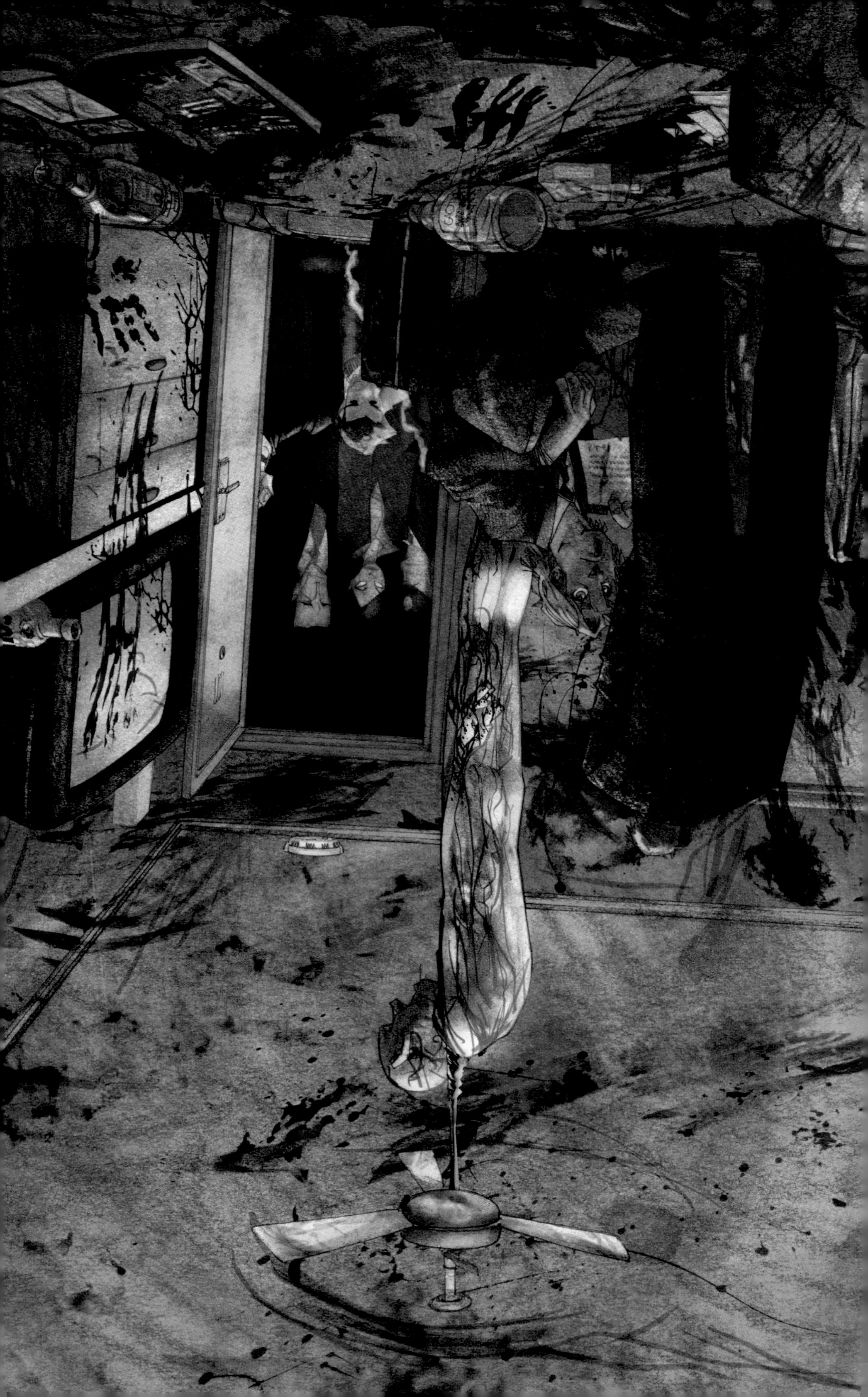

CHAPTER FIVE

House of Cards

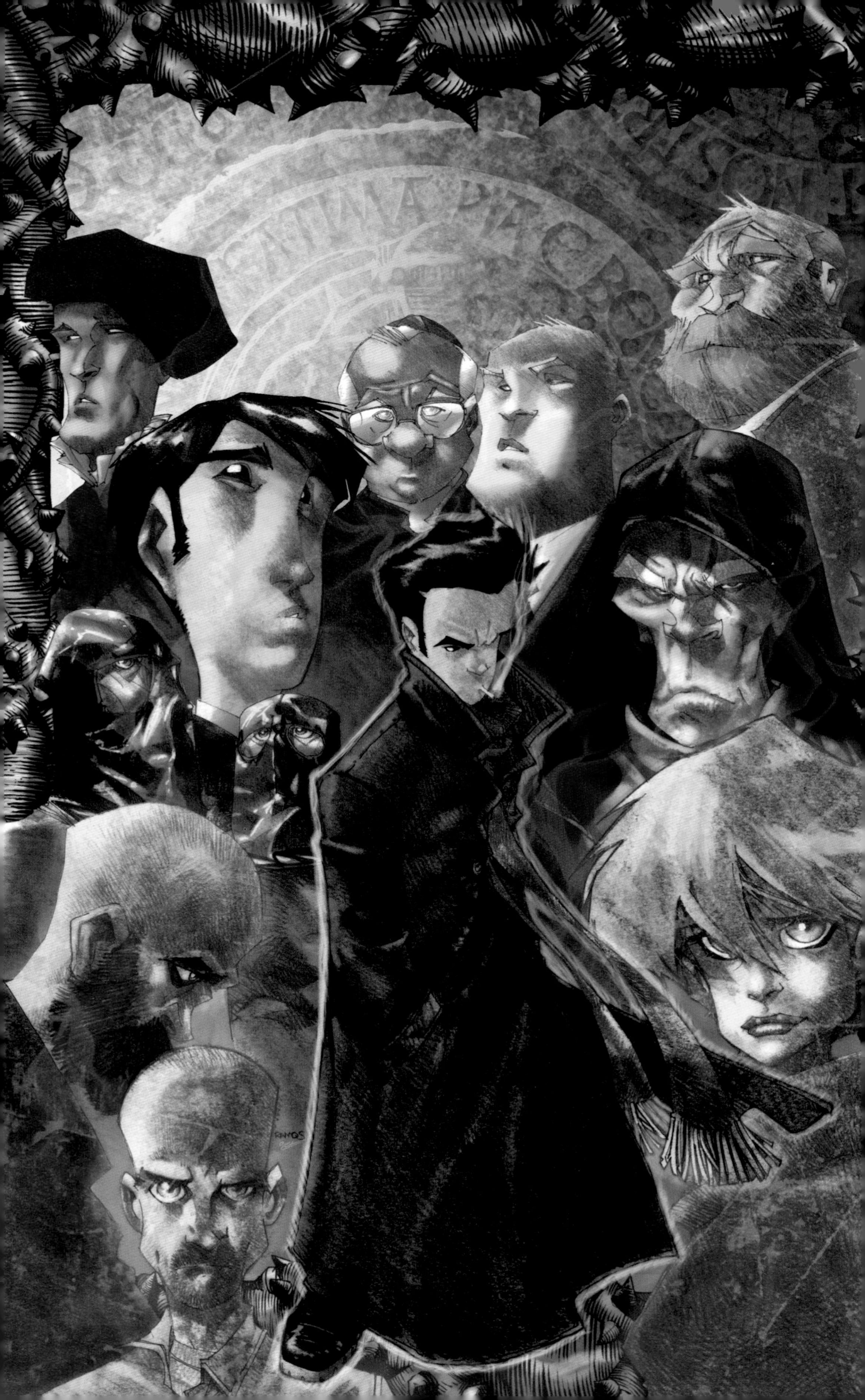

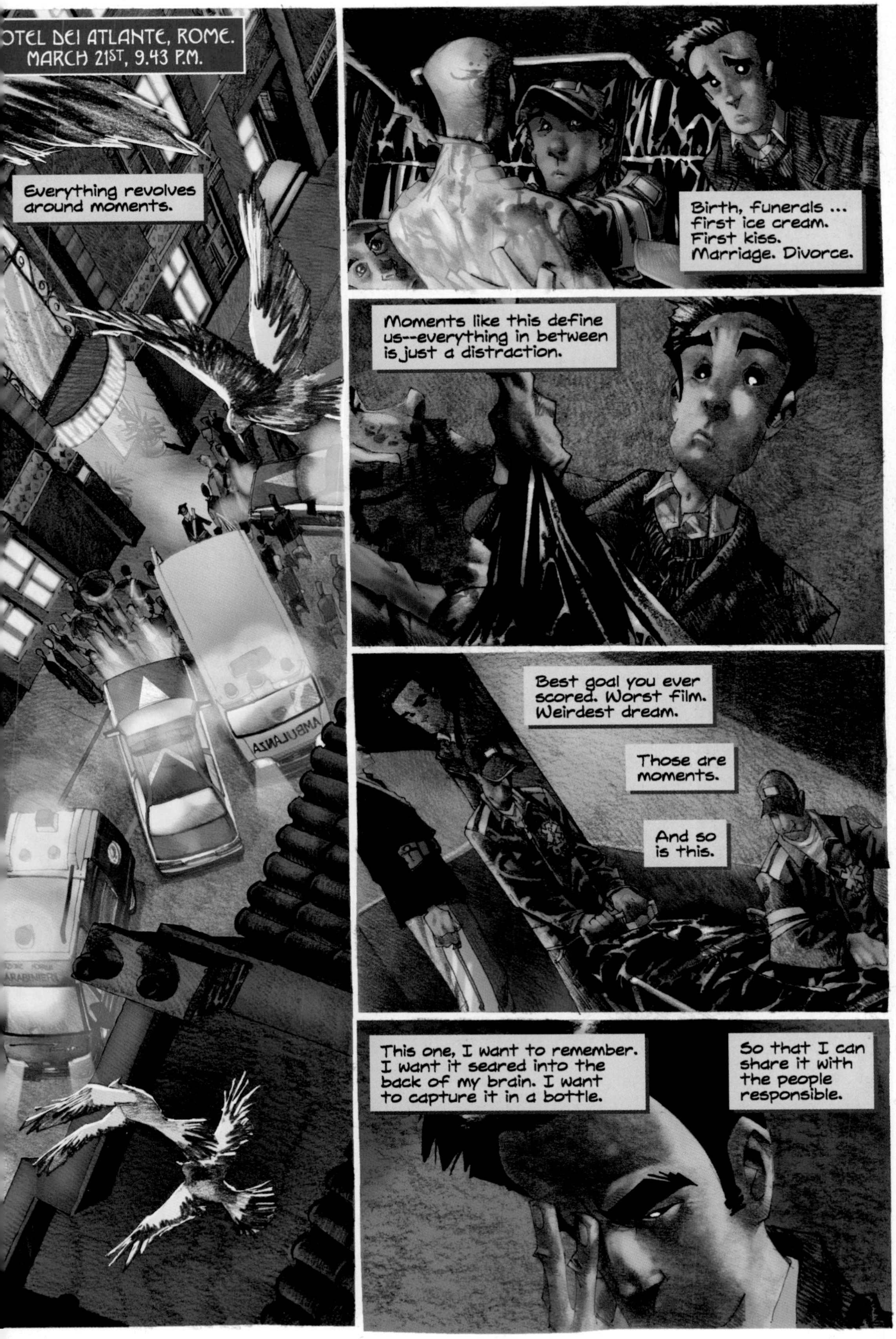

OTEL DEI ATLANTE, ROME.
MARCH 21ST, 9.43 P.M.
Everything revolves around moments.
Birth, funerals ... first ice cream. First kiss. Marriage. Divorce.
Moments like this define us--everything in between is just a distraction.
Best goal you ever scored. Worst film. Weirdest dream.
Those are moments.
And so is this.
This one, I want to remember. I want it seared into the back of my brain. I want to capture it in a bottle.
So that I can share it with the people responsible.

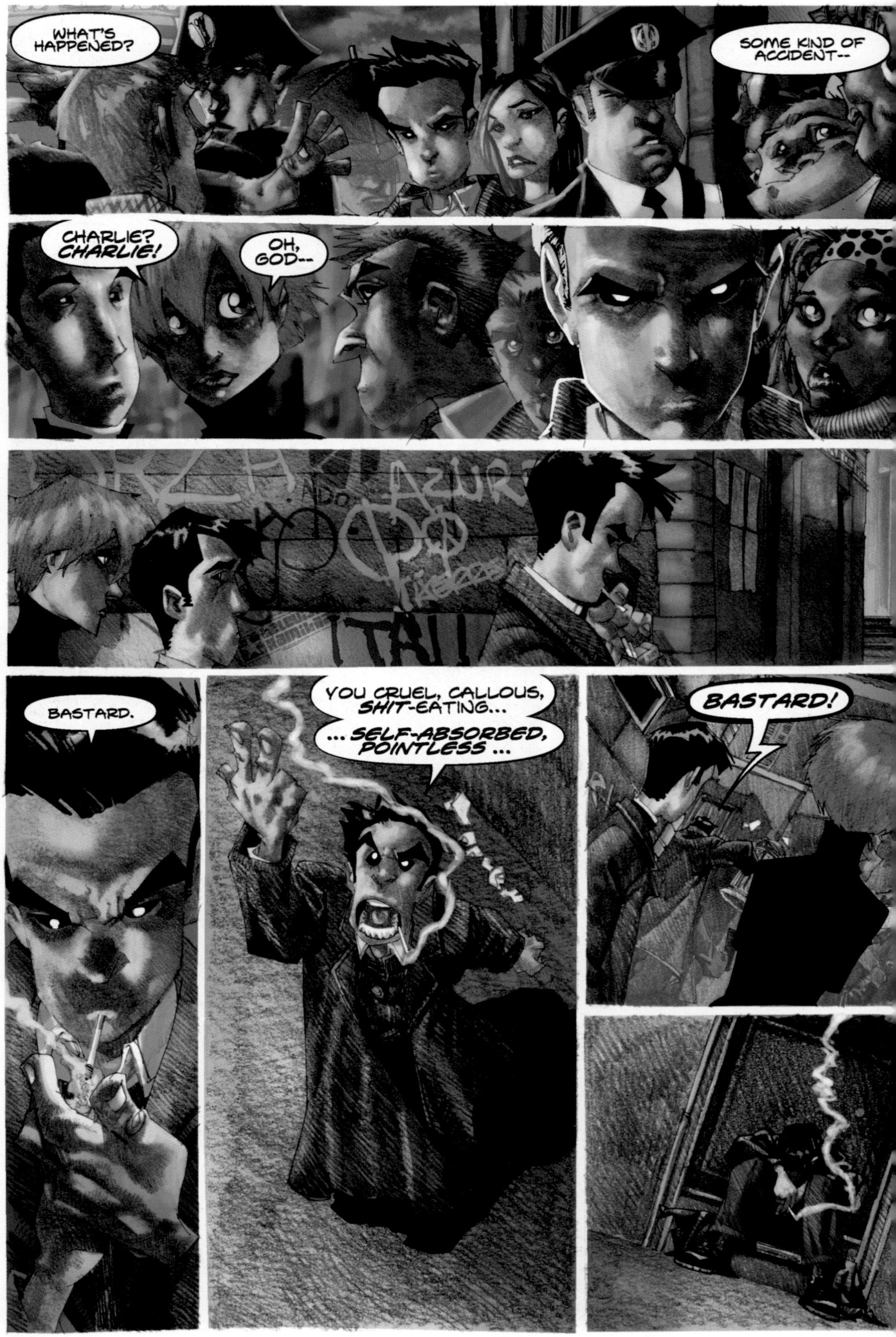
WHAT'S HAPPENED?
SOME KIND OF ACCIDENT--
CHARLIE? CHARLIE!
OH, GOD--
BASTARD.
YOU CRUEL, CALLOUS, SHIT-EATING...
... SELF-ABSORBED, POINTLESS ...
BASTARD!

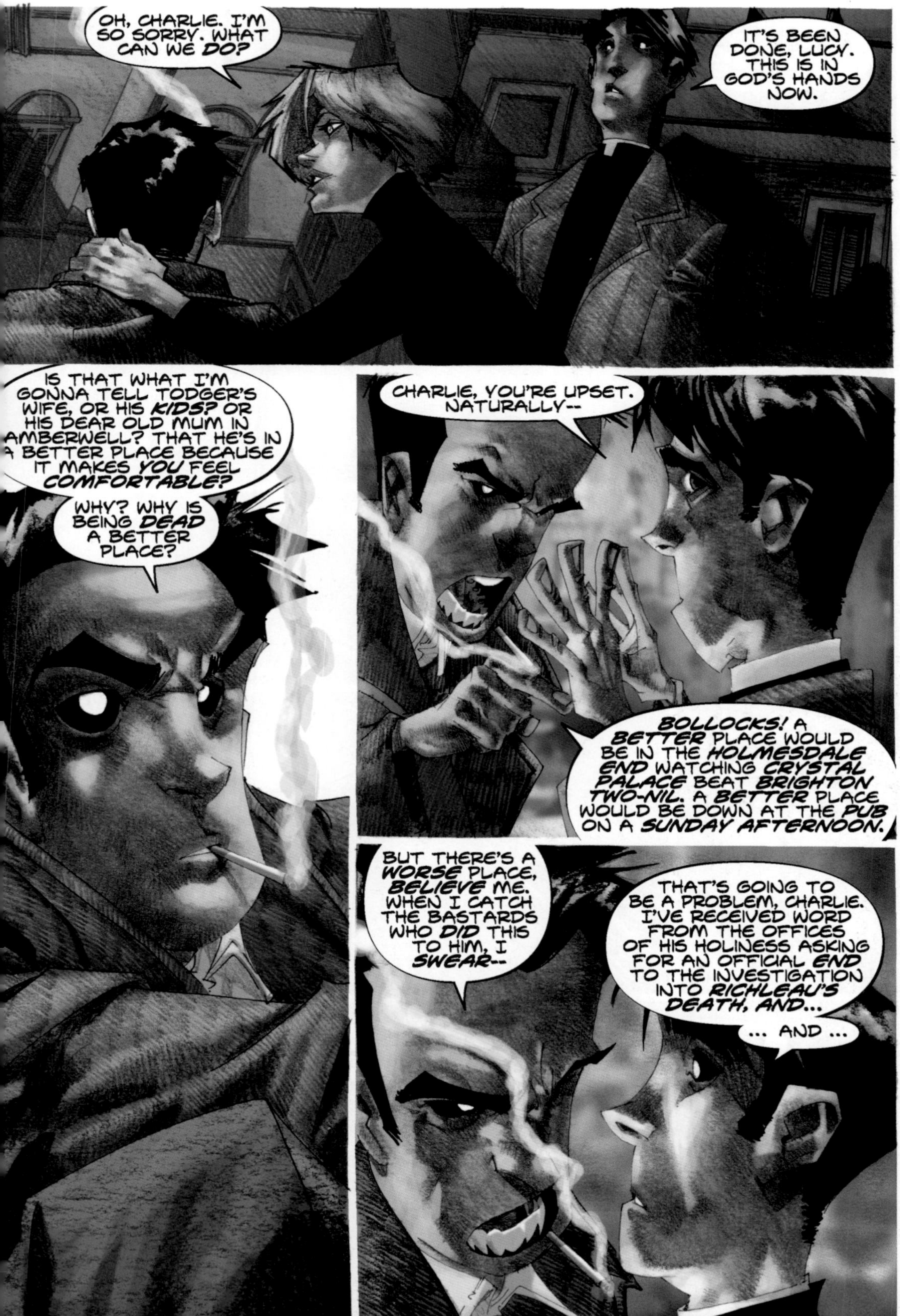
OH, CHARLIE. I'M SO SORRY. WHAT CAN WE DO?
IT'S BEEN DONE, LUCY. THIS IS IN GOD'S HANDS NOW.
IS THAT WHAT I'M GONNA TELL TODGER'S WIFE, OR HIS KIDS? OR HIS DEAR OLD MUM IN AMBERWELL? THAT HE'S IN A BETTER PLACE BECAUSE IT MAKES YOU FEEL COMFORTABLE?
WHY? WHY IS BEING DEAD A BETTER PLACE?
CHARLIE, YOU'RE UPSET. NATURALLY--
BOLLOCKS! A BETTER PLACE WOULD BE IN THE HOLMESDALE END WATCHING CRYSTAL PALACE BEAT BRIGHTON TWO-NIL. A BETTER PLACE WOULD BE DOWN AT THE PUB ON A SUNDAY AFTERNOON.
BUT THERE'S A WORSE PLACE, BELIEVE ME. WHEN I CATCH THE BASTARDS WHO DID THIS TO HIM, I SWEAR--
THAT'S GOING TO BE A PROBLEM, CHARLIE. I'VE RECEIVED WORD FROM THE OFFICES OF HIS HOLINESS ASKING FOR AN OFFICIAL END TO THE INVESTIGATION INTO RICHLEAU'S DEATH, AND...
... AND ...

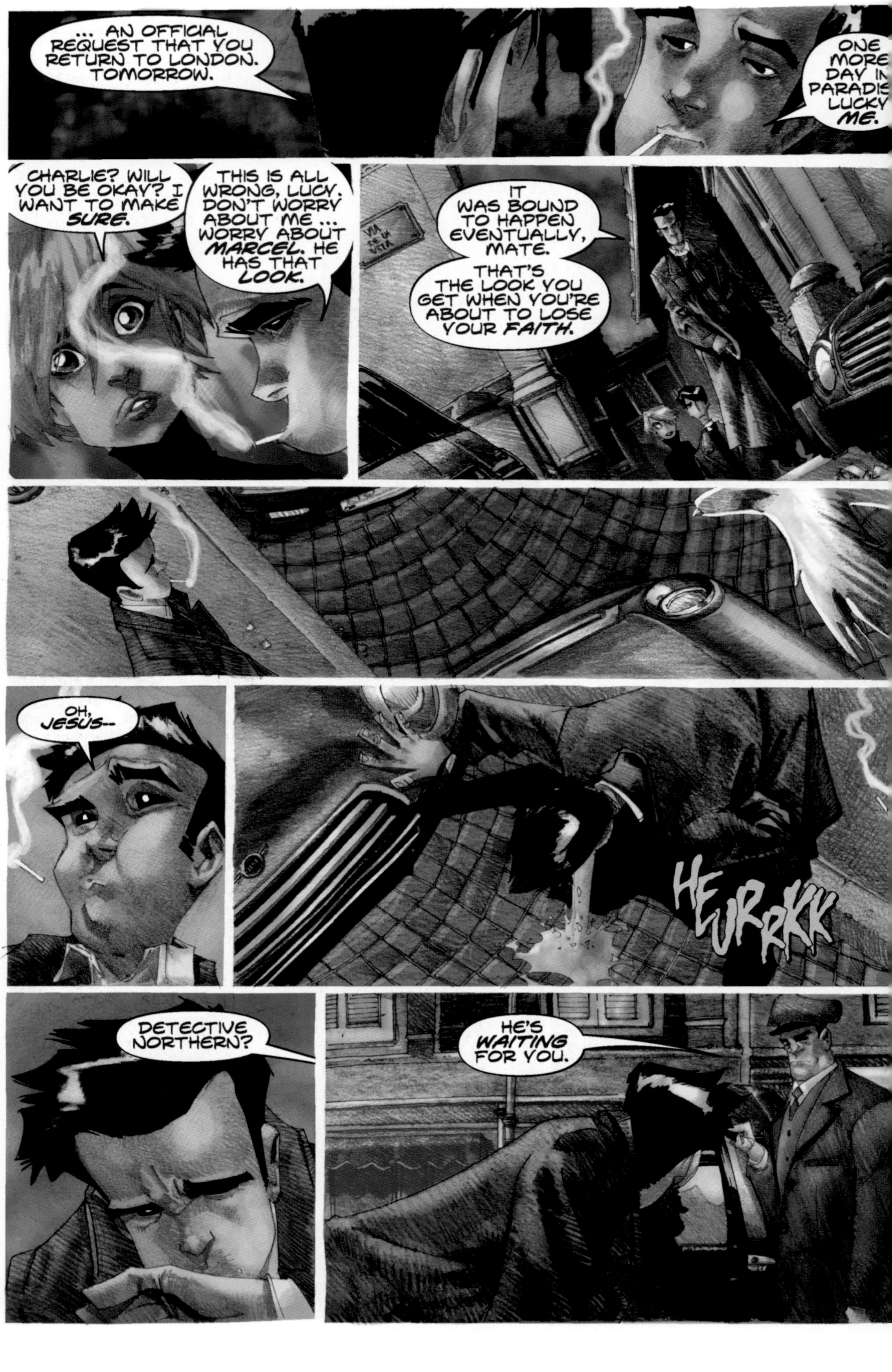

... AN OFFICIAL REQUEST THAT YOU RETURN TO LONDON. TOMORROW.
ONE MORE DAY IN PARADISE LUCKY *ME.*
CHARLIE? WILL YOU BE OKAY? I WANT TO MAKE *SURE.*
THIS IS ALL WRONG, LUCY. DON'T WORRY ABOUT ME ... WORRY ABOUT *MARCEL.* HE HAS THAT *LOOK.*
IT WAS BOUND TO HAPPEN EVENTUALLY, MATE.
THAT'S THE LOOK YOU GET WHEN YOU'RE ABOUT TO LOSE YOUR *FAITH.*
OH, *JESUS--*
HEURRKK
DETECTIVE NORTHERN?
HE'S *WAITING* FOR YOU.

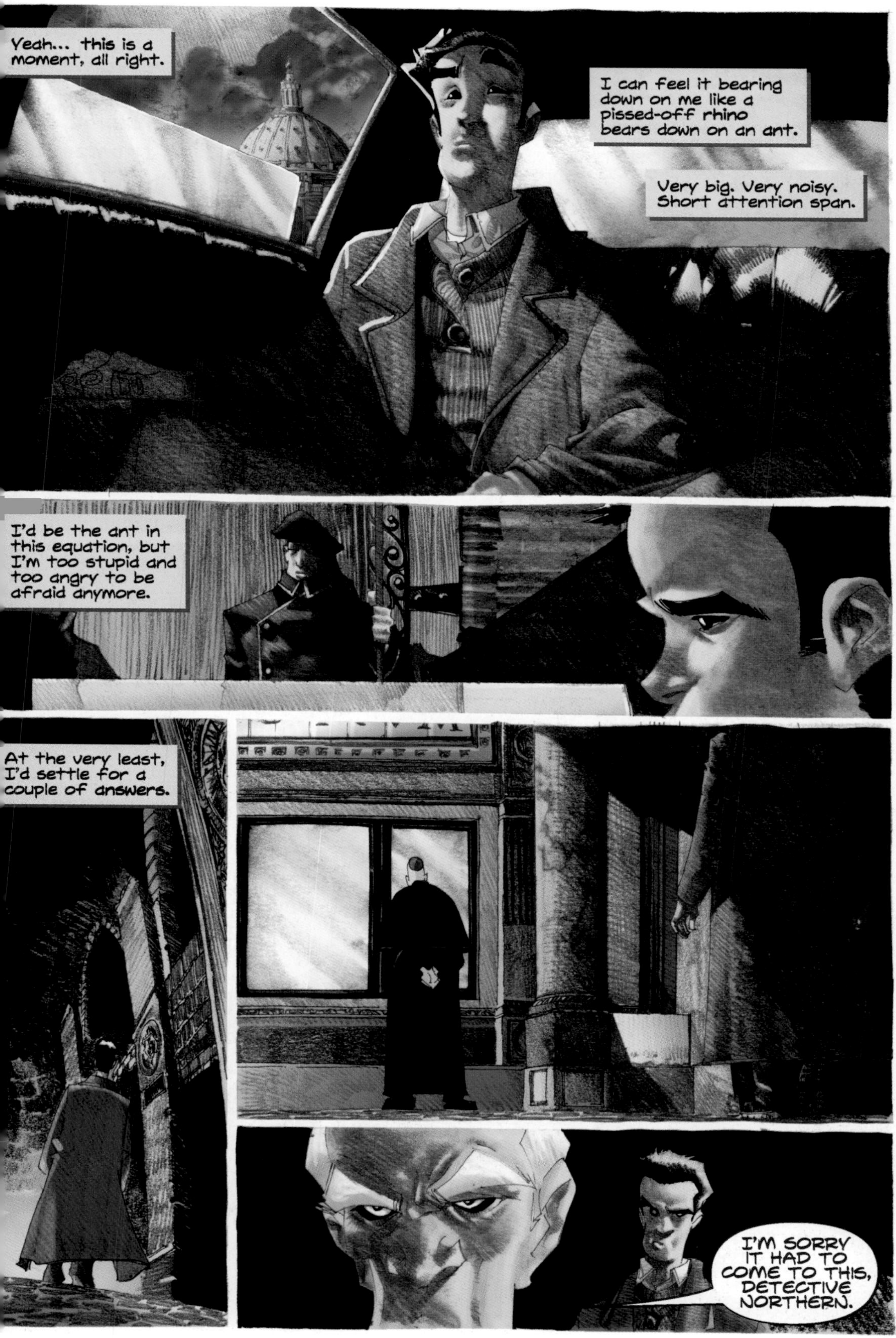
Yeah... this is a moment, all right.
I can feel it bearing down on me like a pissed-off rhino bears down on an ant.
Very big. Very noisy. Short attention span.
I'd be the ant in this equation, but I'm too stupid and too angry to be afraid anymore.
At the very least, I'd settle for a couple of answers.
I'M SORRY IT HAD TO COME TO THIS, DETECTIVE NORTHERN.

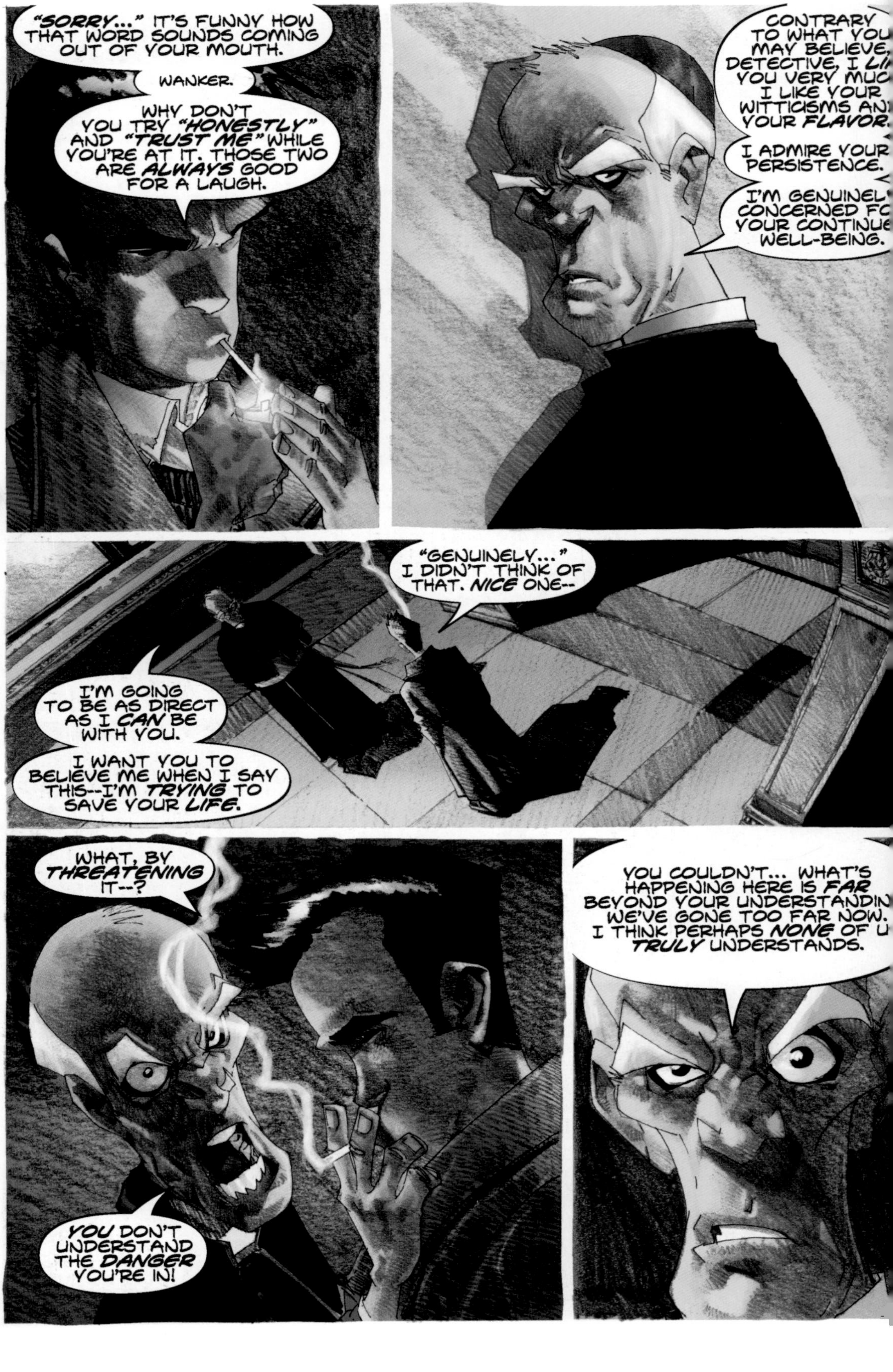

"SORRY..." IT'S FUNNY HOW THAT WORD SOUNDS COMING OUT OF YOUR MOUTH.
WANKER.
WHY DON'T YOU TRY "HONESTLY" AND "TRUST ME" WHILE YOU'RE AT IT. THOSE TWO ARE ALWAYS GOOD FOR A LAUGH.
CONTRARY TO WHAT YOU MAY BELIEVE, DETECTIVE, I LI YOU VERY MUC I LIKE YOUR WITTICISMS AN YOUR FLAVOR.
I ADMIRE YOUR PERSISTENCE.
I'M GENUINEL CONCERNED FO YOUR CONTINUE WELL-BEING.
"GENUINELY..." I DIDN'T THINK OF THAT. NICE ONE--
I'M GOING TO BE AS DIRECT AS I CAN BE WITH YOU.
I WANT YOU TO BELIEVE ME WHEN I SAY THIS--I'M TRYING TO SAVE YOUR LIFE.
WHAT, BY THREATENING IT--?
YOU DON'T UNDERSTAND THE DANGER YOU'RE IN!
YOU COULDN'T... WHAT'S HAPPENING HERE IS FAR BEYOND YOUR UNDERSTANDIN WE'VE GONE TOO FAR NOW. I THINK PERHAPS NONE OF U TRULY UNDERSTANDS.

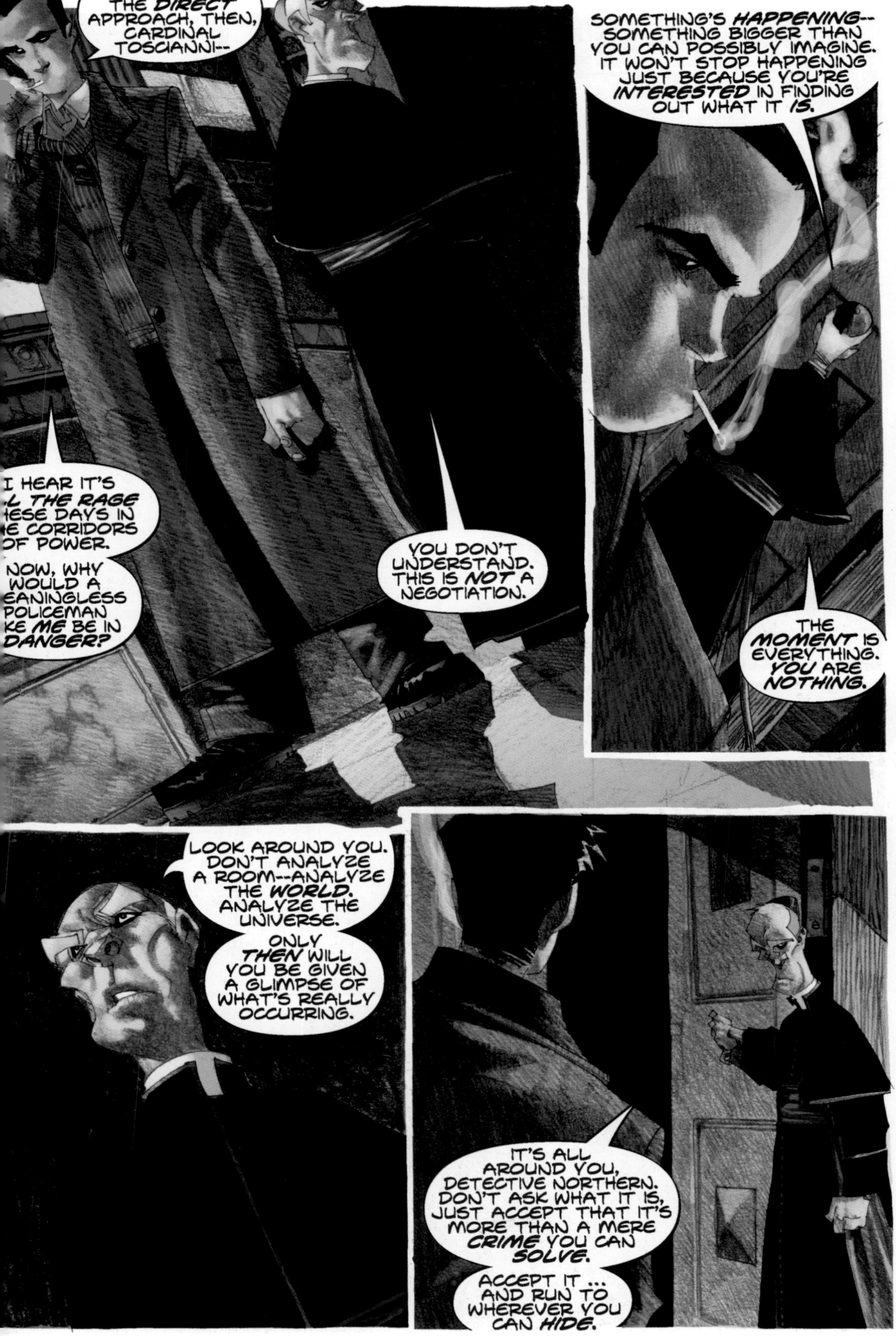
FINE. LET'S TRY THE *DIRECT* APPROACH, THEN, CARDINAL TOSCIANNI--
I HEAR IT'S L *THE RAGE* HESE DAYS IN E CORRIDORS OF POWER.
NOW, WHY WOULD A EANINGLESS POLICEMAN KE *ME* BE IN *DANGER?*
YOU DON'T UNDERSTAND. THIS IS *NOT* A NEGOTIATION.
SOMETHING'S *HAPPENING*-- SOMETHING BIGGER THAN YOU CAN POSSIBLY IMAGINE. IT WON'T STOP HAPPENING JUST BECAUSE YOU'RE *INTERESTED* IN FINDING OUT WHAT IT *IS.*
THE *MOMENT* IS EVERYTHING. *YOU* ARE *NOTHING.*
LOOK AROUND YOU. DON'T ANALYZE A ROOM--ANALYZE THE *WORLD.* ANALYZE THE UNIVERSE.
ONLY *THEN* WILL YOU BE GIVEN A GLIMPSE OF WHAT'S REALLY OCCURRING.
IT'S ALL AROUND YOU, DETECTIVE NORTHERN. DON'T ASK WHAT IT IS, JUST ACCEPT THAT IT'S MORE THAN A MERE *CRIME* YOU CAN *SOLVE.*
ACCEPT IT ... AND RUN TO WHEREVER YOU CAN *HIDE.*

HOTEL SAN SILVESTRO, ROME.
MARCH 22ND, 2.00 A.M.

Toscianni's right, in a way. There's always a big picture. Someone, somewhere, needs there to be so that they can put it on television.

At the Vatican, reports of political maneuvering and cover-ups draw the highest authorities into an emergency session, announced for tomorrow.

His Holiness is unable to attend due to sudden failing health.

His address will be made by an ambitious Cardinal named Toscianni-- a relative newcomer to the scene.

BBC NEWS 24

VATICAN CITY

YOUR HOLINESS VISIBLY ILL, APPEARS TODAY, IN THE VATICAN CITY

A cholera outbreak in sub-Saharan Africa threatens stability in the region.

AFRICA SUFFERS

CNN ▶ CHOLERA OUTBREAK IN KENYA
NA

HUNDREDS OF T

The ebola virus makes an unwelcome appearance in Ken

Poisoned fertilizer and over-farming in Peru results in livestock mutations.

Birth defects quadruple in Russia twenty years after Chernobyl.

FOX NEWS   LIMA, PERU
STRANGE CATTLE MUTATIONS
ON SITE NEWS REPORTER: JOHN WALKER, CLAIMS

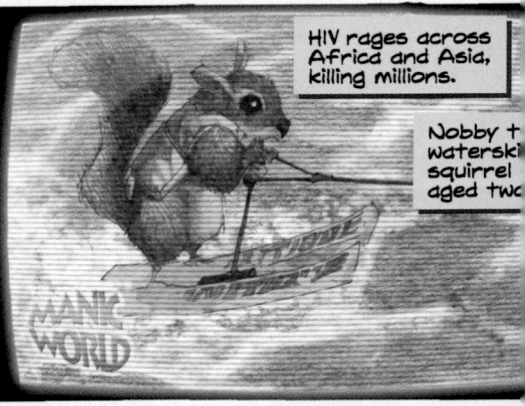

HIV rages across Africa and Asia, killing millions.

Nobby t waterski squirrel aged two

MAN'S WORLD

JUST ANOTHER DAY AT THE OFFICE FOR GOD.

RRRRING

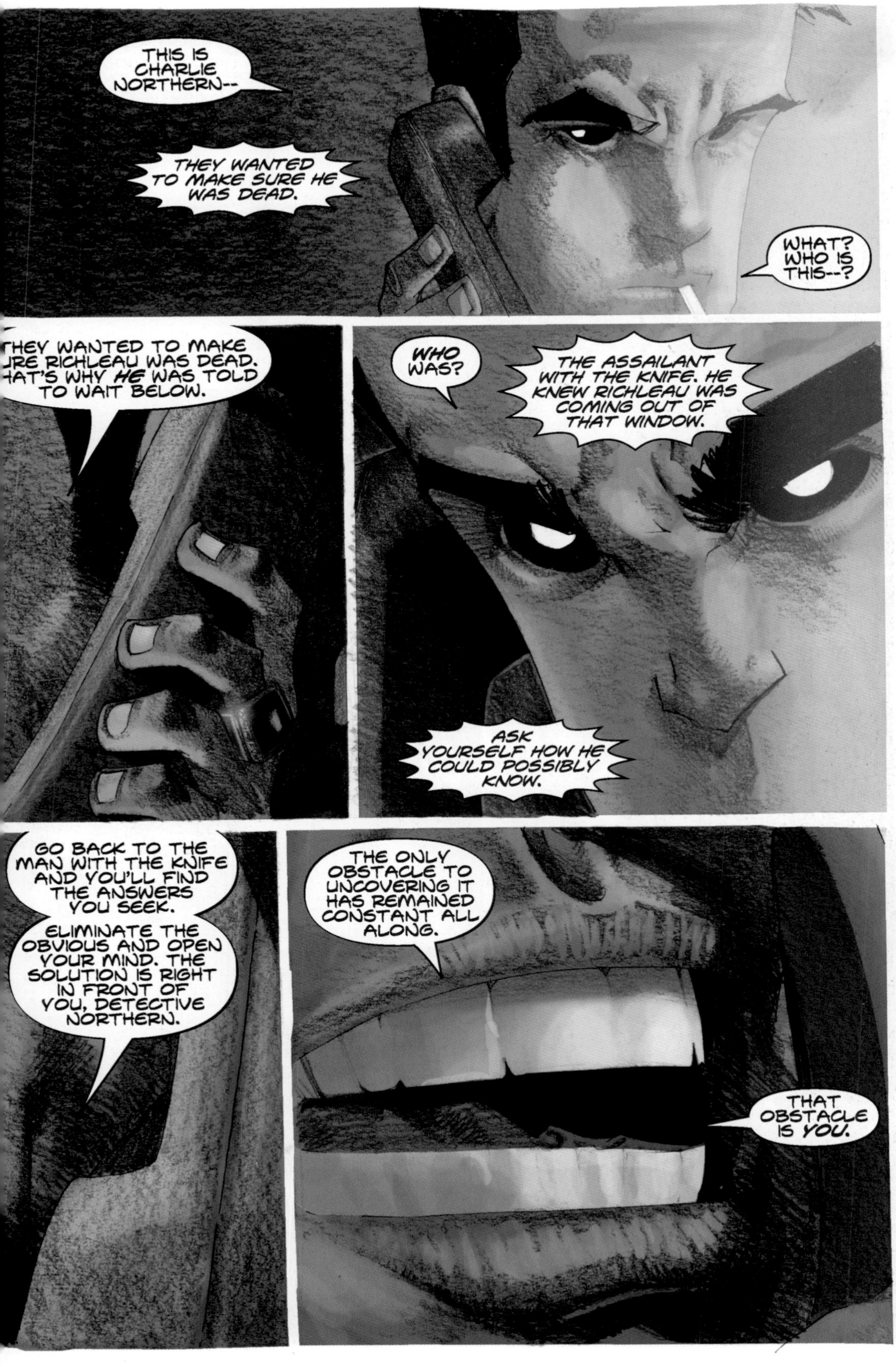
THIS IS CHARLIE NORTHERN--
THEY WANTED TO MAKE SURE HE WAS DEAD.
WHAT? WHO IS THIS--?
THEY WANTED TO MAKE URE RICHLEAU WAS DEAD. HAT'S WHY HE WAS TOLD TO WAIT BELOW.
WHO WAS?
THE ASSAILANT WITH THE KNIFE. HE KNEW RICHLEAU WAS COMING OUT OF THAT WINDOW.
ASK YOURSELF HOW HE COULD POSSIBLY KNOW.
GO BACK TO THE MAN WITH THE KNIFE AND YOU'LL FIND THE ANSWERS YOU SEEK.
ELIMINATE THE OBVIOUS AND OPEN YOUR MIND. THE SOLUTION IS RIGHT IN FRONT OF YOU, DETECTIVE NORTHERN.
THE ONLY OBSTACLE TO UNCOVERING IT HAS REMAINED CONSTANT ALL ALONG.
THAT OBSTACLE IS YOU.

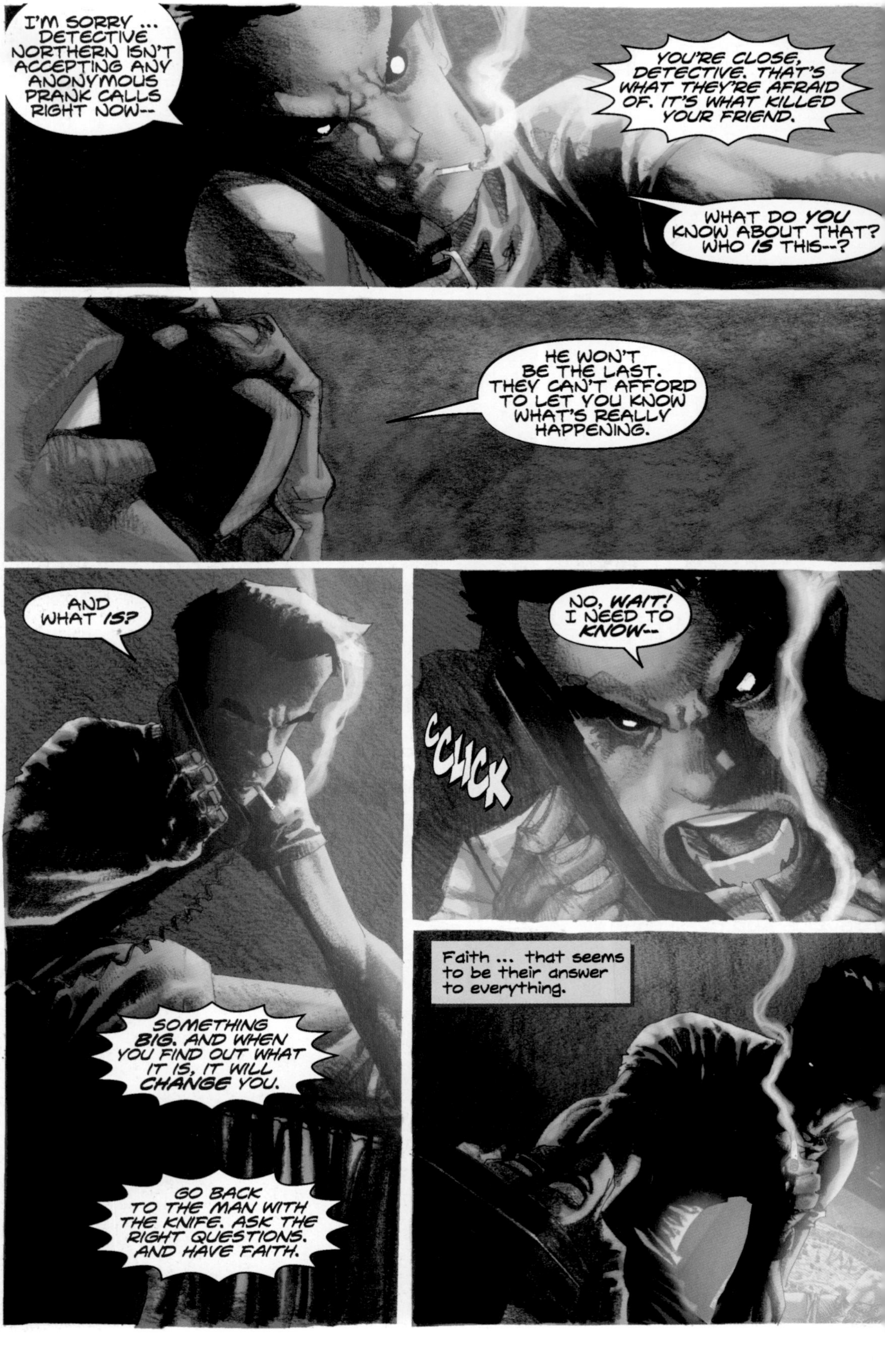

I'M SORRY ... DETECTIVE NORTHERN ISN'T ACCEPTING ANY ANONYMOUS PRANK CALLS RIGHT NOW--
YOU'RE CLOSE, DETECTIVE. THAT'S WHAT THEY'RE AFRAID OF. IT'S WHAT KILLED YOUR FRIEND.
WHAT DO YOU KNOW ABOUT THAT? WHO IS THIS--?
HE WON'T BE THE LAST. THEY CAN'T AFFORD TO LET YOU KNOW WHAT'S REALLY HAPPENING.
AND WHAT IS?
SOMETHING BIG. AND WHEN YOU FIND OUT WHAT IT IS, IT WILL CHANGE YOU.
GO BACK TO THE MAN WITH THE KNIFE. ASK THE RIGHT QUESTIONS. AND HAVE FAITH.
NO, WAIT! I NEED TO KNOW--
CCLICK
Faith ... that seems to be their answer to everything.

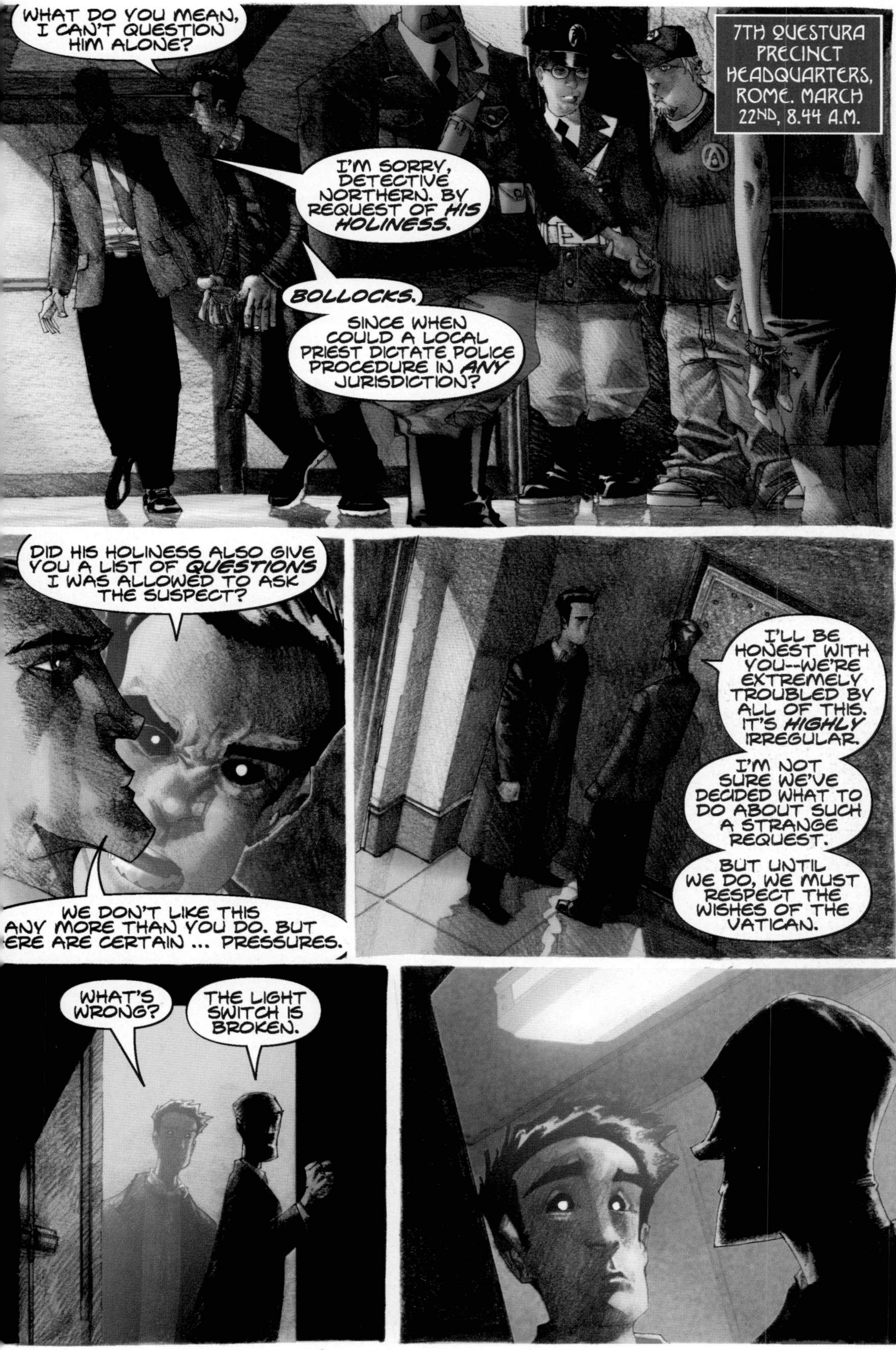
WHAT DO YOU MEAN, I CAN'T QUESTION HIM ALONE?
7TH QUESTURA PRECINCT HEADQUARTERS, ROME. MARCH 22ND, 8.44 A.M.
I'M SORRY, DETECTIVE NORTHERN. BY REQUEST OF HIS HOLINESS.
BOLLOCKS.
SINCE WHEN COULD A LOCAL PRIEST DICTATE POLICE PROCEDURE IN ANY JURISDICTION?
DID HIS HOLINESS ALSO GIVE YOU A LIST OF QUESTIONS I WAS ALLOWED TO ASK THE SUSPECT?
WE DON'T LIKE THIS ANY MORE THAN YOU DO. BUT
ERE ARE CERTAIN ... PRESSURES.
I'LL BE HONEST WITH YOU--WE'RE EXTREMELY TROUBLED BY ALL OF THIS. IT'S HIGHLY IRREGULAR.
I'M NOT SURE WE'VE DECIDED WHAT TO DO ABOUT SUCH A STRANGE REQUEST.
BUT UNTIL WE DO, WE MUST RESPECT THE WISHES OF THE VATICAN.
WHAT'S WRONG?
THE LIGHT SWITCH IS BROKEN.

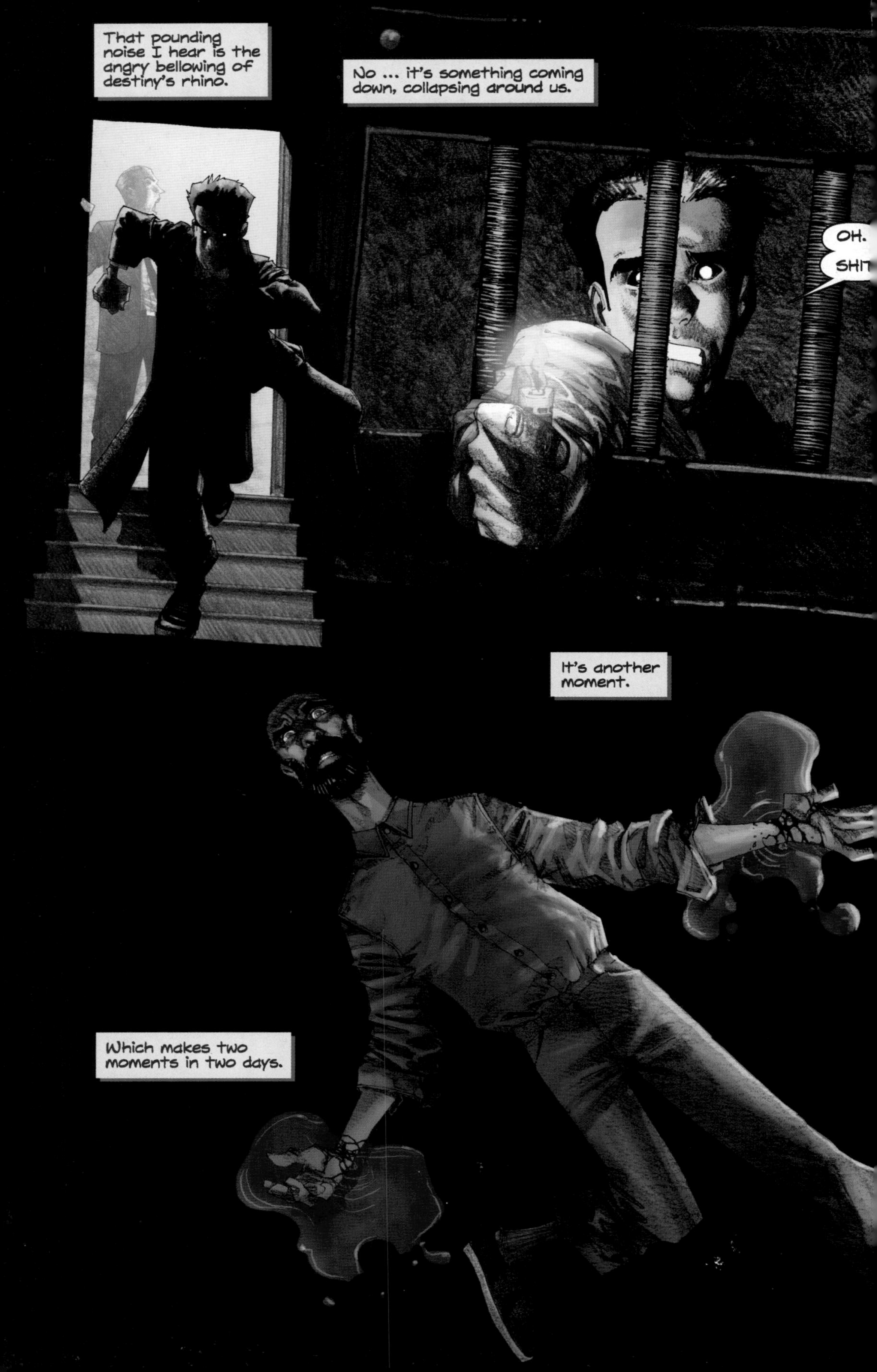

That pounding noise I hear is the angry bellowing of destiny's rhino.
No ... it's something coming down, collapsing around us.
OH.
SHIT
It's another moment.
Which makes two moments in two days.

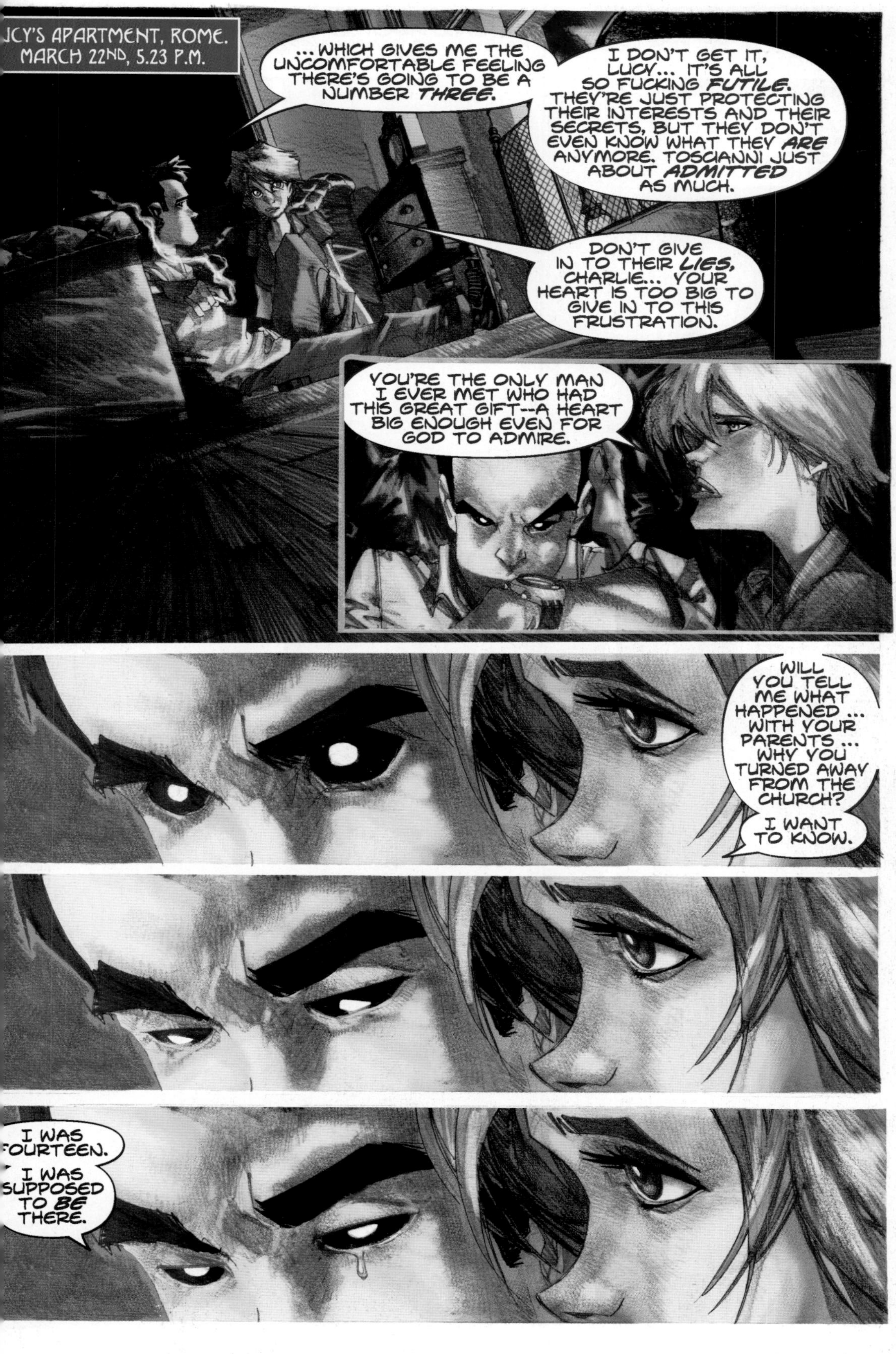
UCY'S APARTMENT, ROME. MARCH 22ND, 5.23 P.M.
...WHICH GIVES ME THE UNCOMFORTABLE FEELING THERE'S GOING TO BE A NUMBER *THREE*.
I DON'T GET IT, LUCY... IT'S ALL SO FUCKING *FUTILE*. THEY'RE JUST PROTECTING THEIR INTERESTS AND THEIR SECRETS, BUT THEY DON'T EVEN KNOW WHAT THEY *ARE* ANYMORE. TOSCIANNI JUST ABOUT *ADMITTED* AS MUCH.
DON'T GIVE IN TO THEIR *LIES*, CHARLIE... YOUR HEART IS TOO BIG TO GIVE IN TO THIS FRUSTRATION.
YOU'RE THE ONLY MAN I EVER MET WHO HAD THIS GREAT GIFT--A HEART BIG ENOUGH EVEN FOR GOD TO ADMIRE.
WILL YOU TELL ME WHAT HAPPENED ... WITH YOUR PARENTS ... WHY YOU TURNED AWAY FROM THE CHURCH?
I WANT TO KNOW.
I WAS FOURTEEN.
I WAS SUPPOSED TO *BE* THERE.

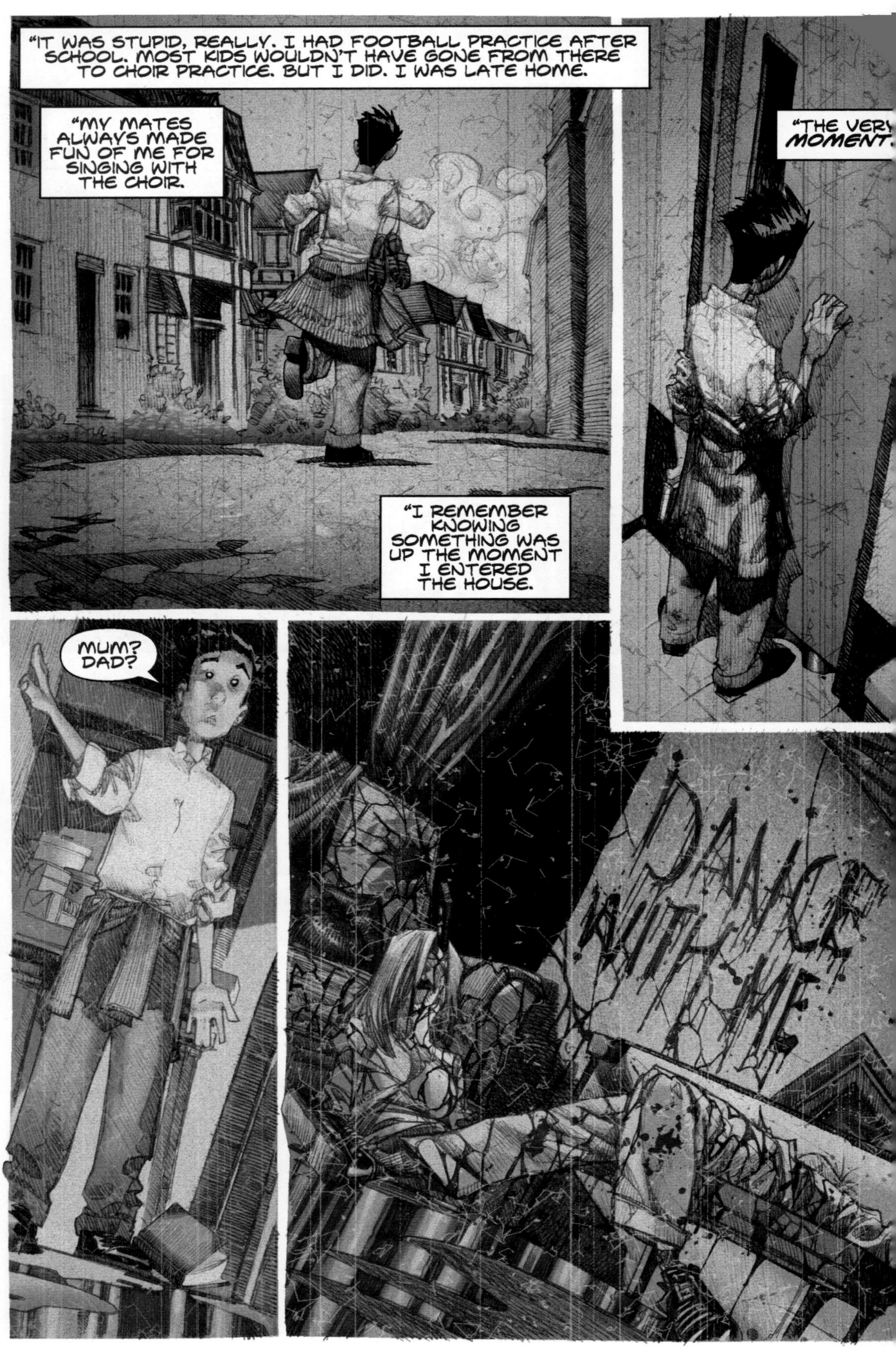

“IT WAS STUPID, REALLY. I HAD FOOTBALL PRACTICE AFTER SCHOOL. MOST KIDS WOULDN'T HAVE GONE FROM THERE TO CHOIR PRACTICE. BUT I DID. I WAS LATE HOME.
“MY MATES ALWAYS MADE FUN OF ME FOR SINGING WITH THE CHOIR.
“I REMEMBER KNOWING SOMETHING WAS UP THE MOMENT I ENTERED THE HOUSE.
“THE VER
MOMENT.
MUM? DAD?
DANCE WITH ME

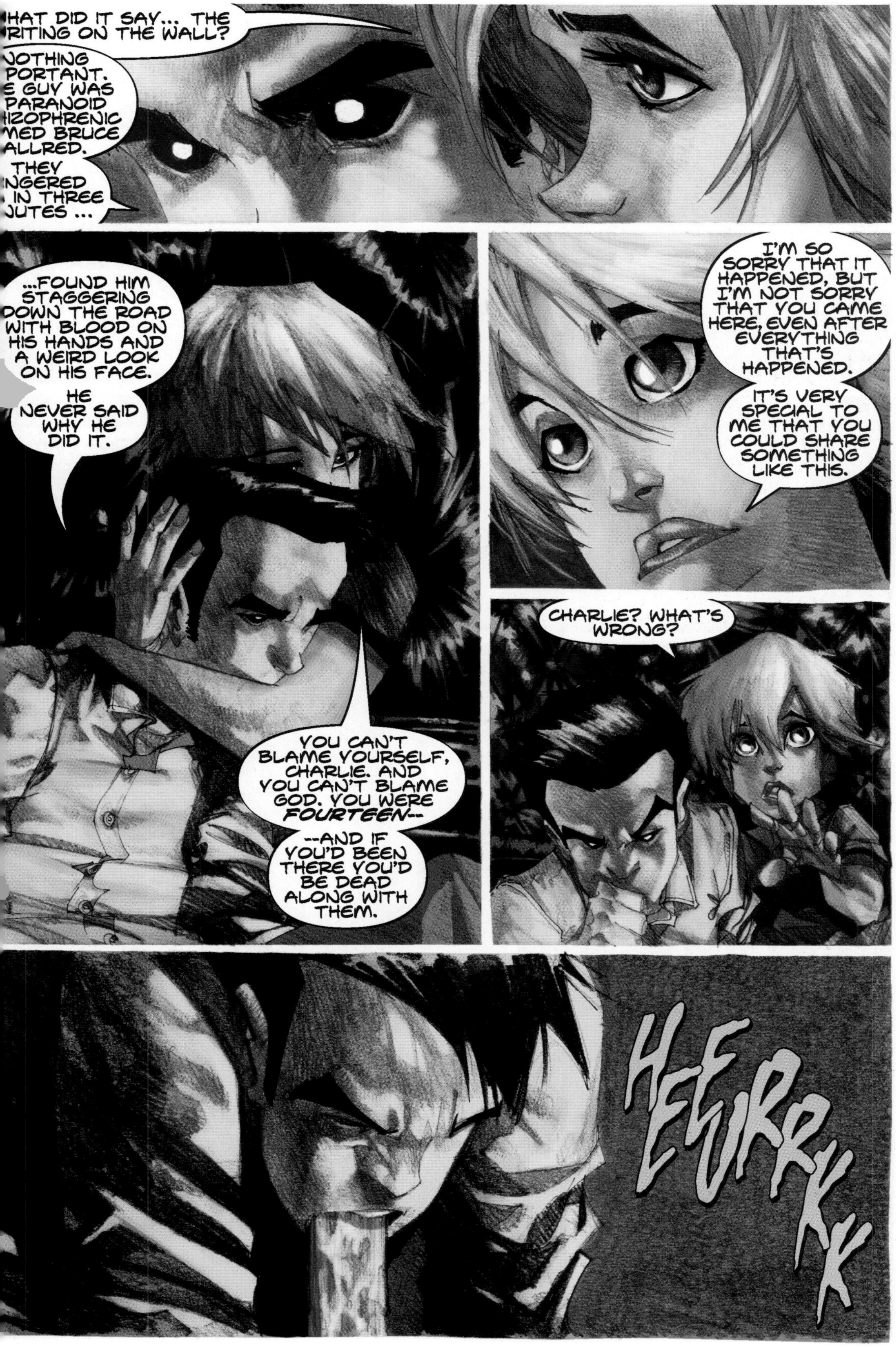
HAT DID IT SAY... THE RITING ON THE WALL?
NOTHING PORTANT. E GUY WAS PARANOID HIZOPHRENIC MED BRUCE ALLRED.
THEY NGERED IN THREE NUTES ...
...FOUND HIM STAGGERING DOWN THE ROAD WITH BLOOD ON HIS HANDS AND A WEIRD LOOK ON HIS FACE.
HE NEVER SAID WHY HE DID IT.
YOU CAN'T BLAME YOURSELF, CHARLIE. AND YOU CAN'T BLAME GOD. YOU WERE *FOURTEEN*--
--AND IF YOU'D BEEN THERE YOU'D BE DEAD ALONG WITH THEM.
I'M SO SORRY THAT IT HAPPENED, BUT I'M NOT SORRY THAT YOU CAME HERE, EVEN AFTER EVERYTHING THAT'S HAPPENED.
IT'S VERY SPECIAL TO ME THAT YOU COULD SHARE SOMETHING LIKE THIS.
CHARLIE? WHAT'S WRONG?
HEEURRKK

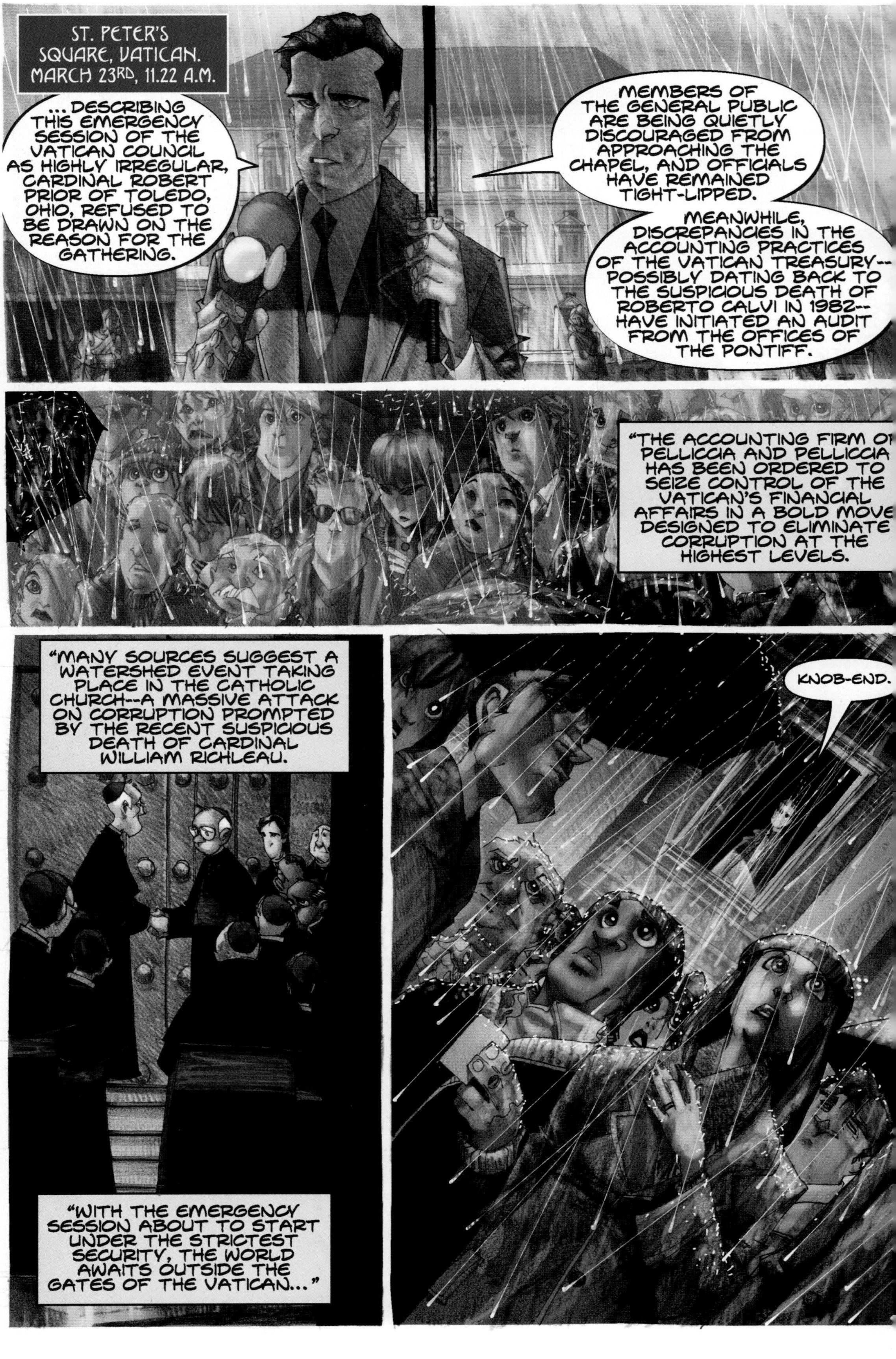
ST. PETER'S SQUARE, VATICAN. MARCH 23RD, 11.22 A.M.
...DESCRIBING THIS EMERGENCY SESSION OF THE VATICAN COUNCIL AS HIGHLY IRREGULAR, CARDINAL ROBERT PRIOR OF TOLEDO, OHIO, REFUSED TO BE DRAWN ON THE REASON FOR THE GATHERING.
MEMBERS OF THE GENERAL PUBLIC ARE BEING QUIETLY DISCOURAGED FROM APPROACHING THE CHAPEL, AND OFFICIALS HAVE REMAINED TIGHT-LIPPED.
MEANWHILE, DISCREPANCIES IN THE ACCOUNTING PRACTICES OF THE VATICAN TREASURY--POSSIBLY DATING BACK TO THE SUSPICIOUS DEATH OF ROBERTO CALVI IN 1982--HAVE INITIATED AN AUDIT FROM THE OFFICES OF THE PONTIFF.
"THE ACCOUNTING FIRM OF PELLICCIA AND PELLICCIA HAS BEEN ORDERED TO SEIZE CONTROL OF THE VATICAN'S FINANCIAL AFFAIRS IN A BOLD MOVE DESIGNED TO ELIMINATE CORRUPTION AT THE HIGHEST LEVELS.
"MANY SOURCES SUGGEST A WATERSHED EVENT TAKING PLACE IN THE CATHOLIC CHURCH--A MASSIVE ATTACK ON CORRUPTION PROMPTED BY THE RECENT SUSPICIOUS DEATH OF CARDINAL WILLIAM RICHLEAU.
"WITH THE EMERGENCY SESSION ABOUT TO START UNDER THE STRICTEST SECURITY, THE WORLD AWAITS OUTSIDE THE GATES OF THE VATICAN..."
KNOB-END.

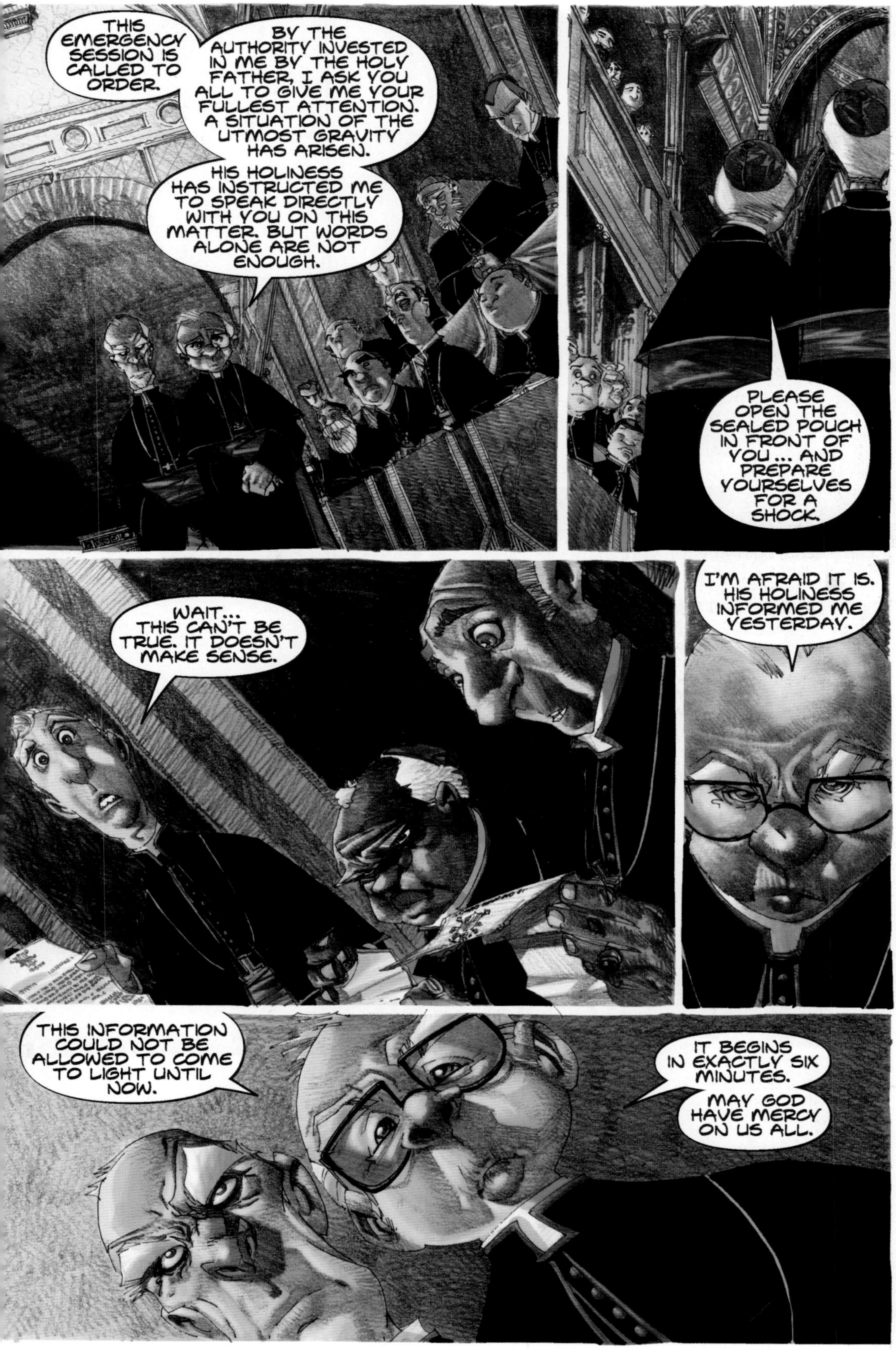
THIS EMERGENCY SESSION IS CALLED TO ORDER.
BY THE AUTHORITY INVESTED IN ME BY THE HOLY FATHER, I ASK YOU ALL TO GIVE ME YOUR FULLEST ATTENTION. A SITUATION OF THE UTMOST GRAVITY HAS ARISEN.
HIS HOLINESS HAS INSTRUCTED ME TO SPEAK DIRECTLY WITH YOU ON THIS MATTER. BUT WORDS ALONE ARE NOT ENOUGH.
PLEASE OPEN THE SEALED POUCH IN FRONT OF YOU ... AND PREPARE YOURSELVES FOR A SHOCK.
WAIT... THIS CAN'T BE TRUE. IT DOESN'T MAKE SENSE.
I'M AFRAID IT IS. HIS HOLINESS INFORMED ME YESTERDAY.
THIS INFORMATION COULD NOT BE ALLOWED TO COME TO LIGHT UNTIL NOW.
IT BEGINS IN EXACTLY SIX MINUTES.
MAY GOD HAVE MERCY ON US ALL.

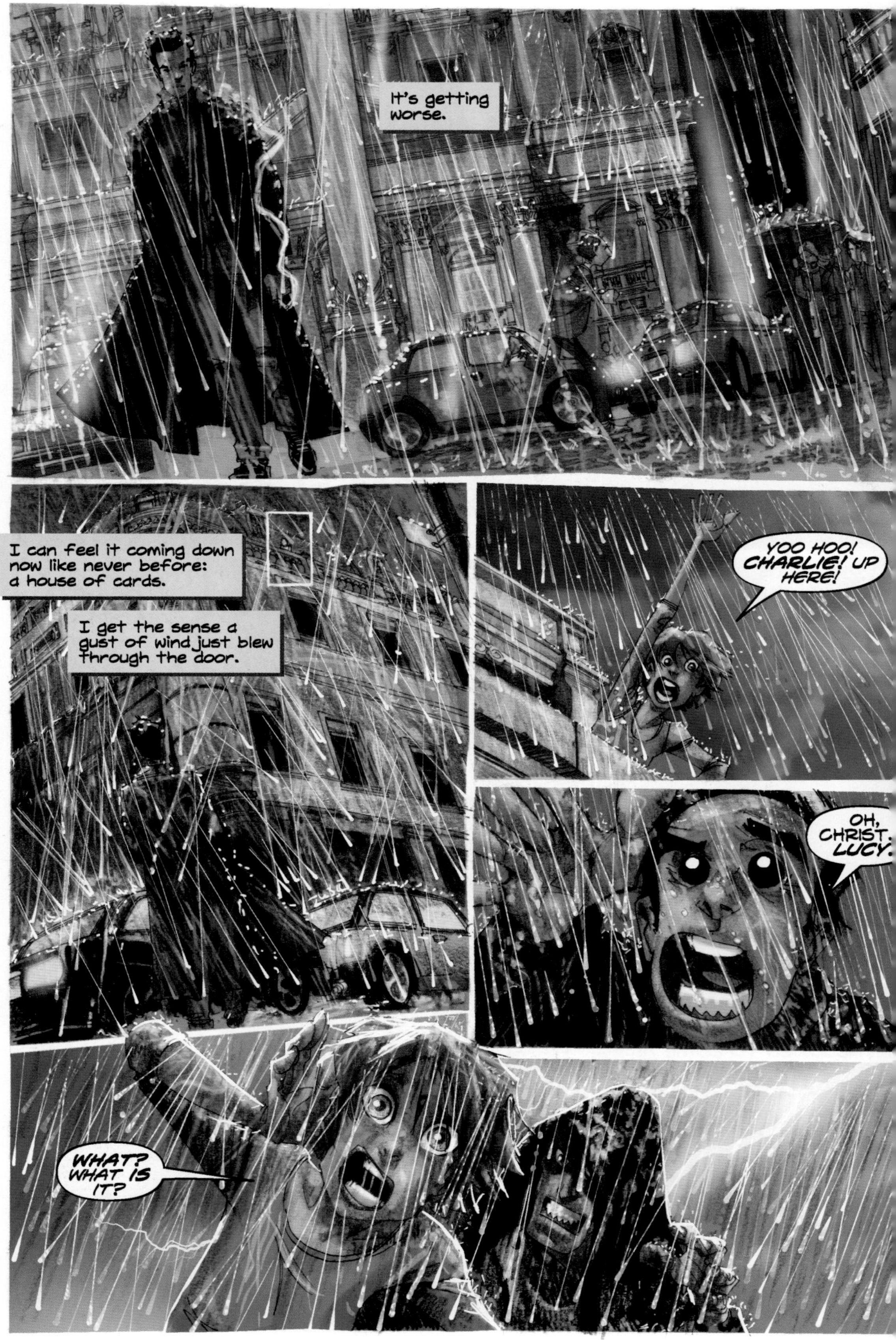
It's getting worse.
I can feel it coming down now like never before: a house of cards.
I get the sense a gust of wind just blew through the door.
YOO HOO! CHARLIE! UP HERE!
OH, CHRIST. LUCY.
WHAT? WHAT IS IT?

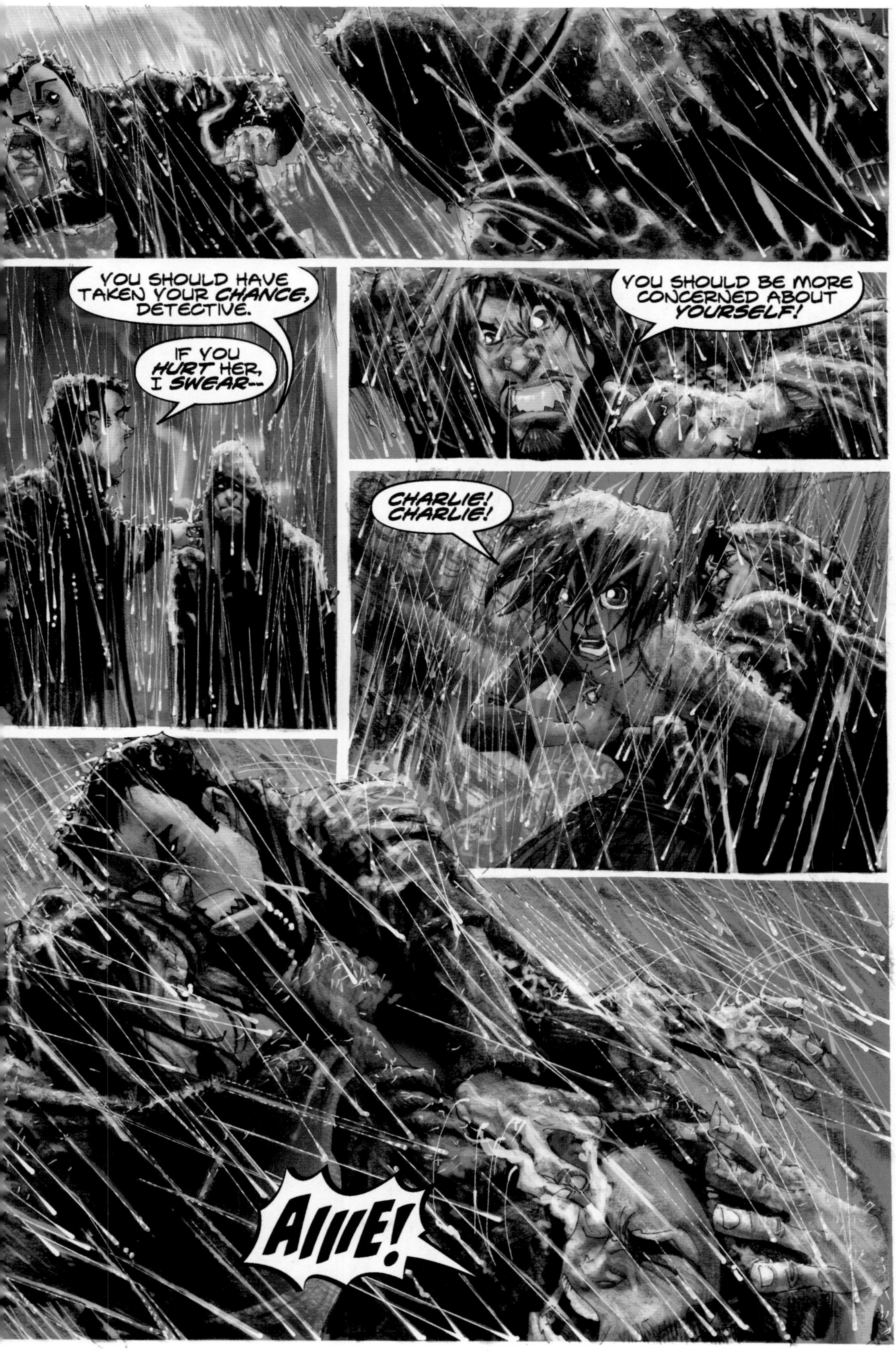
YOU SHOULD HAVE TAKEN YOUR *CHANCE,* DETECTIVE.
IF YOU *HURT* HER, I *SWEAR*--
YOU SHOULD BE MORE CONCERNED ABOUT *YOURSELF!*
CHARLIE! CHARLIE!
AIIIE!

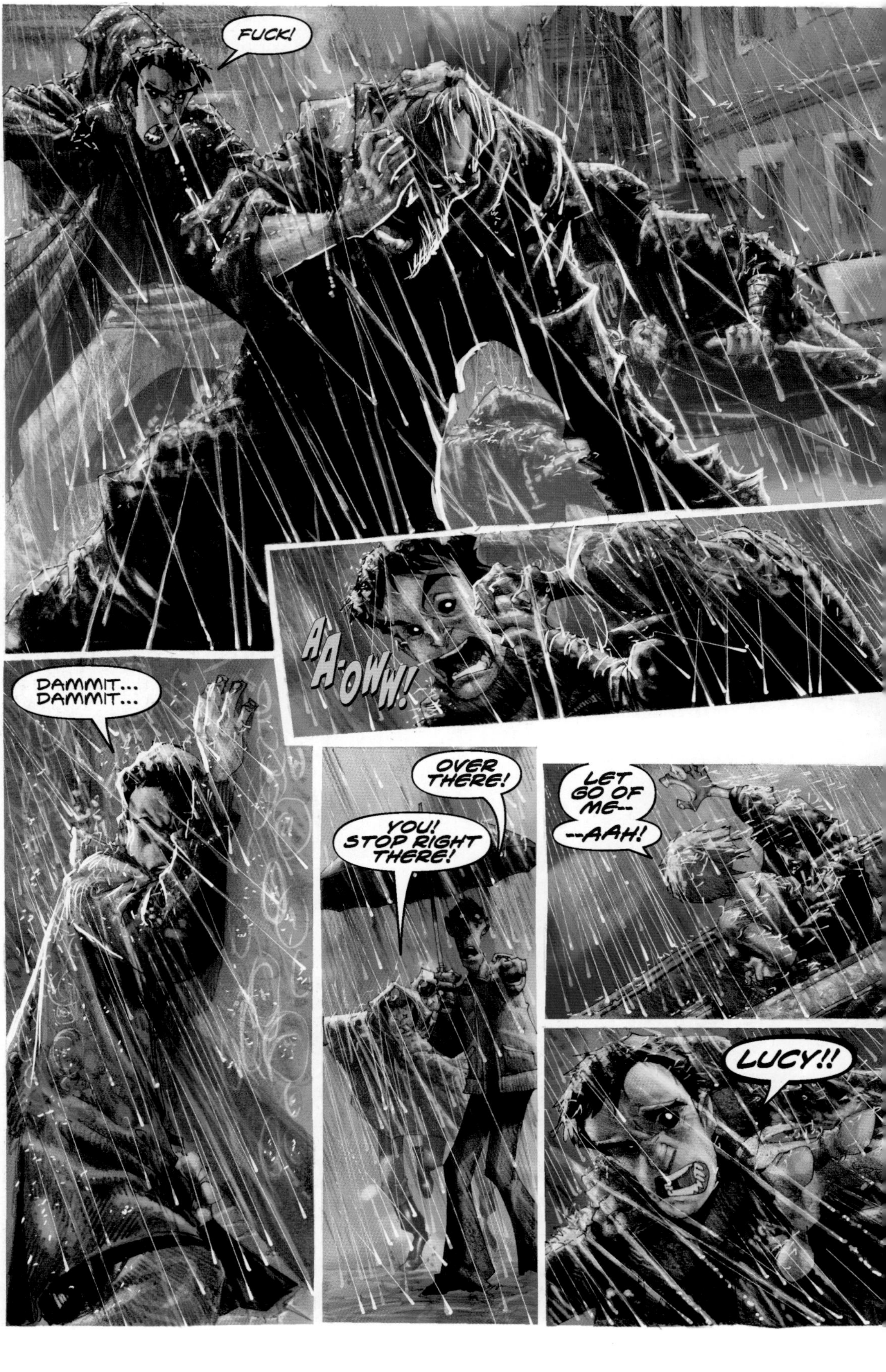
FUCK!
AA-OWW!
DAMMIT... DAMMIT...
OVER THERE!
YOU! STOP RIGHT THERE!
LET GO OF ME--
--AAH!
LUCY!!

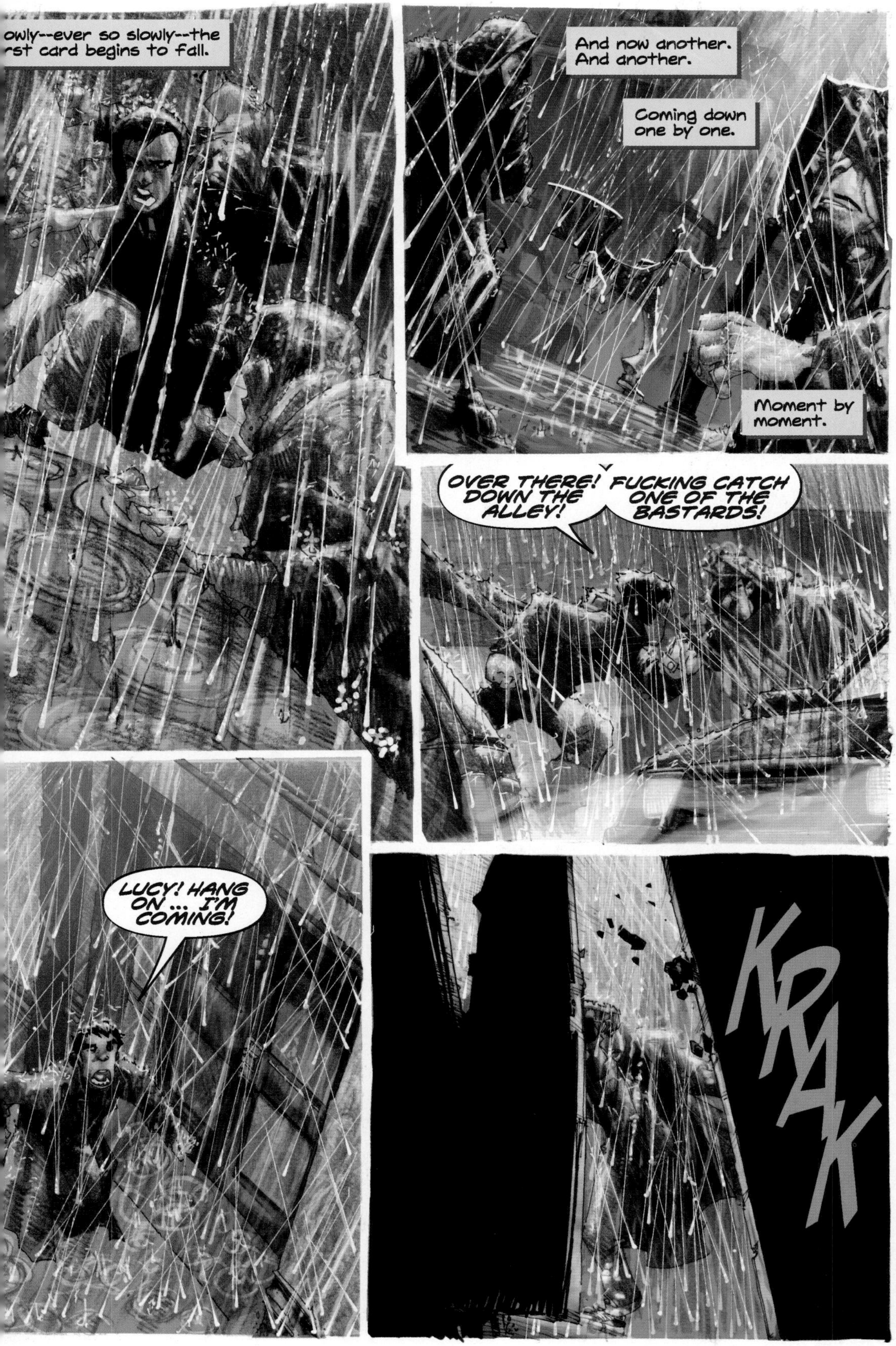
owly--ever so slowly--the
rst card begins to fall.
And now another.
And another.
Coming down
one by one.
Moment by
moment.
OVER THERE! DOWN THE ALLEY!
FUCKING CATCH ONE OF THE BASTARDS!
LUCY! HANG ON ... I'M COMING!
KRAK

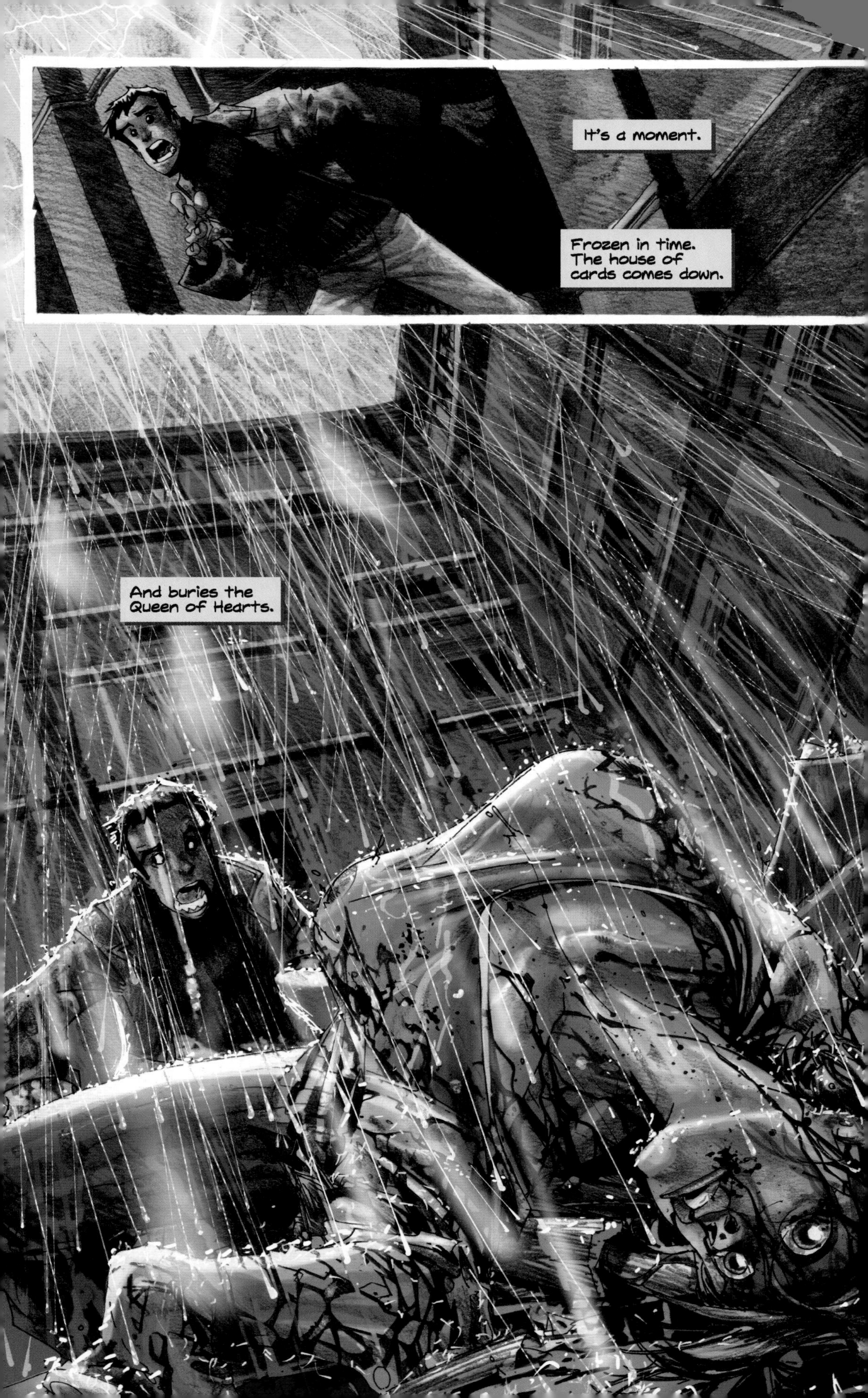
It's a moment.
Frozen in time. The house of cards comes down.
And buries the Queen of Hearts.

CHAPTER SIX

Dance with Me

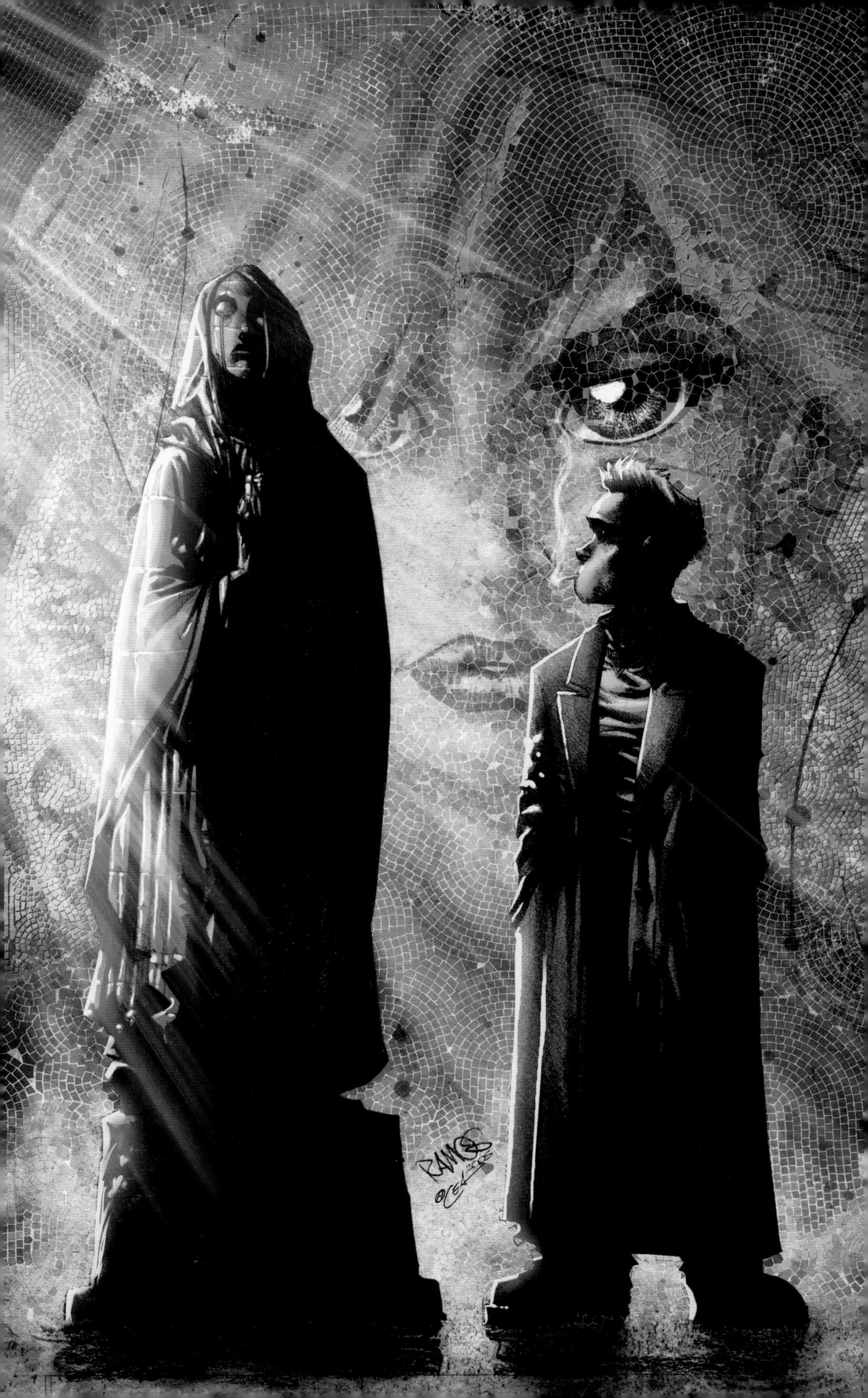

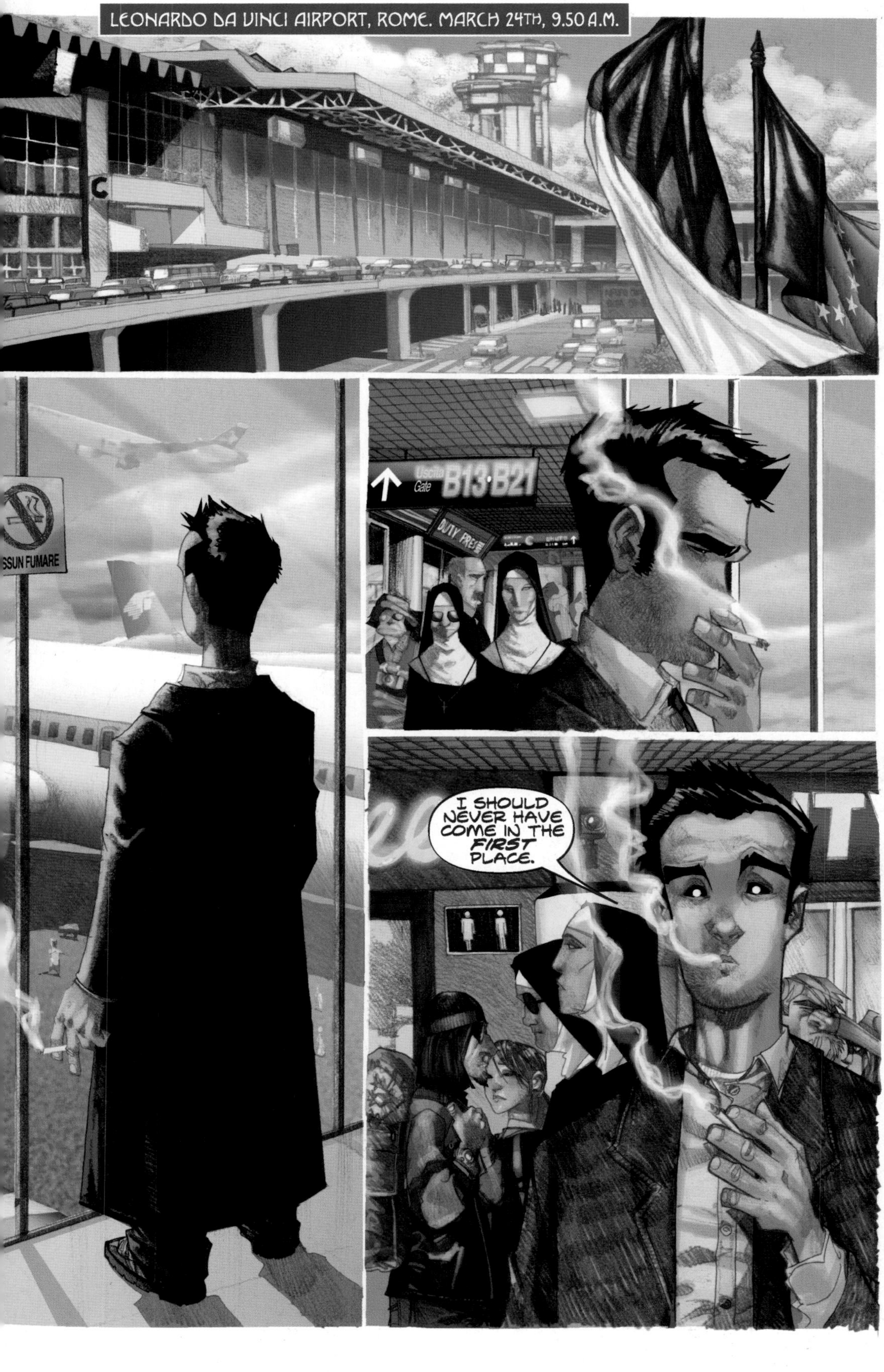
LEONARDO DA VINCI AIRPORT, ROME. MARCH 24TH, 9.50 A.M.
SSUN FUMARE
Uscita Gate B13·B21
DUTY FREE
I SHOULD NEVER HAVE COME IN THE FIRST PLACE.

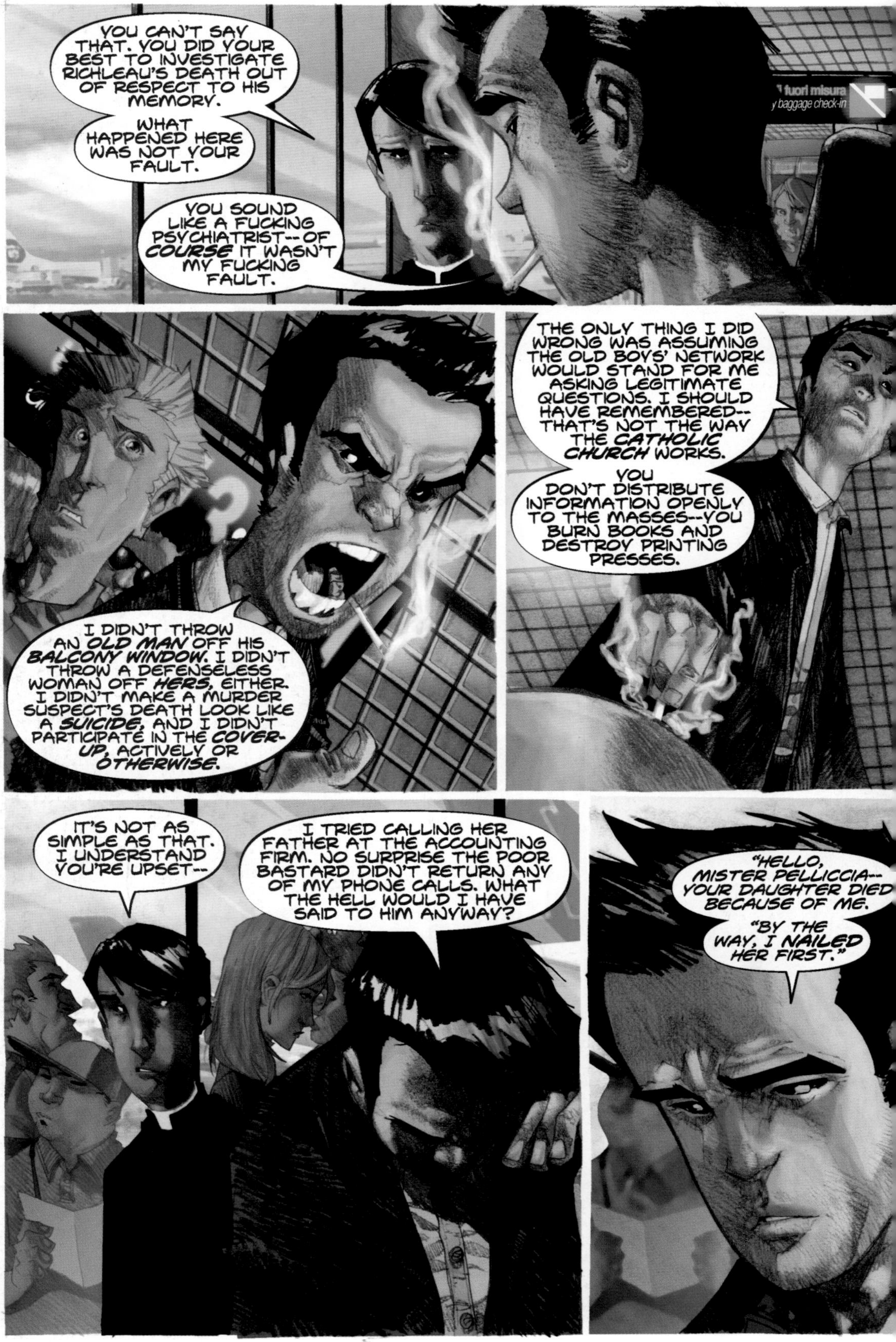
YOU CAN'T SAY THAT. YOU DID YOUR BEST TO INVESTIGATE RICHLEAU'S DEATH OUT OF RESPECT TO HIS MEMORY.
WHAT HAPPENED HERE WAS NOT YOUR FAULT.
YOU SOUND LIKE A FUCKING PSYCHIATRIST--OF *COURSE* IT WASN'T MY FUCKING FAULT.
fuori misura
baggage check-in
I DIDN'T THROW AN *OLD MAN* OFF HIS *BALCONY WINDOW*. I DIDN'T THROW A DEFENSELESS WOMAN OFF *HERS*, EITHER. I DIDN'T MAKE A MURDER SUSPECT'S DEATH LOOK LIKE A *SUICIDE*, AND I DIDN'T PARTICIPATE IN THE *COVER-UP*, ACTIVELY OR *OTHERWISE*.
THE ONLY THING I DID WRONG WAS ASSUMING THE OLD BOYS' NETWORK WOULD STAND FOR ME ASKING LEGITIMATE QUESTIONS. I SHOULD HAVE REMEMBERED--THAT'S NOT THE WAY THE *CATHOLIC CHURCH* WORKS.
YOU DON'T DISTRIBUTE INFORMATION OPENLY TO THE MASSES--YOU BURN BOOKS AND DESTROY PRINTING PRESSES.
IT'S NOT AS SIMPLE AS THAT. I UNDERSTAND YOU'RE UPSET--
I TRIED CALLING HER FATHER AT THE ACCOUNTING FIRM. NO SURPRISE THE POOR BASTARD DIDN'T RETURN ANY OF MY PHONE CALLS. WHAT THE HELL WOULD I HAVE SAID TO HIM ANYWAY?
"HELLO, MISTER PELLICCIA--YOUR DAUGHTER DIED BECAUSE OF ME.
"BY THE WAY, I *NAILED* HER FIRST."

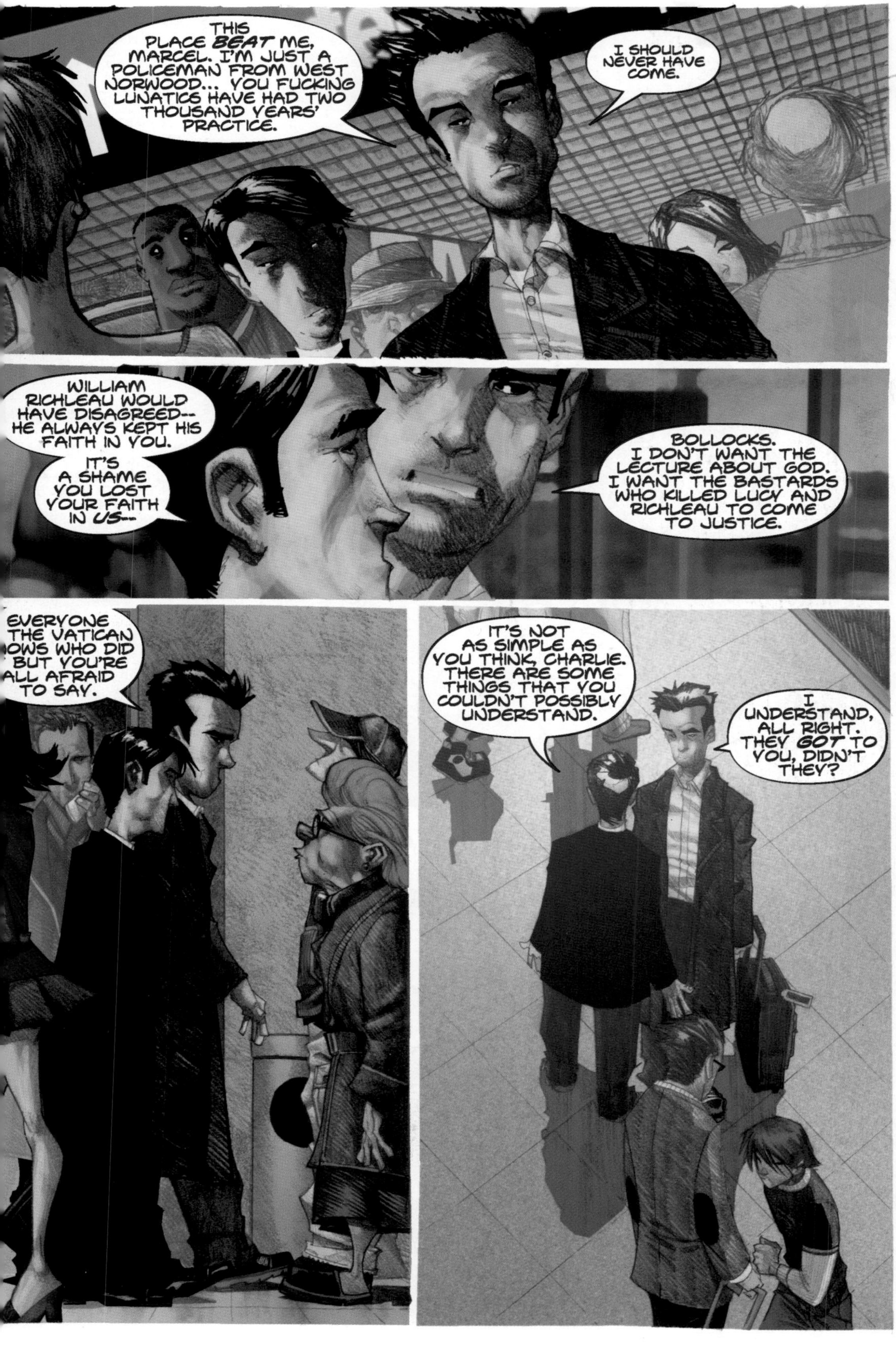
THIS PLACE BEAT ME, MARCEL. I'M JUST A POLICEMAN FROM WEST NORWOOD... YOU FUCKING LUNATICS HAVE HAD TWO THOUSAND YEARS' PRACTICE.
I SHOULD NEVER HAVE COME.
WILLIAM RICHLEAU WOULD HAVE DISAGREED-- HE ALWAYS KEPT HIS FAITH IN YOU.
IT'S A SHAME YOU LOST YOUR FAITH IN US--
BOLLOCKS. I DON'T WANT THE LECTURE ABOUT GOD. I WANT THE BASTARDS WHO KILLED LUCY AND RICHLEAU TO COME TO JUSTICE.
EVERYONE THE VATICAN OWS WHO DID BUT YOU'RE ALL AFRAID TO SAY.
IT'S NOT AS SIMPLE AS YOU THINK, CHARLIE. THERE ARE SOME THINGS THAT YOU COULDN'T POSSIBLY UNDERSTAND.
I UNDERSTAND, ALL RIGHT. THEY GOT TO YOU, DIDN'T THEY?

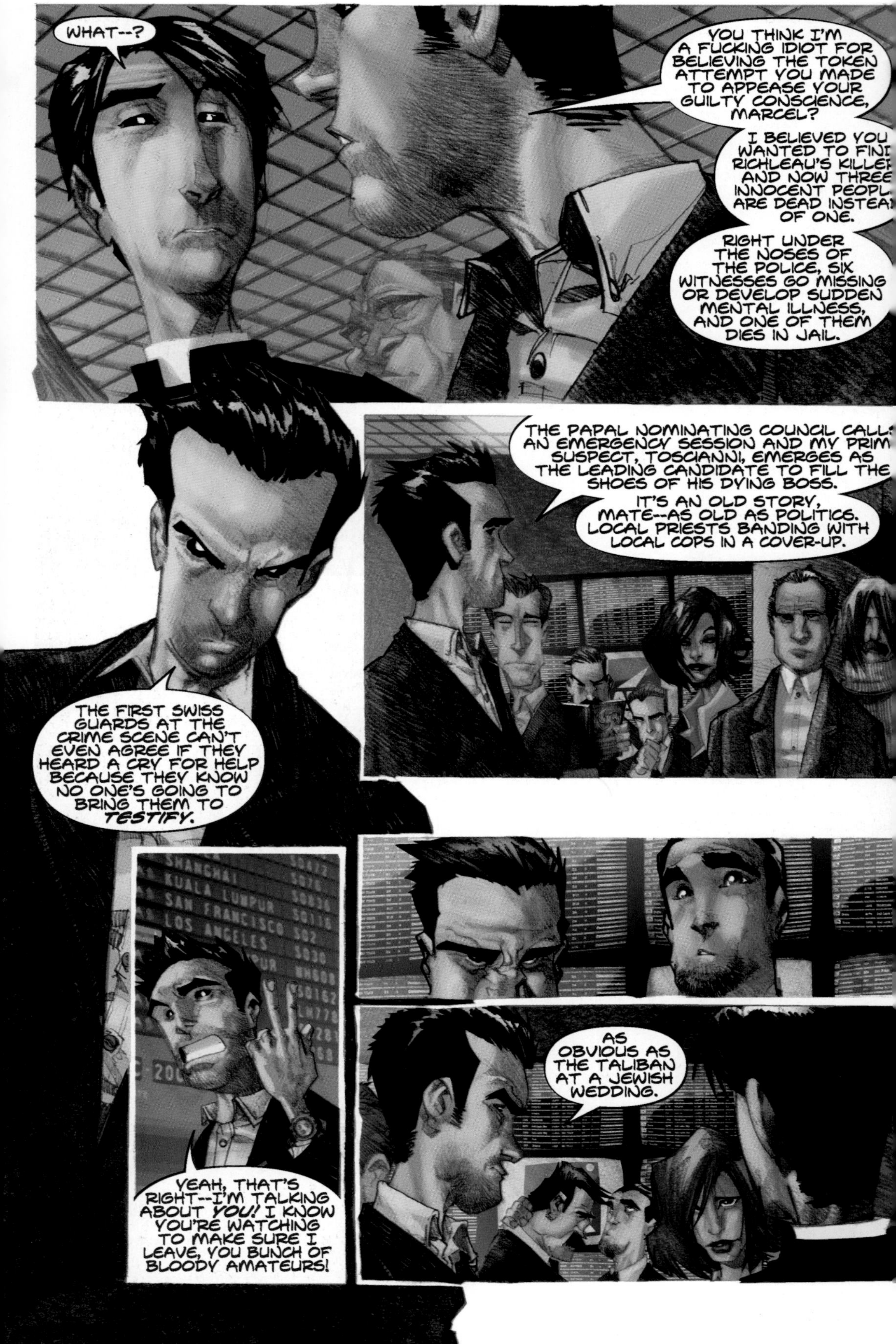
WHAT--?
YOU THINK I'M A FUCKING IDIOT FOR BELIEVING THE TOKEN ATTEMPT YOU MADE TO APPEASE YOUR GUILTY CONSCIENCE, MARCEL?
I BELIEVED YOU WANTED TO FIND RICHLEAU'S KILLER AND NOW THREE INNOCENT PEOPLE ARE DEAD INSTEAD OF ONE.
RIGHT UNDER THE NOSES OF THE POLICE, SIX WITNESSES GO MISSING OR DEVELOP SUDDEN MENTAL ILLNESS, AND ONE OF THEM DIES IN JAIL.
THE PAPAL NOMINATING COUNCIL CALLS AN EMERGENCY SESSION AND MY PRIME SUSPECT, TOSCIANNI, EMERGES AS THE LEADING CANDIDATE TO FILL THE SHOES OF HIS DYING BOSS.
IT'S AN OLD STORY, MATE--AS OLD AS POLITICS. LOCAL PRIESTS BANDING WITH LOCAL COPS IN A COVER-UP.
THE FIRST SWISS GUARDS AT THE CRIME SCENE CAN'T EVEN AGREE IF THEY HEARD A CRY FOR HELP BECAUSE THEY KNOW NO ONE'S GOING TO BRING THEM TO TESTIFY.
YEAH, THAT'S RIGHT--I'M TALKING ABOUT YOU! I KNOW YOU'RE WATCHING TO MAKE SURE I LEAVE, YOU BUNCH OF BLOODY AMATEURS!
AS OBVIOUS AS THE TALIBAN AT A JEWISH WEDDING.

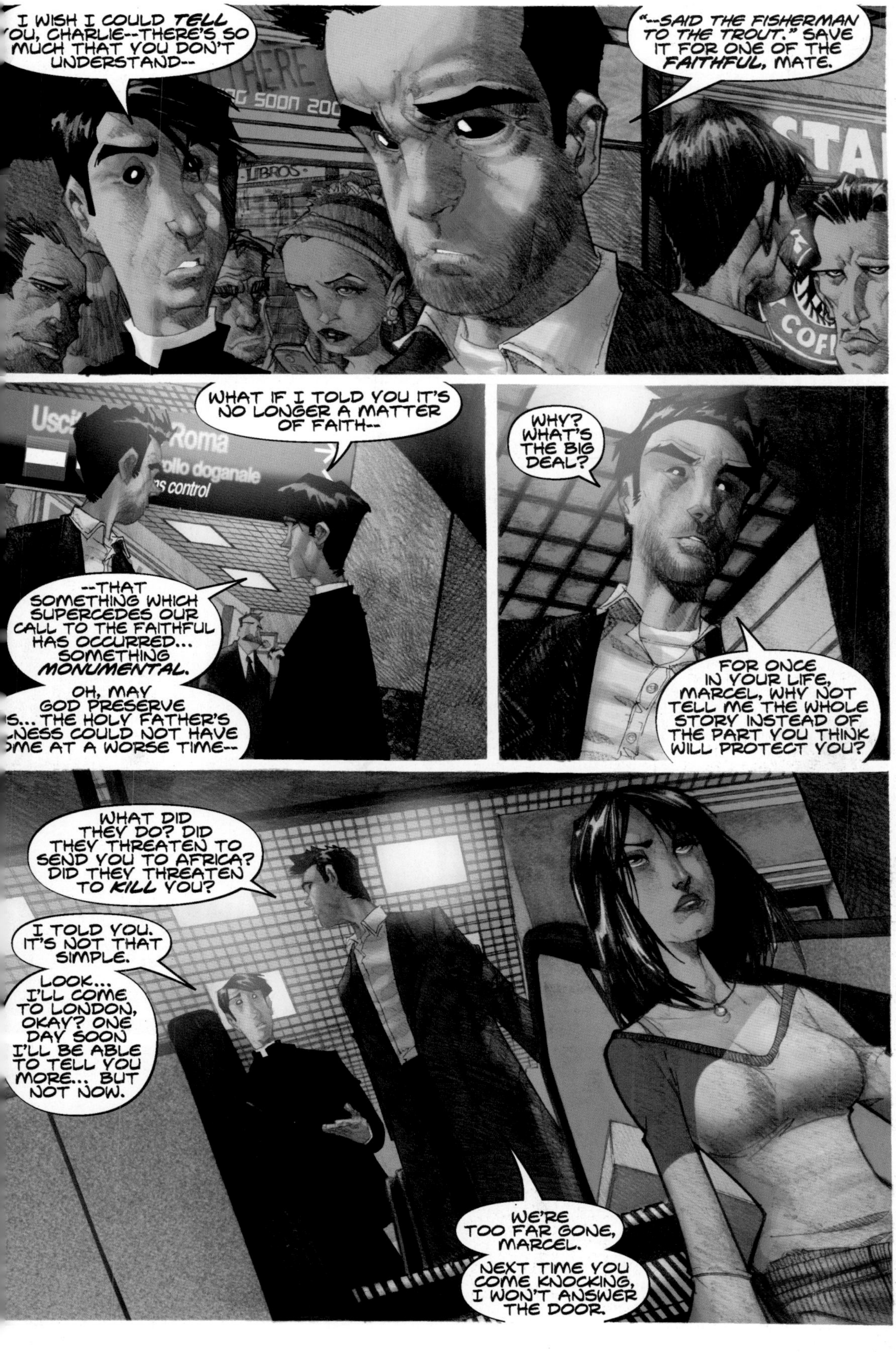
I WISH I COULD *TELL* YOU, CHARLIE--THERE'S SO MUCH THAT YOU DON'T UNDERSTAND--
"--SAID THE FISHERMAN TO THE TROUT." SAVE IT FOR ONE OF THE *FAITHFUL*, MATE.
WHAT IF I TOLD YOU IT'S NO LONGER A MATTER OF FAITH--
Roma
ollo doganale
s control
--THAT SOMETHING WHICH SUPERCEDES OUR CALL TO THE FAITHFUL HAS OCCURRED... SOMETHING *MONUMENTAL*.
OH, MAY GOD PRESERVE US... THE HOLY FATHER'S ILLNESS COULD NOT HAVE COME AT A WORSE TIME--
WHY? WHAT'S THE BIG DEAL?
FOR ONCE IN YOUR LIFE, MARCEL, WHY NOT TELL ME THE WHOLE STORY INSTEAD OF THE PART YOU THINK WILL PROTECT YOU?
WHAT DID THEY DO? DID THEY THREATEN TO SEND YOU TO AFRICA? DID THEY THREATEN TO *KILL* YOU?
I TOLD YOU. IT'S NOT THAT SIMPLE.
LOOK... I'LL COME TO LONDON, OKAY? ONE DAY SOON I'LL BE ABLE TO TELL YOU MORE... BUT NOT NOW.
WE'RE TOO FAR GONE, MARCEL.
NEXT TIME YOU COME KNOCKING, I WON'T ANSWER THE DOOR.

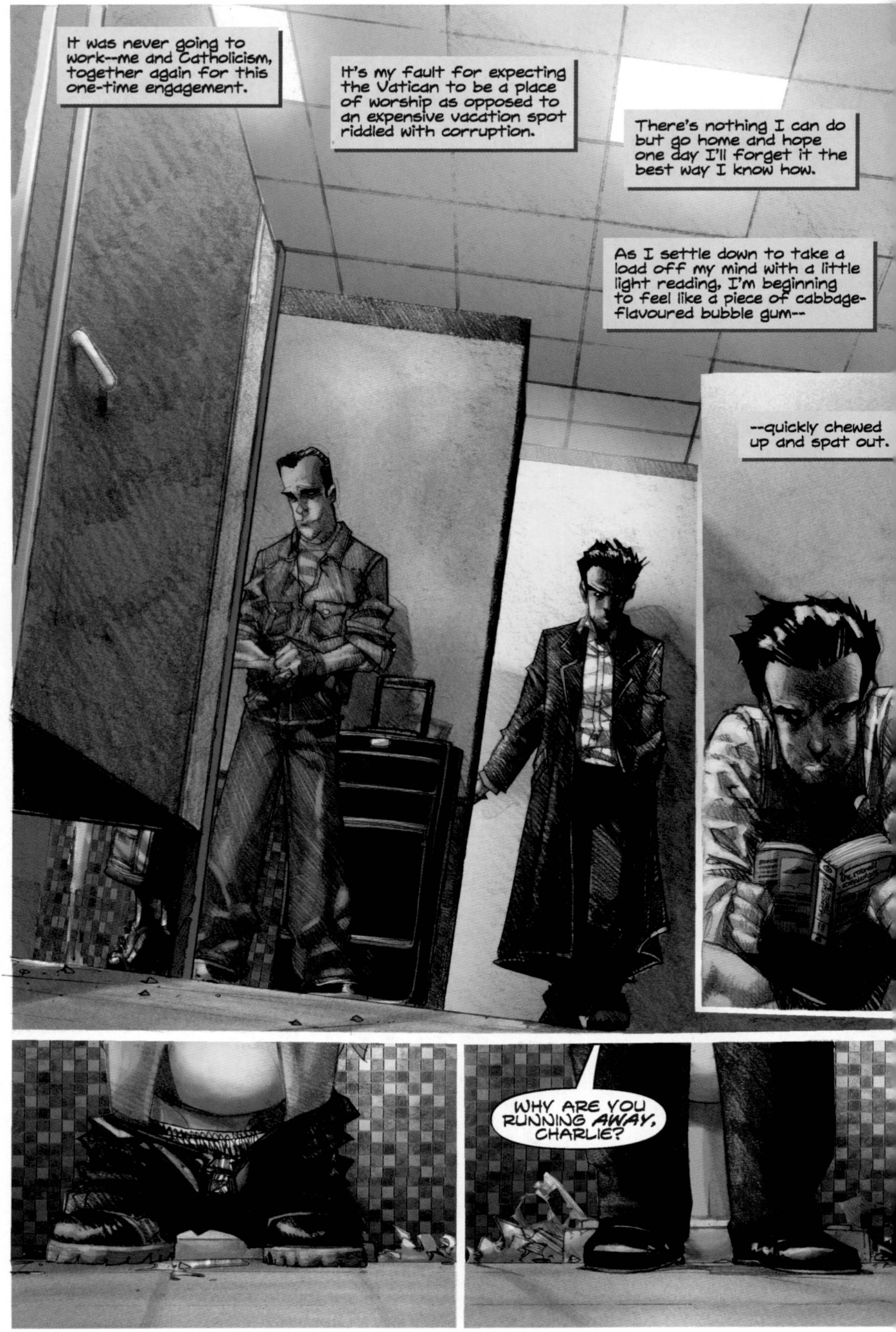
It was never going to work--me and Catholicism, together again for this one-time engagement.
It's my fault for expecting the Vatican to be a place of worship as opposed to an expensive vacation spot riddled with corruption.
There's nothing I can do but go home and hope one day I'll forget it the best way I know how.
As I settle down to take a load off my mind with a little light reading, I'm beginning to feel like a piece of cabbage-flavoured bubble gum--
--quickly chewed up and spat out.
WHY ARE YOU RUNNING AWAY, CHARLIE?

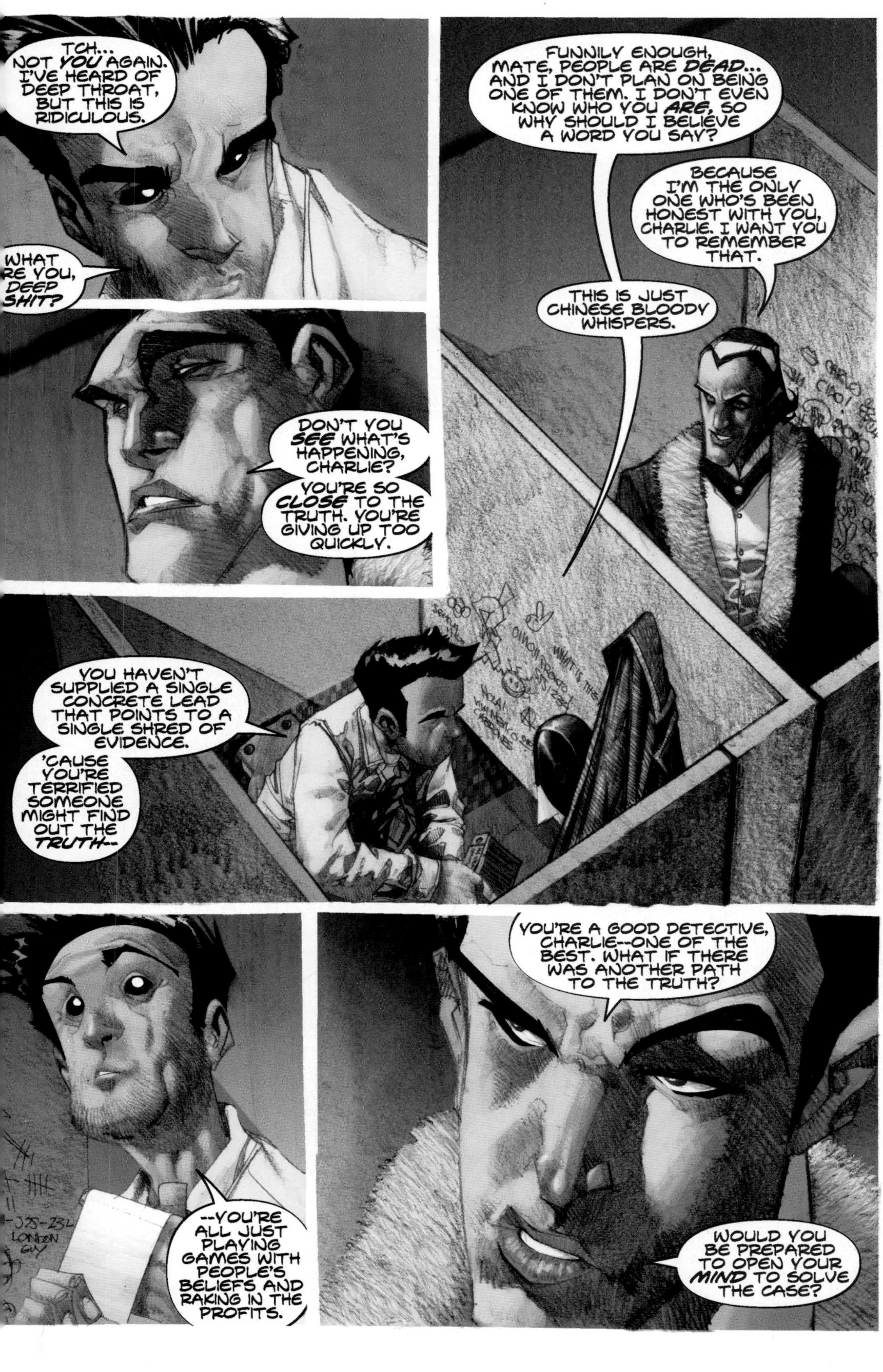
TCH... NOT *YOU* AGAIN. I'VE HEARD OF DEEP THROAT, BUT THIS IS RIDICULOUS.
WHAT ...RE YOU, DEEP *SHIT?*
DON'T YOU *SEE* WHAT'S HAPPENING, CHARLIE?
YOU'RE SO *CLOSE* TO THE TRUTH. YOU'RE GIVING UP TOO QUICKLY.
FUNNILY ENOUGH, MATE, PEOPLE ARE *DEAD*... AND I DON'T PLAN ON BEING ONE OF THEM. I DON'T EVEN KNOW WHO YOU *ARE*, SO WHY SHOULD I BELIEVE A WORD YOU SAY?
BECAUSE I'M THE ONLY ONE WHO'S BEEN HONEST WITH YOU, CHARLIE. I WANT YOU TO REMEMBER THAT.
THIS IS JUST CHINESE BLOODY WHISPERS.
YOU HAVEN'T SUPPLIED A SINGLE CONCRETE LEAD THAT POINTS TO A SINGLE SHRED OF EVIDENCE.
'CAUSE YOU'RE TERRIFIED SOMEONE MIGHT FIND OUT THE *TRUTH*--
--YOU'RE ALL JUST PLAYING GAMES WITH PEOPLE'S BELIEFS AND RAKING IN THE PROFITS.
YOU'RE A GOOD DETECTIVE, CHARLIE--ONE OF THE BEST. WHAT IF THERE WAS ANOTHER PATH TO THE TRUTH?
WOULD YOU BE PREPARED TO OPEN YOUR *MIND* TO SOLVE THE CASE?

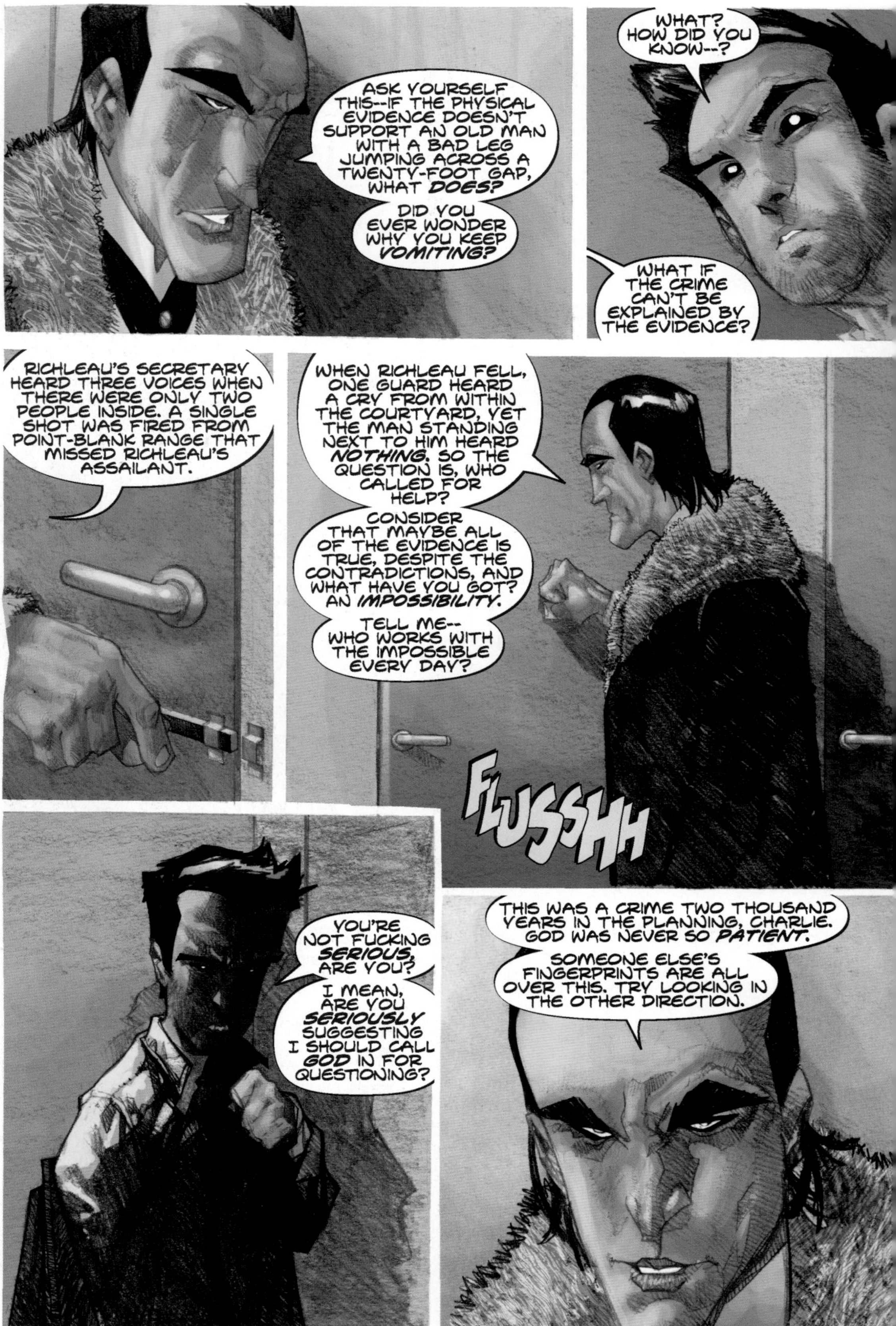
ASK YOURSELF THIS--IF THE PHYSICAL EVIDENCE DOESN'T SUPPORT AN OLD MAN WITH A BAD LEG JUMPING ACROSS A TWENTY-FOOT GAP, WHAT *DOES*?
DID YOU EVER WONDER WHY YOU KEEP *VOMITING*?
WHAT? HOW DID YOU KNOW--?
WHAT IF THE CRIME CAN'T BE EXPLAINED BY THE EVIDENCE?
RICHLEAU'S SECRETARY HEARD THREE VOICES WHEN THERE WERE ONLY TWO PEOPLE INSIDE. A SINGLE SHOT WAS FIRED FROM POINT-BLANK RANGE THAT MISSED RICHLEAU'S ASSAILANT.
WHEN RICHLEAU FELL, ONE GUARD HEARD A CRY FROM WITHIN THE COURTYARD, YET THE MAN STANDING NEXT TO HIM HEARD *NOTHING*. SO THE QUESTION IS, WHO CALLED FOR HELP?
CONSIDER THAT MAYBE ALL OF THE EVIDENCE IS TRUE, DESPITE THE CONTRADICTIONS, AND WHAT HAVE YOU GOT? AN *IMPOSSIBILITY*.
TELL ME-- WHO WORKS WITH THE IMPOSSIBLE EVERY DAY?
FLUSSHH
YOU'RE NOT FUCKING *SERIOUS*, ARE YOU?
I MEAN, ARE YOU *SERIOUSLY* SUGGESTING I SHOULD CALL *GOD* IN FOR QUESTIONING?
THIS WAS A CRIME TWO THOUSAND YEARS IN THE PLANNING, CHARLIE. GOD WAS NEVER SO *PATIENT*.
SOMEONE ELSE'S FINGERPRINTS ARE ALL OVER THIS. TRY LOOKING IN THE OTHER DIRECTION.

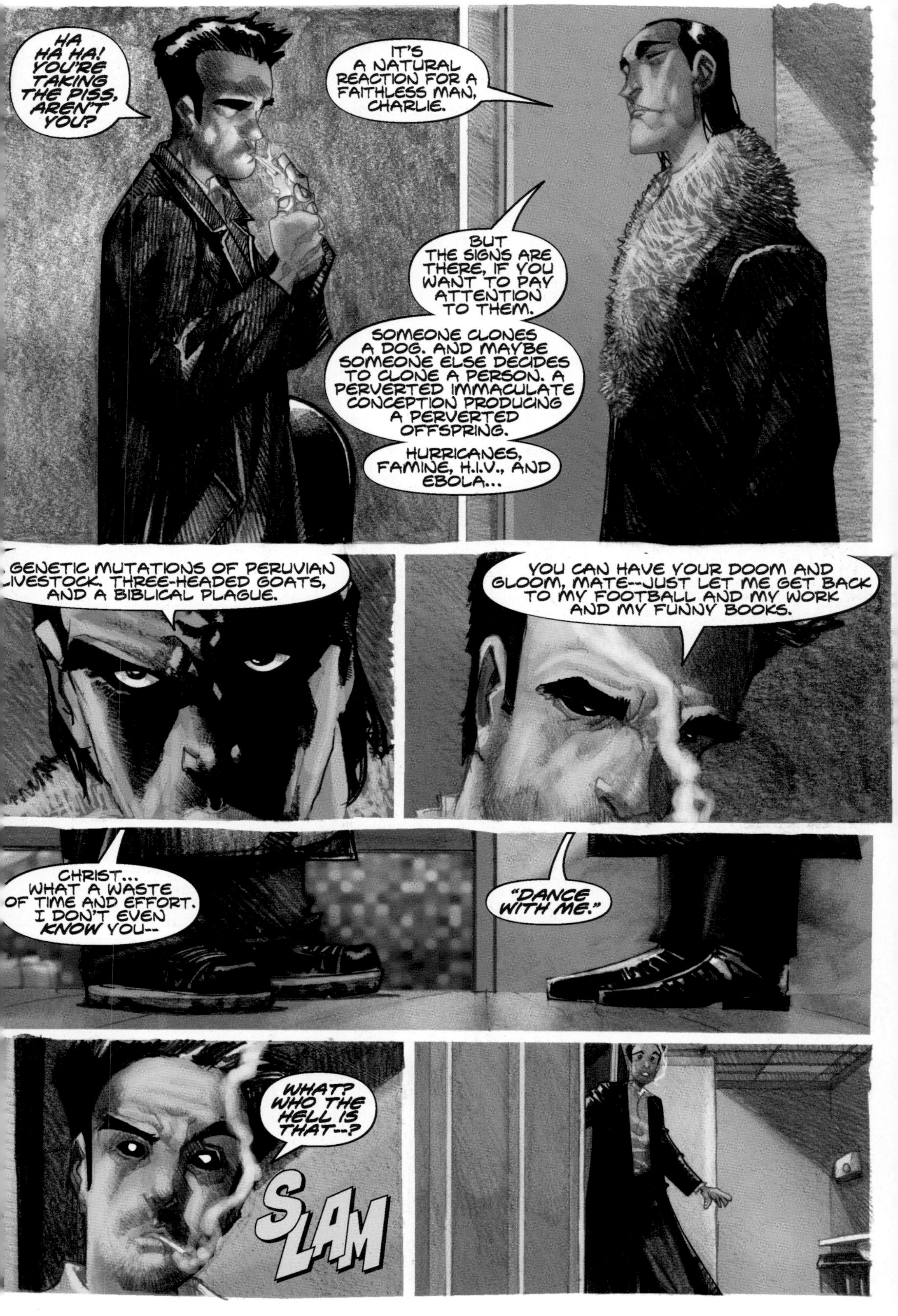
HA HA HA! YOU'RE TAKING THE PISS, AREN'T YOU?
IT'S A NATURAL REACTION FOR A FAITHLESS MAN, CHARLIE.
BUT THE SIGNS ARE THERE, IF YOU WANT TO PAY ATTENTION TO THEM.
SOMEONE CLONES A DOG. AND MAYBE SOMEONE ELSE DECIDES TO CLONE A PERSON. A PERVERTED IMMACULATE CONCEPTION PRODUCING A PERVERTED OFFSPRING.
HURRICANES, FAMINE, H.I.V., AND EBOLA...
GENETIC MUTATIONS OF PERUVIAN LIVESTOCK. THREE-HEADED GOATS, AND A BIBLICAL PLAGUE.
YOU CAN HAVE YOUR DOOM AND GLOOM, MATE--JUST LET ME GET BACK TO MY FOOTBALL AND MY WORK AND MY FUNNY BOOKS.
CHRIST... WHAT A WASTE OF TIME AND EFFORT. I DON'T EVEN KNOW YOU--
"DANCE WITH ME."
WHAT? WHO THE HELL IS THAT--?
SLAM

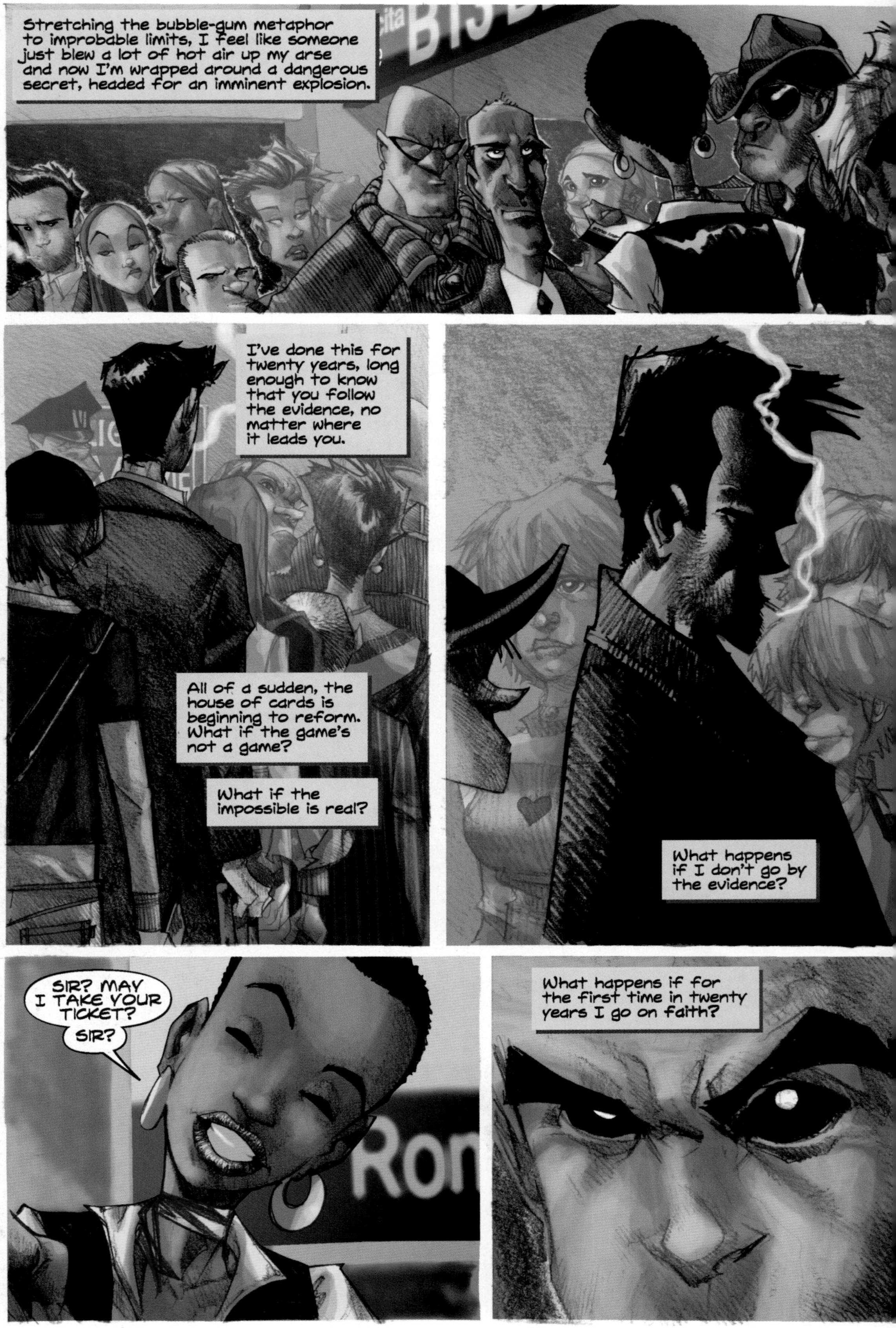

Stretching the bubble-gum metaphor to improbable limits, I feel like someone just blew a lot of hot air up my arse and now I'm wrapped around a dangerous secret, headed for an imminent explosion.
I've done this for twenty years, long enough to know that you follow the evidence, no matter where it leads you.
All of a sudden, the house of cards is beginning to reform. What if the game's not a game?
What if the impossible is real?
What happens if I don't go by the evidence?
SIR? MAY I TAKE YOUR TICKET? SIR?
What happens if for the first time in twenty years I go on faith?

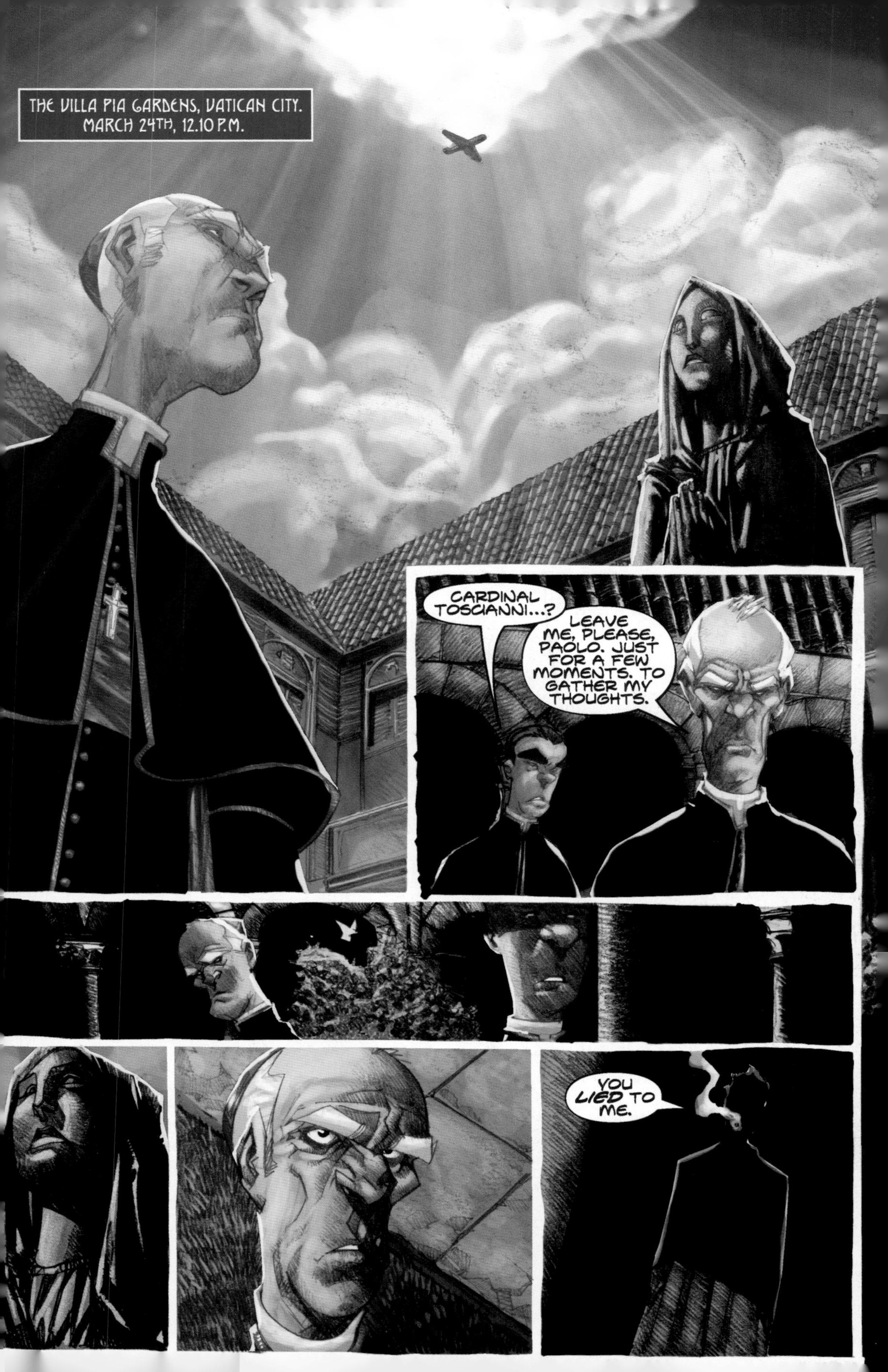
THE VILLA PIA GARDENS, VATICAN CITY. MARCH 24TH, 12.10 P.M.
CARDINAL TOSCIANNI...?
LEAVE ME, PLEASE, PAOLO. JUST FOR A FEW MOMENTS. TO GATHER MY THOUGHTS.
YOU *LIED* TO ME.

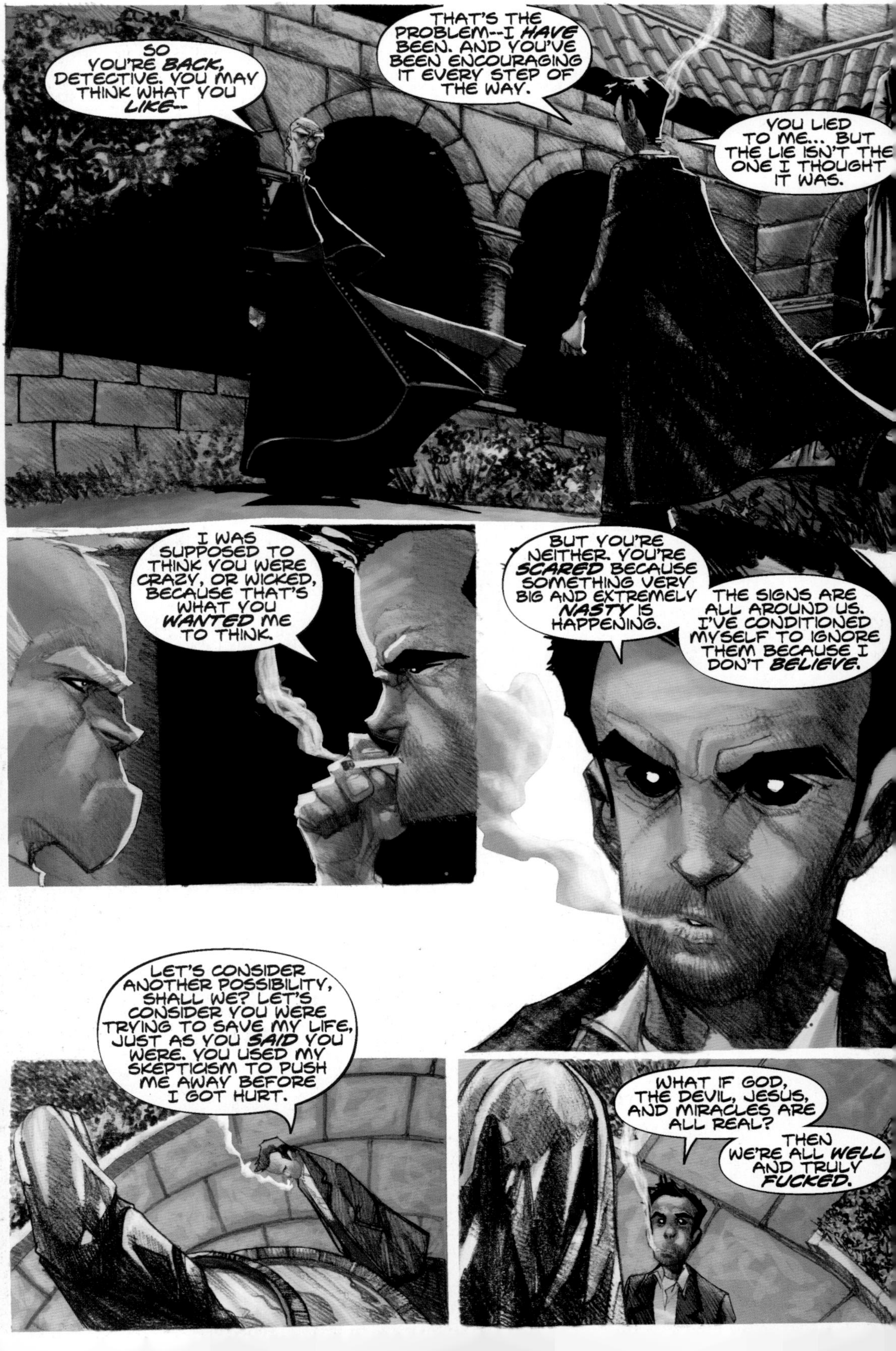
SO YOU'RE BACK, DETECTIVE. YOU MAY THINK WHAT YOU LIKE--
THAT'S THE PROBLEM--I HAVE BEEN. AND YOU'VE BEEN ENCOURAGING IT EVERY STEP OF THE WAY.
YOU LIED TO ME... BUT THE LIE ISN'T THE ONE I THOUGHT IT WAS.
I WAS SUPPOSED TO THINK YOU WERE CRAZY, OR WICKED, BECAUSE THAT'S WHAT YOU WANTED ME TO THINK.
BUT YOU'RE NEITHER. YOU'RE SCARED BECAUSE SOMETHING VERY BIG AND EXTREMELY NASTY IS HAPPENING.
THE SIGNS ARE ALL AROUND US. I'VE CONDITIONED MYSELF TO IGNORE THEM BECAUSE I DON'T BELIEVE.
LET'S CONSIDER ANOTHER POSSIBILITY, SHALL WE? LET'S CONSIDER YOU WERE TRYING TO SAVE MY LIFE, JUST AS YOU SAID YOU WERE. YOU USED MY SKEPTICISM TO PUSH ME AWAY BEFORE I GOT HURT.
WHAT IF GOD, THE DEVIL, JESUS, AND MIRACLES ARE ALL REAL?
THEN WE'RE ALL WELL AND TRULY FUCKED.

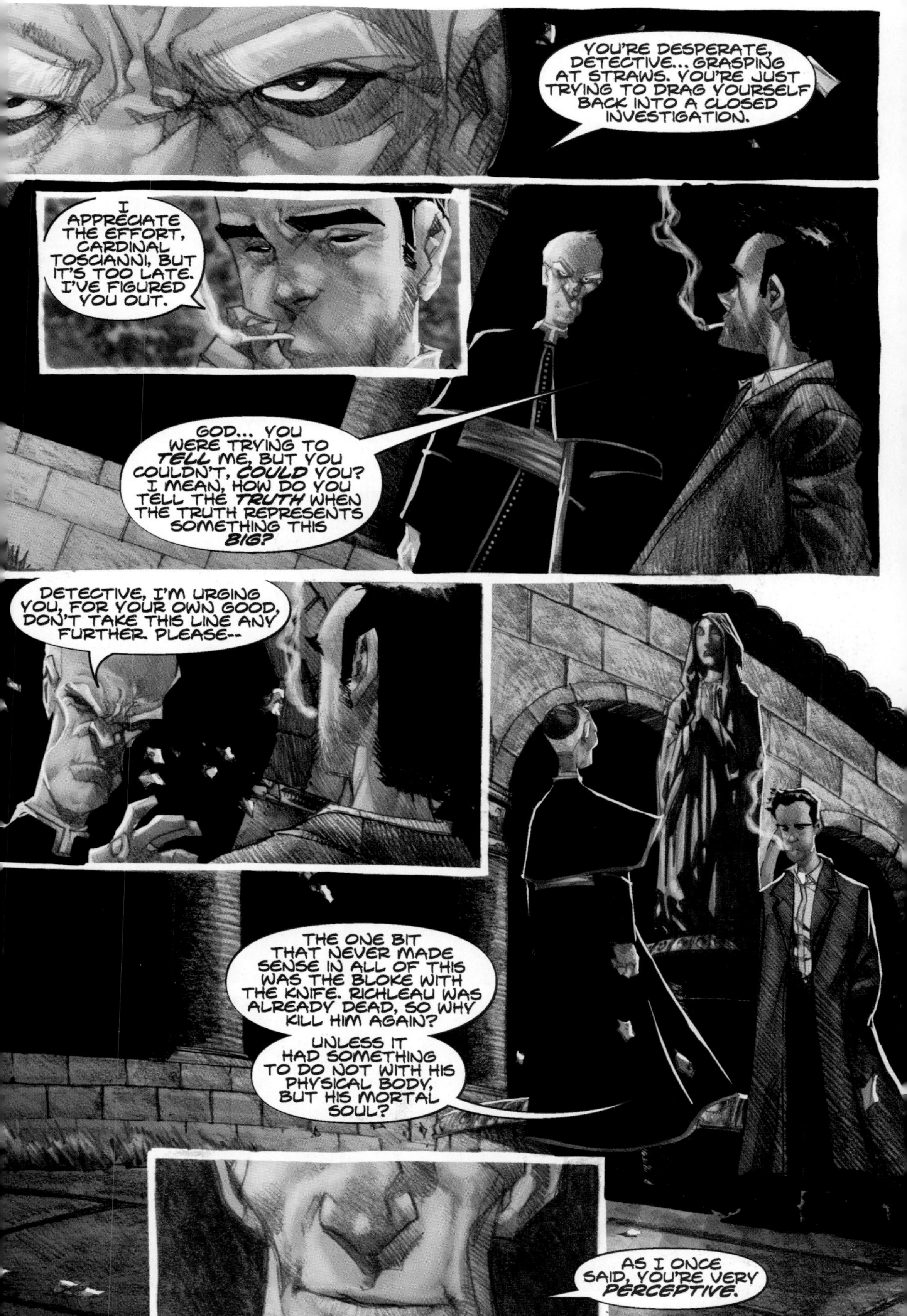
YOU'RE DESPERATE, DETECTIVE... GRASPING AT STRAWS. YOU'RE JUST TRYING TO DRAG YOURSELF BACK INTO A CLOSED INVESTIGATION.
I APPRECIATE THE EFFORT, CARDINAL TOSCIANNI, BUT IT'S TOO LATE. I'VE FIGURED YOU OUT.
GOD... YOU WERE TRYING TO *TELL* ME, BUT YOU COULDN'T, *COULD* YOU? I MEAN, HOW DO YOU TELL THE *TRUTH* WHEN THE TRUTH REPRESENTS SOMETHING THIS *BIG?*
DETECTIVE, I'M URGING YOU, FOR YOUR OWN GOOD, DON'T TAKE THIS LINE ANY FURTHER. PLEASE--
THE ONE BIT THAT NEVER MADE SENSE IN ALL OF THIS WAS THE BLOKE WITH THE KNIFE. RICHLEAU WAS ALREADY DEAD, SO WHY KILL HIM AGAIN?
UNLESS IT HAD SOMETHING TO DO NOT WITH HIS PHYSICAL BODY, BUT HIS MORTAL SOUL?
AS I ONCE SAID, YOU'RE VERY *PERCEPTIVE.*

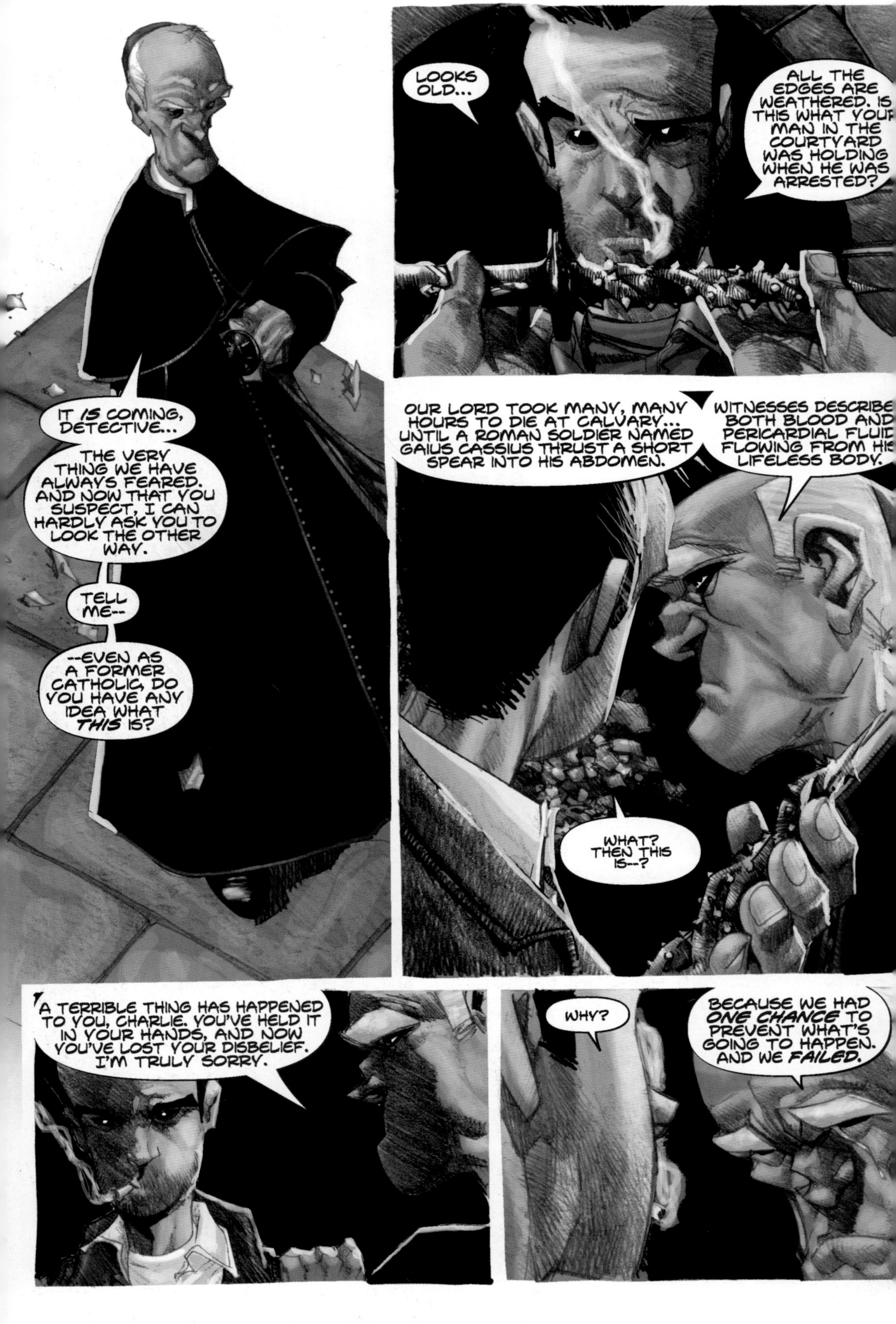
IT *IS* COMING, DETECTIVE...
THE VERY THING WE HAVE ALWAYS FEARED. AND NOW THAT YOU SUSPECT, I CAN HARDLY ASK YOU TO LOOK THE OTHER WAY.
TELL ME--
--EVEN AS A FORMER CATHOLIC, DO YOU HAVE ANY IDEA WHAT *THIS* IS?
LOOKS OLD...
ALL THE EDGES ARE WEATHERED. IS THIS WHAT YOUR MAN IN THE COURTYARD WAS HOLDING WHEN HE WAS ARRESTED?
OUR LORD TOOK MANY, MANY HOURS TO DIE AT CALVARY... UNTIL A ROMAN SOLDIER NAMED GAIUS CASSIUS THRUST A SHORT SPEAR INTO HIS ABDOMEN.
WITNESSES DESCRIBE BOTH BLOOD AND PERICARDIAL FLUID FLOWING FROM HIS LIFELESS BODY.
WHAT? THEN THIS IS--?
A TERRIBLE THING HAS HAPPENED TO YOU, CHARLIE. YOU'VE HELD IT IN YOUR HANDS, AND NOW YOU'VE LOST YOUR DISBELIEF. I'M TRULY SORRY.
WHY?
BECAUSE WE HAD *ONE CHANCE* TO PREVENT WHAT'S GOING TO HAPPEN. AND WE *FAILED*.

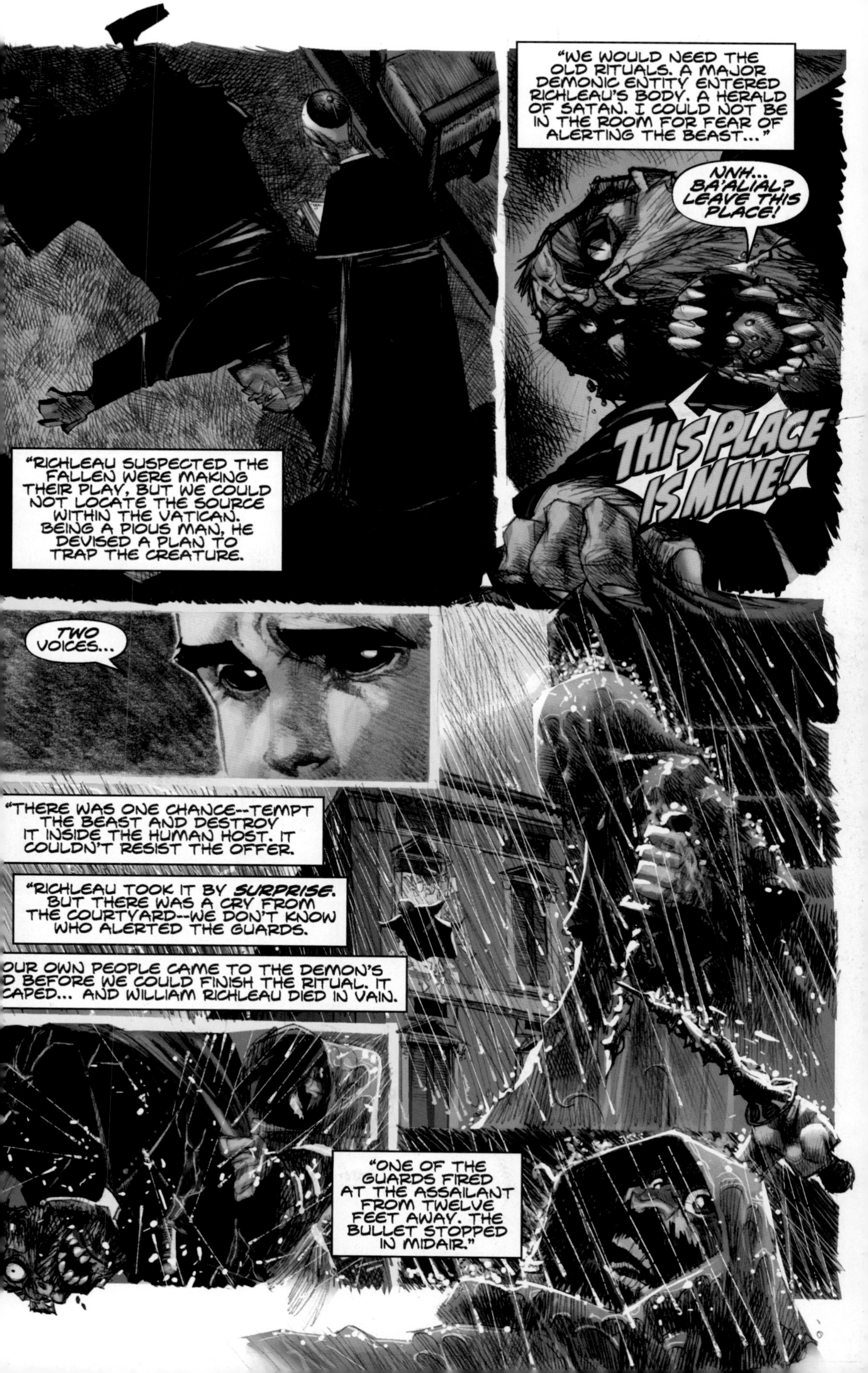
"RICHLEAU SUSPECTED THE FALLEN WERE MAKING THEIR PLAY, BUT WE COULD NOT LOCATE THE SOURCE WITHIN THE VATICAN. BEING A PIOUS MAN, HE DEVISED A PLAN TO TRAP THE CREATURE.
"WE WOULD NEED THE OLD RITUALS. A MAJOR DEMONIC ENTITY ENTERED RICHLEAU'S BODY. A HERALD OF SATAN. I COULD NOT BE IN THE ROOM FOR FEAR OF ALERTING THE BEAST..."
NNH... BA'ALIAL? LEAVE THIS PLACE!
THIS PLACE IS MINE!
TWO VOICES...
"THERE WAS ONE CHANCE--TEMPT THE BEAST AND DESTROY IT INSIDE THE HUMAN HOST. IT COULDN'T RESIST THE OFFER.
"RICHLEAU TOOK IT BY SURPRISE. BUT THERE WAS A CRY FROM THE COURTYARD--WE DON'T KNOW WHO ALERTED THE GUARDS.
OUR OWN PEOPLE CAME TO THE DEMON'S D BEFORE WE COULD FINISH THE RITUAL. IT CAPED... AND WILLIAM RICHLEAU DIED IN VAIN.
"ONE OF THE GUARDS FIRED AT THE ASSAILANT FROM TWELVE FEET AWAY. THE BULLET STOPPED IN MIDAIR."

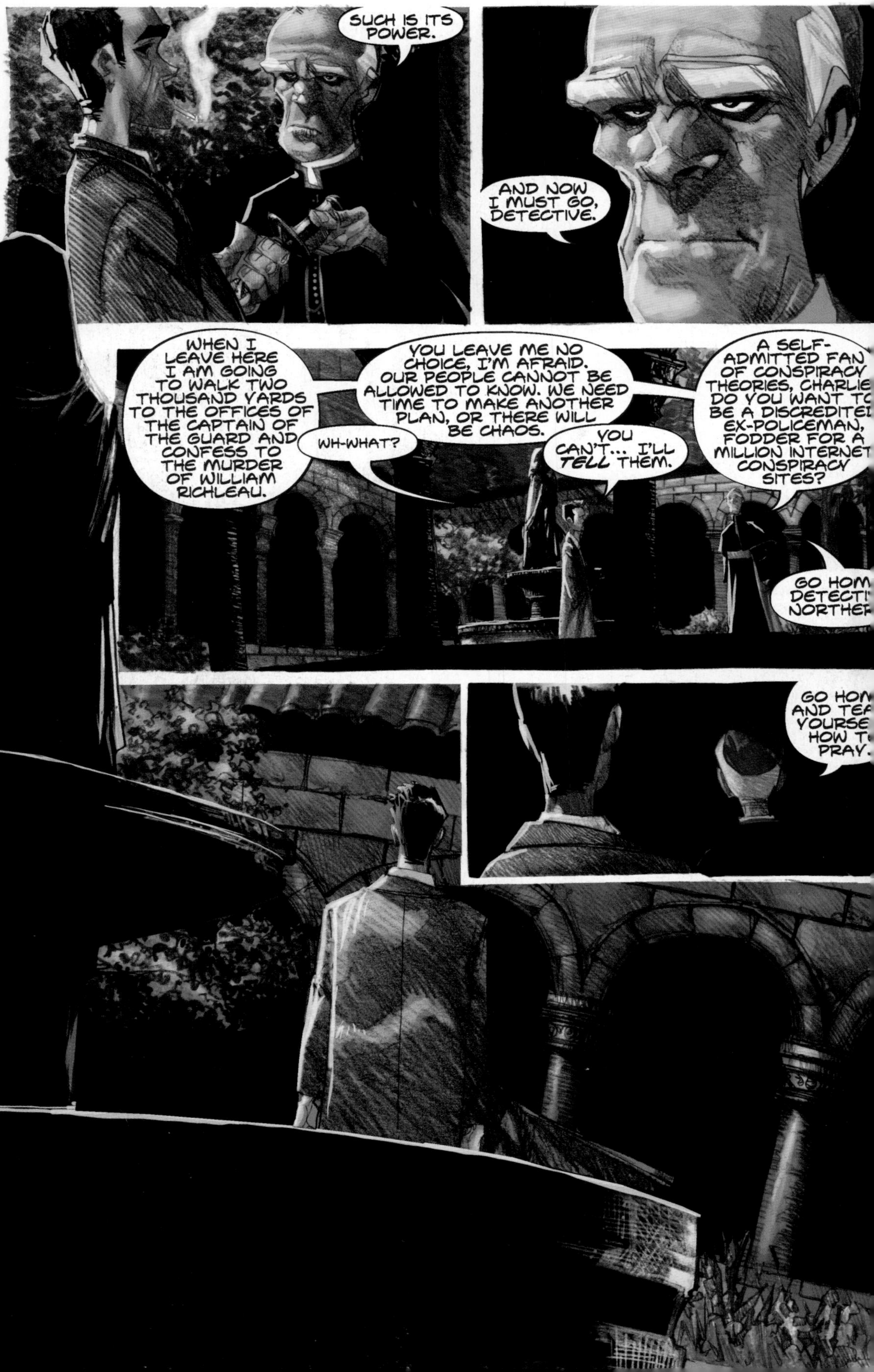
SUCH IS ITS POWER.
AND NOW I MUST GO, DETECTIVE.
WHEN I LEAVE HERE I AM GOING TO WALK TWO THOUSAND YARDS TO THE OFFICES OF THE CAPTAIN OF THE GUARD AND CONFESS TO THE MURDER OF WILLIAM RICHLEAU.
WH-WHAT?
YOU LEAVE ME NO CHOICE, I'M AFRAID. OUR PEOPLE CANNOT BE ALLOWED TO KNOW. WE NEED TIME TO MAKE ANOTHER PLAN, OR THERE WILL BE CHAOS.
YOU CAN'T... I'LL *TELL* THEM.
A SELF-ADMITTED FAN OF CONSPIRACY THEORIES, CHARLIE DO YOU WANT T BE A DISCREDITE EX-POLICEMAN, FODDER FOR A MILLION INTERNE CONSPIRACY SITES?
GO HOM DETECTI NORTHE
GO HOM AND TE YOURSE HOW T PRAY.

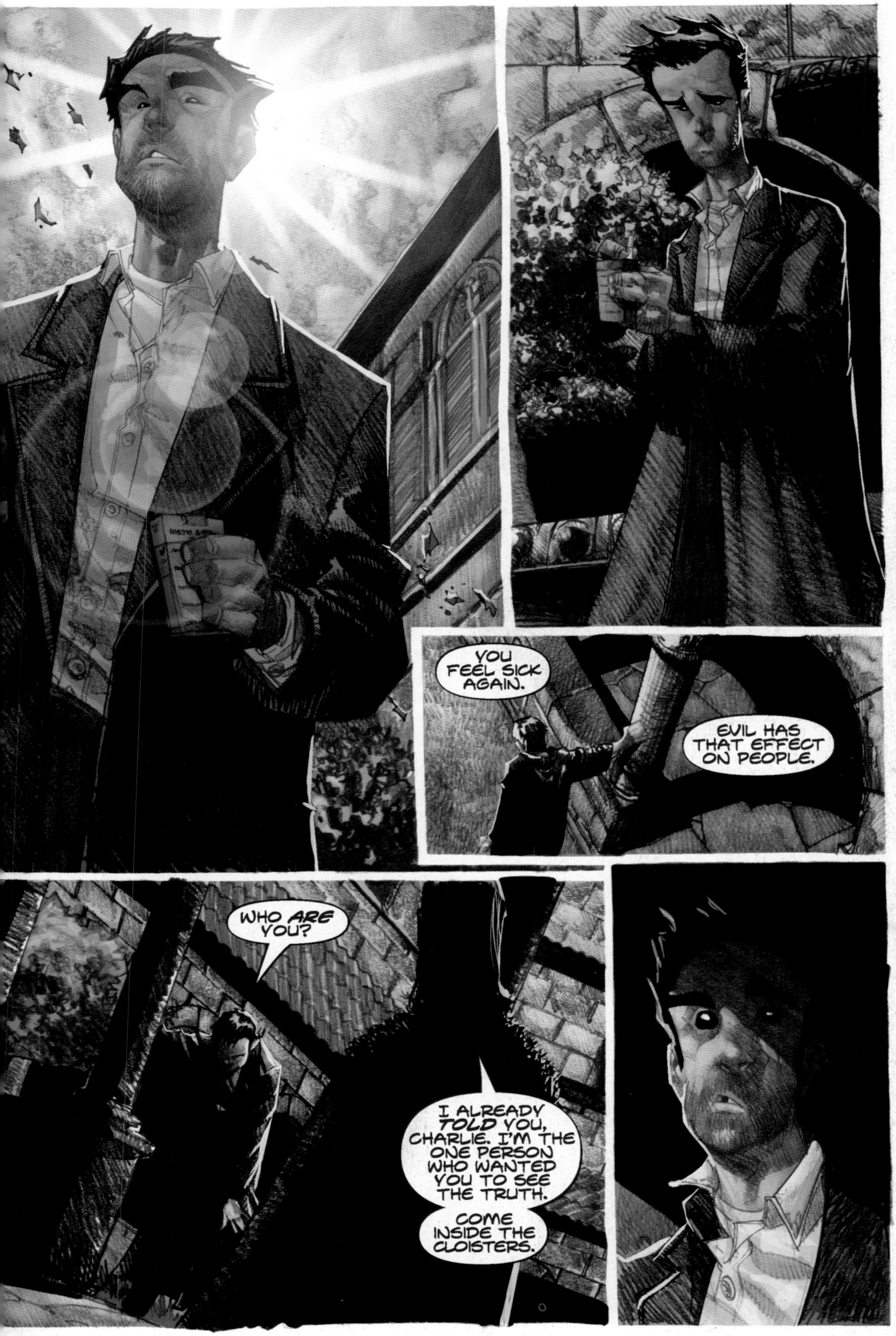
YOU FEEL SICK AGAIN.
EVIL HAS THAT EFFECT ON PEOPLE.
WHO *ARE* YOU?
I ALREADY *TOLD* YOU, CHARLIE. I'M THE ONE PERSON WHO WANTED YOU TO SEE THE TRUTH.
COME INSIDE THE CLOISTERS.

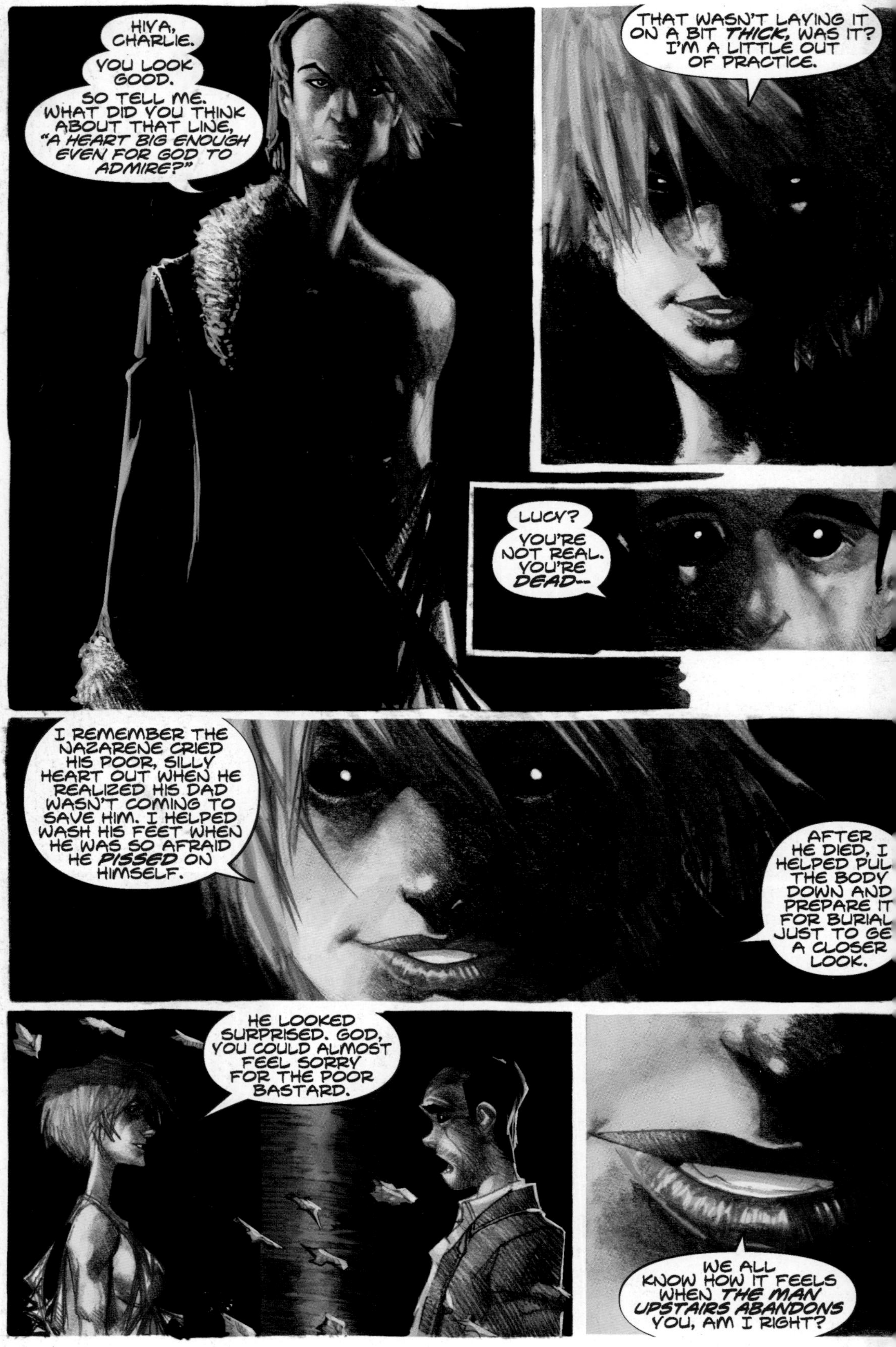
HIYA, CHARLIE.
YOU LOOK GOOD.
SO TELL ME. WHAT DID YOU THINK ABOUT THAT LINE, *"A HEART BIG ENOUGH EVEN FOR GOD TO ADMIRE?"*
THAT WASN'T LAYING IT ON A BIT ***THICK,*** WAS IT? I'M A LITTLE OUT OF PRACTICE.
LUCY?
YOU'RE NOT REAL. YOU'RE ***DEAD--***
I REMEMBER THE NAZARENE CRIED HIS POOR, SILLY HEART OUT WHEN HE REALIZED HIS DAD WASN'T COMING TO SAVE HIM. I HELPED WASH HIS FEET WHEN HE WAS SO AFRAID HE ***PISSED*** ON HIMSELF.
AFTER HE DIED, I HELPED PUL THE BODY DOWN AND PREPARE IT FOR BURIAL JUST TO GE A CLOSER LOOK.
HE LOOKED SURPRISED. GOD, YOU COULD ALMOST FEEL SORRY FOR THE POOR BASTARD.
WE ALL KNOW HOW IT FEELS WHEN ***THE MAN UPSTAIRS ABANDONS*** YOU, AM I RIGHT?

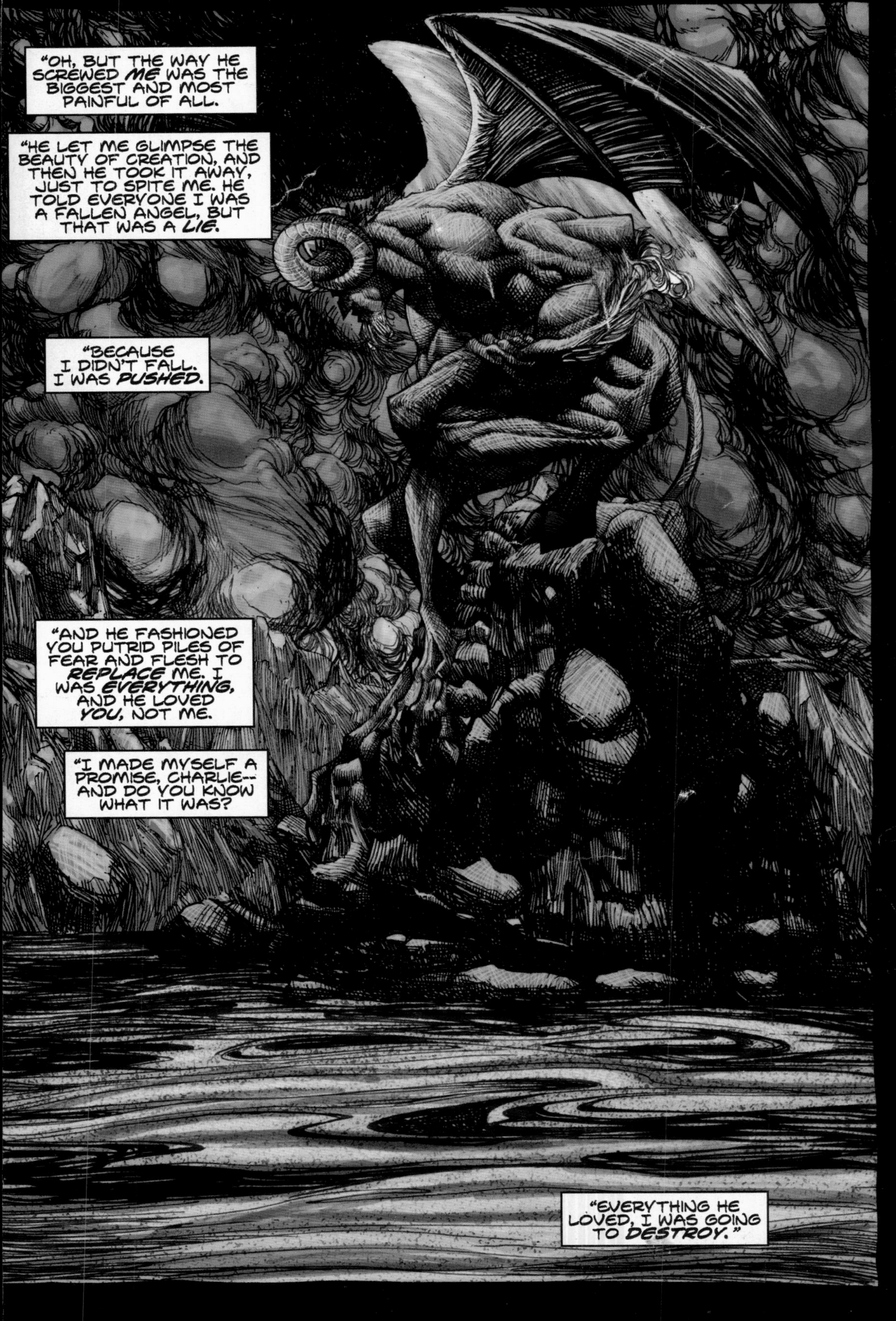
"OH, BUT THE WAY HE SCREWED *ME* WAS THE BIGGEST AND MOST PAINFUL OF ALL.
"HE LET ME GLIMPSE THE BEAUTY OF CREATION, AND THEN HE TOOK IT AWAY, JUST TO SPITE ME. HE TOLD EVERYONE I WAS A FALLEN ANGEL, BUT THAT WAS A *LIE*.
"BECAUSE I DIDN'T FALL. I WAS *PUSHED*.
"AND HE FASHIONED YOU PUTRID PILES OF FEAR AND FLESH TO *REPLACE* ME. I WAS *EVERYTHING*, AND HE LOVED *YOU*, NOT ME.
"I MADE MYSELF A PROMISE, CHARLIE-- AND DO YOU KNOW WHAT IT WAS?
"EVERYTHING HE LOVED, I WAS GOING TO *DESTROY*."

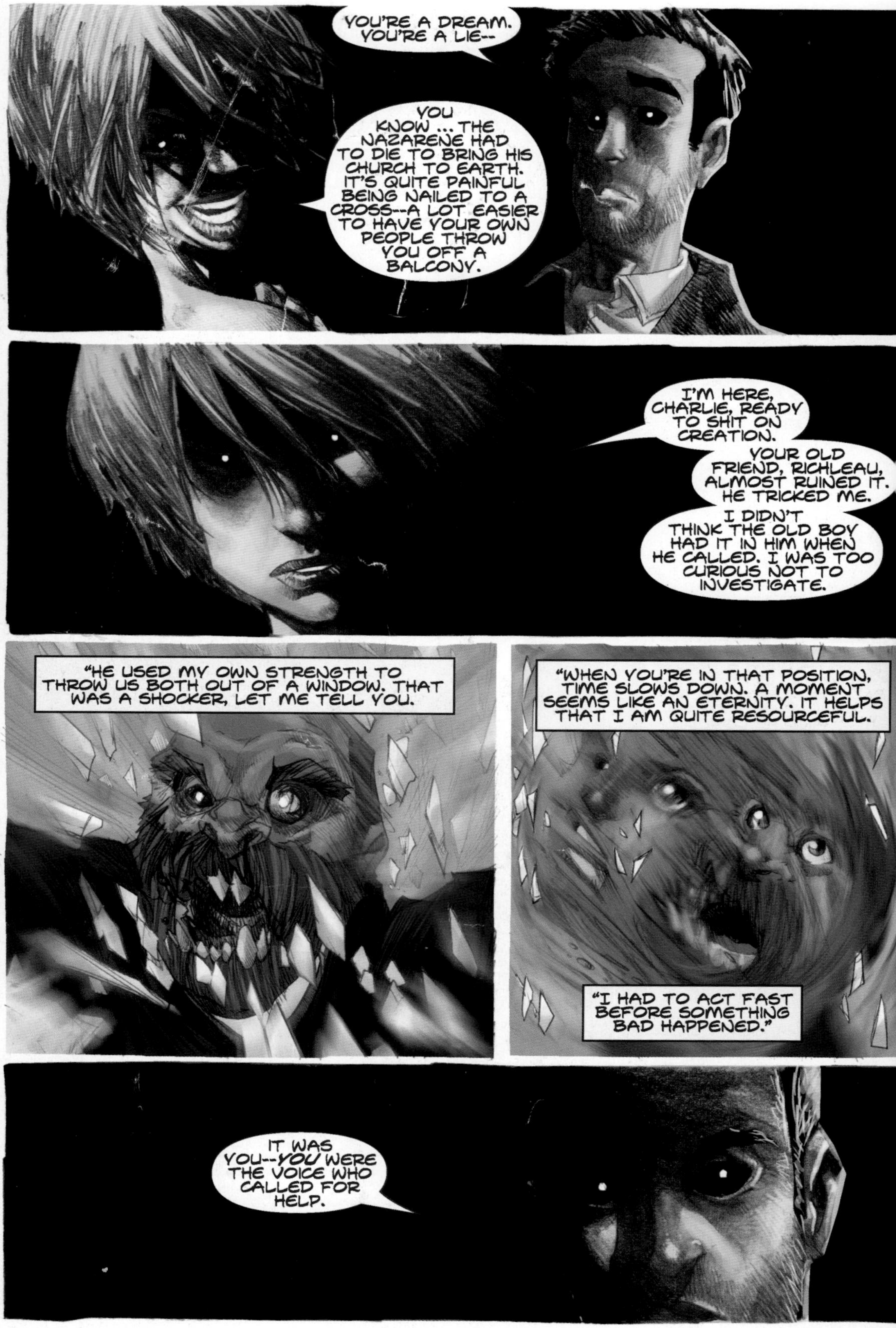
YOU'RE A DREAM. YOU'RE A LIE--
YOU KNOW ... THE NAZARENE HAD TO DIE TO BRING HIS CHURCH TO EARTH. IT'S QUITE PAINFUL BEING NAILED TO A CROSS--A LOT EASIER TO HAVE YOUR OWN PEOPLE THROW YOU OFF A BALCONY.
I'M HERE, CHARLIE, READY TO SHIT ON CREATION.
YOUR OLD FRIEND, RICHLEAU, ALMOST RUINED IT. HE TRICKED ME.
I DIDN'T THINK THE OLD BOY HAD IT IN HIM WHEN HE CALLED. I WAS TOO CURIOUS NOT TO INVESTIGATE.
"HE USED MY OWN STRENGTH TO THROW US BOTH OUT OF A WINDOW. THAT WAS A SHOCKER, LET ME TELL YOU.
"WHEN YOU'RE IN THAT POSITION, TIME SLOWS DOWN. A MOMENT SEEMS LIKE AN ETERNITY. IT HELPS THAT I AM QUITE RESOURCEFUL.
"I HAD TO ACT FAST BEFORE SOMETHING BAD HAPPENED."
IT WAS YOU--YOU WERE THE VOICE WHO CALLED FOR HELP.

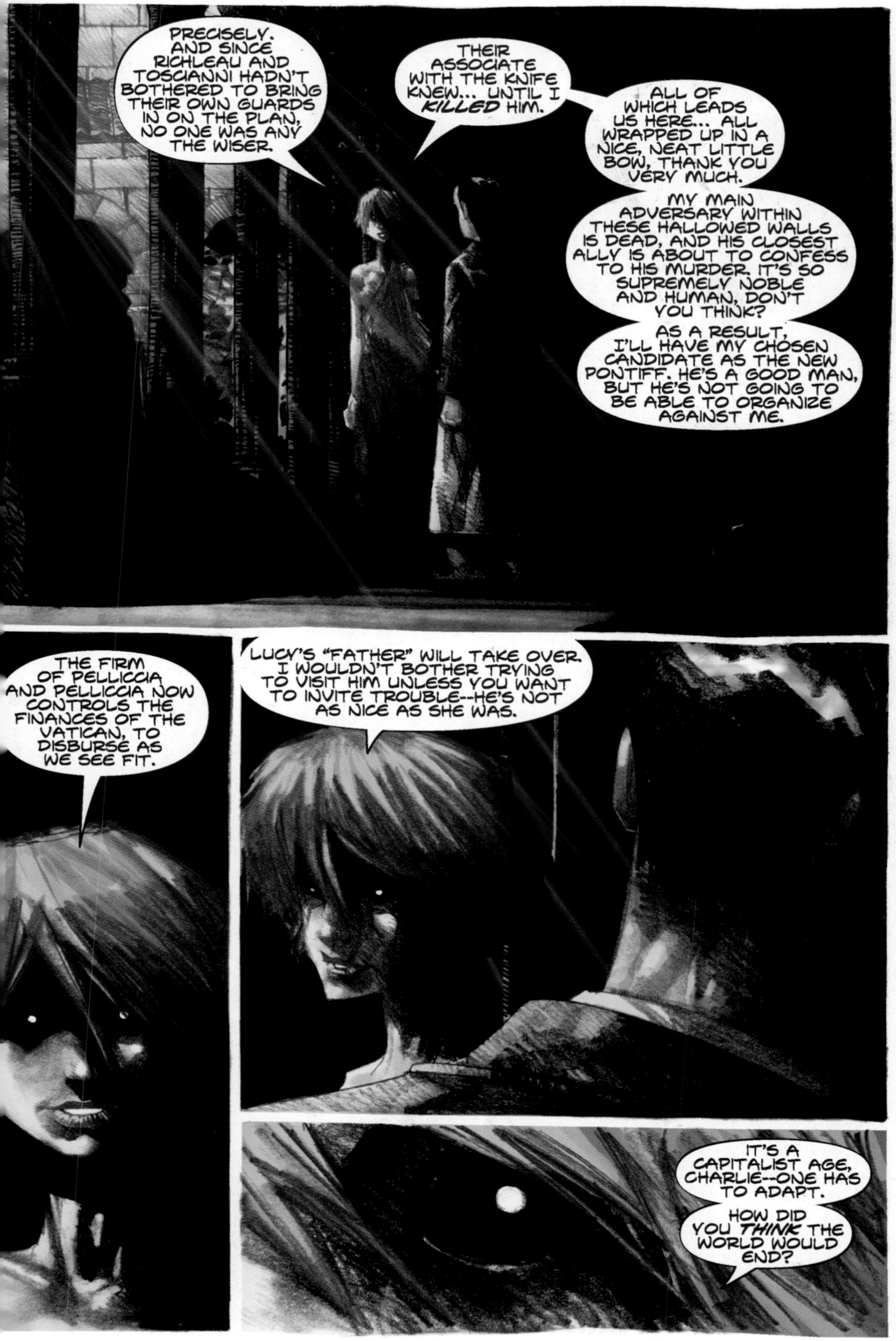
PRECISELY. AND SINCE RICHLEAU AND TOSCIANNI HADN'T BOTHERED TO BRING THEIR OWN GUARDS IN ON THE PLAN, NO ONE WAS ANY THE WISER.
THEIR ASSOCIATE WITH THE KNIFE KNEW... UNTIL I *KILLED* HIM.
ALL OF WHICH LEADS US HERE... ALL WRAPPED UP IN A NICE, NEAT LITTLE BOW, THANK YOU VERY MUCH.
MY MAIN ADVERSARY WITHIN THESE HALLOWED WALLS IS DEAD, AND HIS CLOSEST ALLY IS ABOUT TO CONFESS TO HIS MURDER. IT'S SO SUPREMELY NOBLE AND HUMAN, DON'T YOU THINK?
AS A RESULT, I'LL HAVE MY CHOSEN CANDIDATE AS THE NEW PONTIFF. HE'S A GOOD MAN, BUT HE'S NOT GOING TO BE ABLE TO ORGANIZE AGAINST ME.
THE FIRM OF PELLICCIA AND PELLICCIA NOW CONTROLS THE FINANCES OF THE VATICAN, TO DISBURSE AS WE SEE FIT.
LUCY'S "FATHER" WILL TAKE OVER. I WOULDN'T BOTHER TRYING TO VISIT HIM UNLESS YOU WANT TO INVITE TROUBLE--HE'S NOT AS NICE AS SHE WAS.
IT'S A CAPITALIST AGE, CHARLIE--ONE HAS TO ADAPT.
HOW DID YOU *THINK* THE WORLD WOULD END?

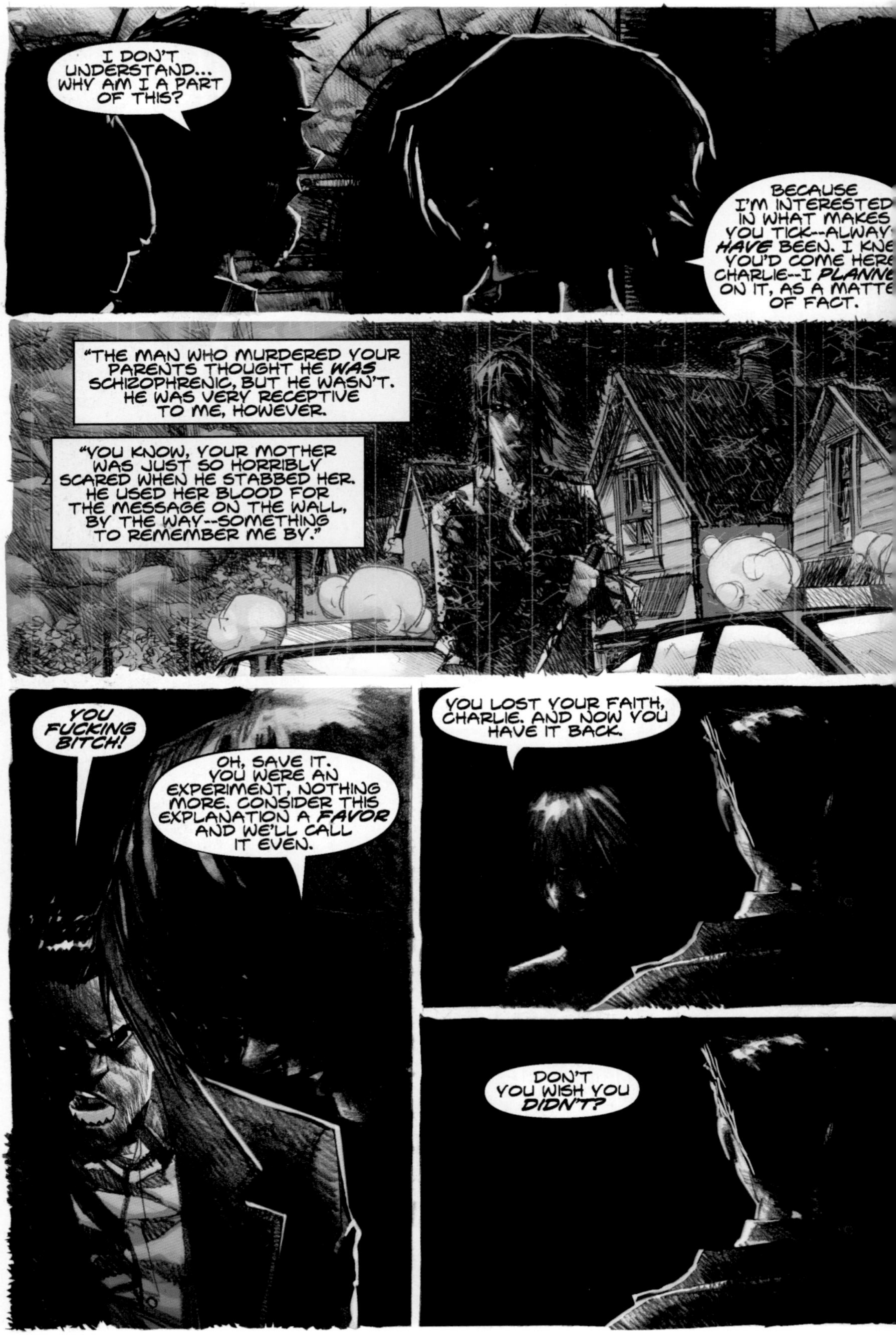
I DON'T UNDERSTAND... WHY AM I A PART OF THIS?
BECAUSE I'M INTERESTED IN WHAT MAKES YOU TICK--ALWAY HAVE BEEN. I KNE YOU'D COME HERE CHARLIE--I PLANNE ON IT, AS A MATTE OF FACT.
"THE MAN WHO MURDERED YOUR PARENTS THOUGHT HE WAS SCHIZOPHRENIC, BUT HE WASN'T. HE WAS VERY RECEPTIVE TO ME, HOWEVER.
"YOU KNOW, YOUR MOTHER WAS JUST SO HORRIBLY SCARED WHEN HE STABBED HER. HE USED HER BLOOD FOR THE MESSAGE ON THE WALL, BY THE WAY--SOMETHING TO REMEMBER ME BY."
YOU FUCKING BITCH!
OH, SAVE IT. YOU WERE AN EXPERIMENT, NOTHING MORE. CONSIDER THIS EXPLANATION A FAVOR AND WE'LL CALL IT EVEN.
YOU LOST YOUR FAITH, CHARLIE. AND NOW YOU HAVE IT BACK.
DON'T YOU WISH YOU DIDN'T?

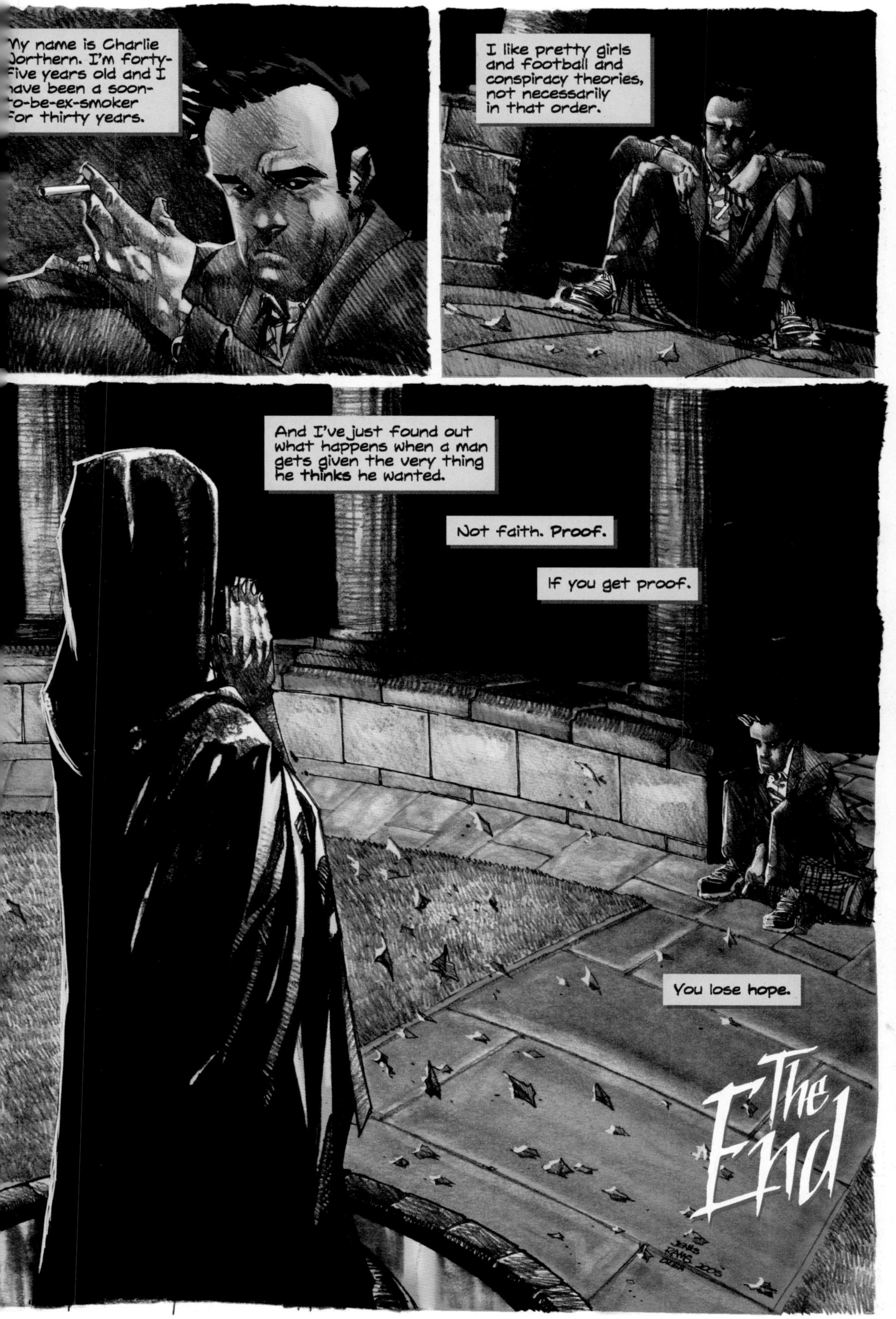
My name is Charlie Northern. I'm forty-five years old and I have been a soon-to-be-ex-smoker for thirty years.
I like pretty girls and football and conspiracy theories, not necessarily in that order.
And I've just found out what happens when a man gets given the very thing he thinks he wanted.
Not faith. Proof.
If you get proof.
You lose hope.
The End

HUMBERTO RAMOS'S

REVELATIONS

Sketchbook

Presenting concepts and
character designs from the sketchbook
of HUMBERTO RAMOS.

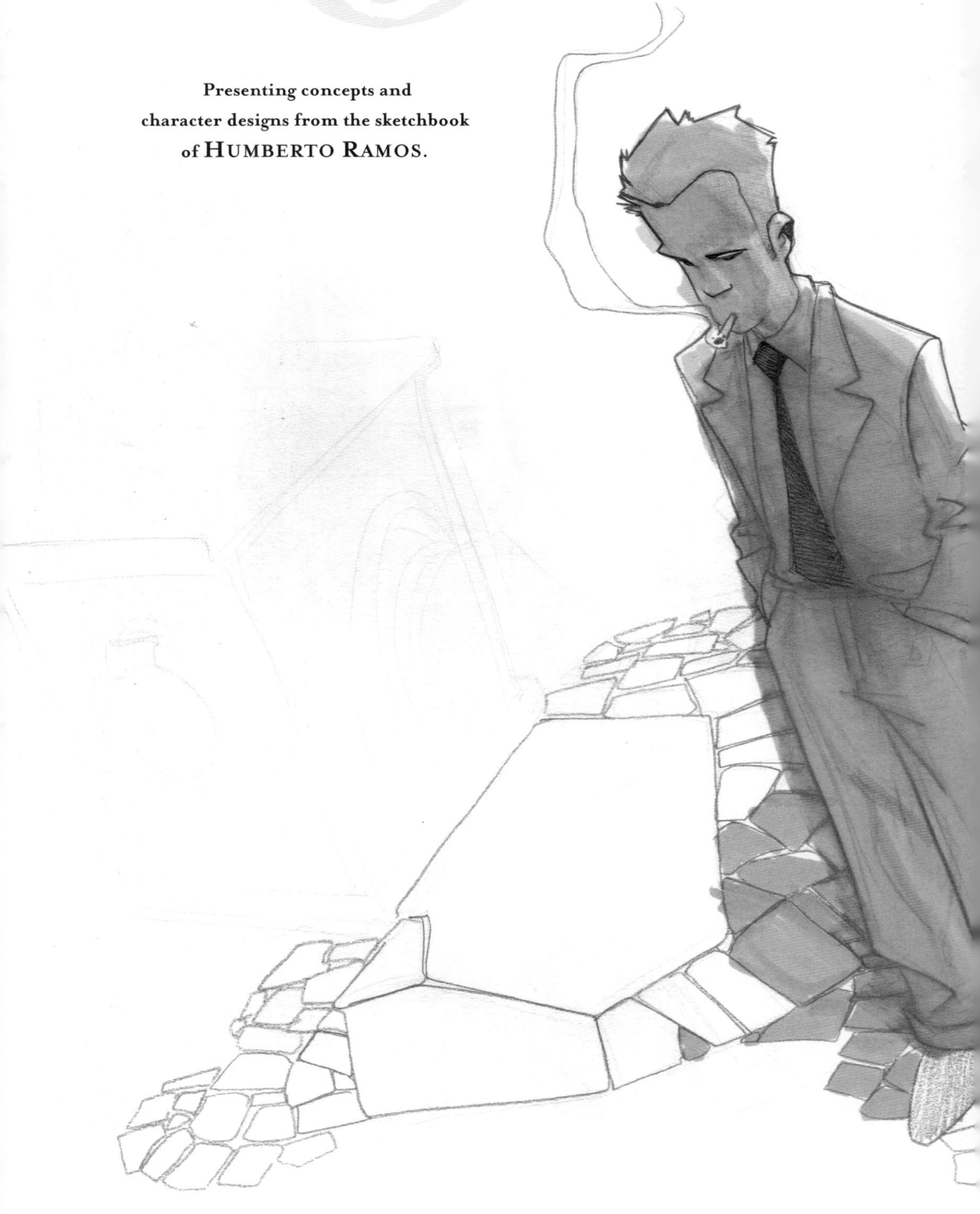

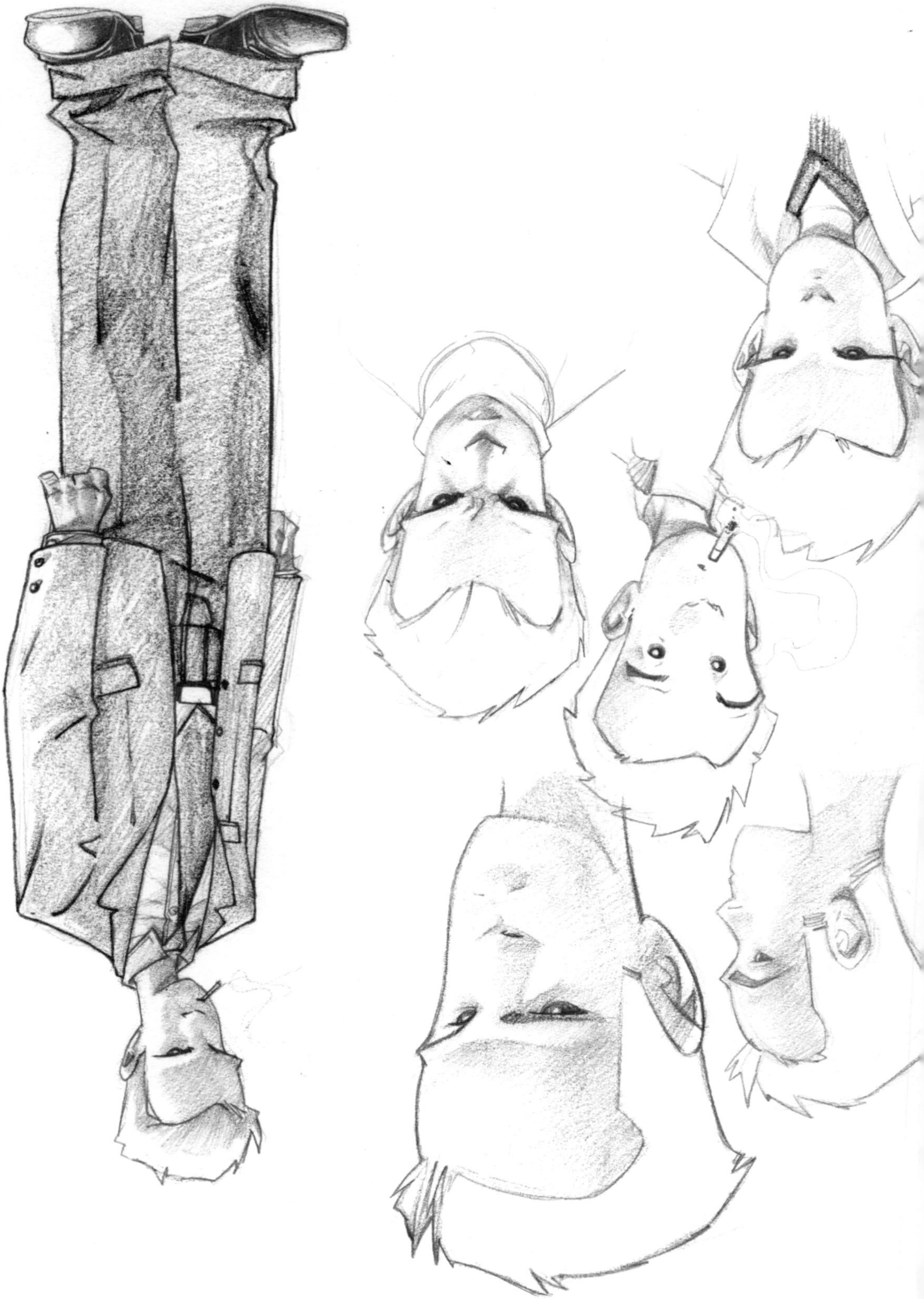

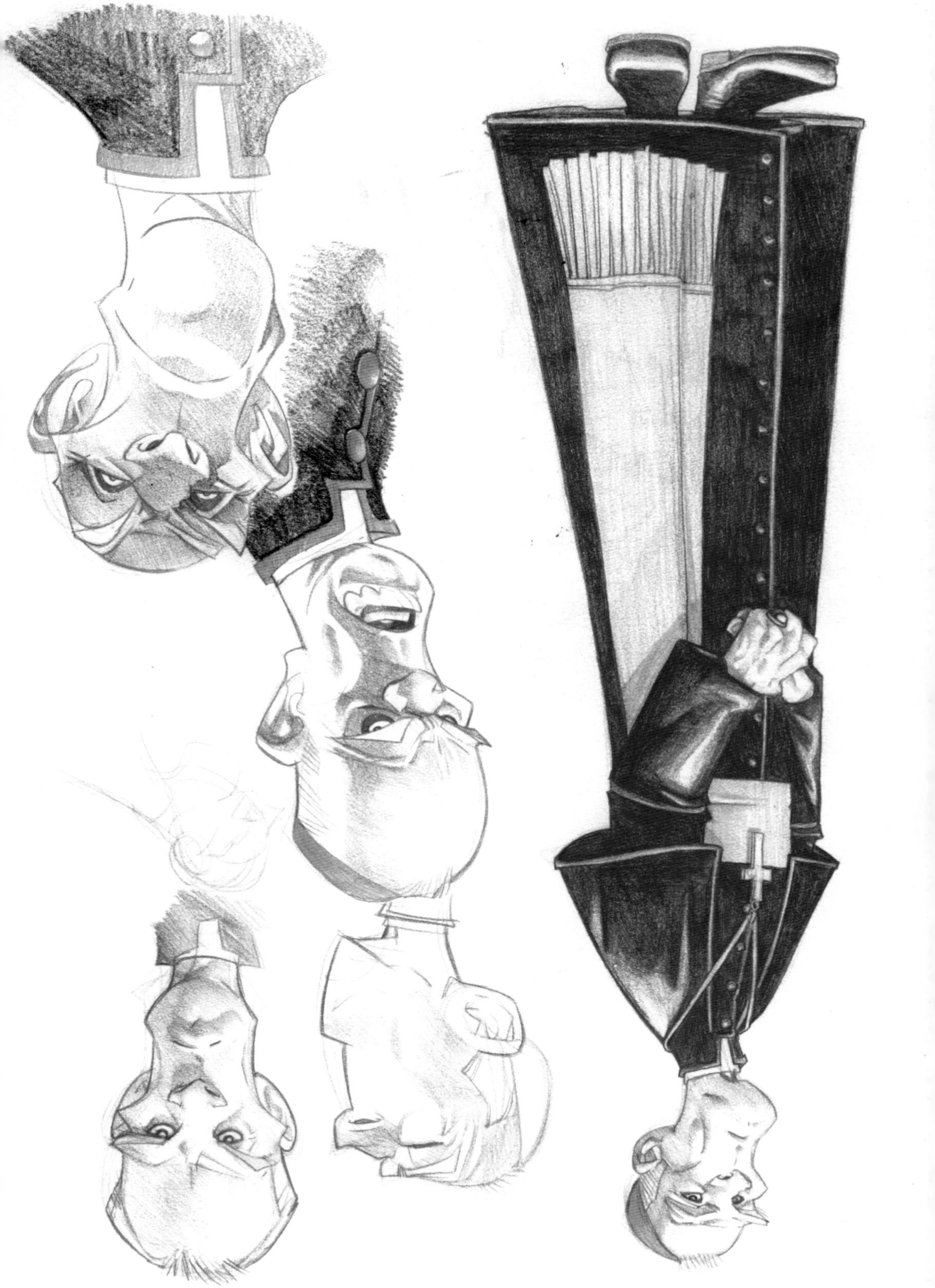

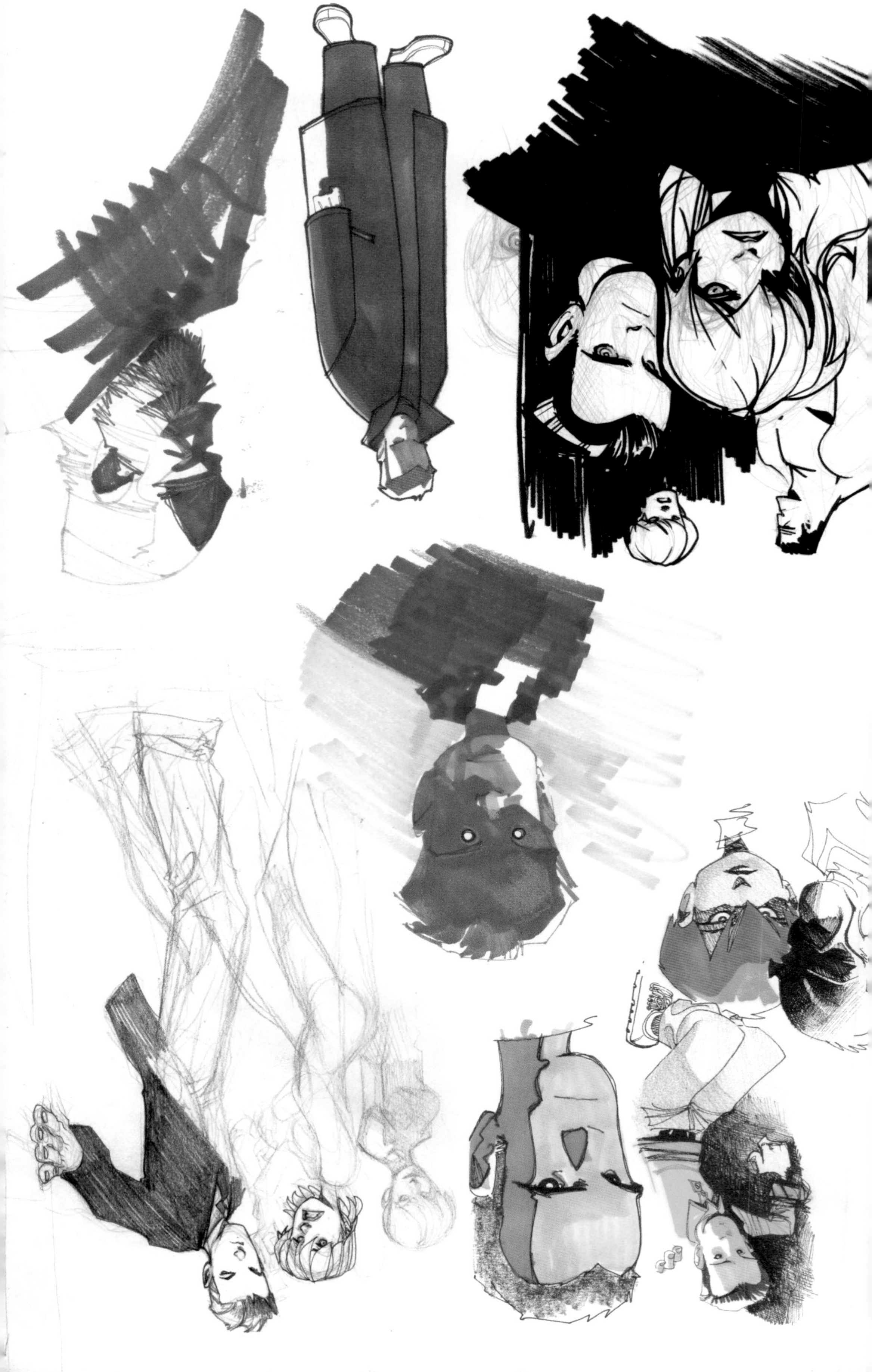

Uncolored pencil cover to the first issue.

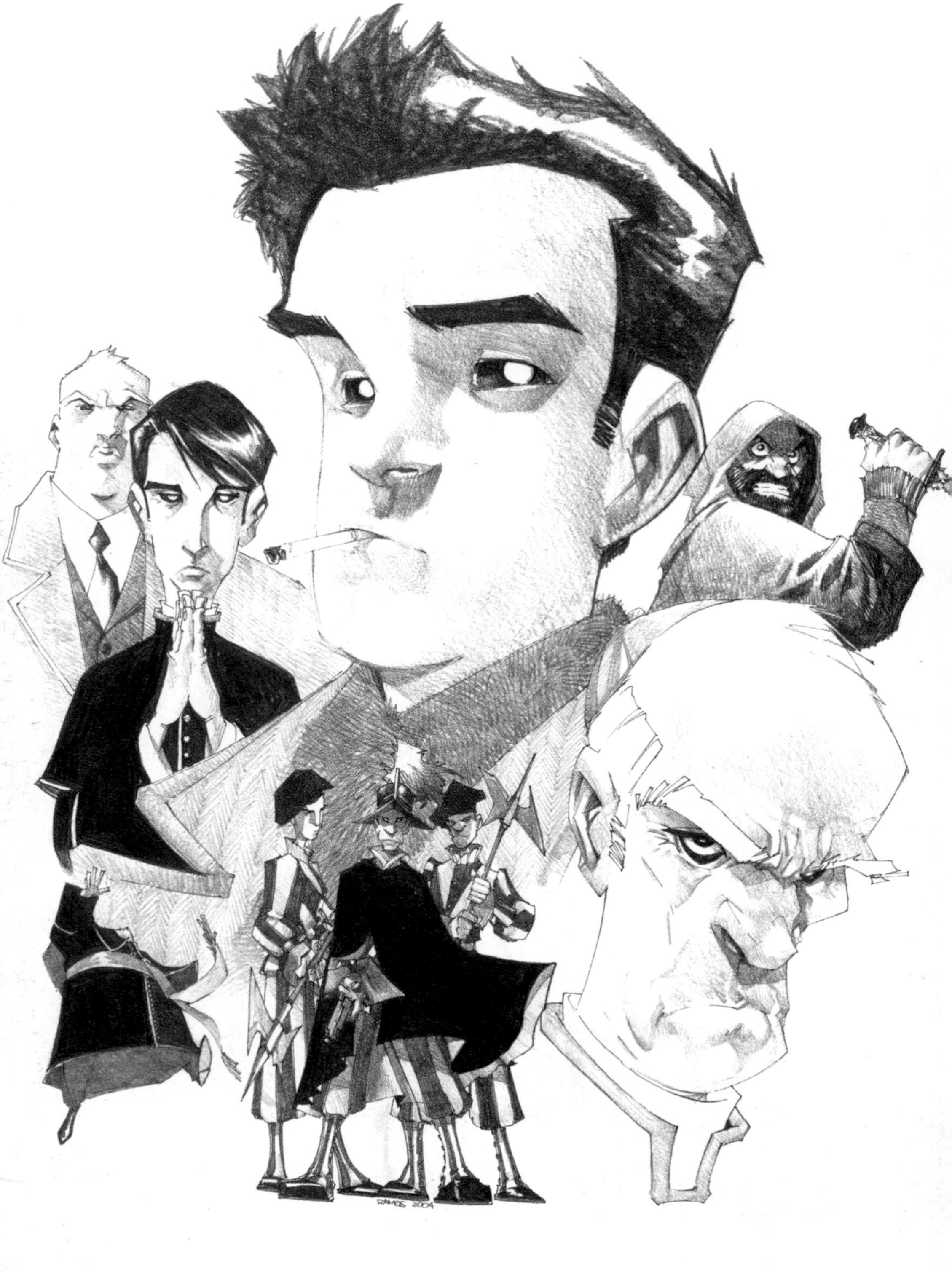
RAMOS 2004

Second-issue cover—a mix of colored pencil and ink—by Humberto Ramos, before digital colors by Leonardo Olea. Following page—original cover pencils to this edition.

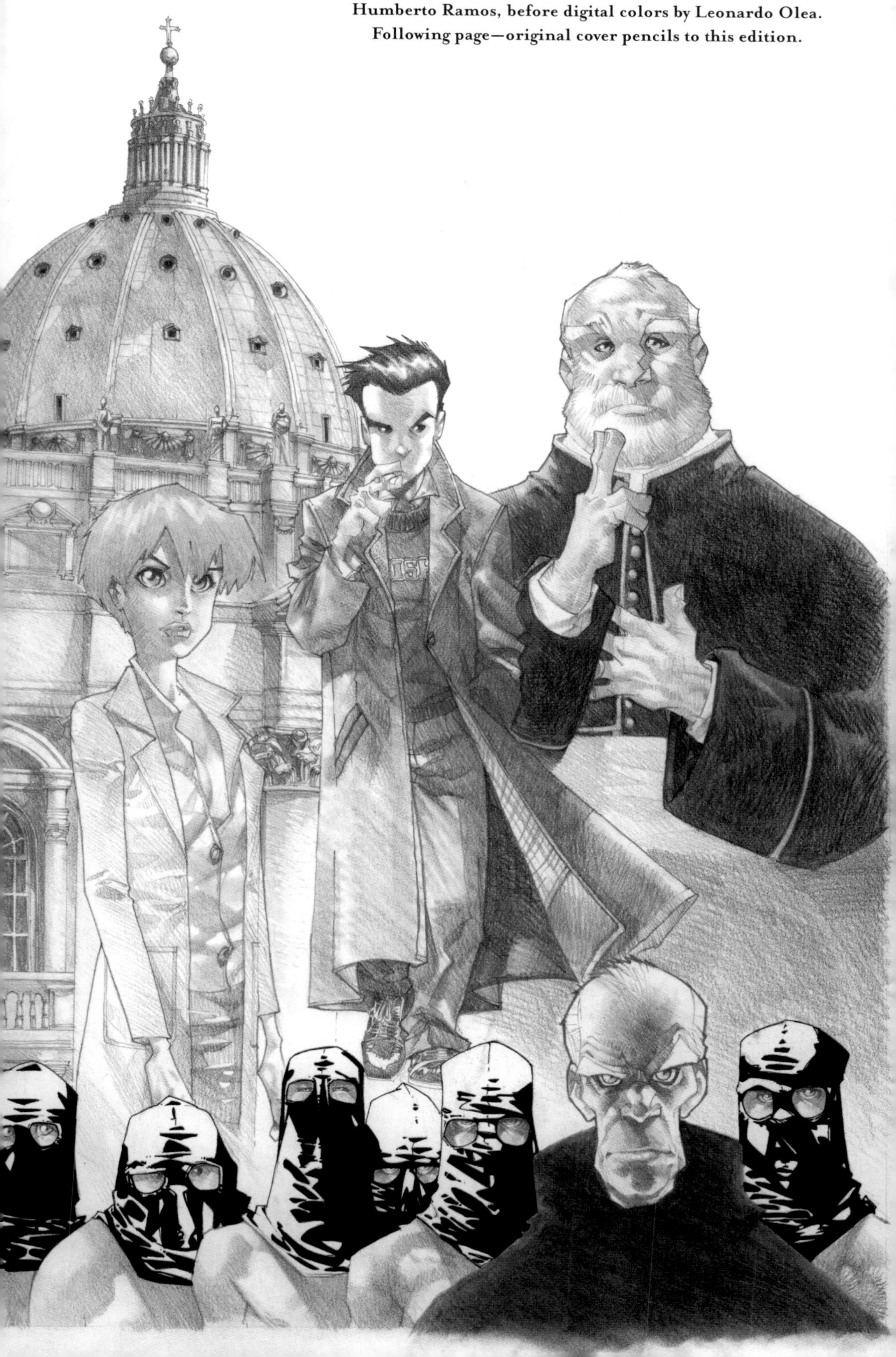

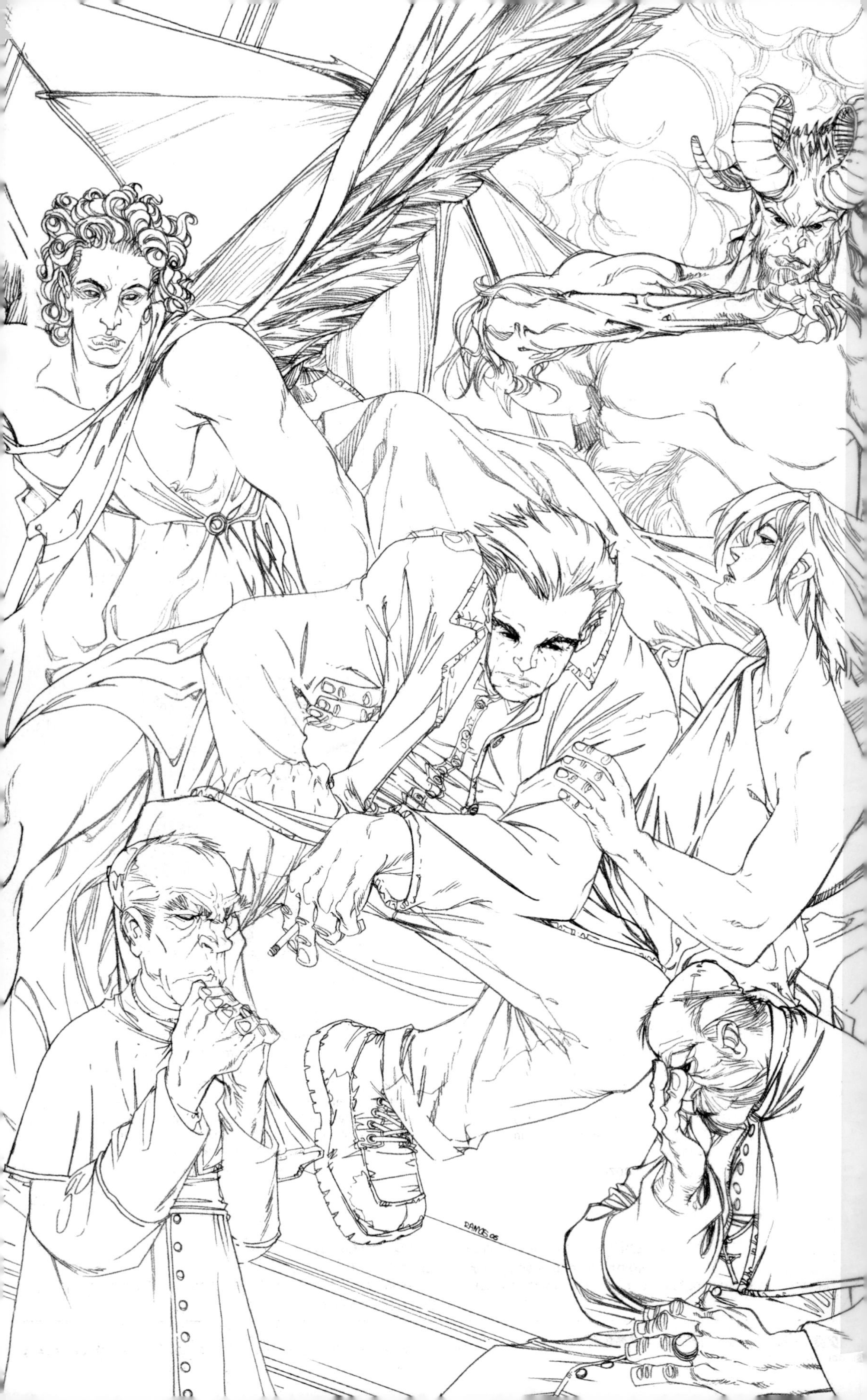
RAMOS 05

ALSO FROM DARK HORSE BOOKS

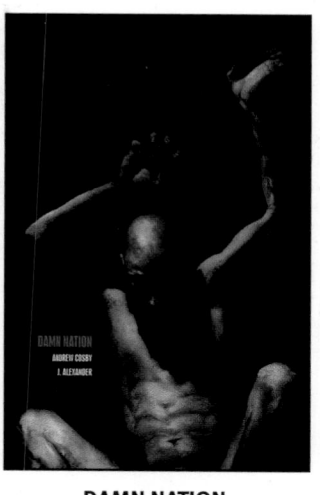

DAMN NATION
Andrew Cosby and J. Alexander

Overrun by a vampire plague, the United States is quarantined from the world. When scientists trapped inside the U.S. discover a cure, it's up to a Special Ops team from the president's current offices in London to go get it. Yet, not everyone on earth wants to see America cured.

$12.95, ISBN: 1-59307-389-5

FREAKS OF THE HEARTLAND
Steve Niles and Greg Ruth

Under the weathered skies of America's heartland, and in the wounded hearts of every family in one tiny rural town, a terrible secret has been kept for too many years. Now, a young boy must try to keep his younger brother from falling victim the tragic secret that binds the town's families together.

$17.95, ISBN: 1-59307-029-2

13TH SON: WORSE THING WAITING
Kelley Jones

Born to a young woman driven to insanity and black magic by the deaths of her previous children, the 13th Son is a creature like nothing this world has seen before. Humans are not his target. It's the other monsters who walk this earth who live in fear of his enormous and terrifying powers.

$12.95, ISBN: 1-59307-551-0

THE BLACKBURNE COVENANT
Fabian Nicieza and Stefano Raffaele

Someone is following Richard Kaine, someone interested in knowing how he came up with his best-selling historical-fantasy novel. How could he have written about an event that has been meticulously erased from every chronicle of human history? Who are the Blackburne Covenant, and why are they trying to kill Richard Kaine?

$12.95, ISBN: 1-56971-889-X

AVAILABLE AT YOUR LOCAL COMICS SHOP OR BOOKSTORE
To find a comics shop in your area, call 1-888-266-4226
For more information or to order direct visit darkhorse.com or call 1-800-862-0052 • Mon.-Fri. 9 A.M. to 5 P.M. Pacific Time
*Prices and availability subject to change without notice

DARK HORSE COMICS™ *drawing on your nightmares*
darkhorse.com

ALSO FROM DARK HORSE BOOKS

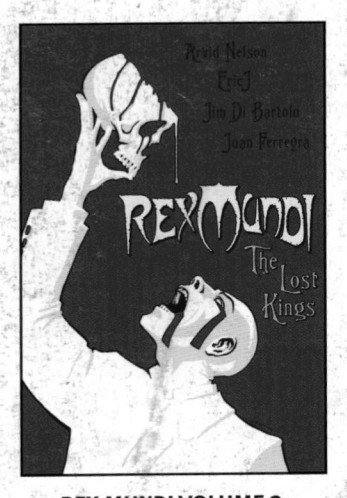